Science, Values
and Politics
in
Max Weber's Methodology

D1596334

H. H. BRUUN

Science, Values
and Politics
in
Max Weber's Methodology

MUNKSGAARD · COPENHAGEN

This book was set in Intertype Baskerville
and printed by
Aarhuus Stiftsbogtrykkerie A/S

ISBN 87 16 00993 2

TO MY PARENTS

Preface

On one point at least, this book will surprise and probably dismay the reader: in many places, passages quoted in it are left in the original, mostly in German, unaccompanied by a translation into English. This may seem paradoxical and even perverse in a work the purpose of which is avowedly to help the reader to understand the complexities of Max Weber's thought, since this help is of course above all required when the reader is not prepared to read Weber in the original German.

However, the practice indicated has been adopted precisely because of the peculiar, and peculiarly difficult, character of Weber's German text. In fact, Weber's thought, at least in the field of methodology, is far from clear. His arguments do not progress in straight lines and logical chains, but on the contrary derive much of their effect from being rich in ramifications, modifications, digressions and exemplifications. This tortuous, even tortured, density of Weber's intellectual texture is reflected in his language, which is full of long, involved, carefully balanced sentences (sometimes running to half a page or more). These intricate linguistic constructions pose an almost insuperable problem to the would-be translator. If they are rendered accurately, they grow very obscure; and if the translator opts for clarity, he runs the risk of destroying the intricate balance of Weber's thought. To this must be added a second difficulty: The meaning of many of Weber's concepts "shimmers" and is difficult to grasp accurately; thus, any *translation* of his text automatically implies an *interpretation* which, like all interpretations (particularly of Weber's thought), is debatable.

On the balance, it has therefore seemed preferable to leave the major part of the passages quoted, whether from Weber or from the, often equally involved, discussions by others of his work, in their original form. This should at least ensure that the profusion of Weber's thought and text is respected and that the text is separated from the interpretation.

On all major poins, I hope that the discussion in English makes the argument clear even to readers who do not understand German. Moreover, I have tried to alleviate the rigour of the main principle of quotation a little: first, by translating a number of passages from which an exclusively

English-speaking reader would otherwise derive no sense at all, or which seem so trivial that there would be no sense in keeping them in the original language; secondly, by sometimes appending an *approximate* English translation to central terms when they appear for the first time; and, thirdly, by providing, at the end of the book, a comparative page index, which, for most of the passages quoted from Weber's work, indicates the corresponding page numbers of the current English translations, and thus enables the reader to check fairly easily with the latter in case of doubt.

The first reference to books and articles gives their full title, place, date, and page number. Subsequent references are abridged, giving only the author's name, a shortened title, the year of publication, and the page number. The shortened titles are given together with the full ones in the bibliography at the end of the volume. Max Weber's own books, and his more important essays, are referred to throughout in the abbreviated form given in the list preceding the main account.

The unpublished documents quoted are all, with a very few exceptions, part of the large collection of Weber's letters and manuscripts (original or copied) found in Repository no. 92 of the German Central Archives, Historical Section II (Deutsches Zentralarchiv, Historische Abteilung II). Merseburg (GDR). They are denoted by the abbreviation "DZA II, Rep. 92" followed by the number and, in some cases, the volume number of the file in which the document in question is found.

My thanks are due to the following publishers for permission given me to quote passages of some length from works of other authors:

Routledge and Kegan Paul, Ltd.: Gunnar Myrdal, *The Political Element in the Development of Economic Thought,* London 1953.

Princeton University Press: Arnold Brecht, *Political Theory.* Copyright 1959 by Princeton University Press.

University of Chicago Press: Leo Strauss, *Natural Right and History.* Copyright 1953 by University of Chicago; and Eric Voegelin, *The New Science of Politics.* Copyright 1952 by University of Chicago.

Alfred A. Knopf, Inc.: H. Stuart Hughes, *Consciousness and Society.* Copyright 1958 by H. Stuart Hughes.

I wish to express my gratitude to the Danish State Council for Social Science Research (Statens Samfundsvidenskabelige Forskningsråd) which, through a generous grant, made it possible for me to publish this book. My sincere thanks are also due to the University of Aarhus, Denmark, whose ready financial aid permitted me to work under the best possible conditions.

From the Institute of Political Science, University of Aarhus, I have received every help throughout. In particular, I wish to record my deep gratitude to Professor Erik Ramussen and Professor H. P. Clausen, who, together, launched me on the venture, and whose unfailing support was a great help to me.

The Max Weber Institute of the University of Munich extended all its facilities to me and in fact, for a year, became my second home. My warmest thanks are due to its Director, Professor Johannes Winckelmann, who with great kindness put his vast knowledge of Weber's life and thought at my disposal; and to Dr. Constans Seyfarth, who introduced me to many things besides Max Weber.

The staff of the German Central Archives, Historical Section II, Merseburg (GDR), greatly facilitated my studies by finding material and by occasionally deciphering Weber's undecipherable handwriting.

Professor Brian D. Beddie was a patient listener and a wise critic during our discussions in Munich, and with his family kept my courage up during what sometimes seemed a very long winter; and my heartfelt thanks are due to him, and to David Beetham, who was an inspiring companion during my second stay in Munich, for undertaking the difficult task of correcting and of instilling a minimum of grace into my continental English. I am painfully aware of the stylistic imperfection of this book; but it is undoubtedly much improved by their efforts.

I am thankful to many others who helped me in the course of my studies; but among them, I particularly wish to mention three: Aase Bay, who was a constant source of invaluable advice on, and gentle criticism of, my work, which she followed with warm enthusiasm until her sudden and tragic death a few months ago. And my parents, who saw me through, and to whom this book is dedicated, in deep affection.

Copenhagen, January 1972.   *H. H. B.*

Abbreviated titles of Weber's writings

GARS	*Gesammelte Aufsätze zur Religionssoziologie, I–III*, Tübingen 1920–21 (photographic reprint 1963 (vol. I) and 1966 (vols. II–III)).
Zw. betr.	pp. 536–73: "Zwischenbetrachtung" (1916).
GASW	*Gesammelte Aufsätze zur Sozial- und Wirtschaftsgeschichte* (ed. Marianne Weber), Tübingen 1924.
GASS	*Gesammelte Aufsätze zur Soziologie und Sozialpolitik* (ed. Marianne Weber), Tübingen 1924.
GAW	*Gesammelte Aufsätze zur Wissenschaftslehre* (3. ed.; ed. Johannes Winckelmann), Tübingen 1968.
	pp. 1–145: "Roscher und Knies und die logischen Probleme der historischen Nationalökonomie" (1903–06).
Roscher	pp. 3–42: "Roschers "historische Methode" " (1903).
Knies I	pp. 42–105: "Knies und das Irrationalitätsproblem" (1905).
Knies II	pp. 105–45: "Knies und das Irrationalitätsproblem II" (1906).
Objektivität	pp. 146–214: "Die "Objektivität" sozialwissenschaftlicher und sozialpolitischer Erkenntnis" (1904).
Kritische Studien	pp. 215–90: "Kritische Studien auf dem Gebiet der kulturwissenschaftlichen Logik" (1906).
Stammler	pp. 291–359: "R. Stammlers "Überwindung" der materialistischen Geschichtsauffassung" (1907).
Nachtrag	pp. 360–83: "Nachtrag zu dem Aufsatz über R. Stammlers "Überwindung" der materialistischen Geschichtsauffassung" (posthumous).
Grenznutzlehre	pp. 384–99: "Die Grenznutzlehre und das "psychophysische Grundgesetz" " (1908).

Energ. Kult. th.	pp. 400–26: " "Energetische" Kulturtheorien" (1909).
Kategorien	pp. 427–74: "Über einige Kategorien der verstehenden Soziologie" (1913).
Typen der leg. Herrschaft	pp. 475–88: "Die drei reinen Typen der legitimen Herrschaft" (1922 (posthumous)).
Wertfreiheit	pp. 489–540: "Der Sinn der "Wertfreiheit" der soziologischen und ökonomischen Wissenschaften" (1917).
Wiss. Beruf.	pp. 582–613: "Wissenschaft als Beruf" (1919).
Gutachten	*Äußerungen zur Werturteilsdiskussion im Ausschuß des Vereins für Sozialpolitik,* 1913, pp. 83–120.
PE I	*Die protestantische Ethik* (ed. Johannes Winckelmann), Munich/Hamburg 1965.
Vorbem.	pp. 9–26: "Vorbemerkung".
Meth. Schr.	*Methodologische Schriften* (ed., intr. Johannes Winckelmann), Frankfurt a/ Main 1968.
GPS[1]	*Gesammelte Politische Schriften,* Munich 1921.
GPS	*Gesammelte Politische Schriften* (2. ed.; ed. Johannes Winckelmann, intr. Theodor Heuß), Tübingen 1958.
Antrittsrede	pp. 1–25: "Der Nationalstaat und die Volkswirtschaftspolitik" (1895).
Zwei Ges.	pp. 139–42: "Zwischen zwei Gesetzen" (1916).
Wahlr. u. Dem.	pp. 233–79: "Wahlrecht und Demokratie in Deutschland" (1917).
Parl. u. Reg.	pp. 294–431: "Parlament und Regierung im neugeordneten Deutschland" (1918).
Pol. Beruf.	pp. 493–548: "Politik als Beruf" (1919).
WG	*Wirtschaft und Gesellschaft. Grundriß der verstehenden Soziologie, I–II* (ed. Johannes Winckelmann), Cologne/Berlin 1964.

Furthermore, the following abbreviations will be used:

Archiv	Archiv für Sozialwissenschaft und Sozialpolitik.
Gesellschaft	Deutsche Gesellschaft für Soziologie.
Verein	Verein für Sozialpolitik.

Table of contents

Introduction

It may be useful, at the very beginning of the present work, to try to explain the reasons behind the severe limitations which admittedly characterize it, both as regards its character, its subject, and its method.

Character. The horizon of the work is very restricted. It does not aim at presenting a *development* of Weber's thought, but is only meant as an *exposition* and *exegesis*. In principle, it does not go beyond 1920, the year of Weber's death. Works appearing after that year have not been used directly, but only to throw light into the past, onto the problems of interpretation which present themselves.

Moreover, I have tried to keep this interpretative account as neutral in tone as possible. Of course, the choices of subject and of approach are in themselves indications of the selective interest of the scholar, and consequently introduce an inevitable element of subjectivity. But I have tried not to go beyond this: no *defence* of Weber's views has been attempted; and if the interpretations of other commentators are occasionally criticized, the criticism is only intended as an "immanent" one, i. e., as a correction or modification of interpretations which seem difficult to uphold when confronted with Weber's own text.

These limitations of scope are deliberate. Today, more than fifty years after Max Weber's death, his thought has been commented on, developed, modified, and attacked, so often, and in so many different contexts, that Weber himself occasionally seems to vanish behind a mountain of references and commentaries. It may not therefore be inappropriate to concentrate, in this book, on the original sources by themselves. This method of discussion may be useful by making clear what Weber actually said, and perhaps what he actually meant; but it also has another, independent function. When Weber's ideas are extricated from later constructions and misconstructions, analysed and, wherever possible, related to each other, they turn out to possess far greater present interest than might have been expected. Today, the problems which Weber discussed are still debated, and his own arguments and solutions have lost little of their capacity to provoke and inspire. An interpretation of Weber on his own premises and in his own context may have the independent value of bringing out with renewed clarity the strangely modern quality of his thought.

Subject. Not only the general character of this work, but also its special subject, and the material on which it is based, are characterized by self-imposed limitations. Although Weber doubtlessly felt that his most important efforts lay in the field of empirical sociology, the present account only deals with his methodology. Furthermore, the account of these methodological questions is to a very large extent based only on those parts of Weber's production which explicitly *deal with* such questions, whereas his empirical works have largely been neglected as sources of material. Finally, even within these already narrow limits, the focus of attention has been narrowed still further, since this book deals only with the relations of science and values, in their various manifestations, in Weber's methodological thought.

There are, however, certain reasons for these rigorous restrictions. In many respects, Weber's theory of science (methodology) seems, even to himself, to contain little more than a repetition of the views of earlier thinkers in the field; but on closer analysis, he often turns out to modify these views profoundly by placing them in a different setting. Although he himself often seems unaware of the fact, Weber's methodology, on a number of decisive points, breaks with the past and lays the foundations for the future.

This process of innovation is often evident in Weber's empirical sociology quite as much as in his theory of science; and several commentators [1] therefore claim that it is not sufficient to take his methodological writings into account; his empirical works should, in their opinion, be analysed as well, to supplement—and to a certain extent perhaps also to correct—the methodological essays. However, the question is not quite simple. It is undoubtedly true, as Andreas Walther puts it, that Weber's "vergleichend-kulturhistorisches Arbeiten von einer ungewöhnlichen, ursprünglichen Instinktsicherheit getragen [wird], die als Korrektiv gegen Einseitigkeiten und Engen der methodologischen Theorie durchgehend wirksam war" [2]; but this formulation at the same time points to the central problem: unless we hold preconceived

1. For instance Alexander v. Schelting, *Max Webers Wissenschaftslehre*, Tübingen 1934, p. 362; Reinhard Bendix, *Max Weber. An Intellectual Portrait*, New York (Doubleday Anchor Books) 1962, p. xxii; Raymond Aron, "Introduction", Max Weber, *Le savant et le politique* (tr. Julien Freund) Paris 1963, p. 11.
2. ([that Weber's] "comparative sociological work is supported by an unusually and naturally sound instinct, which to a large extent effectively corrected the one-sidedness and limited scope of his methodological theses"). Andreas Walther, "Max Weber als Soziologe", *Jahrbuch für Soziologie* (ed. G. Salomon), Vol. 2, Karlsruhe 1926, p. 2.

opinions as to the "soundness" or "unsoundness" of Weber's intuition, we cannot be sure whether an example from his empirical work which is at variance with his theoretical writings should be interpreted as a deliberate correction of the latter (i. e., as a kind of "methodology in disguise") or as a (probably unwitting) deviation without theoretical importance. This problem is particularly acute with regard to the methodological questions discussed in the present work, which largely deals with the fundamental logical *conditions* of scientific activity rather than with Weber's reflections on more concrete scientific approaches. If Weber practices "intuitive" ("verstehende") sociology or "causal imputation" ("kausale Zurechnung") in a way which does not conform to his own description of these methods, the deviant practice must be regarded as an important correction of the theoretical definition [3]. But even a deluge of value judgments and metaphysical concepts in his work would hardly, for instance, in itself invalidate his demand for the value freedom of scientific inquiry. Thus, while Weber's non-methodological scientific production has of course been taken into account as a possible source, it will only infrequently appear as an actual one.

The particular subject chosen: science and values in Weber's methodology, may seem too specific. However, I hope that the book will make clear that the intention has not been simply to produce an isolated discussion of a narrow range of problems. On the contrary, the account is designed to show that the two main concepts, "science" and "values", are fundamental co-ordinates of Weber's methodology, in fact of his scientific work altogether. And through the incarnation of the sphere of values in the concept of political action, the tension between these two co-ordinates turns out to be even more general: in a fundamental sense, Weber's own inner and outer life is profoundly influenced by the field of force defined by the relations of scientific contemplation and political action. In the light of this, it does not seem inappropriate to adapt the treatment of Weber's methodology to this essential dichotomy governing Weber's existence, what Karl Jaspers has called his "concrete philosophy" [4].

Method. This work was originally prepared as a thesis, and it admittedly still exhibits what is usually felt to be the limitation of a thesis: an almost exaggerated concern to document and substantiate any argument put forward, to the evident detriment of both the originality and the readability of the result.

3. The examples quoted by Aron (*Introduction,* 1963, p. 11) and Schelting (*Wissenschaftslehre,* 1934, p. 362) to illustrate the necessity of going beyond Weber's theoretical works are precisely of this kind.
4. See for instance Karl Jaspers, *Max Weber. Politiker. Forscher. Philosoph,* Munich 1958, p. 13.

However, I have felt that a need might yet exist for an account in English, but based on the original published and unpublished German sources, of a number of fundamental problems in Max Weber's methodology. And in such a work, which to a large extent consists of interpretations of complicated texts written in a foreign language, one has to take special pains to ensure that the conclusions can everywhere be tested against the original material. This may make the reading rather heavy going; but I hope that the reader will at least be sure where the argument is leading him, and feel the ground fairly firm beneath his feet.

Preliminary questions

A. *The problem of the systematic intentions behind Weber's methodological work*

1. All Weber's methodological writings were originally published as articles in scientific journals; and it was only after his death that they were published together in GAW. It therefore seems natural to raise the question whether, on the basis of this collected publication, it is justified to regard Weber's methodology as a systematic whole. It is necessary to deal with this question before passing on to the actual discussion, since the answer it receives will have an important influence on the whole of the subsequent account: if we have to conclude that GAW does contain a complete methodological system, the results of the various interpretations of Weber's text must be adapted to this larger systematic framework. On the other hand, a complete rejection of the systematizing point of view would rather lead to the highlighting of the individual peculiarities of Weber's articles.

On this point, we find two main tendencies among the commentators:

2.1. The first tendency above all dominates in the older literature on Weber. To a certain extent, it is met with as early as in Marianne Weber's biography of her husband [1], and it is definitely present in Alexander v. Schelting's *Max Webers Wissenschaftslehre* [2] (as well as in numerous other works); but it is most consistently formulated by Dieter Henrich. Henrich's thesis (which is already evident from the title of his work: *Die Einheit der Wissenschaftslehre Max Webers* [3] is that only a radically systematizing interpretation does full justice to Weber's methodology:

"[Der Weg der Untersuchung] soll zu der Einsicht führen, daß der Sammelband der Aufsätze [GAW] nicht nur an zufälligem Orte Einzelanalysen und Meinungen eines

1. Marianne Weber, *Max Weber. Ein Lebensbild,* (2. ed.), Heidelberg 1950.
2. Tübingen 1934.
3. Tübingen 1952. In his intervention at the 1964 Sociological Congress in Heidelberg (Otto Stammer (ed.), *Max Weber und die Soziologie heute,* Tübingen 1965, pp. 82–83), Henrich discusses a number of serious inconsistencies in Weber's work. His approach is still systematizing; but although he reaffirms his central thesis of the unity of Weber' methodology, he now gives it a more hypothetical formulation: *we* may perhaps, according to Henrich, see Weber's theory of science as a coherent whole; but this unity is no longer presented as being inherent in Weber's work.

Spezialforschers versammelt, sondern eine theoretische Einheit ausdrückt, deren Ge-
schlossenheit umso mehr in Verwunderung setzt, weil sie nicht offen sichtbar und
vielleicht nicht einmal Max Weber selbst bewußt gewesen ist" [4].

To this systematizing principle of interpretation, Henrich adds the claim
that Weber's methodology is fully developed from the very beginning [5].
2.2. Against this, Friedrich H. Tenbruck, for instance, maintains that a
systematizing interpretation makes it more *difficult* to understand Weber [6].
Instead, one should concentrate on the "historical co-ordinates" of Weber's
methodological writings:

"... Webers methodologische Betrachtungen [definieren und präzisieren sich] in
einem ganz bestimmten Fragezusammenhang seiner Zeit ..., dessen Kenntnis er als
selbstverständlich voraussetzt. Die Begriffe stammen aus ganz bestimmten Diskussionen und Traditionen, die Argumentation richtet sich gegen wohlumrissene Gruppen
und Lager, und die Arbeit gilt der Lösung eines besonderen zeitgenössischen Problems" [7].

2.3. The arguments by which the commentators try to support their respective principles of interpretation are closely interwoven with their differing
views of the *importance* of Weber's thought (and often even of Weber as a
person), which are largely irrelevant to the present account. Consequently,
we have to go beyond these arguments, to the primary sources, i. e., to Weber's
own text, in order to decide the point.

3.1. It is clear from GAW that Weber did not see himself in the role of an
original thinker in the field of methodology; he simply wishes to apply the
general results reached by "professional" philosophers to the more concrete
problems of the social sciences [8]. Thus, he regards his methodological work
not as an *aim* in itself, but as a *means* of arriving at a deeper understanding
of the character and potentialities of a number of scientific disciplines,
"their logical structure, and the limits and preconditions of their validity" [9].
This already indicates that we cannot be sure of finding large coherent discussions of methodological points in the essays collected in GAW, nor should
we expect to come across wholehearted attempts on Weber's part to co-
ordinate these essays to a systematic whole. And this indication is further
supported by passages in which Weber explicitly declares that he has not
worked out, or even tried to work out, a complete methodology:

4. Henrich, *Einheit*, 1952, p. 2.
5. *Ibid.,* p. 6.
6. Friedrich H. Tenbruck, "Die Genesis der Methodologie Max Webers", *Kölner
   Zeitschrift für Soziologie und Sozialpsychologie,* Vol. 11 (1959), p. 574.
7. *Ibid.,* p. 576.
8. *Cf.* GAW, pp. 1n1, 7n1, 215, 288n1.
9. ("ihre logische Struktur, die Grenzen und die Voraussetzungen ihrer Geltung").
   Schelting, *Wissenschaftslehre,* 1934, p. 69n2.

"... der Versuch, an Stelle der Aneinanderreihung einiger methodologischer Gesichtspunkte eine *systematische* Untersuchung treten zu lassen, [ist] hier ganz unterlassen worden ... Es soll hier nicht Logik getrieben, sondern es sollen bekannte Ergebnisse der modernen Logik für uns nutzbar gemacht, Probleme nicht gelöst, sondern dem Laien ihre Bedeutung veranschaulicht werden" [10].

3.2. To this, we may add a number of arguments of a more formal kind:

The title of the collection, *Gesammelte Aufsätze zur Wissenschaftslehre,* did not emanate from Weber but was formulated by his widow who edited the collection. In fact, the expression "Wissenschaftslehre" never occurs in GAW [11]. This point is not wholly unimportant, since the concept of "Wissenschaftslehre" has *philosophical* antecedents, going back to Fichte; in the work of Rickert—from whom Marianne Weber undoubtedly borrowed the term [12]—the concept still covers a wide area in the field of epistemology and of the philosophy of science. Thus, when both Schelting and Henrich choose—with a definite systematic intention—to incorporate the word "Wissenschaftslehre" in the titles of their respective works, this terminology should not be taken at its face value [13].

Many of Weber's methodological essays were produced for special occasions, and often take the form of critical, or even downright polemical, comments. Only *Wertfreiheit,* and the (in this connection) less significant essays *Kategorien, Grundbegriffe* and *Typen der leg. Herrsch.* do not seem to come under this heading [14]. Weber wrote *Objektivität* on the occasion of his taking over the editorship of the *Archiv* (with Werner Sombart and Edgar Jaffé). *Roscher* and *Knies I–II* were begun as the result of an invitation of the editors of a memorial volume in honour of Heidelberg University [15]. *Wiss. Beruf* and *Pol. Beruf* are based on shorthand notes of two lectures delivered by Weber to a student society in Munich. As for *Kritische Studien, Stammler* (with *Nachtrag*), *Grenznutzlehre* and *Energ. Kult.th.,* they are all critical discussions of the works of other thinkers.

10. GAW, p. 146n1. Tha passage in itself only refers to *Objektivität;* but the argument seems valid *a fortiori* for GAW as a whole. See also GAW, p. 292 and Marianne Weber, *Lebensbild,* 1950, p. 350.
11. We do find it, however, in two titles of books quoted in GAW by Weber; *cf.* Tenbruck, *Genesis,* 1959, pp. 573–74.
12. Cf. *ibid.,* p. 573; Heinrich Rickert, *Die Grenzen der naturwissenschaftlichen Begriffsbildung,* Tübingen 1902, pp. 15, 22. Marianne Weber prepared a dissertation on Fichte under Rickert's guidance, *cf.* letters from Weber to his wife of Aug. 7th and 10th, 1898 (copies in DZA II, Rep. 92, No. 30, Vol. 1).
13. It is consequently to be welcomed that Johannes Winckelmann, in his new edition of a number of Weber's methodological essays, prefers the more accurate title *Methodologische Schriften (cf. Meth. Schr.,* pp. XVII–XVIII).
14. It should be noted, however, that *Wertfreiheit* is based on the *Gutachten* which was Weber's written contribution to a methodological debate in the *Verein (cf. infra,* p. 19.
15. Marianne Weber, *Lebensbild,* 1950, p. 296. The essays were not finished in time and were instead published in *Schmollers Jahrbücher.*

Moreover, the greater part of the methodological essays collected in GAW were left unfinished in the sense that Weber, at the end of each of them, holds out the prospect of an additional essay, which is, however, never written, let alone published [16].

On the other hand, it must be admitted that the essays contain numerous cross-references, not only to discussions of central concepts like "ideal type" [17] or "value relation" ("Wertbeziehung") [18], but also on a number of subsidiary points which have apparently, in Weber's opinion, received sufficient treatment in an earlier work [19].

4. In the light of all this, it seems reasonable to conclude that there are not sufficient formal grounds for supposing that Weber, in writing the methodological articles reprinted in GAW, aimed at constructing a systematic methodology. This means that it is not *necessary* to organize the present account in conformity with some systematic framework provided by GAW; and moreover, it does not, as a general rule, seem *warranted* to try to remove inconsistencies in Weber's thought, or to supply missing links in the chain of his argument, simply in order to conform to such a hypothetical framework. This seemingly negative conclusion also has positive consequences: it enables us to regard a possible "unevenness" or intellectual jump in Weber's thought as a fruitful problem which does not necessarily detract from his greatness as a thinker. And on the other hand, nothing seems to debar us from choosing a systematic *method of presentation,* cutting across the lines of argument of the separate essays, as long as the individual peculiarities of form or content of the various essays are noted and given their proper weight [20].

B. *The problem of the philosophical basis of Weber's methodology*

1. Commentators often discuss the question to what extent Weber's theory

16. *Cf.* GAW, p. 145n1 (*Roscher* and *Knies I–II*), 290n4 (*Kritische Studien*) and 359n1 (*Stammler;* here, Weber began work on the promised additional essay, which was published posthumously as *Nachtrag*). As for the problems discussed in *Objektivität,* Weber himself expresses the hope that he will later on find time to deal with some of them at greater length (*Cf.* GAW, p. 131n1). However, there are no grounds for supposing, as Henrich seems to do (*Einheit,* 1952, p. 30n2), that Weber regarded *Objektivität* as *particularly* imperfect.
17. GAW, pp. 131n1, 330n1, 548n1, 562n1.
18. GAW, pp. 122n1, 512.
19. Henrich (*Einheit,* 1952, p. 6) takes these cross-references as sufficient proof of his thesis that Weber never even envisaged a revision of his opinions. This seems like investing purely formal arguments with more weight than they can carry.
20. Even the radically "fragmentating" Tenbruck admits that such a systematical presentation is permissible (*Genesis,* 1959, p. 576).

of science is influenced by, or even dependent on, certain *philosophical* positions, particularly those of the "South-West German" variety of neo-Kantian philosophy (Windelband, Rickert). In principle, it seems entirely justified to pose the problem in this way: Weber's methodological work is filled with references to philosophical works [21]; and he nowhere defines his position in a way which explicitly *rejects* the idea of the existence of philosophical elements in it. On the contrary, many of his statements seem to indicate that his methodology is in fact based on philosophical considerations. While it is generally recognized that Weber was not a philosopher in the proper sense of the word [22], it is certain that his methodology deals with questions which are at the same time legitimate subjects of philosophical inquiry.

However, the problem of the possible philosophical basis of Weber's theory of science is, in the form stated, largely irrelevant to the present account, which tries to keep within the context of the empirical discipline of political science. Here, the demonstration that Weber's methodology is, on certain points and to a certain extent, based on, say, neo-Kantian philosophy, is not very useful. On the contrary: to the ordinary student of political science, the relevance and fruitfulness of Weber's methodological arguments will probably be a function of the possibility of understanding and employing these arguments *independently* of a particular philosophical position. He will instead ask whether it is *necessary* to inscribe Weber's methodology in a philosophical framework, or, more pointedly, to what extent it is justified to *do without* such a framework. This is the line followed in the present account: instead of pursuing the lines of thought connecting Weber's theory of science "upwards" with philosophy, I have tried to establish to what extent it is legitimate to ignore these lines of thought and to push Weber's methodology "downwards", to the point where its conclusions are valid in the same sense as those of empirical science [23]. In fact, it seems *possible* to discuss Weber's theory of science without reference to its philosophical affiliations. And moreover, Weber's methodological thought is, in my opinion, particularly valuable and fruitful because it is able to *dispense with* the safety net of philosophy. It may be useful, even at this early stage, to try to substantiate this claim a little further, and, in so doing, to define the problem more accurately.

21. Apart from the works of Windelband and Rickert, Weber refers to those, for instance, of Wundt, Lask and Husserl.
22. *Cf.* Heinrich Rickert, *Die Grenzen der naturwissenschaftlichen Begriffsbildung* (5. ed.), Tübingen 1929, p. XXV; Marianne Weber, *Lebensbild*, 1950, pp. 350, 366; and for instance GAW, pp. 1n1, 215.
23. In the following, the term "philosophy" will therefore be used to denote types of argument going beyond what is regarded as valid in the empirical disciplines.

2. As an empirical discipline, political science relies on a criterion of scientific truth defined by the observance of a number of formal conditions which we may, with Arnold Brecht, call Scientific Method [24]. One of these conditions is the observance of the fundamental rules of logic [25]; this on the other hand implies that the *validity* of true propositions of analytical logic must by necessity be accepted by anyone who regards the results of empirical science as valid. From this, it seems possible to conclude that methodological arguments must be accepted as valid by political scientists as long as these arguments remain within the bounds of Scientific Method (including, in particular, the bounds of logic). Conversely, arguments going beyond these limits may be described as philosophical, in the sense that they can no longer be regarded as valid solely on the basis of the criteria of truth imposed by empirical science.

3. At first, it seems as if Rickert, for instance, believed that Weber's methodology kept *within* the bounds of Scientific Method; in *Grenzen* [5], he states that Weber believed the possibilities of scientific philosophy to be very restricted, "... i. e., in fact he only believed in "logic" " [26]. However, the discipline of "logic", as defined by the neo-Kantian philosophers, goes further than the traditional Aristotelian rules of correct thinking and includes the study of "the process of cognition as such in its formal structure" [27]; it comprises not only the scientific processing of empirical reality (Scientific Method), but also *pre*-scientific cognition: in fact, "Logik" would, in the current philosophical terminology, correspond to logic *plus* methodology *plus* epistemology. To the neo-Kantians, a strict delimitation of these three concepts was of little importance [28], because the demonstration of the objectivity of certain intellectual categories, which was their main concern, was in their opinion possible with regard both to pre-scientific and to various forms of scientific cognition. To a modern social science, however, the distinction is vital, first because the idea of objective intellectual categories cannot lay claim to scientific validity [29],

24. Arnold Brecht, *Political Theory*, Princeton 1959, p. 71.
25. *Ibid.*, pp. 28–29, 55–59.
26. ("... d. h. er glaubte eigentlich nur an die "Logik" "). Rickert, *Grenzen* [5], 1929, p. XXV.
27. ("die Erkenntnisbetätigung als solche in ihrer formalen Struktur"). Alexander v. Schelting, "Die logische Theorie der historischen Kulturwissenschaft von Max Weber und im besonderen sein Begriff des Idealtypus", *Archiv*, Vol. 49 (1922), p. 628.
28. Although Rickert does, in the *Grenzen* (1902, pp. 156n1, 601–02) distinguish between "methodologische" (methodological) and "erkenntnisstheoretische" (epistemological) questions, his distinction is rather vague; and both kinds of questions lie within what Rickert calls "Wissenschaftslehre".
29. Brecht (*Theory*, 1959, pp. 99, 113–15) admits that Scientific Method, too, is based on a number of immanent methodological *a priori* conditions (consubjectivity, causality, etc.); but the neo-Kantian categories discussed here differ from such

and secondly because epistemology, so to say, looks behind the façade of empirical reality, whereas Scientific Method has to take the latter for granted [30]. In the sense defined above, epistemology is philosophy, while methodology and logic are non-philosophical disciplines.

In Weber's terminology, "Logik", "Methodologie" and "Erkenntnistheorie" are all employed to denote reflections on the preconditions of human perception and cognition [31]. Therefore, the problem is whether the reflections denoted by these terms include more than the analysis of *scientific* activity, i. e., whether Weber's "logic" covers the whole neo-Kantian scale of "Logik". This is denied by a number of the most important commentators, among them Schelting, Henrich and Winckelmann [32].

However, while Schelting goes further still, and denies that Weber's methodology depends in any way on philosophical positions, Henrich—followed by Winckelmann—limits his rejection to the influence of Rickert's epistemology on Weber. To Henrich, Weber's theory of science does have its roots in philosophy, in a certain view of the essential nature of man, i. e., in a *philosophical anthropology*, which in its turn gives rise to a particular theory of *ethics* propounded by Weber [33].

Thus, the problem of the possible philosophical basis of Weber's methodology will concretely manifest itself in the attempt to show that it is legitimate to interpret Weber's text without reference to, a) an epistemology of prescientific cognition, and, b) a philosophical anthropology and an ethical theory derived from this anthropology.

conditions by being completely *deductive* and by going beyond a purely *formal* categorization of the process of cognition. *Cf. infra,* pp. 116–17.

30. "... in a sense, the observable world *is* the real world to Scientific Method" (Brecht, *Theory,* 1959, p. 52).
31. See for instance GAW, p. 214, where all three expressions occur.
32. Schelting, *Wissenschaftslehre,* 1934, pp. 66–67; Henrich, *Einheit,* 1952, p. 15; Johannes Winckelmann, *Legalität und Legitimität in Max Webers Herrschaftssoziologie,* Tübingen 1952, pp. 21–24. Marianne Weber, on the other hand, implies (*Lebensbild,* 1950, pp. 353, 366) that Weber drew the boundary at the same point as Rickert.
33. Henrich, *Einheit,* 1952, p. 3. It may not be irrelevant to point out that Henrich's book is a rewritten version of a *philosophical* dissertation.

The general plan of the work

Leaving aside for the moment the accurate definition of the two concepts involved, we can logically distinguish a number of different possible relations between scientific inquiry and values.

Since the concept of scientific inquiry must be supposed always to imply the notion of a person, the *investigator,* dealing with some particular *object of research,* it is possible to make a first distinction between the *research level* (the level of the investigator) and the *object level* of scientific inquiry. Accordingly, the relation between values and scientific inquiry can exist on either of these two levels, and it is an important—but often neglected [1]—rule when discussing a particular problem always to make perfectly clear on what level the discussion is being conducted.

As regards the relation of values to the *research level* of scientific inquiry, we can formulate two sets of questions [2]: First: Can we find value elements which must be regarded as illegitimate in certain relations on the research level of scientific inquiry? If so, what are these value elements, and what are the relations in which they are illegitimate? This set of questions expresses a problem of definition concerning the concept of scientific inquiry: Do we define "scientific inquiry" in such a way that particular value elements on its research level fall with necessity *outside* the definition? The *second* set of questions can be formulated as an inversion of this problem of definition: Is the definition of "scientific inquiry" of such a kind that certain value elements lie *within* its scope? If so, does this mean that the value elements in question are a *necessary* part of the definition, or simply that a particular course of inquiry does not lose its "scientific" character even if these value elements are present in it [3]?

1. *Cf. infra,* p. 28.
2. *Cf.* Ralf Dahrendorf, "Sozialwissenschaft und Werturteil", *Pfade aus Utopia,* Munich 1967, p. 77.
3. Apparently, Hans Albert, *Traktat über kritische Vernunft,* Tübingen 1968, pp. 63–64, sees this last problem ("das [Problem] der Wertbasis der Wissenschaften") as independent of the first one. Although his classification is based on a careful distinction between various related forms of discussion, I think that the one adopted here, while being somewhat cruder than his, is warranted, and possibly a little closer to Weber's line of thought.

On the *object level,* we can formulate two similar sets of questions which may, without distortion, be reduced to the single one: Does the definition of "scientific inquiry" include value elements on the object level? If so, what are these value elements?

Each of the three first chapters of the following work is devoted to one of these three sets of questions, as they are discussed by Max Weber. The problem of values as illegitimate elements on the research level, of values as a *problem of scientific inquiry,* is treated in ch. 1; the legitimate, indeed to a large extent the necessary, role of values on the research level of the social sciences in particular: their status as a logical *precondition of scientific inquiry,* is discussed in ch. 2; and ch. 3 concerns the relation of values to scientific inquiry on the object level, as an *object of scientific inquiry.* Two further chapters have been added: ch. 4 contains a discussion of a concept, defined and elaborated by Weber, which has the peculiarity of being both based on and primarily useful for the investigation of values on the object level of social science; this concept, the so-called ideal type, is an example of values being employed as an *instrument,* albeit an abstract one, *of scientific inquiry.* In the last chapter, the concept of *politics,* as the epitome of social value orientation, is discussed, both in itself and in its relation to its conceptual opposite, *scientific inquiry.*

1. Values as a problem of scientific inquiry: value freedom

As mentioned above [1], one of the fundamental problems arising out of the relation of values to scientific inquiry is the question whether the definition one adopts of "scientific inquiry" excludes certain value elements from the predicate "scientific", and, if so, what value elements and in what connections. More succinctly, the question can be formulated as follows: is the sphere of scientific inquiry defined in such a manner that we can point to a sphere of value elements separated from it by this definition?

It is quite obvious, indeed a commonplace to anyone who has worked on the methodology of the social sciences, that this question can be answered in the affirmative in the case of Max Weber. At least in certain connections, Weber demands a complete separation of the value sphere from that of scientific inquiry; in these connections, values are, in his view, illegitimate elements in the process of scientific inquiry. This principle or demand (both terms will be used in the following) Weber calls the demand for the "Wertfreiheit", the *value freedom* of scientific inquiry [2].

It is certain that Weber was not the first scholar to formulate a principle of this kind. As Arnold Brecht has pointed out [3], scholars like Georg Simmel,

1. Pp. 13–15.
2. The term "value freedom" has been chosen as the *linguistically* most correct and idiomatic rendering of "Wertfreiheit". As will appear in the course of the discussion, the German term "Wertfreiheit" adopted by Weber is in itself extremely unfortunate, since it evokes—as do his terms "Objektivität" and "Idealtyp" (*cf. infra*)—precisely those associations which Weber in his discussion tries to rid it of: a "wertfrei" science is *not* free from all value elements. Unfortunately, this unequivocal interpretation of the concept is only carried over into Weber's *terminology* by means of the inverted commas put around the word "Wertfreiheit" in the title of *Wertfreiheit* (*cf.* the same kind of typographical scepticism in the inverted commas of "Objektivität" in the title of *Objektivität*); consequently, the risk of misunderstanding still exists. To eliminate it, the German editor of Weber's works, professor Winckelmann, and certain other authors (René König, Hans Albert), have substituted the term "Werturteilsfreiheit" for the Weberian one, a coinage which is far more accurate. In view of Weber's own preference, however, I have kept to the term "value freedom" in this work, the more so as the term "freedom from value judgments" has nothing to recommend it from an aesthetic point of view.
3. Brecht, *Theory*, 1959, pp. 215–21; see also Fritz Loos, *Zur Wert- und Rechtslehre Max Webers*, Tübingen 1970, pp. 38–42.

Heinrich Rickert and Georg Jellinek had, each in his own field (ethics, philosophy and political science, respectively), advanced similar ideas before Weber's first complete formulation of the demand (1904). The logical assumptions underlying it have an even longer history, since in their essentials they reach back to Aristotelian logic, and may be found in their relevant form in Hume and Kant [4]. Weber, however, was the first to extend the principle of value freedom to all the social sciences, and to give its central concepts the meaning which is by and large still today accepted as the basis for the discussion of this question.

The principle of value freedom in itself, however, by no means exhausts the question, and raises more varied and greater problems than those which it disposes of. Although the paternity of the principle as such must be attributed to other scholars, more important is the fact that Weber was the first to think out its premises thoroughly, in all their ramifications, to apply it in a number of different fields, and to demonstrate its scope and consequences: in short, to discuss exhaustively what he himself called "the *meaning* (Sinn) of value freedom" (italics mine). As the present work endeavours to show, Weber's treatment of the various aspects of the principle of value freedom has for the most part remained valid even today. Viewed from this angle, the claim that Weber was the true author of the principle of value freedom, as this principle is currently understood and discussed, does not seem unwarranted [5].

To explain why it was Weber, rather than another scholar, who came to explore the principle of value freedom in all its details, some reference is necessary to the circumstances under which it came to be formulated. From the point of view of the theoretical discussion of the principle, these circumstances are of no particular importance [6]; but they form the background to its formulation and growth, and put it in its proper polemical context. It may therefore perhaps not be out of place to give a brief sketch of this context of the problem.

4. Brecht, *Theory*, 1959, pp. 200–215; see also Loos, *Wertlehre*, 1970, pp. 36–38.
5. As a matter of curiosity, it may be noted that the use of the *term* "Wertfreiheit" to cover the concept of value freedom (as defined by Weber) probably originates with him. In his own works, the term first occurs in the title of *Wertfreiheit* (1917) and in the text of that essay. The adjective "wertfrei" occurs once in *Knies I* (GAW, p. 74), and in letters to E. Jaffé (from 1907; reprinted in Eduard Baumgarten, *Max Weber. Werk und Person,* Tübingen 1964, p. 647) and Karl Voßler (letter of Nov. 14th, 1905; copy in DZA II, Rep. 92, No. 30, Vol. 4); in the letter to Voßler, however, the word may denote a somewhat broader concept.
6. It is consequently rather unfortunate, in my view, that T. S. Simey, *Social Science and Social Purpose,* London 1968, devotes the major part of his chapter on "Value Freedom" (pp. 88–108) to a presentation and discussion of the principle from the point of view of the immediate, external causes of its formulation.

1.1. The external context of Weber's demand for value freedom

From the very beginning, Weber's demand for value freedom was hotly debated. The first fairly complete formulation of the principle of value freedom, its premises and consequences, was given by him in 1904 in *Objektivität*. The immediate cause was peaceful enough, viz, the taking over of the *Archiv* by a new team of editors; but Weber's declaration, on behalf of the new editors, that the periodical, "als Vertreterin einer empirischen Fachdisziplin" [1], would observe the principle of value freedom, was a thinly veiled declaration of war on the "historical" school of economics under the leadership of Gustav Schmoller. In *Knies I–II*, Weber's critique of the philosopher Wundt was in part guided by the same main principles as those governing the argument of *Objektivität*. In the following years, the same fate befell the jurist Rudolf Stammler (in *Stammler)* and the "energeticist" biologist, Professor Ostwald (in *Energ. Kult. th.*) who was strongly influenced by the methods of natural science. At the same time, Weber raised the problem of value freedom in the stronghold of historico-ethical economics, the *Verein,* first, at the 1905 congress, in a tentative way, then vigorously, at the 1909 congress in Vienna where Werner Sombart backed him up.

The reaction inside the *Verein* to this offensive was extremely cool [2]. This was unquestionably one of the main reasons why Weber was insistent in having the principle of value freedom written into the statutes of the *Gesellschaft,* a new sociological society founded, partly on his own initiative, in 1909. This measure, however, aggravated the problem instead of solving it. Already at the first congress of the *Gesellschaft,* a strong anti-value-free group emerged under the leadership of Rudolf Goldscheid; and Weber consequently felt it necessary to intervene in a large number of the debates, which ranged very widely (from economic to biological problems) because of the interdisciplinary character of the then infant study of sociology. At the second congress, the differences of opinion grew critical: in Weber's view, almost all the speakers offended against the officially established principle of value-freedom, and the discussions became, in the words of one observer, " a veritable chase after the supposed or actual prescriptive demands of the

1. ("since it represented an empirical discipline"). GAW, p. 149.
2. *Cf.* Franz Boese, *Geschichte des Vereins für Sozialpolitik 1872–1932,* Berlin 1939, pp. 135–37, who quotes disapproving letters to Schmoller from, among others, Philippovich, Fuchs and Knapp; a letter of Weber's to his wife Marianne, dated Oct. 13th, 1909 (copy in DZA II, Rep. 92, No. 30, Vol. 1), concerns a subsequent meeting of the main committe of the *Verein* in Leipzig, where Weber's views on value freedom met with little approval.

speakers" [3]. When, shortly afterwards, Goldscheid was elected president of the *Gesellschaft,* Weber left the society [4].

Simultaneously, the discussion of the principle of value freedom in the *Verein*—a discussion which, characteristically, was often given the name of "Werturteilsstreit" ("value controversy") by later observers—came to a head. On Weber's initiative [5], the assiciation decided to place the question of value freedom in the science of economics on the agenda for an enlarged meeting of the main committee (from which, unlike the ordinary congresses, the public was excluded). Prospective participants were requested to send in in advance a short summary of their views on four aspects of the question, viz, "1. die Stellung des sittlichen Werturteils in der wissenschaftlichen Nationalökonomie, 2. das Verhältnis der Entwicklungstendenzen zu praktischen Wertungen, 3. die Bezeichnung wirtschafts- und sozialpolitischer Zielpunkte, 4. das Verhältnis der allgemeinen methodologischen Grundsätze zu den besonderen Aufgaben des akademischen Unterrichts" [6]. Weber's contribution to the symposium, the *Gutachten,* was far more comprehensive than those of the other contributors, and put his own views in their most systematic form as yet (although the subjects singled out for discussion did lead him to concentrate on particular aspects of the question)[7]. The small volume (*Äußerungen*) containing the printed contributions to the symposium was never put on sale, and probably only existed in some two hundred copies [8]. Apparently, the *Verein* was anxious to ensure that the methodological brawl would not be known in detail to a larger public. This concern was manifested even more clearly at the meeting itself, on January 4th and 5th, 1914, where it was

3. ("eine wahre Jagd auf die vermeintlichen oder wirklichen Soll-Forderungen der Redner"). Leopold v. Wiese, "Die deutsche Gesellschaft für Soziologie", *Kölner Zeitschrift für Soziologie und Sozialpsychologie,* Vol. 11 (1959), pp. 12–13. Only excerpts from Weber's contributions are known, since is was decided—probably because of the internal crisis of the *Gesellschaft*—not to publish the complete protocol of the debates.
4. Marianne Weber, *Weber,* 1950, pp. 468–69, who quotes Weber's disappointed and bitter declaration of withdrawal.
5. *Cf. Verhandlungen des Vereins für Sozialpolitik in Nürnberg 1911,* Leipzig 1912, p. 163, and Boese, *Geschichte des VfS,* 1939, p. 145, who is unnecessarily coy in speaking only of an "Anregung von bestimmter Seite".
6. ("1. the position of ethical value judgments in the science of economics, 2. the relation of "lines of development" to practical valuations, 3. the designation of goals for economic and social policy, 4. the relation of general methodological principles to the special tasks of academic teaching"). Boese, *Geschichte des VfS,* 1939, p. 145.
7. It is very difficult, and not very fruitful, to analyse in detail the influence which the circumstances surrounding the composition of the *Gutachten* may have had on Weber's arguments in that essay. One does notice, however, that the wording of the *Gutachten* is often more *cautious* and more *precise* than might have been excepted. This *may* be due to a wish on Weber's part to avoid, if possible, an open break with Schmoller.
8. Boese, *Geschichte des VfS,* 1939, p. 145.

decided, on Schmoller's proposal, to keep no record of the debates. Consequently, we possess only rather vague accounts of the discussions, and especially of Weber's contributions to them; but this much seems certain, that the proceedings soon took a not very fruitful turn, and that Weber in particular defended his position with great heat. The debate came to a dramatic conclusion:

"Da ... die [Weber] widersprechenden oder wenigstens teilweise widersprechenden Meinungen sich mehrten und wesentlich nur Sombart volle Zustimmung äußerte, erhob sich Max Weber noch einmal zu einer wuchtigen Äußerung, die ziemlich unverblümt den Widersprechenden zu verstehen gab, sie verstünden nicht, worauf es ihm (Max Weber) ankomme, und verließ dann unwillig die Sitzung" [9].

For a number of reasons (the war, Weber's preoccupation with other scientific and practical problems), this stormy discussion was followed by a period of relative calm; Weber's only subsequent contribution to the question was the publication (in 1917) of the *Gutachten* in revised and enlarged form. In *Wiss. Beruf* and *Pol. Beruf,* we still find echoes of the problem, but with different accents, particularly in the form of an added interest in practical politics.

As we have seen, Weber discusses the principle of value freedom with reference to numerous disciplines: logic, pure and applied economics, sociology (including the sociology of religion and of law, and the biological-organicist school), law and politics. Obviously, these diverse points of reference explain his extension of the demand to cover the social sciences in general, as well as his careful discussion of its applicability and application in each of the fields mentioned. But, paradoxically, this important reason for the *scope* and *depth* of Weber's discussion must at the same time be reckoned among the main causes of its *fragmentary character.* Weber treats the demand for value freedom in sections, bringing the central principle to bear now in one direction, now in another; the various aspects of the problem are singled out for attention according to the need of the moment.

To ensure that the general view of the problem is kept clear in the present account, where Weber's basic position is of greater importance than his various immediate reasons for stating it with regard to this or that particular discipline, I have adopted a more systematic approach: after a short

9. ("As ... the number of opinions wholly or partly hostile to Weber increased, and in fact only Sombart declared himself in complete agreement with him, Max Weber rose once more and delivered himself of a forceful statement which, in rather blunt terms, gave his opponents to understand that they did not see his point; he then left the meeting in anger"). *Ibid.,* p. 147. Weber's last "intervention" is said, according to contemporary observers, to have run as follows: "It is impossible to argue with idiots", followed by a crash, as the door slammed shut behind the departing scholar. Boese's version should be read in the light of his frankly pro-Schmoller and anti-Weber attitude.

initial exposition of the *general* principle of value freedom, as formulated by Weber, the discussion will concentrate on his treatment of the various groups of problems raised by this principle.

1.2. The principle and its premises in their most general form

As mentioned above, Weber most often discusses the principle of value freedom with regard to some particular discipline and in a polemical context. This is probably the reason why his formulations of the principle are similarly limited in scope. In fact, general statements of the demand for value freedom are quite rare. Most of them are found in *Objektivität* [1], and in the published report of the 1909 congress of the *Verein* [2]; but *Kritische Studien* and *Wertfreiheit,* as well as certain reports of other debates in the *Verein* and the *Gesellschaft,* contain similar general formulations of the principle of value freedom [3].

1. The definition implied above of the principle ("complete separation, in certain relations, of the sphere of values and the sphere of scientific inquiry") raises a problem which may at first seem slight, but which turns out to be of considerable importance.

Formally, the demand that two spheres, A and B, are to be kept separate may be expressed in three different ways: 1): "A must be kept free from elements of B"; 2): "B must be kept free from elements of A"; 3): "A and B must be kept free from elements of each other". We can call the last formulation the *symmetrical,* and the two first ones the two *asymmetrical* demands. In our case, the symmetrical demand for value freedom would be couched in roughly the following terms: "Scientific inquiry and values must be kept separate", while the two asymmetrical formulations would run: "Scientific inquiry must be kept free from value elements" and "the value sphere must be kept free from scientific elements" respectively [4].

On closer examination, it appears that Weber, whenever he is stating the principle of value freedom in general terms, tends to express it in either of the two asymmetrical forms, whereas the symmetrical formulation is very rarely met with. One of the few passages which does—probably [5]—belong in this

1. For instance GAW, pp. 146n1, 149, 151, 152.
2. For instance GASS, pp. 417, 418, 419, 420.
3. For instance GAW pp. 225, 557; GASS, pp. 402, 476–77.
4. This double aspect is clearly brought out by Ernst Troeltsch, *Der Historismus und seine Probleme,* Tübingen 1922 (photographic reprint, Aalen 1961), p. 569: "Wertfreie, reine Kausalitätsforschung ... und wissenschaftsfreie, von jedem Geltungsrationalismus und jeder Metaphysik, auch jeder Religion und Spekulation befreite Wertposition: das ist es, was dem klaren Denker ziemt".
5. It is not quite clear from the context whether Weber is referring to the demand as such or to the logical premises on which it is based.

last category is the introductory footnote to *Objektivität,* GAW, p. 146nl, where it is said that the three editors of the *Archiv* (Jaffé, Sombart and Weber) hold similar views on a number of fundamental points, particularly concerning "der Forderung ... der strengen *Scheidung von Erfahrungswissen und Wert-urteil,* wie sie hier—natürlich ohne den Anspruch, damit etwas "Neues" zu fordern—vertreten wird".

It is also rare to find general statements in Weber's works asserting that scientific inquiry should be kept free from value elements, that is, expressing, in its strict sense, the principle of the value freedom of science. The only passage which quite clearly reflects this asymmetrical aspect, is Weber's famous passionate outburst at the 1909 congress: "... das Hineinmengen eines Seinsollens in wissenschaftliche Fragen ist eine Sache des Teufels" [6].

The other asymmetrical formulation, which, properly speaking, does not demand the value freedom of scientific inquiry, but the freedom of the value sphere from allegations of scientific demonstrability, appears far more frequently. As a paradigm of this type, we can take the continuation of Weber's intervention at the 1909 congress quoted above: "... eine empirische Wissenschaft gibt es nicht anders als auf dem Boden des Seins, und sie besagt *nichts* über das Sollen" [7]; but *Objektivität* contains many of these "asymmetrical" formulations as well [8, 9].

This material is clearly too slight and too provisional, and the analysis too formal and rudimentary, to warrant any far-reaching conclusions. But it is worth noting that the asymmetrical dominance described above reappears continuously as a fundamental feature of Weber's discussion of the problems reviewed below.

2.   Weber seems to advance only one *argument* for his demand for value freedom: the fact that the sphere of scientific inquiry and the value sphere are logically absolutely different [10]. He sees this difference as fundamental,

---

6. ("The introduction of a prescriptive demand into scientific questions is the work of the Devil"). GASS, p. 417. Weber adds sourly: "...which the *Verein* has, however, quite often carried out with ample sufficiency".
7. GASS, p. 417.
8. For instance GAW, pp. 149, 151, 152.
9. At the Sociological Congress in Heidelberg in 1964 (Stammer (ed.), *Weber,* 1965, p. 123), Carl J. Friedrich seems to advance a thesis diametrically opposed to the one outlined above, asserting that Weber, even in his scientific work, was deeply concerned with formulating and substantiating value judgments. The grounds for this assertion are not quite clear; but the indication is that Friedrich believes that Weber tried to adduce scientific proof of the value of parliamentary democracy and of bureaucracy (*cf.* Carl J. Friedrich, *Man and his Government,* New York 1963, pp. 65–68). If this is indeed Friedrich's opinion, it must be described as a simple misunderstanding. Weber did not even regard the values in question as necessarily positive, still less as scientifically demonstrable.
10. A hypothetical second argument, based on the change of values through time, is criticized by Weber; *cf. infra,* pp. 51–52.

as "der allerelementarste Gegensatz: der zwischen "Sein" und "Sollen" " [11]. The two categories belong, in his view, to separate theoretical "provinces", on separate logical "planes" [12]: "... die Geltung eines praktischen Imperativs als Norm und ... die Wahrheitsgeltung einer empirischen Tatsachenfeststellung [liegen] in absolut heterogenen Ebenen der Problematik..." [13].

One gets the impression that this position—which is repeated again and again—was accepted as self-evident, almost a logical commonplace, by Weber. One indication of this is that he nowhere discusses the logical and philosophical foundations of the argument more thoroughly; another is the nonchalant air of a statement like the following: "... weil es sich da [i.e., concerning the difference between "Sein" and "Sollen"] nun einmal um heterogene Probleme handelt" [14]. One practical instance of Weber's apparent belief in the self-evidence of the argument is the speed with which he denies, in a few introductory sentences to *Pol. Beruf,* that there is any connection between the question of *what* policy to pursue and the other one asking what politics *is* and what it *can* come to mean; he then immediately, with the words: "Damit zur Sache", hurries on to deal with the latter problem in its various ramifications [15, 16].

3. We find a considerable variety of terms being used by Weber to designate the spheres of scientific inquiry and of values respectively, in his fundamental statements of the principle of value freedom as well as in his arguments supporting it. This terminological variation does not seem to indicate any wavering in Weber's mind about the fundamental and absolute character of the logical difference between the two spheres; but it does warrant a certain preliminary hesitation as to his views on the exact definition and designation of these spheres.

It is a reasonable supposition that the analysis of the *terms* used by Weber to designate the two spheres might add to our knowledge of how he defined their respective *characteristics*. The need for such an analysis, however, is not the same in the two cases. Weber's discussion of the question of values as a problem in scientific inquiry takes the form of a close analysis of the positive characteristics of the sphere of *science,* so that a study of the terms chosen to designate the latter concept adds little to our knowledge. On the other hand, Weber treats the value sphere in itself so briefly [17] that an

11. GAW, p. 127n1.
12. GASS, pp. 450 and 418 respectively.
13. GAW, p. 501.
14. GAW, p. 500; see also for instance GAW, pp. 212, 261, 381, 491.
15. GPS, p. 493.
16. The fact that the notes on which the lecture was based (now in the archives of the Max-Weber-Institut, Munich) contain no mention of this logical aspect of the question, seems to show that Weber regarded the point as wholly unproblematical.
17. This does not mean that Weber is less *concerned with* the value sphere; but even

examination of the various designations used for it may be able to shed more light on his view of its characteristics. Thus, the discussion below of the sphere of scientific inquiry is not based on a semantic analysis and is on the whole limited to a short exposition of what Weber regarded as the fundamental quality of scientific inquiry and its results; the value sphere, on the other hand, is given more exhaustive treatment, which to a large extent concentrates on the various terms that Weber used.

1.3. The logical premises of the principle

1.3.1. The definition of the logical spheres

1.3.1.1. The sphere of scientific inquiry

The terms used by Weber to designate the sphere of scientific inquiry and its content ("Wissenschaft", "Erfahrungs-" or "empirische Wissenschaft", "Erfahrungswahrheit" and "(empirische) Tatsachenfeststellung" are the ones most frequently used)[1] are, taken by themselves, relatively opaque; and the exemplification found in certain passages of Objektivität, viz, that the aim of scientific inquiry is "denkende Ordnung der empirischen Wirklichkeit"[2], does not increase our knowledge very much. If we limit ourselves to this kind of data, the only conclusion we can draw is that Weber's concept of "scientific inquiry" apparently designates a perception of reality laying claim to some kind of truth.

The concept of truth, however, is by no means unambiguous, but on the contrary raises a number of questions concerning the concrete criteria of the "truth" referred to, its sphere of validity, etc., in short, the material definition of the sphere of scientific inquiry. On this point, Weber's discussion of the principle of value freedom is peculiar in that it almost completely concentrates on the separation between the sphere of scientific inquiry and the value sphere: his arguments justifying the principle do not go beyond a simple simple statement of logical fact; and his exposition and discussion of the corresponding practical demand accordingly tend to remain negative, simply

when his analysis is wholly concentrated on the latter (as in the case of the problems treated in ch. 5), he largely seems to regard the question of its content as trivial.
1. "Wissenschaft" ("science") for instance GAW, pp. 212, 611; GASS, pp. 402, 417. "Erfahrungs-/empirische Wissenschaft" ("empirical science") for instance GAW, pp. 149, 151, 508; GASS, p. 418.
"Erfahrungswahrheit" ("empirical truth") for instance GAW, p. 261.
"(Empirische) Tatsachenfeststellung" ("empirical ascertaining of facts") for instance GAW, pp. 311, 501, 601; GASS, p. 419.
2. ("intellectual ordering of empirical reality"). GAW, pp. 150, 160; see also GAW pp. 155, 213.

postulating an unbridgeable gap between "Sein" and "Sollen", "Is" and "Ought". The question of the criteria of scientific truth in Weber's methodology will therefore not be discussed at this point [3].

The only specification of Weber's concept of scientific truth which it may be useful to offer at this stage, is derived from his insistence that scientific truth, as defined by him, is *objective:* "... sie [will] überindividuell als "objektive Wahrheit" *gelten* ..."[4]. Considering that Weber does not at all discuss the concrete criteria and conditions of validity of scientific truth, such a "specification" apparently only amounts to a change of name; but it does add the material characteristic that scientific truth reaches out beyond the individual and his subjective will and preferences [5], and thus separates *objective* truth from mere subjective conviction, although the latter may have the status of *absolute* truth *in the eyes of the individual concerned.* This specification is certainly not unproblematical, even in relation to the wholly formal and negative discussion of the principle of value freedom [6]. But it is still useful to be able to assert, even at this preliminary stage, that Weber's concept of scientific inquiry implies a perception of reality which (on the basis of a number of empirical and logical criteria not concretely defined) can lay claim to *objective truth,* i. e., which may be said to be valid even for persons who have not *subjectively* accepted it as valid for themselves [7].

1.3.1.2. The value sphere

Philosophically, it may be possible to work out a systematic classification of the various logical forms in which a valuational element can manifest itself. As might be expected in view of his general scepticism concerning philosophy [1], systematic intentions of this kind were alien to Weber. Although the diversity of his formulations probably is not quite fortuitous, nothing indicates that his methodology was influenced by philosophical considerations or even that he wished to work out an analytical classification of the concepts

---

3. Parenthetically, it may be observed that the problem of the criteria of truth is not treated by Weber in the course of his positive discussion of the implications and possibilities of science. *Cf. infra,* pp. 137–38.
4. GAW, p. 89.
5. Weber illustrates this with the example: that an empirical or theoretical scientific assertion should aim at being valid even for a Chinese. *Cf.* GAW, pp. 155–56.
6. *Cf.* for the question of the relationship truth value–value of truth *infra,* pp. 32–34, and for the possible relativation of truth value by, for instance, psychological, biological or historical knowledge, *infra,* pp. 46–50.
7. The parallel to the monopoly of "intersubjectively transmissible knowledge" possessed by Scientific Method, as Arnold Brecht defines it (in *Political Theory*), is obvious.
1. *Cf. supra,* p. 12.

involved [2]. I have consequently felt justified in grouping below the various terms found in Weber's work without regard to any *intended* classification on his part.

1. Considering that Weber himself calls his imperative principle a demand for "Wertfreiheit" and that he several times uses the same terminology in derivatives like "wertfrei", it is remarkable that the closer discussion in his methodological works of this demand mainly relies on other terms: apart from one passage [3] where "die "Geltung" [der] "Werte" " is opposed to "die Geltung [der] Erfahrungswahrheit", we only find the term as a part of the compound "Wertsphäre" ("value sphere"), where it denotes an un-defined, general concept [4]. When the *term* "Wert" occasionally appears else-where, in the discussion of the concrete implications of the principle of value freedom, it carries the meaning of "importance", not "value" [5].

2.1. Among the terms used by Weber to denote the value element which the principle of value freedom aims at eradicating from science, "Wertung", "Werturteil" and their linguistic satellites ("Werten", "Bewerten", "Wert-beurteilung") hold a very prominent place [6]. This seems to reflect a deliber-ate attempt on Weber's part to carry through the discussion of value freedom by means of precisely these terms. They are carefully defined and con-spicuously placed. *Wertfreiheit* opens with the definition of "Wertung"; and the definition of "Werturteil", which follows ten pages later, is also given a key position, introducing the positive discussion of value freedom [7]. Further-more, before entering into the concrete discussion of his theme, Weber fol-lows up his definition of "Wertung" by an explicit, although indirect, indi-cation to the effect that the term "Wertfreiheit" in the title of the essay

2. *Cf.* GAW, p. 501, where Weber refuses to discuss the question whether subjective judgments of taste are on a different (implicitly: a lower) level than practical, particularly ethical, valuations: "das sind Probleme der Wertphilosophie, nicht der Methodik der empirischen Disziplinen". In a letter to Robert Liefmann of July 15th, 1907, Weber also takes a severely practical view of the concept of value: the important point, to him, is the *utility* of the concept, i. e., what it *covers* or *explains* (copy in DZA II, Rep. 92, No. 30, Vol. 7). *Cf.* Loos, *Wertlehre*, 1970, p. 46.
3. GAW, p. 261. Of course, the term "Wert", as well as the various other terms discussed below ("Wertung", "Sollen", etc.), is met with far more frequently in GAW than in this one passage; but the present discussion has been deliberately restricted to Weber's direct and fundamental formulation of the principle of value freedom and of its logical premises.
4. As for instance GAW, pp. 523, 537.
5. For instance GAW, p. 345, where the term appears together with its opposite, "Unwert".
6. "Wertung" for instance GAW, pp. 155, 489–91, 508, 540; GASS, p. 431. "Werturteil" for instance GAW, pp. 61, 146n1, 149, 313, 425, 495, 499, 557, 602; GASS, pp. 421, 476.
7. GAW, pp. 489 and 491 respectively.

should be understood as "Wertungsfreiheit" (this again to be interpreted in the light of the definition of "Wertung") [8]. Finally, the essay taken as a whole shows that Weber, in describing the typical characteristics of the value sphere, mentions just those contained in the definitions of "Wertung" and "Werturteil".

What are these characteristics? GAW, p. 489 gives the following description:

"Unter "Wertungen" sollen nachstehend, wo nicht ein anderes gesagt oder von selbst ersichtlich ist, *"praktische"* Bewertungen einer durch unser Handeln beeinflußbaren Erscheinung als verwerflich oder billigenswert verstanden sein."

and on p. 499, roughly the same qualities are enumerated in the definition of "Werturteil":

"Unendliches Mißverständnis und vor allem terminologischer, daher gänzlich steriler, Streit hat sich an das Wort "Werturteil" geknüpft, welches zur Sache offenbar gar nichts austrägt. Es ist, wie eingangs gesagt, ganz unzweideutig, daß es sich bei diesen Erörterungen für unsere Disziplinen um *praktische* Wertungen sozialer Tatsachen als, unter ethischen oder unter Kulturgesichtspunkten oder aus anderen Gründen, praktisch wünschenswert oder unerwünscht, handelt."

These definitions have at least two things in common: the stress laid on the "practical" aspect of the concepts defined; and the view of their logical structure as dualistic, either positive or negative: "verwerflich"–"billigenswert", "wünschenswert"–"unerwünscht". By emphasizing in this way the practical (as opposed to the theoretical) and evaluative elements in value judgments [9], Weber characterizes the sphere of valuation as opposed to that of empirical science (in a manner which would probably still be accepted as valid today, at least for the purposes of political science), and thus underpins his assertion of the *logical* gap between the two. But the wording of the definition, apart from indicating this "external" distinction, also suggests that a particular "internal" aspect of the concept of value as such has seemed important to Weber: that of *action*.

This is already implied by the two common points mentioned above. As regards the dualistic structure of value judgments, it may not be the only logically conceivable one; but it is particularly suitable as a basis for the

8. GAW, p. 489: "Mit dem Problem der "Freiheit" einer bestimmten Wissenschaft von Wertungen dieser Art, mit der Geltung und dem Sinn dieses logischen Prinzips also, in keiner Art identisch ist die ganz andere . . ." See also GAW, p. 515, where Weber speaks of a "wertungsfrei" science, and GAW, pp. 539–40, where the "Wertungssphäre" is contrasted with the "Seinssphäre".
9. Except where the circumstances seem to dictate another course, no distinction will be made below between valuations ("Wertungen") and value judgments ("Werturteile"); either of the terms will be employed, when useful, to cover both concepts. This procedure appears to be justified by Weber's almost identical definition of the two concepts; on the other hand, using only *one* of the English terms throughout for *both* the German ones seemed an unnecessary restriction.

formulation of practical *goals* (one strives to attain a good, or to eliminate an evil) [10]. The term "praktisch" also carries definite overtones of action.

This implicit active aspect is made surprisingly explicit in the definition GAW, p. 489 where, as we have seen, it is assumed that "practical valuations" can only have as their object "eine durch unser Handeln beeinflußbare Erscheinung". Insofar as this assertion is meant to be generally valid, common sense tells us that it cannot be upheld: it seems obvious that we can evaluate a phenomenon without being able to influence it [11]. On the other hand, it is hardly probable that Weber was trying his hand at a recasting of the philosophical theory of value. The most acceptable interpretation accordingly seems to be that which regards the definition quoted as (deliberately or unconsciously) *restrictive:* on this assumption, Weber is limiting the discussion of valuations to cases where such valuational elements are more or less directly used as a basis for, or related to, human action.

One of the most ineradicable misunderstandings current among Weber's critics was that of supposing that "value freedom", as defined by him, entailed the impossibility of making values an *object* of scientific study, in other words, that the object level as well as the research level was to be kept free from value elements [12]. Weber consequently saw it as a major task to underline the distinction between the object level and the research level, and to demonstrate not only the *feasibility* of a value-free treatment of values as an object of study, but also that such a study of values on the object level *presupposed* value freedom (as defined by him) on the research level. If we examine Weber's definitions of "valuations" in this wider perspective, the stress laid on the "active" aspect of value judgments seems to echo his definition of the subject matter of sociology, in which "Handeln" ("action") is similarly made a key concept [13]. To a social science having man as a social *actor* as its subject, the elimination of "action-related" valuations from its research level becomes a particularly vital concern [14].

10. It is open to discussion whether Weber himself regarded the dualistic structure as a logical necessity. Dieter Henrich (*Einheit,* 1952, p. 26) claims that he did, but seems to be contradicted by one of the passages quoted by himself, GAW, p. 123, where Weber describes a "Wert" as something the "validity" of which " "von" uns anerkannt, abgelehnt oder in den mannigfachsten Verschlingungen "wertend *beurteilt"* wird".
11. For certain further consequences of the distinction between "active" and "passive" valuations, *cf. infra,* pp. 76–77.
12. The latest revival of this fallacy seems to have been performed by Simey, *Social Science,* 1968, pp. 75, 77.
13. See the well-known definition from the introduction to WG, GAW, p. 542 (WG, p. 3).
14. See for instance the letter of April 26th, 1920 to Heinrich Rickert (DZA II, Rep. 92, No. 25): "Wertende *Menschen* als *Objekte* der Betrachtung haben wir natürlich vor uns, – aber *wir* sind *nicht* genötigt, zu werten!"
    The symmetry between values on the object level and value freedom on the research

2.2. The practical aspect emphasized here reappears in other of Weber's terms denoting the value sphere:

This is obviously the case with the term "praktisches Wollen" [15]. In the same way, we occasionally [16] find expressions like *"tun* sollen", *"beitragen* sollen", *"handeln* sollen", where Weber's underlining emphasizes the—logically subordinate—"active" aspect.

Finally, it should be noted in this connection that the term "Zweck" ("purpose", "goal") without being, as far as I know, actually used by Weber to indicate the fundamental properties of the value sphere as opposed to the sphere of scientific inquiry, is continuously employed in very close connection with the discussion of the concept of value, and replaces the terms discussed above in passages containing more concrete descriptions or exemplifications of the methodological problem. This transition from more or less philosophical terms to a wholly "formal" concept of value ("formal" in the sense that any situation or phenomenon must automatically be regarded as somehow "valuable" [17] if it is set as a goal for action) is a further indication of the strong emphasis on the concept of practical action which is found in at least parts of Weber's discussion of values [18].

3. Yet another term often employed by Weber to describe the value pole of the dualism values–science is "Ideal" (in one instance [19], "Idee" is used with an identical meaning). This word does not in itself imply any thought of action, nor does Weber's use of it suggest such an implication. On closer examination, however, an "active" aspect is often [20] found to be present in the more indirect way that "Ideale" are described by Weber as being the basis of or the motive for practical action, goals, etc. In other words, Weber apparently sees the value sphere as containing a number of steps or levels,

level of scientific inquiry is noted by several commentators; see for instance René König, "Einige Überlegungen zur Frage der "Werturteilsfreiheit" bei Max Weber", *Kölner Zeitschrift für Soziologie und Sozialpsychologie,* Vol. 16 (1964), p. 12; Albert, *Traktat,* 1968, p. 65; and Loos, *Wertlehre,* 1970, p. 46.
15. GASS, p. 420.
16. GAW, pp. 509, 602.
17. Naturally, this term may cover *negative* as well as *positive* evaluations; in other words, a "Zweck" may consist in the *removal* of something.
18. *Cf.* Schelting, *Wissenschaftslehre,* 1934, p. 22n4, who, in connection with a discussion of values as an object of scientific inquiry, writes: "Wir hätten bei unserer ganzen Analyse der rationalen Klärung der ideellen Grundlagen des Handelns auch die zunächst "unreflektiert sich aufdrängenden Werturteile" über solche "Situationen" zum Ausgangspunkt nehmen können. Wir haben statt dessen die Aufstellung eines konkreten Zwecks gewählt, weil dabei das, worauf es hier ankommt, am klarsten und einfachsten herausgearbeitet werden kann. Max Weber benutzt abwechselnd beide Wege".
19. GAW, p. 150.
20. For instance GAW, pp. 149, 151, 156, 537. Exceptions are GAW, pp. 155, 515; GASS, p. 420.

the "static" higher ones serving as a theoretical basis for the "active" lower ones (goals, valuations etc.).

The idea of such a subdivision is not in itself very original, nor does it appear to be of much interest for our purposes; but one point does merit separate attention.

As mentioned above, a number of the terms employed by Weber to denote the concept of value exhibit a practical aspect, which even seems to dominate some of his concrete discussions. The more Weber stresses this aspect, the more the value element of the concepts recedes: in his treatment of the value sphere, Weber seems more concerned with the fact that something is actually striven for than with the precise nature of the value elements which might be at the root of such a striving[21]. This shift of emphasis is carried to the extreme in the employment, described above, of the term "Zweck".

This subdivision of the value sphere allows us to supplement the concrete, practical aspect, represented by the lower steps, by another more static and general one, which is nearer to a material definition of value. The first aspect reflects the element of striving for goals, the second one represents the *basis* for these practical goals [22].

This conception of an ordering of values does not lead Weber to perform any concrete delimitation of the values which can, or ought to, function as ideals, i. e., as the valuational basis for action. The terms which he applies to this higher order of values cover a wide spectrum, from emotional or affectual attitudes right across to religiously coloured terms; thus, Weber seems to respect in practice his own explicit refusal in theory to venture into the field of philosophical reflections on the exact implications of the concept of value [23]. The element wich distinguishes this "static" aspect from the "active" one is rather to be found in the emphasis laid on the *subjective* character of the concepts exhibiting the former aspect: by setting himself a goal or expressing a value judgment, the individual, whether consciously or uncon-

21. See for instance Weber's refusal (quoted above, p. 26n2) to discuss the relationship between wholly subjective value judgments and ethical ones, and the cursory reference, GAW, p. 499, to "ethische oder Kulturgesichtspunkte oder andere Gründe" as a possible basis for value judgments.
22. This conclusion is supported by one of the few passages where Weber explicitly deals with the structure and modes of valuation, WG, p. 837n1: "... auch in der ... "Wert"-Sphäre treffen [die "Ideen"] sämtlich darin überein: daß sie alle ..., um sich zu objektivieren, also um überhaupt ihre Realität zu bewähren, ein "Ergreifen" oder, wenn man will, Ergriffenwerden von Forderungen des "Werks" bedeuten, und nicht ein subjektives "Fühlen" oder "Erleben" wie irgend ein anderes".
23. The passage, GAW, p. 155, where Weber (distinguishing between the ethical and the more emotional value bases) apparently talks of *three* logical spheres, is an exception from this conclusion. However, the passage can probably be construed to indicate only a subdivision, without fundamental logical significance, of the value sphere.

sciously, with logical necessity commits his personality, his subjectivity, and stakes it on some ideal; potentially, the setting of any goal for oneself can be seen, in Weber's words, as "[die] ganze Subjektivität in Mitleidenschaft ziehend" [24].

1.3.2. The logical gulf between the demand for value freedom and the premises of the demand

As mentioned above [1], Weber bases his demand for the value freedom of scientific inquiry, i. e., the demand that the value sphere and the sphere of scientific inquiry *should* be kept separate, on the sole argument that the two spheres *are in fact* logically different. The principle which, in one of its asymmetrical forms, states that it is logically illegitimate to derive a "Sollen" from a "Sein", seemingly rests on just that kind of illegitimate conclusion.

Theoretically, it is not difficult to resolve this paradox through an interpretation whereby the "Sein" premise ("the value sphere and the sphere of scientific inquiry are logically heterogeneous") is supplemented by a tacit "Sollen" premise ("it is desirable (preferable, etc.) that this logical heterogeneity should be respected in practice") [2]. According to this interpretation, the "Sollen" conclusion (the demand for value freedom) is derived from a combination of "Sein" and "Sollen" premises, a procedure which is quite legitimate in logic.

In principle, this construction only means that the question is shifted, now running: "*Why* is it desirable (valuable, preferable) that this logical heterogeneity should be respected in practice?". But in fact, the transposition often psychologically amounts to a final solution of the problem: to most scientists and scholars, including those working in the field of philosophy, the value of scientific inquiry and of its results, i. e., of objective *truth,* is an *a priori* whose logically uncertain status never worries them or even enters their mind. Insofar as the question of the basis of this value is raised at all, it is usually met by some kind of reflexive argument tending to prove that truth is an objective value for scholars and scientists [3].

Weber's analysis of this problem is interesting: not only does he explicitly subscribe to the "Sollen" premise tacitly introduced above, but he also in the course of the discussion emphasizes that the value of truth and of the pursuit of truth is fundamentally *un*demonstrable and in this sense relative.

A further point of interest in Weber's discussion of the logical premises of the demand for value freedom is the following: the claim that scientific truth

24. GASS, p. 449.
1. Pp. 22–23.
2. For the concrete implications of this "respect in practice", *cf. infra,* pp. 64–70.
3. *Cf. infra,* pp. 47–50.

is a value is a sufficient basis for the "Sollen" premise introduced above, as long as we accept an assumption of *tertium non datur* (what does not belong to the value sphere belongs to the sphere of scientific inquiry). Thus, if we accept the value of scientific inquiry and of its results, we can formulate a complete, symmetrical demand for the value freedom of scientific inquiry without having to take any stand, positive or negative, concerning the value of the value sphere. Nevertheless, Weber several times commits himself to an emphatically positive view of the value sphere, a view which is in fact rather more strongly positive than that which he expresses concerning the sphere of scientific inquiry. In other words, he regards the commitment to certain values, and action motivated by such a commitment, as valuable in itself.

1.3.2.1. The logical status of the sphere of scientific inquiry

1. As we have seen, Weber regards scientific truth as *objective*. On the other hand, he must maintain that this *quality* of objective truth does not in itself prove the practical *value* of scientific inquiry. In general terms, this means that a scientific discipline aiming at or making use of empirical or theoretical evidence cannot itself prove the value of this aim or use. As early as *Knies I,* Weber writes: "... der "Wert" ... [des Zwecks wissenschaftlicher Analyse ist] selbst etwas *aus* der Wissenschaft als solcher ganz und gar nicht begründbares"[1], and this view persists unaltered, to be reaffirmed as late as *Wiss. Beruf* (where problems of this kind naturally have a central place): "Vorausgesetzt ist ... [bei jeder wissenschaftlichen Arbeit] ferner: daß das, was bei wissenschaftlicher Arbeit herauskommt, *wichtig* im Sinn von "wissenswert" sei. Und da stecken nun offenbar alle unsere Probleme darin. Denn diese Voraussetzung ist nicht wieder ihrerseits mit den Mitteln der Wissenschaft beweisbar"[2].

1. GAW, p. 60.
2. GAW, p. 599. *Cf.* the analogous formulations GAW, pp. 600, 610; GARS, p. 569. Interestingly, Weber's view that the value of scientific truth is scientifically undemonstrable is shared by Simmel, who expresses it as early as 1892 in his *Einleitung in die Moralwissenschaft* (Berlin 1892, p. 319); it is noted by a large number of commentators, from Marianne Weber (*Lebensbild,* 1950, p. 366) to Hans Albert (*Traktat,* 1968, pp. 62–63). Certain authors, though, interpret Weber differently on this point. This is true of Henrich and—following him—Walther Wegener (Henrich, *Einheit,* 1952, p. 111, and the speech in Stammer (ed.), *Weber,* 1965, p. 84; Walther Wegener. *Die Quellen der Wissenschaftsauffassung Max Webers und die Problematik der Werturteilsfreiheit der Nationalökonomie,* Berlin 1962, pp. 106–07, 268). These scholars maintain that Weber, in fixing objective truth as an absolute value for scientific inquiry, is working from a position belonging to the field of objective ethics (Henrich) or philosophical anthropology (Wegener), according to which truth is an *objective* value and possesses *general validity.* No concrete references are given to passages in Weber's works; Henrich even openly acknowledges that such passages cannot be found: "Max Weber ist dieser Zusammenhang aus nachweisbaren Gründen nicht klar geworden. Aber die

2. A number of scientific disciplines are regarded by Weber as having a "technical" character; they serve "klinische, technische, ökonomische, politische oder andere "praktische" Interessen" [3], i. e., they seek to obtain results which may serve as *means* to some practical end. As far as these disciplines are concerned, Weber derives the value of their results from the value of the end towards which they are seen to be useful, and regards the latter value as scientifically undemonstrable [4]. This view is of interest because of its implicit reference to the practical aspect of Weber's discussion of the value sphere: the ability of a scientific discipline to produce true statements, correct descriptions of facts of some kind, is valuable if, and only if, it is the precondition of the rational attainment of an end. The end, conceived as a value, invests the correct means of attaining it with a corresponding value [5].

When we come to "pure" scientific activity, which is pursued only "um ihrer selbst willen" [6], its value cannot be derived from practical ends, since scientific inquiry is here seen as an end in itself. Consequently, Weber takes great pains to emphasize the relative character of the value of scientific truth and of the activity calculated to obtain this kind of truth:

"Die *objektive* Gültigkeit alles Erfahrungswissens beruht darauf und nur darauf, daß die gegebene Wirklichkeit nach Kategorien geordnet wird, welche ... an die Voraussetzung des *Wertes* derjenigen Wahrheit gebunden sind, die das Erfahrungswissen allein uns zu geben vermag. Wem diese Wahhreit nicht wertvoll ist—und der Glaube an den Wert wissenschaftlicher Wahrheit ist Produkt bestimmter Kulturen und nichts Naturgegebenes—,dem haben wir mit den Mitteln unserer Wissenschaft nichts zu bieten. Freilich wird er vergeblich nach einer anderen Wahrheit suchen, die ihm die Wissen-

Interpretation muß sich auf ihn besinnen und kann ihn aufdecken, ohne auf Willkür der Deutung angewiesen zu sein" (*Einheit,* 1952, p. 111).
    Thus, Henrich's interpretation is deduced from the fundamental systematizing approach which was examined above (*cf. supra,* pp. 7–10) and found irrelevant to the present account. Moreover, both Henrich's and Wegener's views seem to me to contain an extrapolation of certain arguments of Rickert, which will be examined below (pp. 47–50).
    See also Appendix A of this chapter.
3. GAW, p. 60; see also GAW, pp. 599–600.
4. *Cf.* GAW, pp. 60, 599.
5. GAW, pp. 599–600, Weber discusses the case of a number of other disciplines. Although some of these (e. g. law, economics, sociology, political science) are of practical *importance,* in the sense that their results may be put to practical use, Weber does not draw the parallel to the technical sciences in the narrower sense given above. The reason for this omission may be found in the circumstance that Weber in this discussion concentrates on another aspect, viz, the value of the *object* of these sciences. This value is also scientifically undemonstrable; but further treatment of this question would lie outside the scope of this section.
6. GAW, p. 61. One passage, GAW, p. 599, seems to suggest that any scientific discipline can acquire this "pure" character, if the scholar or scientist in question is motivated solely by "die Sache", the pure search for scientific truth, and does not think of the practical results. Here Weber obviously wishes to reserve the term "Beruf" ("vocation") for the scientific inquiry inspired by such "pure" motives.

schaft in demjenigen ersetzt, was *sie* allein leisten kann: Begriffe und Urteile, die ...
[die empirische Wirklichkeit] in gültiger Weise *denkend ordnen* lassen" [7].

What science—in this case, logic—can do is only to set out what results
empirical science can produce, and possibly has a monopoly of producing;
but it cannot force anyone to accept the *value* of such results [8]. As shown in
the passage quoted, Weber does not even reserve the predicate "truth" for
the correct results of the empirical or logical disciplines [9].

The direct consequences of this "relative" conclusion are in Weber's view
purely theoretical. In *Wiss. Beruf*, he writes: "Ich persönlich bejahe schon
durch meine eigene Arbeit die Frage [ob die Wissenschaft wert ist, für
jemanden ein "Beruf" zu werden, und ob sie selbst einen objektiv wertvollen "Beruf" hat]" [10]; and this passage might even suggest that Weber
sees the question of the value of scientific inquiry as, in practice, one of
definition: we are entitled to assume that whoever engages in scientific inquiry thereby implicitly acknowledges the value of scientific activity as such [11].
But since engaging in the activity easily acquires a kind of unconscious self-
evidence, Weber makes a point of demonstrating its implications—which are
logically necessary, and consequently binding upon scholars and scientists in
their capacity as such [12]: the activity of scientific inquiry implies the *choice*
of a particular value. This is put concisely in *Objektivität:* "... wissenschaftliche Wahrheit ist nur, was für alle gelten *will*, die Wahrheit *wollen*" [13].

1.3.2.2. The logical status of the value sphere

It would theoretically have been possible for Weber to put the case for his
demand for value freedom solely in terms of the arguments set out above
concerning the value of scientific inquiry. In that case, valuations would
have been regarded as factors of disturbance in the scientific process, un-

7. GAW, pp. 212–13; see also GAW, pp. 61, 609. Similarly in a letter to Karl
   Voßler of Nov. 14th, 1905 (copy in DZA II, Rep. 92, No. 30, Vol. 4).
8. See also GAW, p. 601.
9. GASS, p. 482 shows a similar tolerance with regard to the term "scientific
   inquiry".
10. GAW, pp. 608–09.
11. See also GASS, p. 449; the point of view which Weber refers to here, advanced
    by Professor Schultze-Gävernitz, was formulated quite radically, and almost
    amounted to the claim that logic was an *objective* value to scholars and scientists.
    Instead of entering into the discussion of the problem, Weber in fact, by means
    of the phrase "für alle unsere Arbeit . . . Vorbedingung", reduces Schultze-
    Gävernitz' fundamental attack to a simple question of definition.
       A very clear statement of Weber's position is found in Loos, *Wertlehre*, 1970,
    p. 49.
12. *Cf.* GAW, p. 600.
13. GAW, p. 184. Analogous passages can be found GAW, pp. 347, 349.

desirable subjective elements which should be eliminated or neutralized as far as possible.

1. In fact, Weber's attitude is quite different. Apart from the question whether values—even in their practical form—are necessary factors in the process of scientific inquiry, Weber makes it quite clear that his demand for value freedom does *not* imply any disparagement of the role of values generally. As he says in *Objektivität*: "*Gesinnungslosigkeit* und *wissenschaftliche* "Objektivität" haben keinerlei innere Verwandtschaft" [1].

This negative formulation is supplemented by a number of passages in which Weber defines his view of the value sphere in a more positive way:

He sees the value sphere as invested with a "spezifische Dignität" [2], presumably comparable to that ascribed to the sphere of scientific inquiry [3]. While Weber sees the "dignity" of the latter as grounded in its monopoly of producing results which are scientifically (empirically or logically) true, the analogous status of the value sphere is based, in his view, on the fundamental importance of values for the human personality [4]: "Und sicherlich liegt die Würde der "Persönlichkeit" darin beschlossen, daß es für sie Werte gibt, auf die sie ihr eigenes Leben bezieht,—und lägen diese Werte auch im einzelnen Falle ausschließlich *innerhalb* der Sphäre der eigenen Individualität . . ."[5].

Thus, not only the value-free search for truth, but also the (logically diametrically opposed) commitment to undemonstrable values is a positive (but not an objective) value in human life, as Weber sees it. And just as the value of scientific truth functions as a premise for a demand for value freedom in the form: "the scholar and scientist must keep his scientific inquiry free from valuations", so the value of "letzte Werte" ("ultimate values") becomes a premise for the complementary conclusion: "human beings—among them scientists and scholars—must choose and defend their personal value orientation in life without hiding behind the assertion that the correctness of

1. GAW, p. 157.
2. ("specific dignity"). GAW, p. 148.
3. *Cf.* GAW, p. 501, where the formulation is quite symmetrical: ". . . die spezifische Dignität *jeder* von beiden [Ebenen] . . ." GAW, p. 491, Weber even indirectly (the immediate subject under discussion is the question whether the university teacher is justified in influencing his students in other ways than by imparting knowledge) suggests that the demand for value freedom might be based solely on the regard for the "dignity" of the *value* sphere. Other passages (GASS, p. 419 and an undated letter (probably written in the spring of 1911) to Heinrich Rickert (DZA II, Rep. 92, No. 25)) seem to express a similar point of view.
4. Admittedly, Weber never explicitly uses this argument to support or prove the "dignity" of the value sphere. But in his discussion of the principle of value freedom, the "dignity" and the "personality" line of thought run quite parallel to each other.
5. GAW, p. 152; see also GAW, p. 213.

such an orientation can be proved or disproved by scientific means". A passage (partly quoted above) from Weber's speech at the 1909 congress of the *Verein* brings this out clearly:

"Der Grund, weshalb ich so außerordentlich scharf bei jeder Gelegenheit ... mich wende gegen die Verquickung des Seinsollens mit dem Seienden, ist nicht der, daß ich die Fragen des Sollens unterschätze, sondern gerade umgekehrt: weil ich es nicht ertragen kann, wenn Probleme von weltbewegender Bedeutung, von größter ideeller Tragweite, in gewissem Sinne höchste Probleme, die eine Menschenbrust bewegen können, hier in eine technisch–ökonomische "Produktivitäts"-Frage verwandelt und zu einem Gegenstand der Diskussion einer *Fach*disziplin ... gemacht werden [6].

Weber's extremely positive attitude to the "dignity" of the value sphere goes even further than the stress placed, in the passage quoted, on the fundamental importance of the "highest" level of values as a basis for commitments of a deeply personal kind. Thus, we find him calling for this commitment to be translated into practice. Sometimes, these requests are indirect, as when Weber speaks of "Eintreten für die eigenen Ideale" [7], or of "praktisches Wollen" [8]. But occasionally, the appeal is overt, and formulated as a demand on any person who wishes to be recognized as a human being in the full sense of the word. This is the case in an aside, GAW, p. 493 [9] and—significantly—at the end of *Wiss. Beruf:*

"Daraus wollen wir die Lehre ziehen: daß es mit dem Sehnen und Harren allein nicht getan ist, und es anders machen: an unsere Arbeit gehen und der "Forderung des Tages" gerecht werden—menschlich sowohl wie beruflich. Die aber ist schlicht und einfach, wenn jeder den Dämon findet und ihm gehorcht, der *seines* Lebens Fäden hält" [10].

As in the discussion of the value of scientific inquiry, we here find the two Weberian aspects of the concept of value: the "committed" and the "active" one. And through both of them runs Weber's firm acceptance of valuation, of practical commitment, as an *ethical* necessity, even for those individuals who, in a different social role, are scientists and scholars and, as such, only committed to the value of scientific inquiry [11].

6. GASS, p. 419. See also GAW, p. 491 and GASS, pp. 449–50, where the essentially *subjective* character of the value sphere is stressed.
7. GAW, pp. 155, 157.
8. GASS, p. 420.
9. "... mag (und: soll) [der Professor] tun, was sein Gott oder Dämon ihn heißt".
10. GAW, p. 613.
11. There seems to be unusually general agreement among the commentators with regard to Weber's positive attitude to values and to active commitment. We do, however, find a few exceptions. Thus, Alvin Gouldner ("Anti-Minotaur: The Myth of a Value-Free Sociology", Irving L. Horowitz (ed.), *The New Sociology*, New York 1964, p. 201), by misinterpreting GAW, p. 493, arrives at the conclusion that Weber denied the right of *university teachers* to believe in and commit themselves to values. This leads Gouldner to define and defend an "opposite view" to Weber's which is in fact identical with Weber's own position (*cf.* Gouldner's "opposite view": "... that professors are, like all others, entitled and

3. It is interesting that Weber, who, in his discussion of scientific inquiry, is at pains to emphasize the *relativity* of the value of scientific truth and, consequently, of scientific inquiry, completely abstains from such verbal and material safeguards in the parallel discussions of the value sphere. The "value of values" is maintained emphatically, at times with a striking intensity [12], but its relativity is nowhere explicitly noted. One explanation is that Weber is trying to establish the "dignity" of the value sphere as being equal to that of the sphere of scientific inquiry, and thus has far less *cause* to insist upon the—logically inescapable—relativation. This explanation of motives may be supplemented by the justification that the intensity of Weber's phrasing is in itself an indirect acknowledgement of the undemonstrable character of the demand for value freedom. Weber nowhere claims that this demand can be *demonstrated* to be valid; instead, he formulates it and supports it with the whole weight of his committed personality.

1.4 The principle in its more specific form

As we saw, the principle of value freedom contains a demand for the separation of empirical science and value judgments (based on fundamental ideals) or, in its two asymmetrical formulations, the demands that scientific inquiry should be kept free of such valuations, and that the latter should not be supported with allegations of scientific demonstrability. If we take the sphere of scientific inquiry as our focal point, the first of these asymmetrical demands emphasizes the *possibilities* of scientific activity, if it is conducted without being disturbed by practical value judgments, while the second stresses the fact that science has *limits* which it cannot, and therefore should not pretend to be able to, overstep.

Turning, as will be done below, to the more concrete formulations of the principle of value freedom, we find that it is logically possible to divide them, too, into two groups: the first comprising the passages where Weber emphasizes the demand that science, in its capacity of being objectively true, should be kept free of valuations in their various forms, while the central point in the passages belonging to the other group is the stress put on the limitations of science relative to practical value judgments.

perhaps obligated to express their values" (*ibid.,* p. 201), compared with Weber's opinion: "In der Presse, in Versammlungen, Vereinen, Essays, in jeder jedem anderen Staatsbürger ebenfalls zugänglichen Form mag (und: soll) er [the professor] tun, was sein Gott oder Dämon ihn heißt" (GAW, p. 493)).

See also Appendix A of this chapter for a discussion of Leo Strauss' views on this point.

12. For instance GPS, p. 536 (*Pol. Beruf*): "... immer muß irgendein Glaube *da* sein. Sonst lastet in der Tat—das ist völlig richtig—der Fluch kreatürlicher Nichtigkeit auch auf den äußerlich stärksten politischen Erfolgen".

The passage GASS, p. 421 suggests that such a distinction was also present in Weber's mind: "Ich bin der Meinung, daß ein echter Naturforscher von einem wahren Schauder erfaßt werden müßte, wenn ihm zugemutet wird, derartig praktische Werturteile in seine Arbeit hineinzutragen oder als deren Resultat auszugeben"; moreover, the quotation shows that the logical distinction made above has a practical correlate, since the first category can be said to relate to the collection of data, the formulation of preliminary hypotheses, etc., while the second one covers generalizations and the formulation of theories on the basis of the data collected. For convenience, the two groups will therefore be referred to below as the demands for the value freedom of the scientific process and of the scientific results respectively.

1.4.1. The demand for the value freedom of the scientific process

In this connection, Weber concentrates his attacks on the risk of introducing valuational elements into the *concepts* employed. This focus of interest probably has its roots in his regard for the neo-Kantian theory of scientific inquiry, particularly in the form given to it by Rickert, according to which the *concept* is the central methodological category. The battle for the value freedom of the scientific process must therefore appear to Weber to be mainly one for the value freedom of the *concepts*.

1. In *Roscher,* Weber discusses a large number of "emanationist" theories, i. e., theories according to which actual behaviour is seen as "emanating" from some concept ("Persönlichkeit", "Geist", "Volk", etc.). Most prominent among the authors treated is Roscher himself, whose views are discussed throughout the essay; but other writers, as for instance Lamprecht and Gierke, with their "organic" theories of the state, are treated as well [1]. Weber does not, however, go beyond a fairly neutral account of the views of the authors discussed: the actual criticism, based on Weber's own positive theory, remains implicit, here as elsewhere in *Roscher*. Nevertheless, it is quite obvious that Weber rejects any kind of "emanationism", both as a consequence of his view that concepts should be regarded as *means,* not as *ends,* of scientific inquiry [2], and—particularly in the case of concepts denoting *collectivities*—because of the individualist bent of his methodological orientation [3].

1. GAW, pp. 24n5 and 35n1 respectively. See also, for instance, a letter to Karl Voßler of Dec. 17th, 1904 (copy in DZA II, Rep. 92, No. 30, Vol. 4), in which Weber voices his suspicion that Voßler's concept of "Sprachgeist" ("the spirit of language") contains emanationist elements.
2. *Cf. infra,* pp. 100–01.
3. See for instance a letter to Robert Liefmann of March 9th, 1920 (copy in DZA II, Rep. 92, No. 30, Vol. 8), where Weber writes: "Wenn ich jetzt nun einmal Sozio-

As for Hegel, who in connection with the discussion of "emanationism" must have seemed to Weber to be *fons et origo malorum* [4], he is mentioned quite often in *Roscher;* but, characteristically, Weber treats him with far more respect and circumspection than he reserves for the other authors [5].

One of the concepts frequently discussed in the later essays is that of "Fortschritt" ("progress"). In *Knies I,* Weber deals with the psychologist and philosopher Wundt, who had propounded a theory arguing for the existence of a law of "growing psychic energy" of the same kind as the law of the conservation of physical energy: an idea which implied the notion of continuous spiritual progress through time. Against this, Weber here [6] demonstrates conclusively that such an idea of "growth" or "progress" does not correspond to anything in the empirical world, being simply a rephrasing in "scientific" terms of the central thesis in Wundt's philosophy of history. Strictly speaking, this procedure constitutes not only an interference from, but a *substitution of* camouflaged value judgments for scientific conclusions, and as such an extreme example of the category of concepts attacked by Weber [7].

A few pages later [8], Weber again turns his attention to the so-called "law" of "growing psychic energy", but this time treats it from a slightly different

loge bin (laut meiner Anstellungsurkunde), dann wesentlich deshalb, um dem immer noch spukenden Betrieb, der mit Kollektivbegriffen arbeitet, ein Ende zu machen. Mit anderen Worten: Auch Soziologie kann nur durch Ausgehen vom Handeln des oder der, weniger, oder vieler, Einzelnen, strikt "individualistisch" in der Methode also, betrieben werden". Reinhard Bendix (Bendix, *Portrait,* 1962 p. 476) remarks that Weber's fear of hypostatizing the conjoint behaviour of individuals into collective concepts with a presumed concrete denotation went so far as to make him replace ordinary nouns ("Wirtschaft", "Gesellschaft", "Handlung") by infinitives used substantively ("Wirtschaften", "Vergesellschaftung", "Handeln"), the latter supposedly retaining the required individual and active aspect.

4. We find an illuminating passage to this effect in a letter from Weber to F. Eulenburg of May 11th, 1909 (copy in DZA II, Rep. 92, No. 30, Vol. 7): "Zwei Wege stehen offen: Hegel oder—*unsere* Art die Dinge zu behandeln".
5. There is a clearly discernible general tendency in Weber towards attacking the lesser prophets, the "epigones", while borrowing from the major ones. Thus, Hegel, Marx and Dilthey, who all had an important—positive or negative—influence on Weber are but rarely mentioned and discussed in his works. Instead, Roscher and Knies (for Hegel), the Marxian epigones and Stammler (for Marx) and Wundt, Croce and others (for Dilthey) have to bear the brunt of the attack. Considering Weber's normally intense love of polemics, it is probably correct to interpret this selectivity as a sign of his respect for intellectual greatness rather than of pusillanimity.
6. GAW, pp. 55–56, 61.
7. Weber directs a similar criticism at the concept "le point de vue social" ("the social point of view") which plays a certain role in a work by the French "energeticist" E. Solvay which bears the awe-inspiring title: "Formules d'introduction à l'Energétique physio- et psycho-sociologique" (*Energ. Kult. th.,* GAW, p. 402n1). On the parallel discussion in *Objektivität* concerning the legitimacy of speaking of "a" social science, without any further differentiation of aspects, *cf. infra,* pp. 137–40.
8. GAW, p. 60.

angle: he outlines a possible line of defence for the unfortunate "law", to the effect that it expresses itself, in part, in the growing ability to acknowledge the validity of logically binding propositions. Since this growing ability may, in principle as well as in fact, be observed empirically, the "law" ought to be regarded as "established" in this sense. Weber, however, does not accept this hypothetical argument. He observes that it is necessary, in order to describe the growing ability to reason logically as "progress", to assume the existence of an *a priori* value, viz, the value of such logical (true) reasoning; accordingly, the argument outlined is still loaded with valuations in disguise. In this case, Weber's criticism is no longer levelled at a pseudo-scientific concept of progress, which disguises undemonstrable philosophical propositions as apparently exact laws, but instead at those scholars who might employ the concept without being conscious of, or at least without properly stressing, its essentially valuational frame of reference (progress—towards what?) [9].

In a discussion in *Wertfreiheit* [10], the concept is once again examined closely. Weber here contrasts the—in his view—value-free term "Fortschritt der seelischen Differenzierung" (in the sense of "quantitative increase in the number of possible forms of behaviour") with the valuationally loaded concept "Fortschritt der seelischen Spannweite" ("increase of psychological scope"), and remarks—with reference to Simmel's "Schopenhauer und Nietzsche"—that the interpretation of the latter concept involves considering a number of different value standards, a process which may perhaps be more complex than one would have thought at the first glance. Weber's point here is the same as in his second argument against Wundt: the use of terms like "Spannweite" tends to obscure the valuational frame of reference. In *Wertfreiheit,* Weber also draws the conclusions from this criticism by trying to elaborate a value-free, "technical" concept of progress to be used in the sociology of art and of music, and in history [11].

2. Weber's only other [12] detailed discussion of the danger inherent in value-laden concepts forms part of his speech at the 1909 congress of the *Verein* in Vienna. At this gathering, one of the subjects under debate was that of "economic productivity", a concept acknowledged by most of the speakers

9. In notes from 1903 (DZA II, Rep. 92, No. 31, Vol. 6), Weber goes even further and describes the concept of evolution as such as a "Werth-Begriff".
10. GAW, pp. 518–27. This discussion is considerably expanded from that of the *Gutachten,* particularly through the introduction of examples from the sociology of art and of music. The most relevant passages in the present context (pp. 518–20, 524) are, however, virtually the same as in the earlier version.
11. *Cf. infra,* pp. 168–69.
12. Not including Weber's numerous attacks on the parading in scientific garb of propositions originating in some philosophy of history; these passage do not seem to me central to the account given in this section. Particular aspects of "emanationist" lines of thought will be dealt with below (pp. 107–09).

to be both vague and complex, but still, in Weber's view, treated too much as a matter of course.

Weber's intervention was directly occasioned by some perhaps rather unguarded remarks by Professor Liefmann. Liefmann had tried to construct a value-free, economically "correct" concept of productivity, by means of the concept of "Volkswohlstand" (defined as the greatest possible income for all members of a given group); and one of his examples of behaviour conducive to "Volkswohlstand", and consequently to productivity, was the destruction of goods in the case where selling them would have resulted in a lower total revenue [13].

Against this construction, Weber advances the same arguments as against "steigende psychische Energie" and "Fortschritt": the concept of "Volkswohlstand" is quite indefinite in itself; and if one wishes to define it more closely, *ethical* problems will arise concurrently with—perhaps even to a greater extent than—economic ones [14]. And if we try, as Liefmann does, to exclude this ethical element, to construct a purely economic definition, this definition will, on the one hand, not turn out to be ethically indifferent (since it will have ethically relevant consequences); and on the other hand, it does not even dispose of all the economic problems involved, since its apparent self-evidence hides certain well-defined economic value judgments [15].

Weber also criticizes other vague conceptualizations, like "Rasse" ("race") [16], "landwirtschaftliche Interessen" ("agricultural interests") [17] and (implicitly) "Klasse" ("class") [18]. These discussions, however, do not turn on the introduction of a *valuational* element into the concept, and have therefore been left out of account here.

3.   Apart from the conceptual criticism referred to above, Weber now and then deals with the question of the influence of value judgments on other parts of the scientific process.

Thus, for instance, he points out that the personal ideals or wishes of the individuals engaging in research may affect their estimate of the relative weight of various causal factors [19], and consequently influence their formulation and acceptance of research hypotheses. His warning against invest-

---

13. *Verhandlungen des Vereins für Socialpolitik in Wien 1909* (Schriften des Vereins für Socialpolitik, Vol. 132), Leipzig 1910, pp. 577–80.
14. I take this to be the meaning of the passage: "In dem Begriff des "Volkswohlstandes" steckt offensichtlich alle Ethik der Welt, die es gibt" (GASS, p. 416).
15. GASS, pp. 416–17.
16. GASS, p. 459.
17. GAW, pp. 210–12.
18. GAW, p. 212; *cf.* WG, pp. 680–81.
19. GAW, p. 151.

ing research methods and approaches with the dignity of a philosophy of
life, and thereby loading them with valuations, is another case in point [20].

4. Weber's formulations of the demand for the value freedom of the scientific
process, as it has been discussed above, may be divided into two main categories:

The first category comprises concepts which are too general to be operational without further specification, and which moreover have the peculiarity
that all propositions referring to them are empirically undemonstrable, no
matter what concrete definitions are given to the concepts as such. Since
such propositions are fundamentally incapable of verification or falsification,
they cannot pretend to any scientific status, but are to be regarded as speculative constructions in borrowed scientific plumes [21]. Examples of such constructions are, in Weber's view, the various "emanationist" theories and the
law of "steigende psychische Energie".

The second category includes the concepts which share with those of the
first one the characteristic of being too general to be immediately operational.
These concepts, however, may be defined in such a way as to allow empirical
testing of the propositions referring to them. Accordingly, they do not fall
completely outside the realm of science, but they are imperfect, warped instruments of scientific inquiry, since their form makes them pretend to a
generality of application which they cannot in fact lay claim to. They represent a variant of the well-known single-factor theories, in the sense that
a proposition whose validity only holds inside a particular field is formulated
so as to seem valid for a larger area of facts, i. e. for situations with a greater
number of variable conditions. Instances of this intrusion of value judgments
are the concepts of "Fortschritt" and "Volkswohlstand" discussed by Weber.

Both these categories represent problems of considerable interest to modern
political science. Without entering into a more thorough discussion, we can
mention a few examples. Good specimens of the first category are to be found
in, for instance, Eric Voegelin's *The New Science of Politics* [22]. Among the

20. This point is clearly made, for instance, in Weber's notes from 1903 (DZA II,
    Rep. 92, No. 31, Vol. 6).
21. In unpublished notes and letters, Weber openly characterizes both Roscher's and
    Wundt's constructions in point as "metaphysics". (Note from 1903 in DZA II,
    Rep. 92, No. 31, Vol. 6 (concerning Roscher); letter to Willi Hellpach of Oct.
    10th, 1905 in DZA II, Rep. 92, No. 17 (concerning Wundt)).
22. Chicago 1952. *Cf.* the following characteristic argument of Voegelin's: "In order
    to degrade the politics of Plato, Aristotle, or St. Thomas to the rank of "values"
    among others, a conscientious scholar would first have to show that their claim
    to be science was unfounded. And that attempt is self-defeating. By the time the
    would-be critic has penetrated the meaning of metaphysics with sufficient thor-
    oughness to make his criticism weighty, he will have become a metaphysician
    himself" (*Politics*, 1952, p. 20).

abundant examples of the second group, we can point to the—now obsolete—definition of politics as constitutionally relevant activity, and to the highly ambiguous concept of "democracy".

The particular danger of the concepts of the second group—if we abstract from instances of scholars who in deliberate bad faith manipulate their concepts to further their own valuational ends—lies in the *unconscious* character of the generalization of a specialized value aspect. This often prevents a sufficiently thorough causal analysis [23]; and in a practical (political) context, an insufficient awareness of the valuational element present in a concept may in fact diminish the ability to realize the ideals implicit in the valuations in question. Weber himself gives a striking example of this in his speech at the 1909 congress of the *Verein:* this association had been founded by "academic socialists", i. e., scholars who, often on the basis of quite conservative political views, concerned themselves with social questions. The "academic socialists" turned against the laissez-faire of classic liberalism, and instead tried to establish more general principles of social justice, especially with regard to the workers, to guide economic policy. But, as Weber demonstrated in his speech, the general concepts established in this manner were by no means free of valuational bias, which in the case of the concept of "economic productivity" expressed itself in the exclusive concern with the "capital" aspect of production [24]; consequently, the concrete norms deduced from these general concepts were, in the eyes of many workers, no less inimical to the working class than the laissez-faire system which the *Verein* was founded to combat.

1.4.2. *The demand for the value freedom of the scientific results*

1. The main point of Weber's discussion of the value freedom of the results of scientific inquiry is expressed clearly in, for instance, the following passage from *Knies I:* "Es gibt schlechterdings keine Brücke, welche von der wirklich *nur* "empirischen" Analyse der gegebenen Wirklichkeit mit den Mitteln kausaler Erklärung zur Feststellung oder Bestreitung der Gültigkeit *irgendeines* Werturteils führt..." [1] But the formulations are so varied that it is still worthwhile to discuss them a little more closely and to deal with certain problems arising out of them.

23. GAW, p. 524; see also GAW, p. 602.
24. "Es sind ausschließlich Unternehmerinteressen, die hier zugrunde gelegt wurden" (GASS, p. 417).
 1. GAW, p. 61. Considering the stress laid on the *empirical* sciences, it should be noted that Weber frequently (GAW, pp. 47n1, 362, 496, 537; GASS, pp. 401–02) expresses the same idea in relation to disciplines like epistemology and law, which can hardly be said to belong to the group of empirical sciences proceeding by causal analysis.

44

2. The distinction made above [2] between the two aspects of the value sphere, the committed, "passive" one, and the motivating, "active" one, is reflected in Weber's more concrete demands for value freedom: he formulates some passages in general and fundamental terms, simply pointing out the boundary between demonstrable science and undemonstrable values, while in other cases he gives himself a looser rein, touching on practically all the aspects of the tension between theory and practice [3].

Within the category of "active" formulations, we can single out a special group, consisting of the passages where Weber maintains the impossibility of making scientifically correct choices between different values. This point of view of Weber's is derived from a theory of the fundamental conflict of values with each other, rather than from the principle of value freedom as discussed above. The passages in question have been mentioned here all the same, since they *may* also be interpreted as special forms of the demand for value freedom [4].

3. Two variants of the demand for the value freedom of the results of scientific inquiry merit separate treatment because of their connexion with questions treated later in this work, and because they partly also touch on problems of particular interest to the political sciences.

3.1. For one thing, Weber repeatedly [5] emphasizes that the demonstration of the *empirical* existence of cultural values (i. e., values actually held by civilized societies) is logically quite a different operation from that of establishing *ethical* duties, and that consequently the first one cannot legitimately be used as a basis for the second one: "Nur positive Religionen ... vermögen dem Inhalt von *Kulturwerten* die Dignität unbedingt gültiger *ethischer* Gebote zu verleihen. Außerhalb ihrer sind Kulturideale, die der Einzelne verwirklichen *will*, und ethische Pflichten, die er erfüllen *soll*, von prinzipiell verschiedener Dignität" [6]. This view, which is strengthened and elaborated by means of other theoretical arguments [7], is important for evaluating the rela-

---

2. Pp. 29–31.
3. Examples of "passive" formulations are Weber's assertions of the impossibility of demonstrating "Werte" or "Ideale" (see for instance GAW, pp. 47n1, 151–52, 223, 604; GASS, p. 488; GPS, p. 16); "active" formulations are found, for instance, GAW, p. 152 ("konkrete Normen") and GAW, p. 149 ("Rezepte für die Praxis"); see also *Wiss. Beruf,* where Weber quotes with approval a statement by Tolstoy to the effect that science can give no answer to the question: "Was sollen wir tun? Wie sollen wir leben?" (GAW, p. 598; see also GAW, p. 609).
4. *Cf. infra,* pp. 190–92.
5. GAW, pp. 148, 154, 504; Baumgarten, *Weber,* 1964, p. 399 (letter to Toennies, 1908).
6. GAW, p. 154.
7. Weber links up the discussion with a rejection of the view that it is possible to deduce *normative* cultural values from ethical norms. This conflict between the

tionship between Weber and Heinrich Rickert and thus for the interpretation
of Weber's version of the Rickertian theory of "Wertbeziehung".

3.2. Of particular interest to political science is Weber's discussion of
"lines of development" in history, economics, etc. Older economists had—
sometimes on rather uncritical religious grounds [8]—believed that the discovery of such lines of development could open the way for the definition of
"objective" economic goals [9]. Weber regarded theories of this sort as no less
illegitimate than any other attempt to demonstrate the truth of valuations by
means of empirical statements. In *Roscher,* he criticizes Roscher's naïve belief
in the special role of "lines of development" in the economic disciplines [10],
and in *Wertfreiheit* [11], he couches this criticism in general terms:

> "Der Glaube ist noch immer verbreitet, daß man Weisungen für praktische Wertun-
> gen aus "Entwicklungstendenzen" ableiten solle, müsse oder doch: könne. Allein aus
> noch so eindeutigen "Entwicklungstendenzen" sind eindeutige Imperative des Handelns
> doch nur bezüglich der voraussichtlich geeignetsten Mittel bei gegebener Stellung-
> nahme, nicht aber bezüglich dieser Stellungnahme selbst zu gewinnen" [12].

But while such passages treat the problem of "lines of development" as
a special case (of polemical or institutional interest) of a general complex of
problems in the theory of scientific inquiry, Weber occasionally adopts a
somewhat different and more directly political approach. While, as mentioned
above, the older school of historical economics believed that lines of development pointed unambiguously to particular economic goals, post-Bismarckian
political life in Germany was, in Weber's eyes, characterized by the adaptation
of ends to means, of political goals to short-term lines of development. This
tendency did not spring from the naïve belief in the unity of ends and means
held by Roscher, but rather from a faith in the priority of means *over* ends,
of external over internal factors. This kind of "realist" politics was strongly
attacked by Weber [13] in terms of his fundamental conception of the essence of
political life [14].

Of particular interest in this connection are a couple of pages of the
Antrittsrede [15], where Weber criticizes the belief in "development"—in this
case of the more innocuous historico-economical variety—not on the basis of

sphere of ethical values and the sphere of normative cultural values will be
treated in a larger context below, pp. 179–80.

8. *Cf.* GAW, p. 41.
9. GAW, p. 148.
10. GAW, pp. 38n3, 40n1.
11. As mentioned above, the problem was the third of the four subjects mentioned
in the questionnaire of the *Verein* in 1912; it does not, however, receive very
thorough treatment in *Gutachten* or in *Wertfreiheit.*
12. GAW, p. 512.
13. GAW, pp. 513–15.
14. *Cf. infra,* p. 242.
15. GPS, pp. 17–18.

logical and methodological propositions (which he only arrived at later), but simply because it excludes the possibility of taking an alternative view of economically determined phenomena. The belief in "lines of development" as objective goals either results in a sort of passive determinism or—and this is what is particularly relevant to political science—in an uncritical acceptance of the right of the strongest, in this case of the economically strongest.

4. A line of argument which is in principle nothing more than a special application of the fundamental postulate concerning the gap between empirical truth and undemonstrable values or valuations, but which nevertheless presents particular difficulties, is Weber's rejection of what might be termed the "sociology of knowledge". The latter holds, in short, that the question of the truth, or falsity, of a judgment is affected by *empirical* knowledge concerning the causes and effects of this judgment [16].
4.1. By and large, Weber limits his discussion of this problem to the disciplines which do not study observable phenomena (in the broad sense of the word), i. e., to what we might term the theoretical sciences [17].

Thus, he rejects [18] the view that knowledge, however complete, of the psychological, anatomical or biochemical conditions necessary to our perceiving a judgment to be objectively "true", in any way affects the logical status of the judgment as true or false. A similar discussion [19] deals with the hypothetical case of biology, possibly of the Darwinist variety, being able to demonstrate that the development of the faculty of formulating logically and mathematically correct judgments is conditional on the practical utility afforded by the possession of this faculty. (For instance, persons possessing the faculty in question might be more "fit" for survival in the struggle for existence, and genetic transmission would eventually make the faculty empirically dominant in society). Here again, Weber denies that any such knowledge or demonstration according to which "letztlich als "wahr" nur zu gelten *pflege,* was uns "nützlich" sei" [20], would have *any* legitimate effect on the classification of a judgment as true or false. A third, related, line of argument is Weber's emphasis [21] on the logical distinction between knowl-

16. The problem is thus the diametrical opposite of the question discussed above (pp. 32–34): whether the quality of truth is by itself sufficient proof of the value of striving for such truth or the value of truth as such.
17. At certain times (GAW, pp. 57, 362, 502, 509), Weber does more or less explicitly include the empirical disciplines; but it is probably fair to interpret such passages as focusing on the non-empirical, theoretical aspects of the empirical disciplines.
18. GAW, pp. 57, 59, 225, 362.
19. GAW, pp. 57–59.
20. GAW, p. 58.
21. GAW, pp. 503, 509.

edge of the views actually held by or potentially present within a group of persons, and the classification of such views as correct or incorrect.

4.2. The difficulty inherent in Weber's rejection of the sociology of knowledge is that he clearly assimilates the distinction between empirical causation (or simply existence) and logical correctness to that between empirical knowledge and practical valuations. Thus, GAW, pp. 502–03, he draws a direct parallel between the relation of "realistic" ethics (i. e., the research into the empirical causes and consequences of ethical demands) to normative ethics, and the relation between a similarly "realistic" science of astronomy or mathematics (which would be some kind of *history* of astronomy or mathematics, concentrating particularly on external circumstances causing, furthering or preventing the development of these sciences, and on the empirical consequences of such developments or the lack of them) to the same disciplines in their "normal" form. A few pages later [22], we find a similar parallel; and in *Kritische Studien,* Weber sums up the result of another such discussion (of the science of mathematics in its relationship to ethics and aesthetics) in the general conclusion: "Die kausale Analyse liefert absolut keine Werturteile . . ." [23].

Theoretical disciplines (logic, mathematics, etc.) accordingly seem to occupy a double role in Weber's view: on the one hand, they yield *true* results; but on the other hand, this quality of truth cannot be derived from any true empirical observation or proposition. Truth in the theoretical sciences is different from values, then, in that it is objectively binding; but it is similar to values in that it is empirically undemonstrable.

Weber's grounds for this view seem to be most clearly expressed in a passage, GAW, p. 59:

". . . die Behauptung, daß das Einmaleins "gelte", ist für jede *empirische* psychologische Beobachtung und kausale Analyse einfach transzendent und als Objekt der Prüfung sinnlos, sie gehört zu den *für sie* gar nicht nachprüfbaren logischen Voraussetzungen ihrer eigenen psychometrischen Beobachtungen".

Thus, while Weber rejects the idea of an empirical demonstration of valuations and values because what is to be demonstrated is logically heterogeneous from the chain of demonstration, he rejects the idea of an empirical demonstration of logical truths because what is to be demonstrated is already immanent in the chain of demonstration. For the same reason, the idea of a falsification or relativation of the kind implied by the sociology of knowledge is an absurdity; as Schelting puts it: "denn auch ein solcher Nachweis, der doch *wahr* sein will, ist natürlich auch einmal entstanden und ist durch

22. GAW, p. 509.
23. GAW, p. 225.

48

irgend etwas empirisch bedingt" [24]. In the first case, the demonstration leads to a logical gap; in the second, to a logical circle.

To Weber's postulate of the undemonstrability of the *value* of scientific inquiry is accordingly added the claim that logical *truth* (and consequently empirical truth as well, insofar as the latter is dependent on the former)[25] is in itself based on norms which cannot be falsified and therefore cannot be verified either (since a logical circle implies an endless begging of the question).

4.3. Weber might have taken over the view of truth as being based on an undemonstrable norm from Kant himself [26]; but it seems more reasonable to suppose that Weber's direct source is the neo-Kantian school, above all Windelband and Rickert. The neo-Kantian philosophers regard truth as being defined, in the same way as goodness and beauty, by conformity to a particular *norm* [27]. This norm is essentially different from, for instance, what Arnold Brecht calls Scientific Method: the latter is built up on the assumption that knowledge arrived at in accordance with it has the *factual,* material quality of being "intersubjectively transmissible" *qua* knowledge. The value of the method is assessed on the basis of its results. The neo-Kantian truth is quite formal and undemonstrable; its objective validity "stellt sich in dem empirischen Bewußtsein als unmittelbare Evidenz dar, die absolut nicht erklärt, sondern einfach nur angenommen werden kann" [28]. Its only claim to acceptance is its *evident* quality.

On the other hand, the neo-Kantians regard this norm as *absolute;* it may be violated, like any other norm; but its possible lack of *empirical* validity (frequent logical errors, etc.) does not detract from its normative character [29], just as unethical conduct does not weaken the demands of ethics. In the same way, no explanation, however thorough, of *why* a person accepts, in theory and practice, the norm of truth (i. e., why he wants to, and is able to, think in a logically correct manner) can introduce any relative element into its claim of absolute validity [30].

So far, Weber's lines of thought seem to run quite parallel to those of the neo-Kantians; still, it is noteworthy that Weber never quotes the neo-Kantian definition of truth, as conformity to a certain norm, in its com-

---

24. ("for even such a demonstration, which of course claims to be true, originated somewhere, and is empirically conditioned by certain factors"). Schelting, *Wissenschaftslehre,* 1934, p. 77.
25. GAW, pp. 598–99.
26. *Cf.* Loos, *Wertlehre,* 1970, pp. 37–38.
27. Wilhelm Windelband, "Normen und Naturgesetze", *Präludien,* Freiburg i. B./Tübingen 1884, p. 219.
28. *Ibid.,* p. 226.
29. *Ibid.,* p. 216.
30. *Ibid.,* pp. 227–32.

plete and positive form [31], but only emphasizes its negative corollary, viz, that the status of a proposition as true is unaffected by the empirical circumstances surrounding its formulation.

We may see this as an indication that Weber perhaps did not exclusively rely on the views of the neo-Kantians on this point. And this hypothesis becomes still more plausible if we let the neo-Kantian argument run its full course. The neo-Kantians further argue that the normative character of truth makes it a *value,* albeit only a *theoretical* value, not a practical one related to action [32]. Consequently, a person who thinks correctly, who formulates true propositions, who, in short, acts in accordance with the norm, *eo ipso acknowledges the theoretical value of this norm* [33]. Formulating true propositions implies the acceptance of truth as being objective; and this in turn implies the acceptance of the theoretical *value* of truth as being objective. Such an intimate connection between the truth value of a proposition and the value—even the theoretical value—of truth did not commend itself to Weber, who was firmly committed to the view that the value of science and of scientific truth cannot be demonstrated by scientific means; and we cannot wonder that he nowhere endorses this ramification of the neo-Kantian theory [34].

In the light of this discrepancy, it seems natural to ask whether other scholars might have influenced Weber's thought concerning the truth value of propositions and the relation of this truth value to the value of scientific truth. In this connection, the views of the philosopher and sociologist Georg Simmel merit special attention [35]. In his *Moralwissenschaft I* (1892), Simmel writes:

31. An exception is, possibly, the phrase "... wissenschaftliche Wahrheit ist nur, was für alle gelten *will*, die Wahrheit *wollen*" (GAW, p. 184); the meaning of the seemingly enigmatic expression "gelten *will*" becomes clear when related to the neo-Kantian thesis: truth *will* (i. e. "wants to") be binding because it is a norm imbued with a special, inexplicable, immanent *evidence*. But the whole phrase hardly owes more than its wording to the neo-Kantians.
32. Heinrich Rickert, *Der Gegenstand der Erkenntnis,* Freiburg i. B. 1892, p. 57.
33. "Der Erkenntnissakt selbst kann nur in der Anerkennung des Werthes der Gefühle bestehen. *Erkennen ist Anerkennen oder Verwerfen. (Ibid.,* p. 58).
34. Similarly Loos, *Wertlehre,* 1970, p. 16. A possible exception is the passage, GASS, p. 418, where Weber speaks of "eine logische, also ... jedem theoretisch denkenden Menschen aufzwingbare wissenschaftliche Erörterung". Unless the words "jedem theoretisch denkenden Menschen aufzwingbar" are meant to express the view that the acceptance of the objectivity of scientific truth is optional—a relativation which would be highly uncharacteristic of and dangerous to Weber's thought—the phrase should probably be interpreted in the light of the neo-Kantian argument: in the vocabulary of neo-Kantianism, "theoretisch denkend" means "able to formulate and willing to accept true propositions *as being true, to acknowledge the norm of truth". See the analogous expression "die Wahrheit wollen*" in the passage quoted above (n31).
35. In GAW, Weber refers to several of Simmel's works (but not, admittedly, to *Moralwissenschaft*). Moreover, Simmel was a friend of the Weber family.

"... [es] ist ... eine mangelhafte Einsicht, wenn man meint, die Logik enthielte die Normen, nach denen wir denken sollen; sie zeigt uns vielmehr nur, wie wir denken müssen, wenn unser Denken mit der sinnlich erfahrbaren Wirklichkeit der Dinge übereinstimmen will. Es kann genug Fälle geben, wo dieser Wille nicht vorhanden ist, wo ... unserm Denken die Illusion zuträglicher ist als die Wahrheit. Dann fällt jenes Sollen fort, weil es eben davon abhängig ist, ob die Wahrheit Zweck ist" [36].

Here we find that clear-cut distinction between truth value and the value of truth which was blurred in the argument of the neo-Kantians. Moreover, the passage is interesting because Simmel firmly anchors the truth value of propositions in "die sinnlich erfahrbare Wirklichkeit der Dinge", in the *object* as perceived. As will be shown below [37], this corresponds very closely to Weber's solution of the problem of objectivity.

Simmel, too, however, develops his argument to a point where it becomes unacceptable to Weber. To his contention that truth is defined by reference to reality, to the object, Simmel adds the claim that this definition is essentially decided by *psychological* factors: logic can be reduced to psychology [38]. This lays Simmel open to the attacks of the sociology of knowledge which Weber was precisely trying to defeat with the help of the neo-Kantians.

Thus, Weber seems to be vacillating between the normative truth of the neo-Kantians and Simmel's "reference truth", borrowing from both theories while refusing to follow either to its logical conclusion. There is no doubt, however, that the influence of Simmel is more substantial than that of Windelband and Rickert: in fact, Weber only relies on the neo-Kantians when he is repudiating the conclusions of the sociology of knowledge. In his methodological works, we find no expression of interest in the material conditions necessary for the formulation of objectively valid, "supra-individual" propositions [39]. But even here, he has advanced beyond the doctrine of the immanent evidence of truth, and instead founded his argument on the logical circle inherent in the sociology of knowledge. Only the complicated intertwining of acceptable and unacceptable elements in Simmel's thought seems to prevent Weber from severing his last connections with the neo-Kantian school on this point [40].

36. Simmel, *Moralwissenschaft I*, 1892, pp. 319–20.
37. Pp. 133–35.
38. *Cf.* Loos, *Wertlehre*, 1970, p. 48, with quotations from Simmel.
39. *Cf. infra*, p. 137.
40. The element of neo-Kantian terminology in Weber, and the consequent conceptual fusion of the objectivity with the value of truth, has led certain commentators to conclude—in my view incorrectly—that the passages in question in fact mean that Weber *accepted* this fusion. Thus Wegener, who by and large identifies Weber's arguments supporting the objective character of truth with those advanced by the neo-Kantians (Wegener, *Wissenschaftsauffassung*, 1962, pp. 90, 105), maintains that Weber could not draw the last consequences of his "value scepticism", since this would have called the objective character of truth into question (*ibid.*, pp. 116–17, 252). Schelting (*Wissenschaftslehre*, 1934, pp. 30–31) explicitly rejects the

5. There is a connection between Weber's rejection of the conclusions of the sociology of knowledge and his treatment of an argument occasionally brought up in support of the demand for value freedom. This argument is based on "die empirisch erweisliche Tatsache, daß jene letzten Ziele [i. e. the "higher" values of the value sphere] historisch wandelbar und streitig sind" [41]. In Weber's opinion, of course, this historical change has no bearing on the question of the more or less objective validity of the values involved; and he consequently counters the argument with the remark that "auch die Erkenntnis der sichersten Sätze unseres theoretischen—etwa des exakt natur-wissenschaftlichen oder mathematischen—Wissens ... erst Produkt der Kul-tur [ist]" [42]—from which it follows that the demonstration of the historical change in the structure of the value sphere is itself equally dependent on historically changing factors, and that such a demonstration cannot attain its goal of relativizing certain values without relativizing itself as well.

As part of a criticism of Gustav Schmoller [43], Weber in *Wertfreiheit* [44] rejects a similar argument, but here uses a slightly different approach. Schmoller [45] had implicitly imputed to Weber the view that the subjective character of values had become evident not as a result of essentially logical considerations, but rather as a result of historical or quantitative ones [46]: i. e., that particular value. Schmoller's reply to this imputed position was that values were slowly but surely growing more objective (in this quantitative and historical sense), and that the basis for maintaining a principle of value freedom was therefore slowly crumbling; on the contrary, he saw the education of the public in the direction of more "objective" value judgments as an important task allotted to science.

The first of Schmoller's premises: that values are only subjective in the sense that they change through time and that they possess less than general acceptance, is denied by Weber, who points to the fact that "empirische

assimilation, but still discusses the question of the truth of propositions in terms reminicent of neo-Kantianism, and apparently sees the objectivity of truth as holding only for the theoretical sphere, i. e., the sphere of scientific inquiry.
41. GAW, p. 152.
42. GAW, p. 152.
43. Gustav Schmoller, "Volkswirtschaftslehre", *Handwörterbuch der Staatswissen-schaften* (3. ed.), Jena 1911; quoted from reprint: Gustav Schmoller, *Die Volks-wirtschaft, die Volkswirtschaftslehre und ihre Methodik* (ed., intr. Aug. Skalweit), Frankfurt a/Main 1949.
44. GAW, pp. 501–02.
45. *Volkswirtschaftslehre*, 1949, pp. 78, 80–81.
46. "... ich [würde] ihm [Weber] recht geben ..., wenn ich—wie er—der Ansicht wäre, alle Werturteile seien absolut subjektiv; ... aber es gibt neben den subjek-tiven objektive Werturteile, an denen nicht bloß einzelne Personen und Gelehrte, sondern große Gemeinschaften, Völker, Zeitalter, ja die ganze Kulturwelt teil-nehmen" (Schmoller, *Volkswirtschaftslehre*, 1949, p. 78).

Tatsachenfeststellungen" are often far less generally accepted than the answers to certain questions of value. The second premise: the belief in a progressive conventional agreement concerning the highest values, Weber rejects as being "in schroffem Gegensatz zu meinem entgegengesetzten Eindruck" [47].

While Weber's arguments in *Objektivität* rested on the demonstration of a logical circle in the argument of the opponent, he is on more dangerous ground in *Wertfreiheit:* instead of emphasizing the *essentially* subjective character of valuations of all sorts, and pointing to the existence of a *logical* gap between "Sein" and "Sollen", he rather merges the two spheres into one by demonstrating the "subjectivity" (in Schmoller's sense of the term) of *science* as well as of *values.* The discussion consequently centres around the question whether "objectivation" is to be conceived as a necessarily progressing, or at any rate as a theoretically possible, process; and here again, Weber wards off Schmoller's arguments by means of empirical statements: in fact, the demand for value freedom here seems to stand or fall with the answer to the question whether everybody might conceivably, with time, come to hold the same values.

Weber turns the discussion back into the right channel with his general comments, GAW, p. 502, and with the words: "Allein das scheint mir ohne Belang für die Sache" to a certain extent dissociates himself from his own arguments criticized above. But the passage remains an example of Weber's occasional tendency to make use of the kind of sociology of knowledge which he generally—and rightly—criticizes as being logically unsatisfactory [48].

47. GAW, p. 502.
48. What makes the introduction of any other than a strictly logical and theoretical argument into the discussion of the principle of value freedom particularly dangerous for Weber, is that he himself has pointed to the historical preconditions, the specifically *modern* character of the demand for and the possibility of a value-free, rational science (see for instance PE I, pp. 9–26). This leads Karl Löwith, for instance ("Max Weber und Karl Marx", *Archiv,* vol. 67 (1932), reprinted (with alterations) and quoted from Karl Löwith, *Gesammelte Abhandlungen,* Stuttgart 1960, pp. 11–12), to suppose that Weber saw the progressive "Entzauberung der Welt" not only as a development permitting a growing *awareness* of the logical distinction between "Sein" and 'Sollen", but also as the only *basis* for claiming this distinction to be true; consequently, according to this interpretation, the demand for value freedom must be regarded as valid only for a particular period, and loses its absolute logical basis.

This argument does not seem conclusive. Against it may be marshalled Weber's general rejection of the sociology of knowledge, which certainly also applies to the present case, as is evident, for instance, from a passage like GARS, pp. 541–42: "... die Rationalisierung und bewußte Sublimierung der Beziehungen des Menschen zu den verschiedenen Sphären äußeren und inneren, religiösen und weltlichen, Güterbesitzes drängte dann dazu: *innere Eigengesetzlichkeiten* der einzelnen Sphären in ihren Konsequenzen *bewußt* werden und dadurch in jene Spannungen zueinander geraten zu lassen, welche der urwüchsigen Unbefangenheit der Beziehung zur Außenwelt verborgen blieben".

6. A problem discussed exhaustively by Weber, particularly in the *Stammler* essay, concerns the logical difference between a normative rule and an empirical regularity. For the purposes of his controversy with Stammler, Weber wants especially to emphasize that an empirical regularity does not in itself permit us to infer the existence of a *formal* norm; in fact, the sociology of law usually starts from the opposite assumption, viz, that the *consequences* of formal norms and injunctions bear no necessary relation to their *content.* In both cases, however, it seems to me that the problem is chiefly derived from the existence of the formal norm as an actual, *concrete* injunction, i. e. as an empirical probability that certain sanctions will be brought into play if the norm is not respected; the value structure of the injunction seems to play a secondary role in this connection. Accordingly, the problem will not receive further treatment in the present account.

1.4.3. *The relationship between the two demands*

1.1. Obviously, the distinction applied above to the formulations of the demand for value freedom according to what phase of the scientific process they refer to, must seem artificial and abstract to persons actually engaged in research. Conceptualization and conclusions are interdependent to a much larger degree than the distinction would seem to suggest. Thus, as Arnold Brecht (among others) has pointed out, the process of scientific inquiry often starts off with the formulation of a working hypothesis which is of course of considerable importance for the further course of the scientific process, the concepts used, etc., but which may possibly—if it is verified—only appear in the finished work in the form of a conclusion [1]; on the other hand, the influence of valuational elements on the concepts or on the causal analysis may evidently determine the more or less valuational character of the conclusions [2].

1.2. Weber himself, as we have seen, neglects this unity of the scientific process in his formulations and in practice upholds the distinction between the problems of conceptualization and those of the scientific results; this is probably due to the double concern on which his demand for value freedom is based: the concern for the sphere of scientific inquiry and for the sphere of values respectively.

Not only does Weber uphold the distinction; it is also strikingly evident that one of its elements, viz, the demand for the value freedom of the scientific *results,* appears much more frequently than the other one; this

---

1. Brecht, *Theory,* 1959, p. 29.
2. See for instance the case mentioned above, pp. 40–41, where a vague concept in Professor Liefmann's construction afforded the basis for a conclusion in the form of a practical imperative.

would seem to indicate that Weber is more concerned with defending the value sphere against the unfounded claims of science than with protecting the scientific process from valuational distortions. One might attempt to reduce the importance of this uneven distribution by pointing out that Weber devotes much attention to *positive* discussions of the problems of scientific inquiry [3], and that his huge systematic–empirical works with their profusion of definitions of concepts make up a practical correlate to these methodological discussions. With regard to the *Gutachten* in particular, it might further be argued that the "Bezeichnung wirtschafts- und sozialpolitischer Zielpunkte" was precisely one of the four questions which the *Verein* had singled out for special treatment [4]. Still, one gets the clear impression when reading Weber's discussion that a particular kind of problem was foremost in his mind. I do not think it unjustified to conclude that the uneven distribution of emphasis referred to, whether it be regarded as unconscious or as deliberate, can be taken to indicate an important tendency in Weber's methodology.

2.   A first attempt to relate this imbalance to already established characteristic traits in Weber's discussion of value freedom might be made by pointing to the markedly *active* aspect of a number of Weber's demands for the value freedom of the scientific results. Weber's special emphasis on the latter might, on this interpretation, reflect a wish to formulate the demand for value freedom in relation to a calculation of ends and means, and thereby in the last instance to the political decision-making process and its problems. It is certainly true that many of the passages directly concern the actions of individuals, and the choices which must be made on the basis of a given fund of knowledge; but the *point* of these passages is invariably a negative one, viz, that science is only able to supply knowledge as a foundation for choice, but that is can *never* arrogate for itself the function of choosing. A wish to relate the demand for value freedom as closely as possible to the concern with the rationality of political action would rather have led Weber to stress the *positive* role of science as a supplier of correct knowledge, a role above all safeguarded by the value freedom of the scientific *process* [5].

3. For instance in *Kritische Studien* (historical analysis) and in the discussion of the ideal type (*cf. infra,* ch. 4).
4. *Cf. supra,* p. 19.
5. Ralf Dahrendorf (*Werturteil,* 1967, p. 85) uses the term "Das Problem der *Anwendung*" (my italics) to denote the problem of the value freedom of the *results* of scientific inquiry; the choice of this term is doublessly connected with the "active" structure of the demands for value freedom covered by it, but it is still les than happy: the problem is one of ends, not of application (can science *set* political goals?—not: can science *help* in *attaining* political goals?).

3. A closer examination of Weber's inaugural lecture, *Antrittsrede,* which was delivered in the summer of 1895 on the occasion of Weber's taking up his duties as professor of economics at Freiburg University, opens up interesting perspectives. Its harsh mixture of "Erkenntnis" and "Bekenntnis"[6], of scientific analysis and political commitment—the latter being moreover extremely radical[7]—made a strong, but by no means wholly positive impression on the audience; and Weber referred to the opposition with which it had met as being the main reason why he had it printed in slightly extended form[8]. Since the methodological importance of the lecture is intimately connected with its concrete historical and political content, it may be useful to give a short account of its main lines of argument.

3.1. The *Antrittsrede* opens with an analysis of certain characteristic relations between the economic, social and national structures in the country districts of the German province of West Prussia, with their mixed German and Polish population. In brief, Weber arrives at the following conclusions: the Polish population group is steadily growing relatively to the German one; this development is the result of German migrations away from the economically most prosperous areas, in conjunction with an increase of the Polish population in the economically *least* prosperous areas. This double tendency in its turn partly reflects the greater adaptability of the Polish population group to inferior *economic* conditions (lower agricultural prices), and partly the growing dissatisfaction of the German population group with the traditionalist *social* structures (tenancy system)[9]. In other words, the free play of economic[10] forces in this field leads to the supplanting of the (in Weber's view) economically and socially "superior" German culture by the "inferior"

6. Marianne Weber, *Lebensbild,* 1950, p. 249.
7. Weber himself, in a letter to his brother Alfred of May 17th, 1895 (DZA II, Rep. 92, No. 4) speaks of "die Brutalität meiner Ansichten" ("the brutality of my views").
8. *Der Nationalstaat und die Volkswirtschaftspolitik,* Freiburg/Tübingen 1895; reprinted in GPS, pp. 1–25. As regards the extension, *cf.* GPS, p. 1. I take Weber's statement that he omitted pp. 15–18 "mit Rücksicht auf Zeit und Hörerkreis" to mean that he decided *in advance* not to include the remarks in question in his public lecture, and thus did not simply leave them out in response to a sudden impulse during the actual lecture. The evidence seems to support this hypothesis: the phrasing of the pages left out clearly marks them as an insertion; and the argument of the main text is carried on immediately after the end of the three inserted pages.
9. GPS, pp. 2–10, particularly pp. 6–10.
10. The social factors remain secondary in this connection; they may explain the German migration and consequently determine the estimate of the German culture as socially "superior" (freedom-loving, motivated by ideals); but subsequent developments whereby the old tenancy relationships were replaced by seasonal contracts with Russian and Polish day-labourers, must be regarded as the result of *economic* factors.

Polish one [11]. What Weber sees as the *inferior* culture is thus economically the *stronger* one.

3.2. Weber does not draw the *theoretical* conclusions from this demonstration of a sort of "Gresham's law" for national cultures; instead, he turns to the *practical* aspect of the question and asks: "... was kann und soll hier geschehen?" [12] What chiefly interests him, though, seems to be not so much the concrete measures as such, but rather the *basis* for them: what criteria should guide the elaboration of a policy for the situation described?

3.2.1. The view was widely held that the ideals which were to serve as guides for economic policy could, and should, be supplied by *the science of economics by itself*. A "Volkswirtschaftspolitik", according to this view, should have independent, "volkswirtschaftlich" goals. Weber examines this claim [13] and comes to the conclusion that it is the result of an "optical illusion" [14]. The ideals usually presented as " independent" economic ones on examination turn out to be nothing more than a motley collection of ethical and "eudämonistische" [15] values: "In Wahrheit sind es *keine* eigenartigen und selbstgewonnenen, sondern die *alten allgemeinen Typen menschlicher Ideale,* die wir auch in den Stoff unserer Wissenschaft hineintragen" [16]. If these general ideals are not introduced, the value judgments which can be inferred from the "economic point of view" as such are simply reflections of disguised class interests; the most that the science of economics itself can offer is a technical ideal, i. e., rationality with respect to an *externally* given end or goal [17]. An exclusively economic, "scientifically" defined policy goal does not exist. And against the alternative position: that adequate insight into the laws of economic development can offer sufficiently secure foundations for the elaboration of objective goals of economic policy, Weber demonstrates that such a procedure only serves the purpose of evading the burden of decision, either in the sense that "economic development" is made to justify *any* policy, or by way of legitimating the right of the economically strongest power [18].

3.2.2. Consequently, any criteria for the setting of goals for economic policy must be supplied from *outside,* not from *inside* the science of economics. Among the various external ideals and goals, one might, for instance, choose the "old, general" ideals of traditional economic policy, i. e., ethical

11. GPS, p. 9.
12. GPS, p. 10.
13. GPS, pp. 15–18. This is the part omitted from the actual lecture.
14. ("optische Täuschung"). GPS, p. 16.
15. This probably refers to utilitarian ideals, i. e., to values establishing the happiness or satisfaction of individuals as the fundamental criterion.
16. GPS, p. 16.
17. GPS, p. 16.
18. GPS, pp. 17–18; *cf. supra,* pp. 45–46.

and utilitarian criteria, separately or combined in some fashion. Weber's solution is a different one, however, and one which is implicit in his presentation of the problem. Empirical analysis had shown that national interests were affected negatively by the free and untrammelled development of a particular economic tendency; and the reaction was, as we have seen, a demand for action. This demand already implies the values according to which it is to be satisfied: "Es ist der Umstand, daß unser Staatswesen ein *Nationalstaat* ist, welcher uns das Recht zu dieser Forderung empfinden läßt" [19]. In other words: practical problems are value problems; and the values in relation to which the problem is defined are at the same time the guideline for its solution. In this case, the problem is a national one; consequently, the criteria for its solution are also national.

3.2.3. Taken by itself, however, this argument begs the question, which now runs: "With what *justification* does Weber call for action? What are his reasons for choosing the national rather than the ethical or utilitarian point of view as the starting point of the analysis and as the supreme criterion of economic policy?" The answer to this question falls in two parts:

First, the introduction of the national aspect into the empirical analysis permitted an amplification of its findings. What in the traditional utilitarian view might be conceived simply as a *development* without negative overtones, in the form of analysis guided by the national aspect becomes a bitter *struggle*. True, this struggle is not waged with fire and sword, but remains a "stilles und ödes Ringen des ökonomischen Alltagslebens" [20]; but here, too, some are victors and others vanquished. And the fact that the economic welfare of the individual is increasingly becoming linked to an *international* economic system—a development which might for instance be regarded as an ethically positive trait—does not neutralize the struggle for national existence, but may even deepen it, since economic interests can now run *contrary* to national ones [21].

But the acknowledgement of the *scientific* importance of a national *aspect* is not in Weber's view identical with the commitment to a national *value* as *practically* supreme. He takes this second step by attempting to show that economic policy has fundamentally always implied, and must always imply, the acceptance of the maintenance and furthering of the national culture as a major premise [22]. Moreover, the high standard of human character which in his view should be a fundamental aim of economic policy cannot be defined arbitrarily, and more especially must include a national and cultural reference: "Die Volkswirtschaftslehre als erklärende und analysie-

19. GPS, p. 11.
20. GPS, p. 12.
21. GPS, pp. 13–14.
22. GPS, pp. 12–13.

rende Wissenschaft ist *international,* allein sobald sie *Werturteile* fällt, ist sie gebunden an diejenige Ausprägung des Menschentums, die wir in unserem eigenen Wesen finden" [23]. What the economic policy of today can and ought to strive for is the safeguarding of national and cultural *continuity,* and with it, the *identity* of future generations.

Having thus established the conservation of the national essence as the major goal of economic policy, Weber draws his conclusion and formulates it pithily. Economic policy must subordinate itself to the long-term interests of the nation, in this case of the nation-state; it must serve the enlightened reason of state: "... die Wissenschaft von der Volkswirtschaftspolitik ist eine *politische* Wissenschaft" [24].

3.3.1. One can well understand that the *Antrittsrede* [25], with its extreme political statements and emotional consecration of the principle of nationalism [26], has seemed to many commentators to present a glaring contrast with Weber's later methodology, particularly with his principle of value freedom and with the "value asceticism" which this principle seemed to them to imply. Thus, Tenbruck speaks of "die Gewaltlösung der Freiburger Rede" and of its "Mißachtung aller methodologischen Möglichkeiten" [27]; and Bernhard Pfister, for instance, is of the same opinion [28]. Nevertheless, it seems to me more fruitful to view, with Wolfgang J. Mommsen, the *Antrittsrede* as something more than a mere negation of Weber's later methodological thought: "Es erscheint paradox, ist jedoch für Max Weber höchst charakteristisch, daß gerade in dieser Antrittsvorlesung, die ganz von Politik durchtränkt ist und voll von Werturteilen, die Grundlagen seiner späteren ... Theorie der Wertfreiheit der reinen Wissenschaften gelegt wurden" [29]. In fact, it is probably justified to go still further and to see the *Antrittsrede* as

23. GPS, p. 13.
24. GPS, p. 14.
25. The end of the lecture (pp. 18–25) has not received separate treatment because of its lesser methodological importance. Here, Weber examines the qualifications of the various population groups to lead the German nation-state, and again brings out the tension between economics and politics, since the possession by these groups of *political* power is a consequence of their *economic* potential, from which follows that the nation-state may be governed by groups whose economic interests conflict with the national values.
26. See particularly the last phrases, GPS, p. 25, culminating in a eulogy of "die ernste Herrlichkeit des nationalen Empfindens".
27. Tenbruck, *Genesis,* 1959, p. 581. A similarly negative estimate is found, for instance, in Gerhard Schulz, "Geschichtliche Theorie und politisches Denken bei Max Weber", *Vierteljahreshefte für Zeitgeschichte,* Vol. 12 (1964), pp. 334–35.
28. Bernhard Pfister, *Die Entwicklung zum Idealtypus,* Tübingen 1928, pp. 113–14.
29. Wolfgang J. Mommsen, *Max Weber und die deutsche Politik 1890–1920,* Tübingen 1959, p. 41. Similarly Jürgen Kraft, *Das Verhältnis von Nationalökonomie und Soziologie bei Franz Oppenheimer, Werner Sombart, Max Weber und in der sozialwissenschaftlichen Systembildung des 19. Jahrhunderts,* Diss. Göttingen 1961, pp. 235–36; and Loos, *Wertlehre,* 1970, p. 37.

embodying, in rudimentary form, all the important elements of Weber's methodology.

3.3.2. Thus, we find Weber acknowledging the importance of the ever-changing nature of approaches and aspects, for heuristic as well as for other purposes of science [30]; we find him stressing the element of *conflict* [31] and emphasizing (particularly in the last part of the lecture) the concept of *responsibility* [32].

When it comes to the relevance of the *Antrittsrede* to the problem of value freedom, we can distinguish between two levels of questions. On the one hand, one may ask whether Weber, by his "politicization" of the subject, his passionate defence of a particular ultimate value, his extreme phraseology, in practice violates the principle of value freedom which he formulates some ten years later in *Objektivität* [33]. On the other hand, and more especially, one can look for early material traces of this principle in the *Antrittsrede*.

3.3.3. In this connection, it is beyond doubt that the *intention* of the methodologically relevant passages in the *Antrittsrede* differs sharply from that of the later methodological essays. In the *Antrittsrede,* the point of importance to Weber is to defend an ideal which may serve as a goal for concrete political measures in a given situation: he sets himself a *political* problem which demands a *political* solution.

This general political intention is reflected in the methodologically relevant discussions; here, too, arguments and conclusions are based on *political* premises. We might say that there is a lack of methodological (at least of a critical methodological) *awareness;* we find no trace of the "methodologische Unbehagen" which Pfister [34], rightly, regards as desirable in this connection. However, the lack of methodological awareness does not *eo ipso* mean that the results obtained without it can be discarded offhand; the only *necessary* consequence is that a theoretical dimension remains closed to the scholar in question. In the present case, Weber's methodologically "innocent" point of view does not entail the automatic violation in the *Antrittsrede* of the rules of methodology, but only that the focus of his efforts is mainly [35] located on the concrete, empirical level. In fact, Weber here advances *in concreto* a good number of the views which he later formulates, consolidates, and defends *in abstracto*.

3.3.4. The demand for the value freedom of the scientific process, i. e., the demand that scientific inquiry should be kept free from unconscious value

---

30. *Cf. infra*, pp. 109–14.
31. *Cf. infra*, pp. 178–79.
32. *Cf. infra*, pp. 268–72.
33. For a short discussion of this and similar problems, *cf. infra*, Appendix C.
34. Pfister, *Idealtypus*, 1928, p. 114.
35. Not exclusively: the emphasis on the heuristic and problem-defining function of the aspect adopted already constitutes an explicit methodological element.

judgments, is already suggested in the *Antrittsrede*. The criticism of the vague, "independent" economic ideals [36], of the illusion that it is possible altogether to avoid value elements and valuations, can actually be regarded as a forerunner of the criticism of "value-free" concepts like "Fortschritt" and "Volkswohlstand". Thus, the wish to clarify and confirm the practical political ideal, the *value* sphere, as an independent category, may, as pointed out by Arnold Bergstraesser, result in an extension and consolidation of the sphere of *scientific inquiry* [37].

Still, this embryonic conceptual criticism in the *Antrittsrede* remains isolated, almost casual. A much more prominent role is played by the other asymmetrical demand for value freedom: the rejection of the view that science can provide us with ideals elaborated inside its own sphere, or, generally speaking, that it is possible to arrive at "Sollen" conclusions from "Sein" premises. Weber's argument is direct enough, but, in conformity with the tendency noted above, concrete rather than abstract and paradigmatic. The *conclusion* is only postulated to be valid for the science of economics; and the *grounds* given by Weber for his view are concrete and peculiar to economics: a study of "die Literatur unserer Wissenschaft" [38], i. e. of economic literature, shows that the value judgments found in this discipline are either derived from "foreign" ideals, or give no guidance for the practical action demanded by Weber [39].

Thus, the principle of value freedom is in the *Antrittsrede* mainly formulated and argued in *concrete* terms and *asymmetrically,* the stress being laid on the value freedom of scientific *results*. If we compare it with the fully developed principle as it is formulated for the first time in *Objektivität* and maintained in the later essays, we find that the principle has in the meantime been provided with a complete logical foundation, and has in this sense been *generalized,* inasmuch as it is no longer restricted to the special problems of a single discipline. It is difficult accurately to identify the factors which may have brought about this generalization. One important clue, though,

36. GPS, p. 16.
37. Arnold Bergstraesser, "Max Weber, der Nationalstaat und die Politik", *Politik in Wissenschaft und Bildung,* Freiburg i. B. 1961, p. 69.
38. GPS, p. 16.
39. This shows the limited theoretical scope of the practical conclusion drawn by Weber. As we have seen, his rejection of laissez-faire as a value standard for the solution of the problem was derived from practical considerations, since it was precisely the prevalence of laissez-faire that *created* the problem. Viewed in a general context, however, Weber's rejection must be considered as insufficient, in the sense that the decision to "leave events to take their course" is just as valuational, and logically dependent on some kind of ideal, as practical action. To make a rejection of this particular derivation of a "Sollen" from a "Sein" theoretically and generally valid, Weber would need the *logical* axiom of the heterogeneity of the two spheres, which he only arrived at later.

seems to me to be present in the *Antrittsrede* itself. As will be remembered, Weber here rejects the view that economic policy can be purely "economic" (in the sense of "*correct* according to the science of economics"); on the contrary: the science of economic policy is a *political* science. This latter concept is hammered out: again and again, we find expressions like "politische Macht", "politische Leitung", "politische Herrschaft" [40]. As a correlate to the negative critique of a concept used by a particular discipline, Weber defines a positive and much more general category: the *political* sphere.

3.3.5. Thus, even before the awakening of Weber's "methodological conscience" [41], the "value aspect" of the demand for value freedom is strongly represented in his work, while the "science aspect" is still at a rudimentary stage. The later formulation of the symmetrical demand must accordingly have been in the nature of a completion rather than of an amplification: to a complex of thought whose centre of gravity lies in certain considerations of the essence of the *political* sphere, are added, under the influence of developments in the logical and epistemological field, other lines of thought concerning the distinctive character and independence of *science*. But while the "science aspect" is added on at a late stage, problematical, weak, and defined negatively, the "value aspect" receives its definitive form almost from the beginning, remaining ever afterwards unshaken, clearly and strongly elaborated and positively defined. This, as I see it, is one of the main reasons for the asymmetrical dominance in Weber's principle of value freedom [42].

1.4.4. The field of application of the demand for value freedom

Because of the fragmentary character of Weber's methodological work, it is not easy to establish at the first glance how far-reaching he meant his conclusions, among them the principle of value freedom, to be. For the discussion of this problem, it is necessary to examine the various passages in question a little more closely.

1. The titles of the two important essays, *Objektivität* and *Wertfreiheit* [1], give indications of the framework of the discussions which they contain and indicate the scientific disciplines for which the conclusions are at least presumed to hold.

The title of *Objektivität* speaks of "sozialwissenschaftliche und sozial-

40. See for instance GPS, pp. 18–19, 22–23.
41. ("methodologische Gewissen"). Pfister, *Idealtypus*, 1928, p. 114.
42. *Cf. infra*, Appendix B.
 1. GAW, pp. 146 and 489 respectively.

politische Erkenntnis". This formulation clearly contains a reference to the new name given, at the same time, to the *Archiv:* "Archiv für Sozialwissenschaft und Sozialpolitik" [2], and is probably a little more restrictive than might be supposed, since Weber himself indicates that "Sozialwissenschaft" should be interpreted as: "die geschichtliche und theoretische Beschäftigung mit den gleichen Problemen ..., deren praktische Lösung Gegenstand der "Sozial*politik*" im weitesten Sinne dieses Wortes ist" [3]. Furthermore, this characterization is in its turn linked to the study of phenomena relevant to or caused by *economic* factors. Still, the "Sozialwissenschaft" defined in this fashion covers several fields of study which would today fall under other disciplines [4]; and the actual discussions of the principle of value freedom in *Objektivität* are occasionally still more generally worded [5].

In the *Gutachten,* Weber starts off by delimiting the field of application of his remarks as *"empirische* Disziplinen, wie die uns fachlich interessierende Soziologie (einschließlich der "Politik"), Nationalökonomie (einschließlich der "Wirtschaftspolitik"), Geschichte (aller Arten, also ausdrücklich: einschließlich z. B. der Rechts-, Religions- und Kulturgeschichte) es sind" [6], while *Wertfreiheit,* which no longer contains this introduction, instead carries a programmatic title describing the field of interest of the essay as "die soziologischen und ökonomischen Wissenschaften".

In the light of these definitions, it seems justified to assume that the principle of value freedom propounded in the essays referred to (above all in *Wertfreiheit*) is postulated as being at least valid for all the empirical social sciences [7].

A slightly more awkward problem concerns the hypothetical validity of the principle for the empirical non-social sciences (below referred to for convenience as the "natural sciences") and for the non-empirical sciences.

2.   As far as the natural sciences are concerned, they are covered by the introductory passages of the *Gutachten,* as well as by the terms "Erfahrungswissenschaft" or "empirische Wissenschaft", which are used very frequently. The fact that they are not mentioned explicitly in the course of the discussion

2. Formerly, its name was "Archiv für soziale Gesetzgebung und Statistik".
3. GAW, p. 165.
4. See for instance the discussion of the concepts of "church" and "sect" (GAW, p. 194), of "Christianity" (GAW, p. 197) and of "state" (GAW, pp. 200–01).
5. See for instance expressions like "eine Erfahrungswissenschaft" (GAW, p. 149), "eine empirische Sozialwissenschaft" (GAW, p. 151) and "die Sozialwissenschaften" (GAW, p. 160).
6. *Gutachten,* p. 83.
7. The fact that the historical disciplines are not mentioned in the title of *Wertfreiheit* hardly constitutes sufficient grounds for supposing that Weber wished to accord them some special status in connection with the discussion of the question of value freedom.

is explained partly by Weber's exclusive interest (in this essay) in the social sciences, and partly by the fact that the problem of value freedom and of the logical implications of this principle did not, even at the time, constitute any major difficulty for the natural sciences. If we assume, as was done above [8], that the demand for value freedom acquires a special weight because the element which is seen as illegitimate on the research level is precisely that which is treated on the object level, a demand analogous to the demand for value freedom would in the natural sciences rather deal with the elimination of physical, chemical and other "natural" disturbances from the scientific process, since the object of the latter is singled out for study because of its physical (chemical, etc.) interest. A demand of this kind usually does not raise problems of the same fundamental character; and its practical fulfilment also seems easier to achieve, because the variables to be held constant are normally measurable to the same degree as the object under study, and can be rendered "objective" without inner resistance on the part of the scientists concerned. That the demand may still give rise to fundamental difficulties is shown, for instance, by the discussion of the uncertainty principle in physics. Weber probably would not have seen any particular difficulty in extending his demand for value freedom to embrace the natural sciences explicitly.

3.   Weber does not separately discuss the question of value freedom in those disciplines which do not, like the empirical ones, deal with observable phenomena, and which we might call the theoretical sciences. On the other hand, he obviously acknowledges a logical, i. e., a conceptual and theoretical, truth of the same strength and validity as the empirical one [9]; and the principle of value freedom would consequently seem to apply as much to the theoretical as to the empirical disciplines.

Weber apparently works from the assumption that the theoretical sciences will also be normative ones; as examples of such normative theoretical sciences, he mentions mathematics, logic, ethics, aesthetics, and jurisprudence [10]. The normative element in these disciplines will usually consist in their starting from certain undemonstrable axioms. This by itself need not diminish the relevance of the demand for value freedom, since the normative sciences also, insofar as they wish to qualify as "sciences", as producers of "true" statements [11], depend on correct (i. e., value-free) knowledge.

8. P. 28.
9. *Cf. infra,* pp. 160–61.
10. GAW, pp. 322, 536, 542.
11. Supplemented by an indication of the axiomatic system for which the "true" statements in question are alleged to hold. See for instance GAW, pp. 347, 349, where Weber deals with "juristische Wahrheit", i. e. correct deductions from or subsumptions under normative rules of law.

This rather slight problem has been taken up here because the introduction to the *Gutachten* (quoted above) classifies "Politik" with empirical sociology and "Wirtschaftspolitik" with economics. In contradistinction to ethics, law, etc., politics does *not,* in Weber's view,—for reasons which will become clear later on—belong to the category of the "normative sciences" [12]. Consequently, it seems particularly unfortunate and dangerous that Weber, in the passage quoted, leaves the line dividing science and politics to be held only by a couple of inverted commas, and it becomes all the more necessary to point out that the terms "Politik" and "Wirtschaftspolitik" should be interpreted as "political science" and "the science of economic policies" respectively (or at least the parts of these sciences relevant to practical politics).

1.5. The implementation of the principle

The demand for value freedom must be taken to imply an injunction to observe in *practice* the theoretical (logical) distinction between the value sphere and the sphere of scientific inquiry. The question is now what exactly Weber understands by "observe in practice".

As we have seen, the statement that a logical gap exists between "Sein" and "Sollen" was, in Weber's view, a logically binding one, while the *value* of maintaining this gap in practice was derived from the acceptance of the value of scientific inquiry and/or of personal commitment to values. This acceptance, however, could be assumed to exist in the case of persons claiming some kind of scientific status for their activity and for its results. For such persons, in their capacity as "scientists", the acknowledgement of the desirability, or value, of the distinction between empirical truth and practical valuations is thus a logical necessity.

The practical demand for the observance of the principle of value freedom closely reflects this theoretical foundation, in respect both of its content and of its scope of application. As regards the scope of the demand, it is certain that the latter can only be addressed to the scientist or scholar in his capacity as such, i. e., in fact only to science *qua* science, and that consequently the principle is only logically binding in the fields for which the value of scientific inquiry can be shown to be the *only* ideal and goal. When this condition does not hold [1], as for instance in the case of university teaching, the demand for the observance of the principle of value freedom cannot be maintained, as will be shown in more detail below.

12. GAW, p. 557.
1. As mentioned above, Weber carefully emphasizes that *logical* impossibility, not only actual empirical disagreement on the question, is what counts in this respect. See for instance GAW, p. 491.

1.5.1. The implementation of the principle in fields where the value of scientific inquiry is the only ideal

1. *Within* areas where the value of scientific inquiry is the only value basis (i. e., in all sorts of scientific writings, apart from works which are also meant to serve pedagogic ends), the demand for value freedom merely reflects the acknowledgement of the logical gap, a simple deduction from Weber's axiomatic definition, according to which science can only and may only aim at formulating *true* propositions, and therefore ought to avoid any intermingling of "Sein" and "Sollen", not to mention the disguising of one sphere under the name of the other, since such procedures are not compatible with the aim of providing correct knowledge. This demand is seen by Weber as implicit in the definition of scientific activity [2]; and in this light, his use of the value-laden expression "intellektuelle Rechtschaffenheit" ("intellectual honesty") [3] becomes understandable. What we are dealing with is not a demand based on some undemonstrable value: the observance of the principle of value freedom is a precondition for the legitimate use of the term "scientific inquiry" to denote the activity of a scientist or scholar.

2. On closer examination, Weber sees this "intellektuelle Rechtschaffenheit" as implying *two* duties: "Klarheit und deutliche Trennung der heterogenen Problemsphären durch den Dozenten" [4]. "Klarheit", "clarity", should probably be interpreted along the lines of the following passage from *Objektivität:* "... in jedem Augenblick den Lesern und sich selbst scharf zum Bewußtsein zu bringen, *welches* die Maßstäbe sind, an denen die Wirklichkeit gemessen und aus denen das Werturteil abgeleitet wird..." [5]. The demand for "deutliche Trennung", "clear distinctions", referred to, can be amplified in the same way: "... den Lesern (und—sagen wir wiederum—vor allem sich selbst!) jederzeit deutlich zu machen, *daß* und *wo* der denkende Forscher aufhört und der wollende Mensch anfängt zu sprechen" [6]. The parallel to the demands for the value freedom of the scientific process and of the scientific results respectively, and beyond them to the two asymmetrical demands for value freedom in general, is quite clear.

2. See for instance GAW, pp. 490–91, where the obligation to observe the distinction in practice is assumed to arise directly out of the theoretical acceptance of it ("ein Gebot der intellektuellen Rechtschaffenheit, wenn man einmal die Fremdheit der Sphären zugibt"). Similar passages, GAW, pp. 90, 497.
3. For instance GAW, pp. 491, 601.
4. GAW, p. 497.
5. GAW, p. 156.
6. GAW, p. 157. Similarly, pp. 490, 498.

66

As will be noticed, the principle of value freedom does not in any way debar an author from introducing private value judgments into a work purporting to have a scientific character, just as the principle does not in theory deny the right of scientists and scholars to commit themselves to undemonstrable values of all kinds *outside* their scientific role. Nobody can prevent a scholar from "in einem und demselben Buch, auf einer und derselben Seite, ja in einem Haupt- und Nebensatz einer und derselben syntaktischen Einheit sich einerseits über das eine und andererseits über das andere der beiden heterogenen Probleme zu äußern" [7]. But any value judgment, any "Sollen" in the resulting mosaic of logically heterogeneous statements, must be regarded as an unscientific insertion which is legitimate, perhaps even desirable, but which is in any case something apart from the world of *science* [8]. And precisely because such insertions are different from science and accordingly address themselves to another aspect of the reader's personality [9], because the author, so to speak, introduces a double dialogue between author and reader in their two different aspects: the theoretically contemplating and the actively evaluating one, it is a compelling necessity to make the changes of aspect quite plain by observing in practice the two injunctions defined above [10].

3. Weber's discussion of what he [11] terms "Pseudo-Wertfreiheit" merits special attention. "Pseudo-Wertfreiheit", as he defines the term, consists in paying lip-service to the principle of value freedom, claiming to observe it in

7. GAW, pp. 509–10.
8. GAW, pp. 90, 157.
9. *Cf.* GAW, p. 157: "... *wo* die Argumente sich an den Verstand und *wo* sie sich an das Gefühl wenden".
10. Leo Strauss interprets Weber's position as *prohibiting* all value judgments in scientific works, and contemptuously remarks that "the whole procedure reminds one of a childish game in which you lose if you pronounce certain words, to which you are constantly incited by your playmates" (*Natural Right and History*, Chicago 1953, p. 52). This criticism is based on a misconception. Weber does not prohibit or even attack the use of value judgments as such, but only their being employed in a context where the basic ideal involved has not been expressly declared as a non-scientific valuational premise, and where the value judgments consequently usurp a scientific status for their valuational elements.

One must grant to Strauss, however, that Weber's hunt for value judgments in his own works and lectures does sometimes assume almost comical proportions. See for instance the following episode from the congress of the *Gesellschaft* in 1910: "Was bedeutet denn für die künstlerische Entwicklung beispielsweise, die Klassenevolution des modernen Proletariats, sein Versuch, sich als eine Kulturgemeinschaft in sich—denn das war ja das Großartige an dieser Bewegung—hinzustellen (Der Vorsitzende [Sombart] will den Redner unterbrechen). Das "großartig" war soeben ein Werturteil, wie ich offen zugestehe, und ich nehme es wieder zurück. (Große Heiterkeit). Das war, will ich sagen, das für uns *Interessante* an dieser Bewegung ..." (GASS, p. 452).
11. GAW, pp. 495, 498.

practice, but nevertheless *suggesting* practical value judgments of some kind, while pretending to "let the facts speak for themselves" [12]. It is obvious that such a procedure, which is directly contrary to the demand for "clarity" set out above, does not win Weber's approval. But a comparison of *Wertfreiheit* with the *Antrittsrede* [13], in which a similar difficulty seems to be discussed, raises two problems.

3.1. The first problem is the question whether Weber assumed that the pseudo-value-free procedure was prompted by any deliberate *motive*. *Wertfreiheit* hints darkly at "die pseudowertfreien, tendenziösen, dabei in unserem Fach durch die zähe und zielbewußte Parteinahme starker Interessentenkreise [14] getragenen Elemente" [15], a passage which almost amounts to a covert accusation of bad faith on the part of the scholars concerned. In the *Antrittsrede,* the problem is presented much more flatly: we, says Weber, meaning himself, might suppose, wrongly, that it is possible to *avoid* emitting value judgments altogether; but this opinion would simply have the effect of permitting uncontrolled subjective points of view, perhaps the normative force of the status quo, to take the place of deliberate value judgments. Put in this way, the problem lacks all overtones of hidden motives and strong and tenacious interests conspiring against science; what is presented is a general problem of scientific inquiry.

It seems certain that the "pseudo-value freedom" attacked by Weber, insofar as it is assumed to be deliberate and consequently to be motivated by practical interests of the scholar concerned, is only to be regarded as an extreme case, whose importance to Weber is mainly polemical. His emphasis on the duty of the scholar to try to be conscious of his *own* standards of value [16] clearly implies the possibility of an *unconscious,* and in this sense an "innocent" lack of value freedom in this respect. Thus, it does not seem impossible to reconcile the *Antrittsrede* with later discussions of the problem. Pseudo-value freedom can be the result of deliberate bad faith, but may just as well follow from naïve methodological haziness on the part of the scholar.

3.2. This interpretation, however, immediately raises a new problem: whereas, in *Objektivität* and later essays, Weber calls for clarity concerning the value standard applied in the cases where scholars cannot or do not want to stick to empirical fact, in the *Antrittsrede* he apparently suggests that it is

12. GAW, pp. 495, 498.
13. GPS, pp. 16–17.
14. The passage quoted above (p. 43n24) from Weber's speech at the 1909 congress of the *Verein* springs to mind here: "Es sind ausschließlich Unternehmerinteressen, die hier zugrunde gelegt wurden" (GASS, p. 417).
15. GAW, p. 495. In the *Gutachten* (p. 89), the hints are even darker and more ominous: for instance, Weber here declares that the pseudo-value-free scholars "[ganz und gar] von der Vertretung ihrer eigenen Wertungen [leben]".
16. This comes out clearly GAW, pp. 156, 490.

impossible to carry on scientific inquiry and communicate its results to others without resorting to value judgments: he speaks of "... diejenige [Illusion], uns des eigenen bewußten Werturteils *überhaupt enthalten* zu können" [17]. Does this mean that Weber in 1895 altogether denied the possibility of a value-free science and that in consequence *Objektivität* marks a complete change in his views on this central point?

In trying to find the answer to this question, one should remember that Weber was not at this early stage conscious of many of the problems and solutions which later came to form the principal part of his methodological production. More especially, it should be noted that Rickert's *Grenzen* had not yet been published and that the refinement and "neutralization" of the concept of value (necessary for the elaboration of Rickert's doctrine of "value relation") which it contained may not yet have been known to Weber. As mentioned above, the ideas advanced and applied in the *Antritts-rede* concerning the different possible aspects of theoretical questions were still somewhat crude and tied to practical problems of the type: how do we evaluate this or that aspect of a particular development? It is therefore reasonable to assume that Weber, in using the term "Werturteil" in the *Antrittsrede,* may denote the theoretical concept of "aspect" as well the practical one of "valuation". His point of view may in that case be reduced from the assertion of the inevitability of value judgments in the sphere of scientific inquiry to the claim that the choice of one or more aspects is the necessary starting point for such inquiry (and for practical valuation) [18].

4. The principle of value freedom, when formulated by Weber as a practical demand, is presented in a sharp and absolute form. This absolute and fundamental character of the demands might be taken to imply that the *obligations* they define, lucidity and sharp distinctions, can also be absolutely *fulfilled* by the conscientious scholar. This assumption, however, is extremely doubtful.

That the observance of the injunctions is at any rate neither self-evident nor a simple detail is shown by Weber's admission, in several instances [19], that it is in practice extremely difficult to separate valuations from scientific results. The context in which these admissions are placed is characteristic and interesting: Weber stresses that the fundamental character of the demands is in no way lessened by any difficulty encountered in observing them [20]: in

17. GPS, p. 16. As early as 1897, however (in a letter to L. Brentano of Jan. 1st, copy in DZA II, Rep. 92, No. 30, Vol. 4), Weber has grown a little more careful, stating simply that it seems *empirically* impossible to avoid mixing up value judgments and scientific statements.
18. *Cf. infra,* pp. 116–20.
19. GAW, pp. 90, 151, 497.
20. GAW, p. 602. It seems doubtful whether GAW, pp. 90, 151, which contain similarly worded passages, go further than the *theoretical* principle of value freedom.

one instance, he apparently goes so far as to say that even the demonstration of the *impossibility* of fulfilling the demands would not weaken his insistence on them:

'Nicht diskutieren möchte ich ferner, ob die Scheidung von empirischer Feststellung und praktischer Wertung "schwierig" sei. Sie ist es. Wir alle, der unterzeichnete Vertreter dieser Forderung ebenso wie andere, verstoßen immer wieder einmal dagegen. Aber wenigstens die Anhänger der sogenannten *ethischen* Nationalökonomie könnten wissen: daß auch das Sittengesetz unerfüllbar ist, dennoch aber als "aufgegeben" gilt"[21].

In other words, the observation of the principle of value freedom in practice should be regarded as an *ideal,* to be striven for even if one knows that it is unattainable.

Perhaps the suggested interpretation, implying the fundamental impossibility of carrying out the principle of value freedom, is a little strained; although it is not contradicted by other passages, its own foundation in the text is somewhat slender. But at least it seems justified to emphasize the abstract and theoretical quality of Weber's attitude. In his view, the observance of the principle of value freedom seems to be above all the *personal* problem of the scholar. In this connection, one can point to the comparison of the (perhaps unattainable) ideal of value freedom with "das Sittengesetz" [22], and to the fact that the violation of the latter is ascribed to "human weakness". Ethical categories like guilt and responsibility seem far more prominent in Weber's thought than considerations of technical and methodological possibilities. It may not be inappropriate to see this as an echo of the neo-Kantian formalization of the truth norm, which puts the latter alongside the norms of aesthetics and ethics [23].

Practical reflections concerning the concrete methods of scientific inquiry are almost entirely lacking in Weber's work. He does mention that "die Fähigkeit [zur faktischen Scheidung] erarbeitet werden will" [24], i. e., that it is possible to *develop* the faculty of distinguishing between "Sein" and "Sollen". But the only help that Weber offers in this respect is the occasional enumeration of factors that may result in a lack of value freedom, and to which it is therefore profitable to turn one's attention if one wishes to eliminate practical value judgments. Among these factors, he mentions the importance of evaluative elements to scientific analysis, the importance of scientific analysis for the evaluation of phenomena (in this case, of a work of

21. GAW, p. 497. Concerning the question of impossibility as a basis for criticism, *cf. infra,* pp. 165–68.
22. GAW, p. 497.
23. The following quotation from Windelband is characteristic: "[Der reife Culturmensch] ... macht sich nicht nur für sein Wollen und Handeln, sondern auch für sein Denken und Fühlen verantwortlich; er wirft sich einen Denkfehler ... nicht minder vor, als eine sittliche Nachlässigkeit" (Windelband, *Normen,* 1884, p. 216).
24. GAW, p. 90.

art)[25] and—as a typical instance of the more critical and heart-searching character of *Wertfreiheit*—the interests of material wealth and prestige tempting the scholar to introduce value judgments into his analysis [26].

1.5.2. The implementation of the principle in fields where other ideals are held besides the value of scientific inquiry

1. The account given above was limited to fields where the search for truth is, according to Weber, by definition the only value premise, and consequently dealt with scientific work in general. Weber expressly excepts university teaching from this category, however, and consequently in the *Gutachten* deplores the inclusion of this consideration among those singled out for discussion by the questionnaire of the *Verein* [1], and its subsequent discussion alongside the true questions of value freedom [2]. He does not believe that there is only one correct answer to the question whether it is legitimate to express value judgments during university lectures: "Die Frage ...: ob man auf dem Katheder *überhaupt* (auch unter dieser Kautel) [the observance of the demands for clarity and clear distinctions] praktisch werten solle oder nicht, ist ihrerseits eine solche der praktischen Universitätspolitik und deshalb letztlich nur vom Standpunkt jener Aufgaben aus entscheidbar, welche der Einzelne von *seinen* Wertungen aus den Universitäten zuweisen möchte" [3]. Weber admits that many professors want university teaching to influence the personality of the students as well as (or rather than) their intellect, and consequently regard "lecture room valuations" as a necessary and legitimate instrument for the realization of this ideal. Other scholars see the task of the university exclusively as "fachmäßige Schulung seitens *fach*mäßig qualifizierter" [4] and accordingly view "lecture room valuations" as undesirable and illegitimate. Weber openly declares for the latter school of thought [5] but, in doing so, emphasizes the fact that the question is in the last resort one involving undemonstrable value attitudes [6].

25. GAW, p. 90.
26. GAW, pp. 497–98.
1. *Cf. supra*, p. 19.
2. *Gutachten*, p. 84: "Ich bedaure die Hineinziehung dieses Problems". It is somewhat curious that Weber in *Wertfreiheit* retains his discussion of the problem, since in this case he had no prescribed set of subjects to prevent him from concentrating on the main themes.
3. GAW, p. 491.
4. GAW, p. 491.
5. GAW, p. 491. Apparently, Weber's first public endorsement of this position dates back to 1909, to a meeting of the main committee of the *Verein* in Leipzig. See his letter to his wife, of Oct. 13th, 1909 (copy in DZA II, Rep. 92, No. 30, Vol. 1): "Ich wollte nun noch mehr erzählen—die Anerkennung, daß die Lehre vom Katheder keine "Werturteile" aufzwingen darf—aber das kapierte die Bande nicht, keine Hand erhob sich zum Beifall."
6. GAW, pp. 489, 491, 495.

2. Weber does not, however, content himself with a naked statement of the two value positions and of their equal status. Instead, he tries to show that the partisans of "lecture room valuations", insofar as they are motivated by a particular regard for the "dignity" of the *value* sphere, have the same fundamental value premises as those from which he derives his "limited" definition of the function of the university, but that they adhere to these premises less consistently than he does.

This attempt to argue from what *might* at least be the position of the opponent reflects Weber's fundamental interest in keeping the distinction between the two spheres, of values and of scientific inquiry, as clear-cut as possible. Though it is impossible to *prove* that universities should only offer intellectual education, it is a fact that university education is *organized* along non-political and technical lines: the imparting of knowledge is unilateral, a monologue against which no criticism is possible [7]. A university teacher who introduces value judgments into his lectures, even when they are clearly distinguishable from the main body of empirical knowledge, and their valuational character openly admitted (i. e., even when the principle of value freedom is observed in practice), still, but in a deeper sense, violates the demand for a distinction between the value sphere and the sphere of scientific inquiry. He exploits an institutional position of strength justified by the laws of one sphere—that of scientific inquiry—to propagate opinions belonging to the other sphere—the sphere of values [8]. One cannot prove that this kind of exploitation is wrong; but Weber brands it as "unverantwortlich" [9]. By expressing "lecture room valuations", the university teacher acts irresponsibly because his position shields him from being held responsible for the value judgments expressed.

3. Weber provides a characteristically cogent discussion of the case of those university teachers who are not *able to* acknowledge fully the logical heterogeneity of "Sein" and "Sollen", nor, accordingly, to respect it in practice. A complete distinction is by definition excluded in this case; at the most one might suppose that value judgments flagrant enough to catch the eye even of the methodologically "innocent" teachers would be left out, whereas the more covert ones would have to be tolerated. Weber firmly rejects this solution [10]. An approximation of this kind would, according to him, simply dis-

7. GAW, pp. 492–93, 602, 606–07.
8. In his letter to L. Brentano, quoted above, of Jan. 1st, 1897, Weber sees the apparent empirical unavoidability of "lecture-room valuations" as an argument in favour of trying to have a number of *different* "schools of thought" represented among the academic teachers, in order that the influence exercised from the chair may not go wholly in one particular direction.
9. GAW, p. 602.
10. GAW, p. 490.

guise the value element inevitably present (since the teachers in question would lack both the ability and the wish to fulfil the demand for value freedom completely), and lead to "pseudo-value freedom". More particularly, this solution would mean that the "political" value judgments, in the *narrow* sense of the term, i. e., the openly partisan, party political valuations, would be the first to disappear. The equally "political" ones (in the *broader* sense of the term) present in the premises or concepts of other disciplines would be allowed to remain, since they would be more difficult to spot—a discrepancy whose basis was as unacceptable to Weber as its consequences [11]. Both in the light of this special difficulty and more generally, the suggested "attempt" to practise value freedom would lead not to an increase, but to a diminution of lucidity and clear distinctions. Weber instead advances the opposite argument [12]: since the teacher cannot promote clarity and convey sharp distinctions through "value asceticism", he must try to do so by *commitment* to values: "Denn gerade durch die Stärke der Affektbetontheit wird der Hörer wenigstens in die Lage versetzt, *seinerseits* die Subjektivität der Wertung des Lehrers in ihrem Einfluß auf eine etwaige Trübung seiner Feststellungen abzuschätzen und also für sich das zu tun, was dem Temperament des Lehrers versagt blieb" [13]. In Weber's view, the superior value remains the same: the possibility for the audience to distinguish between scientific discourse and value judgments.

Appendix A. Leo Strauss' interpretation of Weber's views concerning the logical status of the spheres of scientific inquiry and of values. In the account given by Leo Strauss of Weber's views concerning the logical status of the sphere of scientific inquiry, Strauss, quite correctly, points out that Weber believed the value of objective truth to be scientifically undemonstrable [1]. Taking this as his starting-point, he levels two charges at Weber. First, he seems to accuse Weber of inconsistency. In Strauss' view, a social scientist who, as Weber does, claims that objective knowledge is necessary for the attainment of social goals, proclaims (objective) social science as "a value from every point of view" [2], that is, as an *objective* value. Consequently, Weber at the same time denies and affirms the latter. This criticism is hardly justified, however, since Weber certainly did not share Strauss' idea that objective truth is a value "from every point of view".

Strauss' main charge is that of superficiality: he claims that Webers thesis of the purely subjective value of truth implies a relativism regarding higher values which is not shared by social scientists in general. On the contrary, the latter all seem to be convinced of the absolute value both of truth and of democracy.

---

11. GAW, p. 490.
12. This argument is derived from the demand for the distinction between science and practical valuations; but it is still, and correctly, described as a subjective demand, since the university teachers in question do not accept the value of scientific inquiry as the only value standard for their professional activity.
13. GAW, p. 490.
1. Leo Strauss, "What is Political Philosophy?", *Journal of Politics*, Vol. 19 (1957), pp. 347–48; see also Strauss, *Nat. Right*, 1953, pp. 71–72.
2. Strauss, *Pol. Phil.*, 1957, p. 348.

Their seemingly relativistic conclusions, Strauss claims, only serve to relieve them of the difficulty of clarifying *why* these values are absolute values to them [3].

As Erik Rasmussen has pointed out [4], this last criticism is psychological rather than logical. The fact that the personal attitude of a social scientist runs counter to his theoretical conclusions does not logically impugn the latter. Moreover, it may be objected that the idea of the value of truth as being undemonstrable certainly was not associated in Weber's mind with any lack of interest in scientific truth, its possibilities and limitations (after all, Weber explicitly acknowledges the possibility of making values an object of research) [5]. If anything, we should rather suppose that the social scientist who, without further reflection, accepts the idea of truth as an *objective* value, might be tempted to use this assumption as a bed for intellectual slumbers. Finally, Strauss' accusation is based on a confusion between *objective* and *absolute* values, and on the resultant misconception of the "relativist" strain in Weber's idea of value freedom.

In his book "Natural Right and History", Leo Strauss discusses Weber's views on the logical status of values. Strauss' central claim is that Weber's principle of value freedom is not so much based on the logical heterogeneity of the value sphere and the sphere of scientific inquiry, but rather on "his [Weber's] belief that there cannot be any genuine knowledge of the Ought" [6], and that the adoption of this view leads Weber straight into "nihilism or [7] ... the view that every preference, however evil, base, or insane, has to be judged before the tribunal of reason to be as legitimate as any other preference" [8]. Strauss tries to substantiate his accusation of "nihilism" by examing a number of values which might be thought to hold a particularly high status in Webers eyes and by claiming that Weber cannot, with logical consistency, accept any of these progressively more abstract and "formal" values (the value of *ethics*, of *"good" ideals*, of *any ideal* (whether "good" or "bad"), of any *passionate commitment* (whether it concerns ideals or selfish preferences)), as long as he denies "genuine knowledge of the Ought". "Ought" and "Is" approach each other asymptotically, so to speak, in this reductionist argument, and finally appear to any unbiased observer to merge completely: "The final formulation of Weber's ethical principle would thus be "Thou shalt have preferences"—an Ought whose fulfilment is fully guaranteed by the Is" [9].

To judge these claims and the arguments advanced to support them, it is above all necessary to be quite clear about how to interpret Strauss' expression "genuine knowledge". If we take it to cover Weber's concept of *objective* truth, as defined above, there seems little point in raising objections to Strauss' view, which can in that case be restated as follows: Weber denies that we can, with the validity of scientific truth, know or state anything about values *as values*, and consequently rejects the view that we can state anything about the truth of value systems *as value systems* [10]. From the point of view of science, any value is, as a value, as

3. *Ibid.,* p. 349.
4. Erik Rasmussen, *Komparativ Politik I–II,* Copenhagen 1968–69, p. 37.
5. *Cf. infra,* ch. 3.
6. Strauss, *Nat. Right,* 1953, p. 41.
7. This I take here to mean "i. e.".
8. Strauss, *Nat. Right,* 1953, p. 42.
9. *Ibid.,* p. 47.
10. In commenting on Strauss' assertion that "Weber assumed as a matter of course that there is no hierarchy of values; all values are of the same rank" (Strauss, *Nat. Right,* 1953, p. 66), Brecht (*Theory,* 1959, p. 263) correctly objects that Weber

"legitimate" as any other, since "legitimacy" is in this connection a category appropriate to values, not to science. On this interpretation, Strauss is, if anything, not radical enough, since not even the value of *preferences* is an objective one in Weber's view.

If, on the other hand, "genuine knowledge" is interpreted as referring to a category *broader* than Weber's concept of scientific inquiry, Strauss' claim is unfounded: it is squarely contradicted by Weber's emphasis, noted above, on the value of committing oneself to absolute, subjective values. A person who has thus committed himself to some absolute value may, in Weber's view, have "genuine knowledge" of this value in a *non-scientific sense;* in the same way, it might be accurate to speak about the existence of an absolute, and in that sense "true", value system for such a person. Since "genuine knowledge" is here interpreted as being absolute but not objective, Strauss' justifying argument must be taken as an attempt to show that Weber *himself,* subjectively, did not regard any ideal, be it ever so formal, as better than its logical opposite: i. e., a denial that Weber was committed to any absolute, subjective ideal. Such an argument lies outside the scope of a discussion of Weber's theory of scientific inquiry, since this theory claims scientific validity and cannot be invalidated by reflections on Weber's *own* practice. But, in any case, it is certainly easy to reject Strauss' point: Weber *did* believe in certain values; but it should be remembered that these values were seen by him as undemonstrable by scientific methods [11].

What makes Strauss' treatment of Weber's ideas incorrect, and at the same time elusive, is that the terminology of Strauss' *account* implies that the concept of science referred to is Weber's narrow one, while his *commentaries* and *criticism* are based on his own, wider concept of science [12]. If we assume that the Weberian concept is employed, the account is correct, while the criticism misses its target; if, on the other hand, we suppose that Strauss sticks to his own concept, the account is incorrect, but the criticism becomes justified (in the hypothetical sense that it would be valid against anyone who held the views which Strauss falsely credits Weber with).

> never claimed that values were "equal", but only that they were "equally undemonstrable" (as values); still, this means that values *as values* are equal from the point of view of science *as science;* in this relation, they can only occur as objects of scientific inquiry, and as such they are all equally devoid of positive or negative value. When Brecht (*ibid.,* pp. 263–64) adds that even the "equal demonstrability" only holds for the *highest* value axioms, he seems to me to be over-interpreting Webers term "letzte Werte". Moreover, Weber himself stresses that the adoption of a particular "low", concrete, valuational attitude *already* logically implies the acceptance of one or more of the ultimate value axioms (*cf. infra,* pp. 181, 196–97).
>
> 11. Brecht (*Theory,* 1959, p. 253–55) maintains that Weber does not regard "selfish interests" as a legitimate guide to the individual's choice of values, and seems to imply that Weber claimed some sort of "scientific standing" for this exclusion. This does not see accurate: Brecht refers to Weber's demand that everybody should follow their particular "Dämon" (GAW, p. 613), but this demand is not formulated by him as a scientific, objective statement, but must, in my view, be reckoned among Weber's *personal and subjective* criteria for respecting the attitudes and actions of others.
> 12. The latter is not identical with Weber's concept—a fact that emerges quite clearly from Strauss' work as a whole, and particularly from his distinction between the denial of "genuine knowledge of the Ought" and the assumption of a logical gulf between Is and Ought.

An offshoot of this confusion between different concepts of science has formed the basis of a terminological quarrel which has occasionally been the subject of more interest than it deserves. The question is whether it is correct to level the accusation at Weber's principle of value freedom that it is rooted in or that it leads to a *relativistic* or (to use the term employed by Strauss and others, for instance Aron [13]) a *nihilistic* attitude.

In this connection, it is sufficient to observe that Weber himself emphatically rejects the term "relativism" as being the grossest of the misconceptions concerning the protagonists of the thesis of value conflict [14] and of its corollary, the principle of value freedom [15]. In Weber's vocabulary, the term "relativism" implies that any value is *demonstrably* equal in worth to any other, so that the general value of committing oneself to or against a cause utterly vanishes [16]. An interpretation which ascribes "relativistic" views of this kind to Weber thus adds insult to misconception. The principles for the solution of the conflict of terminology are aptly described in Locke's words: "So the thing be understood, I am indifferent as to the Name" [17].

Appendix B. The causes of the awakening in Germany of the demand for value freedom. The view that the principle of value freedom is already present in embryonic form in the *Antrittsrede*, implies that the explanation given by, for instance, Arnold Brecht of the quick development of the demand in *Germany* in particular, should be modified. Brecht writes:

"The original German relativists were scholars of democratic, liberal, or socialist inclinations who lived in a country run by a semi-authoritarian monarchic government. They were surrounded by a great majority of other scholars who accepted that type of government as ideal and often carried emotional patriotism and conservatism into their lectures and scholarly writings. Disinclined in their own work to bow to authoritarian forms and values, they were driven in self-defense to study the proper relation of science to political evaluations more carefully than their colleagues in democratically governed countries had reason to do" [18].

Whereas it is obviously correct that the opposition of scholars to the conventional norms of society will further their interest in the value freedom of scientific inquiry, in one or both of its asymmetrical forms [19], it seems to me that Brecht, in evaluating the result of this opposition, concerns himself too much with the value freedom of the scientific *process,* the concern for *science.* As for Weber, his interest in the value freedom of the *results* of scientific inquiry, his concern for *values,* is in 1895 far stronger, in fact quite supreme; and his political opposition is anti-liberal and pro-nationalist rather than the reverse. Speaking more generally, I feel

13. Aron, *Introduction,* 1963, p. 39.
14. *Cf. infra,* pp. 178–79.
15. GAW, p. 508.
16. GAW, p. 508; see also below, pp. 190–92.
17. John Locke, *Two Treatises of Government* (ed. Peter Laslett), Cambridge 1960, p. 383. Brecht, *Theory,* 1959, pp. 256–58 contains a more ample discussion of the term "relativism" and of its history.
18. Brecht, *Theory,* 1959, p. 239.
19. H. Stuart Hughes, *Consciousness and Society,* New York 1958, pp. 49–51, 54, convincingly establishes this view by comparing the situation in Germany and France.

that Weber's final formulation of the principle of value freedom is above all indebted to a growing awareness of the importance of *values*, rather than of science.

Appendix C. Problems raised by Weber's own application of the principle of value freedom. A thorough examination of Weber's *own* application in practice of the principle of value freedom does not seem necessary: as mentioned above, he explicitly declares that the ideal character of the demand is *not* influenced by the fact that scholars may not be able to fulfil it; a hunt for value judgments in illegitimate positions in Weber's work would thus only be of interest to an account of Weber the *person*, not of Weber the *scholar*. A few problems in this connection will be briefly discussed, though, since their importance reaches beyond the question of Weber's own application of the principle.

1. A number of authors, among them Friedrich [20] and Mommsen [21], maintain that Weber's "individualist" or "liberal" approach results in the introduction of value judgments favorable to "individualism" or "liberalism" into his work. This, at any rate, was certainly not Weber's *intention:* he explicitly warns that approaches and aspects in scientific work should not be elevated to the dignity of philosophies of life [22]; and he gives this warning a more concrete expression in WG, as regards both his "rationalist" sociology and its "verstehende" character [23].

2. A line of attack similar to that of Mommsen and Friedrich is adopted by Strauss who tries to show that Weber simply could not, and probably deep down inside himself did not want to, fulfil his own demands. To support his claim, Strauss reels off a large number of value judgments included by Weber in his scientific work [24]

Against this comment, one may advance two arguments. In the first place, one might remark, with Arnold Brecht, that "no scientific relativist would condemn words like cruelty, civilization [etc.] ..., wherever they are used within a clear frame of reference as descriptive in accordance with known standards, *as long as these standards are not themselves at issue*" [25]. The underlined condition indubitably holds for many of Strauss' examples. In particular, Strauss seems to ignore completely the *ideal types* elaborated by Weber. These types, although they were not meant as normative ideals, were to function as a frame of reference for hypothetical valuations; and the ideal type itself was often moulded around the description of valuations held by a hypothetical person conforming completely to the type [26].

One may choose a different point of departure, though, and maintain that even obvious value judgments in Weber's work should be regarded as consonant with the spirit, if not with the letter, of the principle of value freedom, *as long as they only concern historical phenomena.* As Bendix remarks, Weber's appreciation of the *unique character* of historical events [27] was highly developed and, by expressing

20. Stammer (ed.), *Weber,* 1965, pp. 121–22.
21. Mommsen, *Weber,* 1959, p. 69.
22. *Cf. supra,* pp. 41–42.
23. WG, pp. 5,9.
24. Strauss, *Nat. Right,* 1953, p. 51.
25. Brecht, *Theory,* 1959, p. 265.
26. *Cf. infra,* pp. 221–22.
27. Reinhard Bendix, "Max Weber's Sociology today", *international social science journal,* Vol. XVII (1965), p. 11.

positive value judgment concerning, say, 17th century art, he would not, in his own view, be laying any legitimate foundation for the contemporary formulation of practical directives, for a new cultural policy, etc. In this connection, it may be useful to point to the limitation in the definition of valuations in *Wertfreiheit* (quoted above [28]) which makes them applicable only to "durch unser Handeln beeinflußbare Erscheinungen" [29].

This line of argument should be used with caution: for instance, it tends to go *against* one of the motives for the elaboration of ideal types; but it may still serve as a useful corrective to Strauss' somewhat indiscriminate interpretations and attacks.

As for Weber's particularly vehement value judgments in the *Antrittsrede*, one must grant him that his "Vorbemerkung" to the lecture explicitly qualifies the claim of the latter to rank as "scientific": "... in welchem speziellen Sinn allein sie [*Antrittsrede*] den Anspruch auf das Prädikat der "Wissenschaftlichkeit" [erhebt], ergibt sich aus der Veranlassung ihres Entstehens. Eine Antrittsrede bietet eben Gelegenheit zur offenen Darlegung und Rechtfertigung des persönlichen und insoweit "subjektiven" Standpunktes bei der *Beurteilung* volkswirtschaftlicher Erscheinungen" [30].

On the other hand, it cannot be denied that at least the demand for clear distinctions between empirical and evaluative statements is grossly neglected, and that it would probably not be an exaggeration to count the lecture among the "lecture-room valuations". In this respect, however, one might make allowance for the fact that the *Antrittsrede* must have impressed its audience so strongly by its passionate commitment that no one could fairly accuse Weber of "pseudo-value freedom". As in the case of Mommsen and Treitschke, the literary pathos allowed the audience to draw that distinction between scientific discourse and value judgments which the speaker himself was unable to provide.

28. P. 27.
29. GAW, p. 489.
30. GPS, p. 1.

2. Values as a precondition of scientific inquiry: value relation.

As mentioned above [1], the problem of the value freedom of scientific inquiry can be interpreted as a problem of the definition of the latter concept. As Weber sees it, this definition excludes certain value elements (practical valuations and value judgments) from scientific proof, and denies the predicate "scientific" to research carried out with the help of concepts containing such value elements [2]. In itself, such a definition only amounts to a formal distinction, a language convention: the predicate "scientific" will be reserved for research which is "value-free" in the sense stated. To this formal definition, however, Weber adds a material description: the results of value-free scientific inquiry (thus defined), he maintains, have the status of *truth*, i. e., they are objectively valid for all individuals, irrespective of the will or valuations of these individuals.

Evidently, there is not much sense in demanding value freedom in scientific inquiry until one has made certain that the value-free science demanded can otherwise lay claim to objective validity. Why eradicate subjective practical valuations from scientific inquiry if what is left is still, in principle, equally subjective? Thus, from a logical point of view the solution of the problem of objectivity is prior to the question of value freedom [3].

This logical relationship finds a nice chronological parallel in the sequence of essays in which Weber discusses the two problems together or separately: whereas the various aspects of the problem of value freedom occupy Weber from 1904 until as late as 1919 [4], his explicit treatment of the question of objectivity is in the main confined to *Objektivität;* the premises on which the argument of this essay relies also serve as the basis for a number of critical discussions of the views of other scholars in *Knies I–II,* and their influence is still fairly evident in *Kritische Studien;* but after 1906, Weber seems to lose interest in this problem. In fact, the key words of the two main

1. Pp. 13–15.
2. *Cf. supra,* p. 16.
3. Pietro Rossi makes a similar distinction between "external" and "internal" preconditions of objectivity (Stammer (ed.), *Weber,* 1965, p. 88).
4. *Cf. supra,* pp. 17–21.

essays, *Objektivität* (1904) and *Wertfreiheit* (1917 (1913)) are succinct indications of the focus of Weber's methodological interest at the time of their publication. Accordingly, his defence of the objectivity of the social sciences can be regarded as a necessary prelude to the formulation of the demand for value freedom, a rearguard action securing the advance of the methodological avantgarde principle of value freedom.

What, then, were the onslaughts on the objectivity of the social sciences [5] which Weber found it necessary to repel in order to make certain that the demand for value freedom remained meaningful? Weber himself gives a clear answer to this question in *Objektivität*:

"Wir haben bisher, indem wir "Werturteile" und "Erfahrungswissen" prinzipiell schieden, vorausgesetzt, daß es eine unbedingt gültige Art der Erkenntnis, d. h. der denkenden Ordnung der empirischen Wirklichkeit auf dem Gebiet der Sozialwissen-schaften tatsächlich gebe. Diese Annahme wird jetzt insofern zum Problem, als wir erörtern müssen, was objektive "Geltung" der Wahrheit, die wir erstreben, auf unserem Gebiet bedeuten *kann*. Daß das Problem als solches besteht und hier nicht spintisierend geschaffen wird, kann niemandem entgehen, der den Kampf um Methode, "Grundbegriffe" und Voraussetzungen, den steten Wechsel der "Gesichtspunkte" und die stete Neubestimmung der "Begriffe", die verwendet werden, beobachtet und sieht, wie theoretische und historische Betrachtungsform noch immer durch eine scheinbar unüberbrückbare Kluft getrennt sind: "*zwei* Nationalökonomien", wie ein verzwei-felnder Wiener Examinand seinerzeit jammernd klagte. Was heißt hier Objektivität?" [6]

The conflict referred to in this passage between the "theoretical" and the "historical" school of economics is the so-called "Methodenstreit", the "con-troversy over method" which raged during the last quarter of the nineteenth century. Since a certain familiarity with the main outlines of this method-ological conflict facilitates the understanding of the problems with which Weber was faced, and of the significance of his solutions, it seems justified to give a brief account of the protagonists, the problems and the perspectives of the debate.

2.1. The precursors

2.1.1. The "controversy over method" ("Methodenstreit" [7])

1.1. In its later stages, classical economics had moved towards an increasing abstraction from reality. The German economists Roscher, Hildebrand and

---

5. Whereas, in the chapter on value freedom, the point that Weber's discussion was in practice concerned with the social rather than with the natural sciences was a minor one, the distinction between the two groups of sciences becomes of crucial importance in the present discussion of the problems of objectivity; here, the attacks are only levelled at the objectivity of the *social* sciences, being in fact based on the affirmation of the objective character of the results of the *natural* sciences.

6. GAW, pp. 160–61; *cf.* GAW, pp. 147–48.

7. References in this section, apart from those involving primary sources, are mainly

Knies (the "elder historical school" of economics) revolted against this "anaemic"[8] tendency and, around 1850, tried to lay the foundations of a historical, and consequently a realistic, science of economics. Their doctrines, however, had little immediate influence on economic thought[9], which was at that time dominated by naturalist and positivist schools of thought[10].

1.2. Eventually, however, political developments gave new actuality and new incentives to the historical school of economics. The classical economists had worked on the theoretical assumption—which was sometimes transformed into a political demand—that government did not interfere with the free play of economic forces; and since the policy of laissez-faire was now being progressively abandoned in practice, it seemed logical to seek a new theoretical foundation for economic policy. The consequence was a revival of the historical aspect of economics: the "younger historical school", with Gustav Schmoller as its acknowledged leader, re-defined and adapted the doctrines of the "elder school"[11].

The intimate connection of the "younger school" with practical economic policy found its institutional expression in the *Verein,* which was created in 1872. As mentioned above[12], the association had a political purpose with strong ethical overtones, viz, to further the economic and social advancement of the growing working class and to secure, partly by means of this advancement, its integration in a harmonious economic whole embracing all the participants in the economic process. The association, in short, tried to exercise a mediating function in the field of politics and economics. By their espousal of this cause, the members of the *Verein,* who were mostly drawn from academic circles, earned for themselves the epithet of "Socialists of the Chair" ("Kathedersozialisten"); and their enthusiastic efforts were a clear manifestation of their view of economics as an *ethical* discipline[13, 14].

to Weber's own historical summaries in *Objektivität* (GAW, pp. 42–43, 148–49, 185–88) and *Wertfreiheit* (GAW, pp. 536–37). These summaries are of course not in any way comprehensive, or even well balanced; but they contain valuable information about Weber's own view of the main stages and problems of the development of economic theory.

8. Schmoller ("Zur Methodologie der Staats- und Socialwissenschaften", *Schmollers Jahrbuch für Gesetzgebung, Verwaltung und Volkswirtschaft,* Leipzig 1883, p. 242) speaks of "geistige Schwindsucht".

9. GAW, p. 42.

10. GAW, p. 42; *cf.* GAW, pp. 536–37.

11. GAW, p. 537.

12. P. 43.

13. GAW, p. 148.

14. Apart from its general wish to further the harmony of economic life, the historical school of economics had a specific claim to a more "ethical" status than the classical theory. The latter had concentrated on one isolated factor: the *enlightened self-interest* of the individual; by abandoning this exclusiveness in favour of a more complex analysis of economic factors, the "younger historicists" were able to maintain that they had superseded the "egoism" of pure theory.

Later, the concrete purpose of the historical tendency waned, partly as a result of the lessened probability of its being carried out in practice; and the conviction that an ethical element was indispensable to economic thought consequently lost its self-evident character and became a methodological problem. It was therefore only natural that a number of Max Weber's demands for value freedom (among them the demand that the scientific process and the scientific results should be free from ethical elements) were in fact formulated in connection with discussions of "die Arbeiterfrage" [15] and within the framework of the congresses of the *Verein*. In this connection, however, the views of the historicists, and their declining importance, were probably the immediate occasion rather than the fundamental cause of Weber's protests. Of far greater importance was the "controversy over method".

2. Two names have above all been associated with this controversy: those of Gustav Schmoller and Carl Menger. There seem to be good reasons for concentrating on these two figures. For one thing, Menger's general attack on the historical school (1883), Schmoller's sharp review of Menger in that same year, and Menger's no less sharp rejoinder (1884) undoubtedly marked the climax of the conflict [16]. Moreover, the specific views of the two protagonists, extreme in Schmoller's case, moderate in Menger's, seem to have isolated them within their respective movements [17].

The controversy raged around the question whether "pure theory", with its attendant sharply defined concepts, had a legitimate place in the science of economics. Although Schmoller had acknowledged the existence of empirical regularities in the field of economics, he firmly denied that they could be identified or formulated by means of classical "pure" theory. In his view, economic phenomena were determined by a complex of, partly non-economic, social factors; and he regarded the method of the classical school, with its elaboration of a system of comparatively abstract "laws", as totally unsuitable for the understanding of the relative weight and importance of these social factors: the classical system, with its clear-cut and "unrealistic" concepts, could only provide a caricature of reality and of real causal connections [18]. Instead, the science of economics ought to concentrate on producing detailed studies of economic history, in which the complexity of the subject-matter was safeguarded by the lack of precise concepts. From such studies in detail,

15. See for instance the remarks in *Objektivität*, GAW, pp. 164–65.
16. Carl Menger, *Untersuchungen über die Methode der Socialwissenschaften und der politischen Oekonomie insbesondere*, Leipzig 1883; Schmoller, *Methodologie*, 1883; Carl Menger, *Die Irrthümer des Historismus in der deutschen Nationalökonomie*, Vienna 1884.
17. GAW, p. 187 ("Der Schöpfer der Theorie" must be taken to be Menger).
18. Schmoller, *Methodologie*, 1883, pp. 242, 244–45, 247.

he imagined that it was possible, by means of some sort of induction, to arrive at a more specific—though no more abstract—formulation of the central concepts and at an understanding of the regularities prevailing in the field of economics. To Schmoller, clearly defined concepts stood at the end, not at the beginning of the scientific process [19].

Faced with this indiscriminate "historization" of the whole of the science of economics, it was not too difficult for Menger to take a more moderate stand, acknowledging, in principle, the value of historical investigations [20], but refusing to accept a "history of minuscules" [21] as a scientific ideal. In his eyes, pure theory was indispensable as an aid to the discovery of economic laws and regularities [22].

3.   One may wonder why the younger historical school did not simply adopt Menger's moderate position with its acknowledgement of *both* theory *and* history as valuable elements of economic science. Viewed in a wider context, however, the problem was complicated by the inclusion of other considerations.

Behind the limited confrontation of science and history in the science of economics lay the general conflict between positivism and historicism (both concepts taken in their widest sense) [23] which was of fundamental importance to the social sciences of the 19th century [24]. The enormous advances of natural science, and the ensuing self-confident claims by its disciples of its methodological monopoly in *all* scientific disciplines kept the historical sciences on a constant defensive. A particularly hard blow to historicism was the growth of a biological science which apparently defined the concept of *development* along the lines of the traditional natural sciences. Here the very core of history seemed to fall into the hands of its positivist opponents [25].

19. Schmoller, *Methodologie,* 1883, pp. 241, 243, 245; *cf.* GAW, p. 537 and Tenbruck, *Genesis,* 1959, pp. 584–85.
20. See for instance Menger, *Untersuchungen,* 1883, p. 98; Menger, *Irrthümer,* 1884, pp. 13, 22, 25.
21. ("historische Mikrographie"). Menger, *Irrthümer,* 1884, pp. 37, 38.
22. See for instance Menger, *Untersuchungen,* 1883, pp. 12, 254–55; Menger, *Irrthümer,* 1884, pp. 48–49, 57. *Cf.* GAW, p. 187.
23. In his wide-ranging study of European social thought 1890–1930, H. Stuart Hughes defines positivism in the broad sense as "the whole tendency to discuss human behavior in terms of analogies drawn from natural science", including under the term the often employed concepts of "mechanism" and "naturalism", which have Newton's physics and Darwin's biology as their respective frames of reference (Hughes, *Consciousness,* 1958, pp. 37–38). Historicism in the broad sense may consequently be defined as the intellectual movement which, instead of drawing analogies from the natural sciences, concentrates on the individuality and individual origin of phenomena (what Weber, with a quite untranslatable term, calls their "So-und-nicht-anders-Gewordensein" (GAW, pp. 171, 186)).
24. Tenbruck, *Genesis,* 1959, pp. 590–91.
25. GAW, p. 186.

Viewed in this light, the debate between Schmoller and Menger takes on a more alarming aspect from the point of view of Schmoller's side. The potential danger to the historical school was that Menger's position, if pushed to its extreme conclusion (a tendency which Menger himself apparently did not ignore) might claim for pure theory a monopoly in the sphere of economics. Such a claim would be able to draw on the seemingly unshakeable prestige of the natural sciences, and of positivism in general, as being "real" science, whereas Schmoller's "historical induction" had methodological feet of clay in this respect [26]. In fact, a number of positivistically oriented economists did advance exorbitant methodological claims, culminating in the idea of an abstract theoretical system of economics from which concrete economic life could be *deduced* [27].

4. Since this dilemma of economics: how to defend the concrete, historical, "inductive" point of view against general, abstract, possibly "deductive" tendencies, was lent added weight by the general conflict between positivism and historicism, it was only natural that the first attempts to give historical method a firm methodological basis came not from the specialized discipline of economics but from the ranks of philosophers and historians with philosophical leanings.

4.1. In 1883, the same year as the "controversy over method" really caught fire, the first of these attempts was made by Wilhelm Dilthey in his "Einleitung in die Geisteswissenschaften". In Dilthey's view, the method of natural science only applied to objects of a physical nature, but not to "Geist", *spiritual* phenomena; the latter instead required a particular kind of intuition and empathy, "Verstehen". In this way, Dilthey raised a number of "Geisteswissenschaften", "spiritual sciences", to the same level as the natural sciences, while preserving for them a materially and methodologically specific domain.

Thus, Dilthey defined his two main categories on the basis of the subject–matter of the disciplines which they contained, and on the distinction between the two corresponding methods, which were also mainly derived from the peculiarities of the scientific *objects*. This way of dealing with the question was certainly in accordance with the view taken by a large number of scholars working in the field of "spiritual sciences"; and this contact with scientific practice made it difficult entirely to reject Dilthey's point of view [28]. On the

26. See for instance Menger, *Irrthümer,* 1884, pp. 49–50 and GAW, p. 187.
27. GAW, pp. 171–72, 184, 187–88, 208.
28. As will be shown below, it is already taken up again by Heinrich Rickert, who needs a connecting link between the object and the method of the historical sciences; in Weber's sociology, this connection is firmly entrenched in the definition

other hand, it was difficult to back up the intuitive plausibility of Dilthey's distinction by sufficiently rigorous logical arguments. The central weakness in this connection was the existence of a psychology working along the lines of the sciences of nature. If the very constituent of the "spiritual sciences", the spirit, was accessible to scientific treatment aiming at general statements, the way seemed open for the natural sciences to subjugate the field of the "spiritual sciences" in its entirety. In that case, generalizing psychology might function as a kind of "historical mathematics" or "historical chemistry", the abstract laws of which simply took concrete shape in the historical subject–matter [29].

4.2. Consequently, the next attempts concentrated on the elaboration of a distinction between the natural sciences and the threatened historical disciplines on grounds of method. In this respect, the Rectoral Lecture "Geschichte und Naturwissenschaft", from 1894, of the philosopher Wilhelm Windelband was of great importance. Here a *methodical* distinction was elaborated between "nomothetische" ("general law-seeking") and "idiographische" ("intuitional") sciences, and between their respective aims, "Gesetz" and "Gestalt".

At the time of its appearance, the lecture was regarded as a "declaration of war on positivism" [30]. Its central thesis remained unquestioned; but the work was very short and, as we shall see below [31], insufficient as a logical basis for the claim that the historical sciences possessed an independent methodological status equal to that of natural science, Consequently, these problems were taken up again by Windelband's pupil Heinrich Rickert.

2.1.2. Rickert's theory of science and the objectivity of history

In Rickert's work "Die Grenzen der naturwissenschaftlichen Begriffsbildung" (finished 1902), the relation between the historical disciplines and the natural sciences is subjected to a thorough and unusually stringent analysis, which in important respects goes beyond the earlier attempts referred to.

1. In the first part of the *Grenzen*, which was published in 1896, Rickert's primary aim is a defensive one. He tries to show that the status of a discipline

of the subject-matter of the discipline (GAW, p. 542), but is not treated as a problem: the conflict with positivism is no longer relevant.
29. *Cf.* Georg Simmel, *Probleme der Geschichtsphilosophie,* Leipzig 1892, p. 2 and GAW, pp. 173–74.
30. Hughes, *Consciousness,* 1958, p. 47, who in his turn quotes an unidentified source (probably Friedr. Meinecke).
31. Pp 87–88.

as empirical not only is not necessarily dependent on its adoption of the methods of natural science, but that there are even aspects of empirical reality which *cannot* be understood by means of this method and demand a different approach. Thus, Rickert tries to reject the "Alleinvertretungsanspruch" (to borrow a term from the sphere of politics) of positivist method by showing that it is neither *necessary* nor even always *sufficient* to proceed by way of generalization and abstraction: his argument is designed to show "in welchen Gebieten die Bildung naturwissenschaftlicher Begriffe einen Sinn hat, und auf welchen Gebieten sie diesen Sinn nothwendig verlieren muß" [1], i. e., where the *limits* of the usefulness of the methods of natural science are to be found—hence the title of the work.

Although this part of Rickert's work is the least original and, in the present context, the least problematical one [2], a brief outline of his discussion may still be useful in order to throw light on the later development of his argument, and on Weber's parallel discussions.

2. As its point of departure, Rickert's analysis takes empirical reality in its unstructured and immediate aspect [3]. Viewed thus, Rickert asserts, empirical reality is fundamentally inexhaustible and boundless: both in space and in time, the number of possible objects of our perception is infinitely great, and any such object may furthermore be divided into an infinite number of lesser objects, each of them different from all the others at least by its place in space and time (since two objects cannot be in exactly the same place at exactly the same time). Empirical reality is an "unübersehbare Mannigfaltigkeit" [4].

Obviously, such an inexhaustible multiplicity of objects cannot be reproduced in its entirety. Any such attempt would result in a never-ending stream of statements, each concerning a particular object in a particular respect. Consequently, a science pretending to embrace the *totality* of its subject-matter, however limited the latter may be (in volume and/or time) is a fundamental impossibility. Conversely, the precondition of any existing science is the necessity of *surmounting* this infinity in some way [5]; scientific work always represents a *processing* of reality: ". . . jedes wissenschaftliche Denken [ist] begriffliches Denken" [6].

Infinite reality is surmounted by means of *concepts* [7]. The simplest kind

1. *Grenzen*, 1902, p. 303.
2. This was Weber's opinion, too. See the letter to L. v. Bortkievicz of March 12th, 1906 (copy in DZA II, Rep. 92, No. 30, Vol. 4).
3. *Grenzen*, 1902, pp. 32–39, particularly pp. 32–36.
4. *Ibid.*, p. 33.
5. *Ibid.*, p. 36.
6. *Ibid.*, p. 140.
7. *Ibid.*, p. 43.

of concept is the everyday *word,* or rather the meaning, the material *reference* of such words [8]; but from the point of view of science, these common-sense meanings and references are too vague and must be replaced by proper definitions, i. e. by statements investing the meaning of the word with the requisite degree of precision [9].

2.1. In a number of disciplines, this process of definition is carried out by summarizing the traits *common* to all the objects covered by the word in question [10]. The definition abstracts from the individual character of particular objects, so that only their general qualities are retained in the concept. For reasons immaterial in this connection, these general concepts in their turn have to be fitted into a framework or system of general regularities, culminating, in principle, in one all-embracing and completely general law of nature [11]. The cognitive aim of these disciplines, which we can call the natural sciences (in the logical sense of the word), is ever-increasing *abstraction.*

2.2. This, in Rickert's eyes, also constitutes the limitation of the method in question. As we have seen, empirical reality is characterized by the fact that its constituent objects are *individual*; and since the method of abstraction seeks to reduce, and in the last resort completely to eliminate, this element of individuality, it can in fact be said to lead away from empirical reality [12]: *"Das, was der naturwissenschaftlichen Begriffsbildung die Grenze setzt, über die sie niemals hinwegzukommen vermag, ist nichts anderes als die empirische Wirklichkeit selbst"* [13]. Now, since our interest is very often connected with the individual, real aspect of things, it has to be satisfied by *another* method which will allow us to understand what individual phenomena really are or were. The science (or group of disciplines) which employs such an individualizing method can be conveniently referred to as historical science [14] (in the logical sense of the word); and since, unlike natural science, it gives information which seeks to approach reality as closely as possible, it can also be given the predicate of "Wirklichkeitswissenschaft" [15]. But it must be borne in mind that this "Wirklichkeitswissenschaft", although it does not *abstract* from reality, still has to *select* from it: the historical point of view, too, is an aspect, not a reproduction [16].

8. *Ibid.,* pp. 39–41, 43.
9. *Ibid.,* pp. 54–55. Rickert himself avoids the word "definition", but only for polemical reasons which do not stand in the way of its being used here (*cf. ibid.,* p. 65n2).
10. *Ibid.,* pp. 50–51.
11. *Ibid.,* pp. 62–74, particularly pp. 68–69, 72–74.
12. *Ibid.,* pp. 228–29, 236–39.
13. *Ibid.,* p. 239.
14. *Ibid.,* pp. 249–51.
15. *Ibid.,* p. 255; the term was originally used by Simmel in his *Geschichtsphilosophie,* 1892, p. 43, cf. Heinrich Rickert, *Die Grenzen der naturwissenschaftlichen Begriffsbildung,* (2. ed.), Tübingen 1914, p. 222.
16. *Grenzen,* 1902, p. 252.

In this way, Rickert constructs a dualism of natural and historical science based primarily on the different methods and cognitive aims of the two categories, and only in a derivative sense on the differences of their objects; as he succinctly puts it: "[*Die empirische Wirklichkeit*] *wird Natur, wenn wir sie betrachten mit Rücksicht auf das Allgemeine, sie wird Geschichte, wenn wir sie betrachten mit Rücksicht auf das Besondere*" [17].

3. Up to this point, Rickert has, by and large, although in far greater detail, repeated the arguments of Windelband's Rectoral Lecture [18]. The problem still remains of constructing a positive theory of the concept formation of historical science. The central difficulty in this connection is the following: It seems beyond doubt that the natural sciences (in the logical sense of the word) are justified in claiming the status of "science"; the criterion according to which they formulate their concepts, hypotheses and laws is objective, in the sense that it seems to relate solely to the *object* under investigation and consequently to be, in principle, independent of the personality of the scientist applying it. On the other hand, it seems very doubtful whether it is possible to find similar "objective" criteria for the formulation of historical concepts. If such criteria cannot be found, the general demonstration of the *raison d'être* of the individual and historical aspect loses its point, since "historical science" would then be *history,* but not *science.* Whenever the need of a scientific treatment of historically relevant material manifested itself, positivism would immediately renew its "Alleinvertretungsanspruch".

3.1. Faced with this dilemma, Windelband had contented himself with a restatement of the classical view of history as a discipline on the borderline between science and art; according to this view, the historian had "an demjenigen, was wirklich war, eine ähnliche Aufgabe zu erfüllen, wie der Künstler an demjenigen, was in seiner Phantasie ist [19]. While this doctrine rendered historical method immune against positivist attacks—since the historian was partly bound to norms different from those of strict science—it meant the renunciation of the scientific status of history.

3.2. This solution was obviously unsatisfactory; but on the other hand, it was difficult to see how the concepts of historical science were to be given an objectivity equivalent to that of natural science. Weber's reaction (as described by Rickert [20]) to Windelband's Rectoral Lecture reflects this difficulty: Weber criticized Windelband's "Aesthetizismus", but admitted that

17. *Ibid.,* p. 255.
18. *Cf. ibid.,* p. 302n2, where Rickert himself acknowledges this fact. The contribution of Simmel in this connection is also pointed out by Rickert (*ibid.,* pp. 301–02).
19. Wilhelm Windelband, "Geschichte und Naturwissenschaft", *Präludien II,* 1914, p. 150.
20. Rickert, *Grenzen* [5], pp. XXIII–XXIV, 758.

the elaboration of a conceptual logic of history was probably an impossible task [21].

This was the task which Rickert set himself in the second part of the *Grenzen* (published 1902).

4. As we have seen, history, although a "Wirklichkeitswissenschaft", remains dependent on a process of selection from the empirical reality which forms its primary subject–matter. The essential must be distinguished from the inessential, and for this distinction it is necessary to have criteria [22]. Thus, the first problem is whether it is possible to find criteria which are sufficiently firm to serve as a basis for *scientific* treatment of these phenomena, and which at the same time preserve the *individual* element constituting the focus of historical interest [23].

In this respect, Rickert's basic contention is that we select, among the infinity of possible phenomena, precisely those which seem important to us because of their special character, their individuality, and which would consequently lose their importance to us if they were analysed into their component parts [24]. To attribute importance to the individuality of certain phenomena again means connecting them with some value in relation to which they acquire their importance [25]. The importance or significance of phenomena in their individual aspect is always derived from their relation to a value; and only this relation permits a selection from the infinite multiplicity of reality which respects the individual character of the phenomena selected, while being rooted in a firm criterion (viz, the value in question). Consequently, the relation between value and phenomenon becomes the pivot of Rickert's further elaboration of a positive theory of history; and since it is also central to the understanding of Weber's methodology, it will receive full treatment in this connection.

4.1. What is the nature of the relation between vaues and phenomena? To answer this question, Rickert first turns to (past or present) real life. This concept, to him, necessarily implies orientation towards "Zwecke", and a person who is "really" living is therefore by definition *value-oriented,* judging and evaluating himself and the surrounding world [26]. Thus defined, man

21. The question, which is not quite simple, of the source value of Rickert's accounts of the relationship between Weber and himself will be gone into below, pp. 95–97.
22. *Grenzen,* 1902, p. 326.
23. *Ibid.,* pp. 336–37, 342.
24. Rickert here makes elegant play with the etymology "indivisible" of the word "Individuum". This—uncharacteristic—linguistic caper on his part has no independent logical significance, however: the "indivisibility" is just a slightly more complicated way of introducing the *values* of the individual concerned into the analysis.
25. *Grenzen,* 1902, pp. 351–52.
26. Rickert's choice of words leaves no doubt on this point: "Wer lebt, d. h. sich

cannot be interested solely in the general regularities of life, but must to a certain extent also pay attention to things in their individual aspect; indeed, it may be held that phenomena attracting attention in, and because of, this individual aspect, constitute reality as such [27]. To Rickert, such an individualizing viewpoint is "die ursprünglichste *historische* Auffassung" [28].

The gist of Rickert's analysis of the object level of historical science is expressed in the following statement: "... die Wirklichkeit wird Geschichte mit Rücksicht auf die Bedeutung, die das Besondere durch seine Einzigartigkeit für wollende und handelnde Menschen besitzt ..." [29].

4.2. By an elegant twist of thought, Rickert now demonstrates that this statement is also valid for the higher, theoretical research level, the level of the historian himself, subject only to two modifications. First, the relation between phenomenon and value, which on the object level took the form of practical *evaluation*, must be, so to speak, defused, and transformed into a theoretical "Wertbeziehung", a *value relation* [30]. And secondly, the value entering into such a value relation must be *generally* valid, not just, as on the object level, rooted in the personal *subjectivity* of the evaluating individual [31].

The first point reflects the concern for the *value freedom* (in Weber's sense) of history; and Rickert takes great pains to emphasize the fundamental difference between value relation and practical valuation: "... es wäre geradezu das schlimmste von allen Missverständnissen, wenn man unsere Ansicht so auffasste, als hielten wir die Fällung von Werthurteilen für eine geschichtswissenschaftliche Aufgabe" [32]. Value relation simply indicates that a certain phenomenon is found to be "worthy of" interest, "worth" assessing—paradoxically speaking: worth evaluating. *What* attitude should be adopted, *how* the phenomenon should be evaluated, remains an open question. Thus, two persons committed to diametrically opposite political values will, by this very opposition of political views, indicate their agreement on

Zwecke setzt und sie verwirklichen will ..." (*ibid.,* p. 353); "... der wirkliche Mensch, der immer ein wollender, werthender, stellungnehmender Mensch ist ..." (*ibid.,* p. 354).

27. *Ibid.,* p. 354. Rickert adds, however, that he is only describing an *aspect,* on the same theoretical level as that of natural science or of art.

28. *Ibid.,* p. 354.

29. *Ibid.,* p. 355.

30. This technical term might of course be left in the original German in order to eliminate any danger of unfortunate connotations in the English translation. However, since the German word is unwieldy, I have preferred to translate it as "value relation", a term which I hope is sufficiently neutral and value-free in tone. The relation between value and phenomenon expressing itself in *practical* valuation (and which Rickert and Weber sometimes refer to as "Wertbezogenheit") will be translated as "value orientation".

31. *Grenzen,* 1902, pp. 355–56.

32. *Ibid.,* pp. 363–64.

the fact that politics is worth discussing, i.e., in their value relation to politics as a theoretical value [33].

The second point is dictated by the concern for the *general validity* of history. The historian selects his material by means of theoretical value relation. If the values entering into this value relation are not shared by his contemporaries, i. e., by his public, his work will be regarded as totally uninteresting; and since historical reality is defined by the interest of certain persons in the individuality of the phenomena in question, a totally uninteresting account cannot, by definition, give any information concerning historical reality: *it simply is not valid as history*. For a historical account to be valid for a person, this person must accept the value relation on which the account is based; thus, if the account is to be valid for everybody, the values entering into the value relation must be accepted by everybody, they must be what Rickert calls "empirisch allgemein". "Everybody", however, does not in this connection mean "anybody at all", but only "everybody in a given "Gemeinschaft" " [34].

The results of Rickert's discussion up to this point are summarized in the following passage:

"[Die Geschichte] ist *Wirklichkeits*wissenschaft, insofern sie es mit einmaligen individuellen Wirklichkeiten als solchen zu thun hat, sie ist Wirklichkeits*wissenschaft*, insofern sie einen für Alle gültigen Standpunkt der blossen Betrachtung einnimmt und daher nur die durch Beziehung auf einen allgemeinen Werth bedeutungsvollen individuellen Wirklichkeiten ... zum Objekt ihrer Darstellung macht" [35].

The key words are: *individual* reality and *value relation* to (empirically) *general values*.

From Rickert's subsequent discussion, only two main problems will be treated here: the question *what values* the historian should relate his material to; and the question of the *objectivity of historical science*.

5. So far, Rickert's definition of history has only involved criteria of logic and method, historical science being seen as an account of reality under a certain *aspect* (albeit a very "realistic" one); and the values on the basis of which the objects of history were selected have been "general" only in the sense that they were common to the historian and the "Gemeinschaft"

33. *Ibid.*, pp. 364–65.
34. *Ibid.*, pp. 380–81. Accordingly, it is possible to speak, for instance, of a valid family history when all members of the family agree that the recorded facts are worth remembering. It is clear that not every more or less fortuitous human grouping can lay claim to the status of a "Gemeinschaft"; but it is not quite obvious what criteria Rickert uses for the purpose of deciding this point, nor whether these criteria are objective. The problems in this connection will be treated more thoroughly below, pp. 93–94.
35. *Grenzen,* 1902, p. 369.

for which he was writing, general, that is, on the research level. Does this mean that any value can be used as a basis for the construction of historical objects, as long as it is endorsed by the historian and by his public?

5.1. This is not Rickert's view. On the contrary, he tries to show [36] that there is a necessary connection between the object and the method of historical science, in the sense that the historian may *theoretically* only relate his raw material to values which have served as a basis for the *practical* value orientation (valuation, etc.) of persons living in the period under investigation. If a certain phenomenon (say, the Magna Charta) has only, in its time, been evaluated as being more or less acceptable or desirable from a *political* point of view, but not (for instance) in terms of its *artistic* (stylistic, calligraphic, etc.) qualities, Rickert would deem it illegitimate to include it in a history of *art*. He describes this connection between object and method in the following terms: "Die leitenden Werthe der Begriffsbildung sind von einer "objektiven" wissenschaftlichen Darstellung stets dem historischen Stoff selbst zu entnehmen" [37]; it might be still more exact to say that the historical raw material implicitly indicates what aspects may *not* be adopted; the material exercises, so to speak, a veto with regard to certain value relations.

The details of Rickert's rather complicated argument to support this thesis are of less importance in this context, and only two points which are relevant to the later discussion should be emphasized. First, the idea that the theoretical value relation is conditional on the existence of a practical value orientation (on the object level, not necessarily on the research level): figuratively speaking, a theoretical aspect cannot "float in the air", but has to represent the sublimation of a practical value judgment. And, secondly, there is the view implicit in the conclusion reached concerning the relation between object and method: that the only angles from which the historian may legitimately regard a phenomenon are those from which it was already regarded and evaluated in its own time. This last assertion in its turn implies that the *human beings* regarding and evaluating the phenomena in their own time must stand at the centre of the historical account.

5.2. Thus, Rickert seems to have anchored the theoretical values guiding the historian firmly in the object of his investigation, and to have "objectified" them in the sense that they can no longer be chosen at random. But if the values present in the historical material set limits to the number of legitimate value relations, the latter in their turn circumscribe the "essential" object of history. This is a consequence of the obligation of the historian always to let his value relations be guided by values which are generally (empirically) valid in the "Gemeinschaft" for which his account is written

36. *Ibid.,* pp. 560–67.
37. *Ibid.,* p. 567.

(i. e., among his public) [38]: only those individuals, on the object level of the historian, who have been practically oriented towards precisely the same empirically general values will stand at the centre of his account.

What are the values, then, which may lay claim to "general validity"? By means of a complicated conceptual exegesis, Rickert arrives at the conclusion that values may only be regarded as generally valid for the "Gemeinschaft" to which the historian addresses his account, if they are a *"gemeinsame Angelegenheit* der Glieder [dieser] Gemeinschaft" [39], i. e., if they can only be incorporated in structures or functions *common* to the "community". We can restate this in the form that the values in question must not only be valid for each separate member *of* the "Gemeinschaft", but must furthermore be valid for the members in their capacity *as* "Gemeinschaft". Among values of this kind we find, for instance, the Church, the State, Law, Science and Art [40]. One or more of such general values—which Rickert calls *cultural values* [41]—must therefore be at the root of human action in a historical process if this process is to be included in a historical account of general validity. "Valid", "objective" history must always be cultural history in the sense that is must be concerned with human behaviour oriented towards one or more cultural values, towards *culture,* and that it must be theoretically related to these same values.

6.   This conclusion has a number of useful implications for Rickert. For one thing, he has established the interdependence of the object and the method of historical science, and consequently demonstrated the existence of firm criteria for the distinction between important and unimportant parts of the material. Moreover, he has been able to define not only the method but also the proper object of history without departing significantly from the actual practice of this discipline: the aspects generally adopted by historical writers are and have always been connected with cultural values in Rickert's sense: politics, art, religion, literature, etc. In the course of his discussion, Rickert has shown the constitutive importance of certain values, the cultural values, for history and for the definition of its proper object. But is it possible for historical science, thus defined, to lay claim to an objectivity of the same degree as that of natural science [42]? Rickert answers this question in the affirmative as far as *empirical objectivity* is concerned [43]; in other words, he believes

38. *Cf. supra,* p. 90.
39. *Grenzen,* 1902, p. 576.
40. *Ibid.,* p. 576.
41. *Ibid.,* pp. 576–77.
42. *Ibid.,* p. 599.
43. The question of the *metaphysical* objectivity of history goes beyond the scope of the present account.

that history as an empirical discipline is just as objective as the natural sciences.

6.1. As a prelude to his discussion of this point, Rickert introduces an important definition. The statement that a discipline is empirically objective, he says, can only be taken to mean that its propositions possess "empirische Geltung", that they are valid, "true", in relation to reality. But since both the natural and the historical sciences are forced to carry out a *selection* from the unstructured reality which is their raw material, and since this selection must in both cases be guided by certain criteria, the problem of objectivity no longer concerns the accordance of the elements of reality present in the concepts and propositions of science with the raw reality from which they have been selected, but instead raises the question of the objectivity, i. e., of the "empirische Geltung", of the *criteria* of selection [44].

6.2. Rickert now claims that this empirical validity is guaranteed only if the scholar employs cultural values actually held in the "Gemeinschaft" to which he addresses himself, and if he can in addition presume that everybody in this "Gemeinschaft" acknowledges these cultural values as "normativ allgemein":

> "Der Historiker, der sich darauf beschränkt, mit Rücksicht auf empirisch gegebene, von einem bestimmten Kreis von Menschen für normativ allgemein gehaltene Kultur- werthe die Vergangenheit in ihrem einmaligen individuellen Verlauf durch historische Begriffe mit individuellem Inhalt darzustellen, erreicht damit ... die höchste Objektivi- tät, die vom empiristischen Standpunkt aus in der Wissenschaft überhaupt erreicht werden kann" [45].

To a modern analysis, it may seem strange that Rickert defines "empirical validity" by reference to a situation where it is empirically established that everybody in a given "Gemeinschaft" regards certain cultural values as being *normatively* valid, i. e., where empirical and normative elements are *combined*. Such a combination is necessary to Rickert's construction, however: a *purely* empirical definition of validity would lead to the absurdity that, for instance, any member of Danish society could render a Danish political history "non-valid" or "non-objective" simply by refusing to see anything interesting in politics. By introducing a normative element, Rickert preserves validity in this and analogous cases, since he may now claim that politics, for instance, is a *normative* cultural value in Danish society. On the other hand, Rickert's solution raises new problems: what, for instance, is the mean- ing of the expression that a cultural value is "normativ allgemein"? The norm *receiver* is of course the "Gemeinschaft" in question; but who is the norm *sender* [46]? This function cannot be assumed by the members of the

44. *Grenzen*, 1902, pp. 626–27.
45. *Ibid.*, pp. 631–32.

"Gemeinschaft" as a whole (since the cultural values would then be empirically general, and, as such, vulnerable to the threat of "resignation" outlined above); instead, we have to suppose that particular, *normatively* designated persons or mechanisms defining cultural values, the "representatives" (in some sense) of society, are regarded by Rickert as the necessary or sufficient senders of cultural norms. In many ways, this is a very reasonable solution; but it still amounts to an—illegitimate—deduction of a "Sollen" from a "Sein", even though it is concealed in a conceptual definition [47]. At one point, this discretely introduced normative element is even presented without any empirical camouflage: here, Rickert defines culture as that which "allen Gliedern einer Gesellschaft am Herzen liegen *sollte,* und deren Pflege von ihnen *gefordert* werden darf" (my italics)[48].

Rickert, however, avoids a closer discussion of this point and simply maintains that cultural values in their function as a basis of theoretical value relation have general empirical validity. On this score, therefore, the historical sciences cannot be shown to be less objective than the natural sciences. (The conceptualization of the latter is generalizing, and consequently guided by the *common traits* of their objects, i. e., by empirically demonstrable criteria [49]).

2.2. *Max Weber and the break-through to a modern social science*

1. As we have seen [1], Weber himself repeatedly refers to the problems of the "controversy over method" as a *basis* for his own discussion of the

46. Rickert eludes the answer to this question by speaking instead (*ibid.,* p. 631) of a group of individuals (a "Gemeinschaft") who *regard* a cultural value as being "normativ allgemein", i. e., who simply *state* that the norm has been sent by somebody to somebody else.
47. The normative tendency of Rickert's argument is probably also responsible for his expression that certain cultural values are "thatsächlich gemeinsam", the latter term being evidently meant as differing from "empirisch allgemein".
48. One would expect Weber to criticize this concept of culture, and that of "Gemeinschaft" *(cf. supra,* p. 90n34), for containing undeclared valuational elements; instead, we find him *defending* Rickert's system in a letter to Gottl-Ottlilienfeld of March 28th, 1906 (DZA II, Rep. 92, No. 11). Here Weber claims that Rickert's expression "allgemein anerkannte Werthe" only refers to a "Zumutung", a *"Stellungnehmen-Sollen* vom Standpunkt des *Historikers* aus". This may be correct; but the violation of the principle of value freedom nevertheless remains. Either the historian's "Zumutung" is purely *theoretical;* in that case, the object of his investigation is provisional and hypothetical, and Rickert's "empirical validity" is not demonstrated conclusively. Or else, the expression "Stellung-nehmen-*Sollen*" is taken seriously, in which case the *historian* must be supposed to be the legitimate person to define the cultural values of his subject-matter; and this would sever the connection between subject–matter and metod which Rickert regards as vital. On the other hand, Weber's defence is an indication of his *own* solution of this problem, a solution which—at least unconsciously—carries him quite far away from Rickert; *cf. infra,* pp. 137–39.
49. *Grenzen,* 1902, p. 628.
 1. P. 79.

objectivity of the historical sciences, above all in *Objektivität*. The influence of the "elder historical school" in this connection is more indirect: admittedly, Weber discusses the thought of two of its leading figures (in *Roscher* and *Knies*); but Roscher, as Weber explicitly remarks[2], is chosen because of his instructive misconceptions, and indeed almost serves as a whipping-boy; and the discussion of Knies' views occupies less than one-third of *Knies I–II*[3], and results in a conclusion of the same negative kind as that concerning Roscher[4]. Accordingly, it is not realistic, either, to expect Roscher or Knies to have furnished Weber with significant elements of his *solution* of the problem of objectivity. The possible influence of the "controversy over method" in this respect will be discussed in various connections below.

2. A more controversial question is that of Weber's methodological dependence on Rickert.

2.1. Weber's work contains numerous *references* to Rickert, above all to his *Grenzen*. In *Roscher*[5], Weber states one of the aims of the essay to be that of trying out ("erproben") "die Brauchbarkeit der Gedanken dieses Autors [Rickert] für die Methodenlehre unserer Disziplin"[6]; and in the introductory footnote to *Objektivität,* the function of Rickert's thought as a basis for Weber's own discussions is similarly stressed: "Wer die Arbeiten der modernen Logiker kennt—ich nenne nur Windelband, Simmel, und für unsere Zwecke speziell Heinrich Rickert—, wird sofort bemerken, daß in allem Wesentlichen lediglich an sie angeknüpft ist"[7]. As a correlate to these frequent references, Weber carries over considerable portions of Rickert's terminology into his own work ("Wertbeziehung", "Kulturwissenschaft", "historisches Individuum", and a number of other terms)[8].

Rickert himself clearly regarded the *Grenzen* as a necessary condition of Weber's early methodological work. In his preface to the 3rd/4th edition of the book, which was published in 1921 (and, characteristically, dedicated posthumously to Weber) the relationship with Weber is described along the

---

2. GAW, p. 1.
3. His name makes a last appearance GAW, p. 64, to re-emerge only GAW, p. 138.
4. GAW, p. 145.
5. It is not quite clear whether the expression "diese Studie" also refers to *Knies I–II*; one problem in this connection is the time of composition of the latter pair of essays.
6. GAW, p. 7n1.
7. GAW, p. 146n1.
8. Weber was not quite happy with Rickert's choice of terms, however. See his letter to Marianne Weber quoted in her *Lebensbild,* 1950, p. 296 ("Gegen die Terminologie habe ich Bedenken") and his concrete hesitation concerning Rickert's term "Naturwissenschaft", in letters to Fr. Eulenburg and L. v. Bortkievicz (Sept. 8th, 1905 and March 12th, 1906, respectively (DZA II, Rep. 92, No. 30, Vol. 4 (copies)) and to Rickert himself (April 28th, 1905 (DZA II, Rep. 92, No. 25)).

following lines: Weber initially doubted the possibility of working out a positive theory of historical science, but was convinced by Part 2 of the *Grenzen* that Rickert was right in characterizing history as an "individualisierende Kulturwissenschaft" working on the basis of theoretical value relation, and "[machte] bald darauf diese Einsicht für seine eigene Wissenschaft fruchtbar ..." [9] In short, Rickert regarded Weber as his methodological and epistemological pupil [10]. Especially, he felt that Weber was indebted to him on the following points: the formation of individualizing concepts; the distinction between theoretical value relation and practical valuation; the view, based on this distinction, of history as a value-free discipline; and the idea that certain kinds of *material* ("Kultur") so to speak *demand* a particular, individualizing, kind of scientific treatment [11].

2.2. Certain attempts have been made to dispute Rickert's account of the relationship between his theory of history and Weber's methodology. Leaving aside criticism based on downright misunderstandings, the objections made all centre around Rickert's absolute system of values and, not unconnected with this, his concept of *objectivity*. On the other hand, all commentators seem to agree that Rickert's analysis of the theoretical value relation influenced Weber strongly [12].

9. *Grenzen* [5], pp. XXIII–XXIV.
10. It is characteristic of his attitude that Rickert in the same preface (pp. XXV–XXVI) draws a parallel from Weber's doubts concerning the "System der Werte" later developed by Rickert, to Weber's earlier scepticism with regard to a positive logic of history, and that Rickert expresses the hope that Weber, had he lived longer, would finally have let himself be convinced, in the words: "Doch er hatte sich nie unbelehrbar gezeigt".

   That the impetus of Rickert's methodological thought remained precious to Weber for a long time is borne out by a letter, probably from 1915 (DZA II, Rep. 92, No. 25) to Rickert, in which he asks the latter to publish his new "Logic" or parts of it as soon as possible: "Wenn *da* einmal etwas kommt, fange ich wieder mit methodologischen Arbeiten an".
11. *Grenzen* [5], p. 758. This last point in particular seems to have been important to Rickert: "Das ist in Wahrheit ... der *zentrale* Gedanke meiner positiven Geschichtslehre, der den *Zusammenhang* von Form und Inhalt erkennen läßt".
12. Eugène Fleischmann denies himself nothing in the way of serious misconceptions concerning the relationship between Weber and Rickert:

    "Les efforts de Rickert font pitié, qui voulait faire adhérer Weber à son "école" philosophique stérile afin de pouvoir montrer les services qu'il aurait rendus à la recherche concrète. De tous les néo-kantiens de l'époque, il était probablement celui pour lequel Weber avait le moins de considération". "En réalité, au témoignage de Troeltsch, Weber ne cite Rickert que par politesse et déférence ..." (Eugène Fleischmann, "De Weber à Nietzsche", *Archives Européennes de Sociologie*, Vol. V (1964), pp. 198–99).

    It is clear from the *Grenzen* [5] that Rickert did *not* attempt to depict Weber as a member of the South-West German school of neo-Kantian philosophy (Rickert, *Grenzen* [5], 1929, p. XXV). The "testimony" of Troeltsch adduced by Fleischmann simply cannot be found; indeed, Troeltsch on the contrary speaks of Weber's

While it is certain that Weber's treatment of the problem of objectivity, and its relation to Rickert's work, merit close investigation, the superficial likeness of Weber's and Rickert's views on value relation may have led commentators to conclude too hastily that these views were fundamentally identical. The question will be taken up below, with the aim of pinpointing possible divergences of Weber's thought from Rickert's, and of analysing the significance of these divergences when viewed in a larger context.

2.3. Before we embark upon the actual analysis of Weber's views, it may be useful to give a brief summary of the general premises of his argument, confronted with the corresponding positions of Rickert, as noted above [13].

The *sphere of application* of Weber's methodology is the science of economics, which is, however, extended in *Objektivität* to include the non-economic causes and consequences of economic phenomena and processes ("ökonomisch relevante" and "ökonomisch bedingte" elements, respectively) [14], an extension which allows Weber to confer on the discipline the title of "Sozialökonomik" ("social economics"). Rickert's focus is in part a different one, viz, history in general.

The *problems* which Weber sets out to solve are closely connected with his sphere of interest. As we have seen, they were defined by the controversy over method, and include both the criticism of the historical and socio-economical point of view, and the question of the legitimate function of non-historical aspects in practical research, particularly with regard to the formation of concepts. In comparison, the complex of problems tackled by Rickert is at the same time wider and narrower: on the one hand, he takes it upon himself to defend and secure the legitimacy of the historical point of view in *all* the scientific disciplines working from it; but this historical point of view is above all regarded and treated as a logically extreme *type,* while Rickert does not deal in detail with actual research, in which the two typical aspects are mixed.

The *method* adopted by Weber also differs from that applied by Rickert:

"enge Anschluß an den Neukantianismus und vor allem an die Rickertsche Geschichtslogik" (*Historismus,* 1922, p. 566). To complete the picture, it may be added that Fleischmann is only able to quote Weber's footnote GAW, p. 7n1 in support of his own thesis because he mistranslates "erproben" by "vérifier" ("test"), although its meaning is clearly "try out", "essay".

In the light of this kind of inaccuracy, it is difficult to take entirely seriously Fleischmann's vehement attacks on the "orthodox" commentators of Weber's work— one of whom, the present editor of Weber's works, Professor Joh. Winckelmann, is accused in more or less veiled terms of bungling and cheating in his scholarly work.

13. This brief summary does not of course pretend to *exhaust* the catalogue of methodological differences between Weber and Rickert, but is only meant to serve as a recapitulation of those divergences of their thought which have already been pointed out.

14. *Cf.* GAW, pp. 161–63.

Weber remains on the methodological level, and perhaps now and then enters the field of epistemology, whereas Rickert apparently plays on the whole register of thought of neo-Kantian philosophy, particularly towards the end of the *Grenzen*.

The different *aims* of Weber and Rickert, naturally enough, mirror the differences of the problems which they set out to solve: they have in common a desire to demonstrate the objectivity of history and "social economics"; but over and above this, Weber wants to analyse the practical consequences of the concept formation of "social economics" to a far greater degree than Rickert.

2.2.1. The theoretical basis

1. Like Rickert, Weber bases his discussion of the logic of history on the view that empirical reality is boundless, an "unübersehbare Mannigfaltigkeit". He repeats this idea in numerous passages of the various essays without modifying it in any important respect; at the most, one may point to a tendency in *Roscher* to keep very close to the Rickertian model [1], while in *Knies I–II,* Weber takes up a more independent position and implicitly reaches out beyond Rickert's conclusions [2]. As might be expected, *Objektivität* contains the most systematic statements of the position, as for instance GAW, p. 171:

> "Nun bietet uns das Leben, sobald wir uns auf die Art, in der es uns unmittelbar entgegentritt, zu besinnen suchen, eine schlechthin unendliche Mannigfaltigkeit von nach- und nebeneinander auftauchenden und vergehenden Vorgängen, "in" uns und "außer" uns. Und die absolute Unendlichkeit dieser Mannigfaltigkeit bleibt intensiv durchaus ungemindert auch dann bestehen, wenn wir ein einzelnes "Objekt"—etwa einen konkreten Tauschakt—isoliert ins Auge fassen,—sobald wir nämlich ernstlich versuchen wollen, dies "Einzelne" *erschöpfend in allen* seinen individuellen Bestandteilen auch nur zu beschreiben, geschweige denn es in seiner kausalen Bedingtheit zu erfassen".

This passage also illustrates a particular point, the consequences of which are given considerable attention by Weber, viz, that the idea of the inexhaustibility of reality in its immediate aspect implies the existence of an equal, or perhaps even greater, infinity of potential causal explanations [3]; any "object", however small, which we want to explain causally, represents an infinite number of qualities, and the individual manifestation of each of these qualities is again the result of the interplay of an infinite number of causal factors. As Henrich puts it: "Das jeweils Wirkliche eines jeden Zeit-

1. GAW, pp. 4–5; see also GAW, pp. 11, 14, 34n1.
2. Examples of the discussions in these essays are GAW, pp. 50, 67, 80, 120.
3. GAW, pp. 67, 177, 184, 232, 271.

punktes hat seine zureichende Ursache lediglich in der Gesamtheit des jeweils zeitlich früheren Seienden" [4].

2. Since this conception of actual reality and of its causal connections is fundamental to an argument which Weber develops along—at least super-ficially—parallel lines to Rickert, it is at this point that one might most plausibly expect to find traces of philosophy or epistemology in Weber's thought. Rickert's discussion of the same problem in the *Grenzen* is in itself apparently free from philosophical elements; but it does evoke overtones of his earlier epistemological work "Der Gegenstand der Erkenntnis" [5]. Can we find similar overtones in Weber's argument?

2.1.1. Weber does not systematically discuss the question; but here and there, he indicates a little more concretely how the perception of immediate reality must be imagined to take place in practice. GAW, p. 67, he writes: "... *jeder* scheinbar noch so einfache individuelle Hergang [enthält] eine inten-sive *Unendlichkeit* des Mannigfaltigen ...., sobald man ihn als eine solche sich ins Bewußtsein bringen *will* ...., and GAW, p. 171, as mentioned above, he speaks of "das Leben, sobald wir uns auf die Art, in der es uns unmittelbar entgegentritt, zu besinnen suchen". In both cases, the perception of imme-diate and infinite reality is presented as the result of conscious *reflection* on the structured, common-sense reality [6].

Put in the form of a paradox, Weber's view is that "immediate" reality is mediate, being the product of logical analysis. It is not, as Henrich supposes, to be equated with a pre-scientific reality, still less, as Tenbruck implies, with Weber's concept of reality altogether (for a more thorough discussion of the views of these two commentators, see Appendix A of this chapter); on the contrary, it is the result of scientific (logical) inference *from* our given, common-sense perception of things around us, from "real" reality in Weber's sense. Weber does *not* claim that we ever *perceive* reality in its infinite and immediate aspect, but only that it can be logically demonstrated that the reality confronting us in our daily lives is the structured version of something immediate and boundless.

2.1.2. From a strictly logical point of view, this shifting upwards of the concept of reality is of course unacceptable; the argument of Rickert, according to which all description implies a processing of reality, remains valid. But this is precisely the crucial point: Rickert's aim is to construct a *logically* consistent chain of argument; accordingly, he has to carry this

---

4. Henrich, *Einheit*, 1952, pp. 10–11.
5. *Cf. ibid.*, p. 15.
6. In a set of rough notes on Gottl's theory of perception, probably written in 1903 (DZA II, Rep. 92, No. 31, Vol. 6), Weber makes a similar point: "Unser "Er-leben" ist vom *Sprechen* u. den *Worten* gar nicht mehr zu trennen".

argument to its logical conclusion, which is that unscientific reality is always, from a strictly logical point of view, completely amorphous. Weber, on the other hand, is more concerned with the *practice* of science: to him, the argument loses its relevance wherever it goes deeper than everyday empirical reality. Formally, the logical chain of argument is retained; but it is only applied to material which is empirically given [7].

Methodologically, too, Weber seems justified in taking as his point of departure reality as actually experienced rather than in its elementary, "immediate" aspect, since, in contradistinction to Rickert, he almost completely ignores the problems of the natural sciences and concentrates on those of social science. While the natural sciences may find it interesting to reflect on and seek information about a world which is not directly observable, i. e., to frame propositions which may be scientifically valid but which lack common-sense evidence (for instance, about the speed of atoms or the chemical properties of certain substances), the interest of social science does not in the same way go beyond what can be directly observed. Weber's implicit, logically unclear, concept of reality corresponds to the needs of the disciplines which stand at the centre of his interest [8].

2.2. This question has been treated at some length because it serves as an introduction to the main thesis of the present account, viz, that Weber broke out of Rickert's system and modified it through the addition of other elements whenever logic threatened to get the better of social science. Moreover, the problem of the structure of reality is of fundamental importance to Weber's theory of the objectivity of scientific results [9].

3.1. Just like Rickert, Weber concludes from the view of reality as boundless that a scientific reproduction of the whole of reality is a practical, indeed a logical, impossibility. This again entails that all scientific disciplines *must*, consciously or unconsciously, make use of concepts, and that such concepts can only embrace *parts* of reality [10]; thus, a scientific discipline is never justified in claiming that its concepts reproduce reality, but only that they represent a *selection from reality*: "...die ... Unendlichkeit und absolute

7. *Cf.* GAW, pp. 231–32, where the discussion of a phenomenon which is indisputably of an empirical nature ("Bismarck") is made to support a conclusion according to which this phenomenon is an "infinite multiplicity"; see also GAW, p. 95n3(3).
8. Insofar as the social sciences try to *explain* human behaviour, it even becomes a *necessity* to adopt the same view of reality as that taken by the persons whose behaviour is to be explained, viz, a purely common-sense view. *Cf.* GAW, p. 437: "... empirische Disziplinen arbeiten, wo immer es sich um die realen beziehungen zwischen ihren *Objekten* (und nicht: um ihre eigenen logischen Voraussetzungen) handelt, unvermeidlich mit dem "naiven Realismus" ..."
9. *Cf. infra*, pp. 133–34.
10. GAW, p. 171.

Irrationalität jedes konkreten Mannigfaltigen [*erweist* wirklich zwingend er-kenntnistheoretisch] die absolute Sinnlosigkeit des Gedankens einer "Abbil-dung" der Wirklichkeit durch irgendeine Art von Wissenschaft . . ." [11]

3.2. Although the parallel to Rickert is quite obvious on this point, it is nevertheless possible to discern a characteristic shift of emphasis. Rickert sees the problem of the concepts of science as a *logical* one; his aim is to show that the constructs of the historical sciences are more than just evocative word-paintings, that they are scientific concepts in the sense that they, like the concepts of natural science, are formed according to firm and "objective" criteria. Thus, the analysis of historical concepts is not the ultimate *purpose* of the discussion, but a—very important—*means* of raising history to a status equivalent to that of natural science. Weber's concern is a different one: as mentioned above, his basic problem is not that of history as a logical type, but rather of economics as a concrete discipline racked by a concrete internal conflict. Since this conflict between historicism and the Menger school fouses on the nature of the *concepts* of economics, the analysis of his issue becomes the chief aim of Weber's discussion.

The detailed analysis of this conceptual discussion comes under the heading of chapter 4, on the concept of the ideal type; but it seems useful already at the present stage to point to the added *weight* which Weber gives to the discussion of concepts, even though the *results* of this discussion do not differ from Rickert's.

4.1. Weber's treatment of concept formation in the natural sciences, of their limits, and of the essence of the historical point of view does not diverge from Rickert's; but here again, a shift of emphasis is noticeable. Thus, the methods of natural science are only briefly touched upon as a separate sub-ject, and then in *Roscher,* in which the influence of Rickert is most imme-diate[12]. As might be expected, Weber simply repeats the Rickertian view that natural science abstracts from reality in its individual and qualitative aspect and seeks to reduce it to general and purely quantitative concepts and laws.

4.2.1. Weber simply accepts and repeats Rickert's thesis of the rooting of historical interest in the *individuality* of the object[13], and, like Rickert,

11. GAW, p. 92n1. Similar statements are found, for instance, GAW, pp. 5, 75n2(1), 113, 192–93, 237, 277.
12. GAW, pp. 4–5, 13–14.
13. For instance GAW, pp. 5–6, 172–73, 177, 245, 352. Weber's formulations are identical whether he is talking of historical or of social science. This is under-standable, since the interest in the *individual* aspect of things is a necessary and *logical* characteristic of *all* non-natural sciences (in the logical sense). The *term* "historical" is only meant by Rickert to mark the opposition to the point of view of natural science, not to limit the discussion to the discipline of history properly speaking.

identifies this individual and qualitative reality with reality as such [14]; Weber, too, refers to disciplines based on a selection of material according to the individuality of the objects as "Wirklichkeitswissenschaft" [15].

4.2.2. Although Weber thus consistently adheres to the positive theory that historical interest is based on the individual aspect of phenomena, he characteristically devotes just as much space and energy to a number of attacks on the positivist position, according to which the essential part of reality is identical with the sum of regularities and *general* qualities which it contains.

Weber already levels his criticism at Roscher (although only in an indirect form: in *Roscher,* Weber usually refrains from overt criticism, preferring to let the impression of the confusion and methodological innocence of Roscher's thought emerge from a neutral, but carefully structured, exposé [16]); the attack recurs in the discussion of Münsterberg's theory of science [17], and is most clearly and completely unfolded in *Objektivität:*

"Das Bedeutsame koinzidiert natürlich auch als solches mit keinem Gesetze als solchem, und zwar um so weniger, je allgemeingültiger jenes Gesetz ist. Denn die spezifische *Bedeutung,* die ein Bestandteil der Wirklichkeit für uns hat, findet sich natürlich gerade *nicht* in denjenigen seiner Beziehungen, die er mit möglichst vielen anderen teilt" [18].

Directly derived from this position is Weber's denial of the possibility of deducing reality from some set of empirical laws [19]. From a purely logical point of view, this denial can be justified simply by pointing to the fact that reality, which is *individual,* cannot be deduced from regularities, which are *general* and abstract. Weber uses a similar argument, but links it up a little more closely with the structure of causal explanation, which seems to him to be the essential form of explanation in the historical sciences; he points

---

14. For instance GAW, pp. 5, 172, 237.
15. GAW, pp. 3, 113, 237 and, in a particularly prominent position, p. 170. Weber's sparing use of the term seems to indicate that he was less than enthusiastic about it; one reason for this may be that the word was a fertile source of misconceptions, particularly in discussions concerning the historicist belief in a science which is able to "reproduce" reality. Tenbruck's view that Weber's use of the term evokes such a theory of "reproduction" (*Genesis,* 1959, p. 591) cannot be accepted: Weber is always most careful to interpret "Wirklichkeitswissenschaft" in the Rickertian sense.
16. GAW, p. 14.
17. GAW, p. 81n1.
18. GAW, p. 176; see also GAW, pp. 171, 175, 180. This *logical* distinction is particularly vital because Weber recognizes that the importance of a phenomenon may *in practice* occasionally be found in those elements which it has in common with other phenomena. Examples from the field of economics and political science are the use of money in economic transactions and the growth of mass movements and of the political parties which Duverger calls "partis de masse".
19. GAW, pp. 13, 75n2(2), 80, 171–72, 174, 188.

out that causal explanation in history consists in tracing back, by means of one's knowledge of the relevant empirical regularities, individual situations to earlier individual situations, just as a prognosis represents a hypothetical development, by means of the same kind of general knowledge, of an individual situation into the future:

> "... die Kausalfrage ist, wo es sich um die *Individualität* einer Erscheinung handelt, nicht eine Frage nach *Gesetzen,* sondern nach konkreten kausalen *Zusammenhängen,* nicht eine Frage, welcher Formel die Erscheinung als Exemplar unterzuordnen, sondern die Frage, welcher individuellen Konstellation sie als Ergebnis zuzurechnen ist: sie ist *Zurechnungsfrage"* [20].

It is interesting that this argument is also used against the younger historical school and its belief in concepts as the aim of scientific inquiry [21]. Here again, Weber departs from the strict logical dualism history/natural science, in order to allow a closer discussion of the problems of a *concrete* discipline (in this case, economics).

2.2.2. *Value relation*

1. How are the elements selected which are to enter into the historical concepts? What is the firm criterion needed to assure the logical equality of these concepts to those of natural science? As we have seen, Rickert claimed that this function was fulfilled by the relation beteeen the "raw" phenomena and certain *values,* what he called the theoretical *value relation.* Weber completely accepts these basic premises of Rickert's argument. But in his interpretation and elaboration of these ideas, in the consequences which he draws from them, and in his final conception of social science, Weber diverges to an increasing extent from Rickert, in my opinion even to an extent greater than commentators on Weber's work have hitherto maintained [1]. As a result of this, the account of Weber's methodological thought, which until now was able to keep very close to the lay-out of Rickert's discussion, will from now on concentrate on presenting Weber's views in their specific, non-Rickertian context; only in the summaries of the main points will attempts also be made to assess the divergence of Weber from earlier theories of the historical sciences, and to estimate the importance of this divergence.

Weber's discussion of the relation of values to phenomena can be divided into two main categories: the first one, which is in the main restricted to *Objektivität,* contains a fairly consistent, constructive and positive formulation of Weber's view, whereas the second one, which is more extensive, cover-

---

20. GAW, p. 178. Similar formulations are found GAW, pp. 75n2(2), 172, 174, 188.
21. GAW, pp. 13n1, 171, 184, 208.
 1. The interpretation which comes closest to that of the present account is that of Schelting in his *Wissenschaftslehre.*

ing *Knies I–II* and *Kritische Studien,* consists of critical commentaries on a number of earlier attempts to fashion a logic of historical investigation.

2. It is natural to turn first to the positive discussion in *Objektivität,* both because it can be supposed to present a more coherent version of Weber's thought, and because *Objektivität* is chronologically prior to at least the later of the critical essays.

2.1.1. In its general form, Weber's description of the relation between value and phenomenon occupies a remarkably inferior place in *Objektivität.* The most important passage is the following:

> "Ein winziger Teil der jeweils betrachteten individuellen Wirklichkeit wird von unserm durch ... Wertideen bedingten Interesse gefärbt, er allein hat Bedeutung für uns; er hat sie, weil er Beziehungen aufweist, die für uns infolge ihrer Verknüpfung mit Wertideen *wichtig* sind. Nur weil und soweit dies der Fall [ist (edit. add.)], ist er in seiner individuellen Egenart für uns wissenswert" [2].

In themselves, these statements do not diverge from Rickert; but it should be noted that the "Verknüpfung mit Wertideen" mentioned by Weber is not explicitly classified as *theoretical* value relation rather than as *practical* value orientation. The careful and deliberate distinction between the object level and the research level is lacking, as is the consequent emphasis on the "sublimated" character of theoretical value relation and on the essential difference between practical valuation (value orientation) and theoretical value relation. Weber's choice of words does not actually contradict these ideas; but the vagueness of the passage suggests methodological hesitation on his part.

2.1.2. Apart from brief references [3], the only other passage in *Objektivität* dealing with the relation between value and phenomenon is found on GAW p. 180:

> "In *welchem* Sinn und in *welchen* Beziehungen dies [the fact that the individuality of objects becomes important to us] der Fall ist, ... entscheidet sich nach den *Wertideen,* unter denen wir die "Kultur" jeweils im einzelnen Falle betrachten. "Kultur" ist ein vom Standpunkt des *Menschen* aus mit Sinn und Bedeutung bedachter endlicher Ausschnitt aus der sinnlosen Unendlichkeit des Weltgeschehens. Sie ist es für den Menschen auch dann, wenn er einer *konkreten* Kultur als Todfeind sich entgegenstellt ... Denn auch zu dieser Stellungnahme kann er nur gelangen, indem er die konkrete Kultur auf seine Wertideen *bezieht* und "zu leicht" befindet".

And a little later:

> "Welches immer der Inhalt dieser [evaluating] Stellungnahme sei,—[die] Erscheinungen [des menschlichen Zusammenseins] haben für uns Kultur*bedeutung,* auf dieser Bedeutung beruht allein ihr wissenschaftliches Interesse" [4].

2. GAW, p. 175.
3. GAW, pp. 176, 213.
4. GAW, p. 181.

Here the difficulty inherent in the first passage reappears: the source of the values entering into the formation of the historical object is still not made explicit. "Wir" or "der Mensch" observe reality and, in so doing, transform it into "culture" [5]; and the interest to *science* of the phenomena rests on an importance which we infer from *practical* value orientation. The imprecision of the first passage is not dissipated: apparently, Weber does not in *Objektivität* make explicit use of the Rickertian distinction between the object level and the research level of scientific inquiry [6].

2.2. Does this mean that Weber also does away with the distinction between value judgments and value relation? A positive answer to this question would be completely at variance with Weber's principle of value freedom, which precisely debars scholars from regarding their own practical valuations of phenomena as being part of the scientific process. On the other hand, it must be admitted that explicit distinctions between value judgments and value relation are hard to find in *Objektivität*. The discussion, cited above, whether a "Beziehung auf Wertideen" implies a *positive* valuation of the phenomenon concerned, is not relevant here, since this discussion does not deal with the difference between value judgments and value relation, but with the distinction between value judgments and *positive* value judgments. In fact, Weber only once, and implicitly, indicates that the scientist who has formed his object through value relation is not allowed, and certainly is not forced, to make value judgments as a part of his scientific treatment of it:

> "Und dieser Satz [the maintenance of the distinction between scientific and non-scientific forms of argument] bleibt richtig, trotzdem ... jene höchsten "Werte" des *praktischen* Interesses für die *Richtung,* welche die ordnende Tätigkeit des Denkens auf dem Gebiete der Kulturwissenschaften jeweils einschlägt, von entscheidender Bedeutung sind und immer bleiben werden" [7].

And even here, it is noteworthy that Weber takes *practical* interest to be the guide of *scientific* inquiry.

2.3. Although Weber's upholding of the fundamental distinction between valuation and value relation is relegated to an inferior place in *Objektivität*, there can be no doubt of his conviction, even in that essay, that the distinction is both legitimate and necessary [8]. This conclusion, on the other hand, raises the problem of what weight and importance should be attributed to the passages quoted above, when the distinction is taken for granted. A reason-

5. For a discussion of this concept, *cf. infra,* pp. 125–31.
6. One of the very few commentators to reach a similar conclusion is Willy Strzelewicz (*Die Grenzen der Wissenschaft bei Max Weber,* Diss. Frankfurt 1933, pp. 20–21), who subjects the question to careful scrutiny.
7. GAW, p. 155. Similarly GAW, p. 158.
8. For instance, one may point to the explicit separation of the two spheres GAW, p. 199: "Es handelt sich hier *nicht* mehr um den rein theoretischen Vorgang der *Beziehung* des Empirischen auf Werte, sondern um Wert*urteile* ..." This

able solution seems to be the following: Weber's discussion of the relation between value and phenomenon is conducted on a general level. What is examined is not primarily the relation of "the scholar" or of "the person observed", but quite generally "man's" or "our" relation to the important, interesting, essential parts of reality. The point, quite simply put, is this: immediate reality in itself *has* no meaning or significance, but only *receives* it when *endowed* with it by man; in a slightly altered version of Goethe's words: "Wir wissen von keiner sinnvollen Welt als in Bezug auf den Menschen".

2.4. This "Bezug", in its turn, is the relation to a value. In extreme cases, this relation may be theoretical from the very beginning: a person *may* be interested in, say, politics without having ever uttered or even formulated in his own mind a single value judgment concerning political matters. But usually, as in the examples given by Weber, at least the point of departure will be a value judgment, a positive or negative attitude to, for instance, some political occurrence. The historical sciences in particular *depend* on such a—practical or theoretical—"Bezug". On the other hand, it should be emphasized that the point of view of science *as such* cannot legitimately be valuational, but must remain theoretical. The conclusion, in other words, is that practical value judgments will often serve as intermediate links for theoretical value relation, not only in the logical sense (as in Rickert's construction) but directly in each actual case, for the individual wishing to obtain historical knowledge. Just as it was demonstrated in the chapter on value freedom [9] that a person may enter into two roles, being the source (or the recipient) of, alternately, scientific and valuational propositions, so we here see that the social scientist will often have to pass through a phase of practical valuation in order to be able to assume his theoretical role. But where the discussion of value freedom made it clear, indeed of paramount importance, that the two roles were separate in principle and that this separation ought to be strictly and consistently preserved in practice, Weber's attitude to the problem of value relation seems far more flexible. Of course, scientific propositions and value judgments are still two entirely different things; but in pointing to

passage has not been quoted above in this connection, since it refers to Weber's concept of the ideal type and consequently does not form part of the discussion of the *principles* guiding the formation of historical concepts.

It seems beyond doubt that Weber's principle of value freedom is sufficiently firmly rooted not to be in any way invalidated by the vague passages quoted above, and that it lends massive indirect support to the claim that Weber accepted the distinction between value relation and value judgments. If the discussion above has concentrated on the—relatively—greater vagueness in this field, the intention has been to demonstrate what new aspects, *apart from* the—implicit but undoubted —maintenance of the principle of value freedom, were introduced by Weber's discussion of theoretical value relation.

9. *Supra,* p. 66.

valuations as a frequent, and legitimate, condition of value relation, Weber hints at the possibility of a more extensive, if still controlled, interplay of practice and theory, interest and perception [10].

3. If, with this provisional conclusion in mind, we turn to Weber's various *negative* discussions in *Knies I–II* and *Kritische Studien* [11], we may initially note that a common trait of most of the scholars attacked by Weber is their view that the specific quality of history resides in its *material,* either in "die spezifischen, diesem Stoff im Gegensatz zum Naturgeschehen *objektiv* zukommenden Qualitäten" (objectivism) or in "die besondere Art seiner [the material's] Gegebenheit" (intuitionism) [12]. Weber's opponents—"victims" is a more fitting term for some of them—are accordingly agreed in their fundamental opposition to Weber's basic premise of the meaninglessness of reality in its immediate aspect. It is therefore reasonable to expect that Weber's criticism will again remain on the general level, shunning the precise Rickertian distinctions belonging to a lower level of abstraction.

3.1. Already the first important discussion, which concerns Wundt's concept "schöpferische Synthese" ("creative synthesis"), confirms this assumption. In Wundt's work, the concept serves to introduce the idea (which violates the principle of value freedom [13]) that history is marked by "steigende psychische Energie"; and Weber in principle attacks the "schöpferische Syn-

10. Tenbruck (*Genesis,* 1959, pp. 591–92), holds that Weber does not and does not try to justify his thesis of value relation in the social sciences on methodological grounds, that is, as a theoretical necessity, but that he *demands* a place for values in the social sciences in the basis of an "aller Methodologie voraufliegende Entscheidung" (*ibid.,* p. 592). Tenbruck apparently interprets a passage from Weber (GAW, p. 170: "Die Sozialwissenschaft, die *wir* treiben wollen, ist eine *Wirklichkeitswissenschaft;* quoted indirectly *Genesis,* 1959, p. 592) as confirming this view.

    Thus, Tenbruck defines Weber's choice as one in favour of a knowledge of concrete reality *by means of value relation.* This implies, first, the existence of *another* way of obtaining concrete knowledge, i. e., that concrete reality may be perceived as such without the intervention of a value relation, and, secondly, that Weber acknowledged the existence of this alternative but that he chose to reject it for his own part. This hypothesis is totally unfounded: Weber never even hints at alternative means of arriving at scientific knowledge in the historical sciences. The passage GAW, p. 170 adduced by Tenbruck does not support his view: in *choosing* to pursue a "Wirklichkeitswissenschaft", Weber is not renouncing natural science but the *normative* sciences (law, etc.).

11. But, characteristically, not in *Roscher,* the essay in which Weber is most directly under the influence of Rickert.

12. Schelting, *Wissenschaftslehre,* 1934, p. 149. Certain other points of view also occur, which cannot be classified under one of the two main headings; particularly prominent among them is Ed. Meyer's doctrine of *causal efficiency* as the criterion of historical importance. Schelting, *Wissenschaftslehre,* 1934, pp. 178–219 discusses the whole complex of problems with great thoroughness.

13. *Cf. supra,* pp. 39–40.

these" on the same grounds: "... man [muß] sich ... sorgsam hüten, in ihm [the concept] etwas anderes finden zu wollen als den Niederschlag einer *Wertung* ..." [14] Particularly, one must beware of thinking that this value judgment can be read off from the material as such. According to Weber, empirical observation of changes occurring in the material may in itself only serve as a basis for the formulation of "Kausalungleichungen", "causal inequations", i. e., statements according to which a particular phenomenon has causal effects that are *unlike* their cause. Such causal inequations are found in every scientific discipline, in natural science as well as in history: oxygen and hydrogen atoms are qualitatively different from the water molecules into which they are incorporated; the various internal and external factors contributing to the growth of the German National Socialist party were qualitatively different from the result which they brought about. Only when causal inequations are transformed, by the introduction of human value judgments, into "Wertungleichungen", "*value* inequations", i. e., when we ascribe to the effect a—positive or negative—value which was not ascribed to the separate causes, does it become legitimate to employ value-laden terms, e. g. "schöpferische Synthese", to denote the changes in question [15].

So far, Weber's criticism of Wundt seems to refer only to a violation of the principle of value freedom, to a vague, indeed a metaphysical, way of constructing scientific concepts [16]. But this criticism, which clearly refers to practical value judgments [17], quickly merges into a discussion of historical concepts in general, of "Wertbeziehung" rather than of "Wertung": "... die Reflexion auf diese Beziehung [to human valuations] [wird] zum entscheidenden *Grund* unseres historischen Interesses" [18]. This emphasis on the role of practical valuations, of *value judgments,* as "triggers" of historical interest, is present throughout the essay [19].

3.2. This discussion of Wundt's conceptual aberrations does not in its conclusion go beyond Weber's main contention: that reality only possesses such meaning as we choose to endow it with. The latter part of *Knies I* does,

14. GAW, p. 49.
15. GAW, pp. 49–50.
16. See a letter from Weber to W. Hellpach of Oct. 10th, 1905 (DZA II, Rep. 92, No. 17) in which he speaks of Wundt's terminology as containing "Metaphysik und keine Psychologie".
17. The hypothetical argument that "Wertung" should not, in Weber's early essays, be interpreted as indicating *practical* valuations, but rather theoretical value relation, is not supported by Weber's text; see for instance GAW, p. 51, where Weber separately discusses the possibility of interpreting "schöpferisch" in this neutral sense *as well,* and GAW, p. 54, where "Beziehung auf Werte" is equated with, among other terms, "Werturteil", which unambiguously refers to practical valuation.
18. GAW, p. 50.
19. For instance GAW, pp. 54, 60.

however—apart from brief references to the role of values in the selection of historical material [20]—contain indications that a more extensive analysis of the methodological principle of value relation is possible. Thus, GAW, p. 100n2, commenting on Simmel's "Probleme der Geschichtsphilosophie", Weber writes:

"Die Verankerung des ganzen Sinns einer Erkenntnis des Individuellen an Wertideen manifestiert sich eben auch in der "schöpferischen" Kraft, welsche eigene starke Werturteile des Historikers bei der Entbindung historischer Erkenntnis entwickeln können". "... hier [treten] die Werturteile in den Dienst der Deutung".

What Weber refers to here is apparently the "Interpretation" which he has briefly touched upon earlier in *Knies I,* and which consists in an "Analyse *möglicher* Wertbeziehungen" [21]. Here Weber, going far beyond Rickert, envisages a proper *theory* of social science method as a supplement to, indeed almost in place of, the purely abstract and formal description of the formation of historical concepts as theoretical value relation; in his own words, he proposes a "Theorie der "Deutung" " [22], in which the formulation of practical value judgments even functions as a rudimentary historical *technique.* In light of this, it seems significant that two references to the distinction between value judgments and value relation are precisely placed in this practical context; in the place of Rickert's logical "sublimation" of value judgments into value relation, Weber formulates an equally strict, but concrete distinction: valuations may function as a means, a technique, but this phase is only a transitory one, which must be followed by theoretical value relation, i. e., by neutral observation [23].

4. Weber now develops the theme of "Wertanalyse" or "Wertinterpretation"—the terms are used interchangeably by him, and will both in the following be translated as "value interpretation"—in *Kritische Studien* and, shortly afterwards, in *Knies II* (the two essays are so close to each other in time that it seems justified to treat them together).

4.1.1. According to Weber, the *occasion* of the value interpretation is furnished by the *valuation* of some phenomenon or event as more or less positive or negative. This practical valuation indicates that the object or event in question has become *important;* but if one wishes to observe and understand this object theoretically, it is necessary, without sacrificing its importance, to remove it, intellectually, to a certain distance; it must be

20. GAW, pp. 86, 92n1, 95n3(2), 99, 100n2.
21. GAW, p. 89n2. It is indicative of the still undeveloped distinction between valuation and value relation that this "Interpretation" is here seen as the prelude to a "Wertung", not to theoretical value relation or to some other scientific activity.
22. GAW, p. 91.
23. GAW, pp. 91, 100n2.

submitted to "afterthought", to "reflection": "... wir [müssen] einem Erlebnis gegenüber erst "objektiv werden" ..." [24]

This intellectual "removal to a distance" liberates the object from the original connection with a value which was expressed in the initial value judgment; consequently, the idea of a relation of the phenomenon to *other* values becomes possible and relevant. This is the actual *substance* of value interpretation: "Die "Deutung" ... in *diesem* Sinn ist Ermittlung der "Werte", welche "wir" in jenen Objekten "verwirklicht" finden *können* ..." [25]. If we take, say, Karl Marx' "Das Kapital" as an example, a value interpretation of the work would consist in making clear what parts of it—if any—would be relevant to (for instance) a strictly Hegelian, a neo-Hegelian, a Soviet Communist, a reformist Communist, a Maoist, a purely historical, but also a literary or an antisemitic valuation. In this way, value interpretation shows up the various possible theoretical value relations [26] of "Das Kapital", and consequently the points of attack of the different valuations of the work; potentially, this illustration even includes the elaboration of the *content* of these various valuations, since a complete knowledge of *where* a potential valuation will be brought to bear also implies knowledge of *what* is the substance of this valuation [27]. The function of value interpretation is seen by Weber as very important: it is the precondition of any historical work, since it makes clear what aspects of the observed phenomenon are relevant to a particular value: "... es ist ... die ganz unvermeidliche "forma formans" für das historische "Interesse" an einem Objekt, für dessen primäre begriffliche Formung ... und für die dadurch erst sinnvoll mögliche kausale Arbeit der Geschichte" [28].

4.1.2. This theory of the formation of potential historical concepts by means of value interpretation is important to Weber not least because it is a factor of *clarity*. Where intuitionism would have defined the task of the historian as a "Nacherleben", a vague "empathy" with times past, Weber's doctrine of value interpretation forces the scholar to *formulate* and *express* exactly what he means: "Denn im Gegensatz zum bloßen "Gefühlsinhalt" bezeichnen wir als "Wert" ja eben gerade das und nur das, was fähig ist, Inhalt einer Stellungnahme: eines artikuliert-bewußten positiven und negativen "Urteils" zu werden ..." [29]. The advantages of this precision are obvious: on the one hand, it has heuristic value, because it makes for clear-cut definitions of the problems involved; and on the other one, it permits subsequent *control* of the sufficency and correct content of the concepts.

24. GAW, pp. 260–61; see also GAW, p. 245.
25. GAW, p. 122.
26. GAW, pp. 123, 246, 252.
27. Thus, GAW, p. 262 speaks of "mögliche Wertungen [des Objekts]".
28. GAW, p. 263; see also, for instance, GAW, pp. 122, 251.
29. GAW, p. 123; see also GAW, pp. 125, 245–46.

Though a special merit of value interpretation is its precision, an "artistic" aspect is by no means excluded. In this connection, Weber remarks that value interpretation may allow certain persons, whose negative value judgments concerning a particular object or event would otherwise have led them to ignore this object, to obtain "neutral" knowledge of its richness of potential meanings. Analysis "at a distance" may thus serve to enlarge the spiritual horizon of the observer. As Weber puts it: "Die "Interpretation" der geistigen, ästhetischen oder ethischen Schöpfung wirkt eben hier, wie diese letztere selbst wirkt . . ." [30].

4.1.3. The function of practical *value judgments* in the process of value interpretation was to supply the *occasion* for such value interpretation. But this does not exhaust their role. Of course, value interpretation does not include the formulation of practical, personal value judgments of the object under investigation; on the contrary, such practical value judgments are only acceptable within an *a priori* frame of reference of norms, which will for the most part be *logical norms:* for instance, the historian may brand Marx' "Das Kapital" as being logically deficient in certain respects [31]. And Weber by no means regards such a normative frame of reference as obligatory [32]. But on the other hand, he points out that a strongly developed "valuational gift" may have great influence on the value interpretation: ". . . "Wertung" [ist] die normale *psychologische* Durchgangsstufe für das "intellektuelle Verständnis" " [33]. In a sense, a great "intellectual distance" between the scholar and his object, or peculiarities and eccentric traits in his value-oriented personality, may have a fruitful influence on his scholarly work, because he may light on value relations which would never have occurred to the mind of the "ordinary" scholar [34]. Here, valuation becomes a positive aid to

30. GAW, p. 247. One may wonder why Weber consistently chooses *intellectual or or artistic products,* the "geistige, ästhetische oder ethische Schöpfungen" mentioned above, to exemplify his theory of value interpretation. Thus, GAW, p. 246, the enumeration of possible objects of value interpretation includes a number of literary works, ranging from Marx to Marie Bashkirtseff, and one work of visual art, but not a single "non-artistic" phenomenon. This circumstance is taken by Henrich (*Einheit,* 1952, pp. 67–68) as the basis of an elaborate construction, which does not, however, seem to have sufficient support in Weber's text. Rather, the explanation should be sought in the special context of Weber's argument. His general point is that *any* object chosen as the point of departure of historical investigation may, and in principle ought to, be subjected to value interpretation (*cf.* GAW, p. 251, where the focus of discussion sudddenly expands to include, for instance, the modern system of international relations and Germany as a State). The only condition is that any object of value interpretation must "embody" human values, a point the importance of which will be explained below (pp. 236–38).
31. GAW, p. 246.
32. GAW, pp. 123, 246.
33. GAW, p. 124.
34. A striking example of such an imaginative and fruitful value interpretation is

scholarship. At the same time, of course, one runs the risk that the eccentricities which may enrich the work of the scholar may also, if they get out of hand, warp it to the same extent [35].

4.1.4. A point of interest is Weber's explicit assertion that a *large number* of value aspects may become important, that a historical object may in fact contain an infinity of valuational points of attack, and that this will increase its historical interest accordingly [36]. The "normal" value aspects which serve to define the various "cultural sciences": politics, art, literature, etc., by no means exhaust the possibilities of the scholar; on the contrary, the latter, if he wishes to break new ground, will also have to go further than the "everyday valuations for household purposes" [37].

4.2. A difficulty which cannot be removed without further analysis is Weber's repeated use of the term "philosophy of history" ("Geschichtsphilosophie") to cover the process of value interpretation. This expression seems to remove the whole procedure from the realm of empirical science and to make it dependent on precisely those premises which the introduction to the present account claimed that it was possible (not: necessary) to dispense with.

4.2.1. Weber's point of view is formulated most directly in *Knies II:* the "Ermittlung der "Werte", welche "wir" in [den] Objekten "verwirklicht" finden *können*" (quoted above), is unambigously labelled: "...—mithin eine geschichts*philosophische* Leistung" [38]. The question is, however, what exactly Weber means by this. If we consider the context, it is at least clear that Weber takes great pains to stress that value interpretation is certainly *not history* in the empirical sense (i. e., the linking up of concrete historical objects with their causes and effects) [39]. This view, which is also encountered in *Kritische Studien* [40], is easy to understand: as we have seen, value interpretation was meant as a preparatory exercise, which did not *in itself* qualify as history, whether it be in Weber's narrow or in a looser sense of that term. Value interpretation consists in the analysis of a phenomenon in the light of a previously given value and consequently, in the last resort, includes the enumeration of the concrete value judgments which would be formulated by a person committed to the value in question. Such an analysis is of course value analysis as well as object analysis [41]; and in a way, it is

Weber's own thesis of the connection between the Protestant ethic and the "spirit" of capitalism.
35. GAW, pp. 124–25.
36. GAW, p. 253.
37. GAW, p. 263.
38. GAW, p. 122.
39. GAW, p. 122.
40. GAW, pp. 248–49, 263.
41. *Cf. infra,* p. 152.

quite fair to regard it as "applied conceptual analysis", in the same way that statements concerning the relation of certain means to certain ends may be termed "applied causal analysis". And just as the means-end analysis, for a given end, has a validity equal to that of the causal laws on which the analysis is based, the "applied conceptual analysis" (value interpretation) must be supposed, for a given historical object, to possess a validity equal to that of theoretical conceptual analysis. And Weber's view that the status of the latter is equivalent to that of ordinary empirical truth, is beyond doubt [42].

4.2.2. The question is now whether Weber *explicitly* states that value interpretation is "applied conceptual analysis" with its clear status as science. In this connection, the continuation of the passage on "Geschichtsphilosophie", GAW, p. 123, is of relevance. Here, Weber writes: "... sie [the normal, non-evaluating value interpretation] [ruht], logisch betrachtet, auf der Grundlage "dialektischer" Wert*analyse* ..." And if we examine the use in Weber's works of the expression "dialektische Wertanalyse" [43] (the meaning of which is not immediately obvious), we find it to cover the conceptual analysis of the inner consistency or lack of mutual contradiction of ideas and values. In the same way, the essence of value interpretation is to connect a valuational attitude with an object and to carry out a conceptual analysis of the various relations in which the object becomes relevant to the value in question.

4.2.3. But if value interpretation, both in Weber's view and to a modern analysis, keeps within the realm of truth of empirical science, i. e., is not "philosophical"—in the sense of the word used in the present account—why then does Weber employ the expression "Geschichtsphilosophie"?

GAW, p. 262, Weber himself, although not quite clearly, defines the concept of "Geschichtsphilosophie": "Wenn wir nun ... diese Wertungen selbst, mit denen wir an die Tatsachen treten, zum Gegenstand der Analyse machen, so treiben wir—je nach dem Erkenntnisziel—entweder Geschichts-*philosophie* oder Psychologie des "historischen Interesses". In other words, the philosophy of history—or at least parts of it—consists in the analysis of the conceptual structure and relations of values (whereas psychology looks for empirical causes, and is not concerned with normative validity). This "philosophical" treatment of values can take various forms. It may try to demonstrate the *objective validity* of certain values; in that case, it comes under the heading of metaphysics, i. e., clearly rates as "philosophy" in our sense of the term. As will be shown below, Weber does not even attempt this kind of demonstration [44]. Another possible variety of "the philosophy of history" is the analysis of the *essential nature* of values (their character as

---

42. This conclusion pre-empts the result of later discussions, *cf. infra,* pp. 160–62.
43. GAW, pp. 151, 312.
44. *Cf.* GAW, p. 47n1.

expressions of will, practical imperatives, etc.); here, we move within the realm of the philosophical theory of values, which is also usually ignored by Weber. Finally, the "philosophy of history" may have a "dialectical" character, i. e., consist in *conceptual analysis;* and in this function, its results possess full scientific validity; they are products of "scientific philosophy" [45].

A renewed examination, in the light of these conclusions, of the passages in which Weber speaks of "Geschichtsphilosophie" [46] shows that they are all covered by the common definition given above ("analysis of values *per se*"), and that, moreover, they all belong to the sub-category of conceptual analysis, that is, non-philosophical (in our sense of the term) and scientific investigation [47].

4.3. The later essays do not shed any new light on the problems of value relation in general and value interpretation in particular. *Wertfreiheit* simply refers to the earlier essays [48]: Weber's attitude does not seem to have changed in the interval. It is therefore not uninteresting to note that the only independent remark in *Wertfreiheit* concerning these problems tends to stress the close connection between value interpretation and conceptual analysis: "[Die Wertdiskussionen] können dem wissenschaftlich, insbesondere dem historisch arbeitenden, Forscher vor allem die Aufgabe der *"Wertinterpretation"* ... weitgehend abnehmen oder doch erleichtern" [49].

5. As we have seen, the concepts of social science were, in Weber's view, formed by means of a relation between immediate reality and one or more values, by which certain parts of reality were selected. This is only a preliminary to the proper task of social science, however. This task, as Weber sees it, consists, at least as far as history in the narrow sense of the word is concerned, either in the causal *explanation* of the phenomena which have attracted the interest of the scholar, or in determining the causal *effects* of these phenomena. At this point, the original problem of the historical sciences reappears:

45. This exegesis of the term "Geschichtsphilosophie" is supported by Weber's use of the term "Sozialphilosophie" (GAW, pp. 150–51) which covers a similar kind of conceptual analysis. (GAW, p. 156, "Sozialphilosophie" refers to philosophy properly speaking, a point which is, however, made quite clear by Weber himself).
46. GAW, pp. 122, 124, 254, 262–63.
47. The only passage which may in this connection give rise to doubts is GAW, p. 254, which may contain a reference to a discussion (a few pages earlier) of the status of values as "Fühlen", "Wollen" or "Sollen", i. e., to an exercise in philosophical value theory. Interestingly enough, the passage in question is a defence of *Rickert's* elaboration of the doctrine of value relation. The whole question will be treated at greater length below, pp. 118–20.
48. GAW, pp. 499n1, 511.
49. GAW, p. 512.

any phenomenon has an infinite number of *possible* causes and effects, both because it is made up of an infinity of partial phenomena, and because any cause or effect determined is in its turn caused by or the cause of an infinitely great number of other phenomena [50]. What criteria should the historian apply in order to select those factors which are to be included in his account?

5.1. The most unambiguous answer to this question is found in *Objektivität* [51]: "... *was* Gegenstand der Untersuchung wird, und wie weit diese Untersuchung sich in die Unendlichkeit der Kausalzusammenhänge erstreckt, das bestimmen die den Forscher und seine Zeit beherrschenden Wertideen ..." [52]. Here, the properly historical work of discovering causes and effects is subjected to the same methodological condition as the primary choice of the historical object: in both cases, *value relation* provides the means of reducing the immense multiplicity to a clear structure.

On the other hand, we have Weber's claim that the results of historical science are *objectively* true [53]. This claim is advanced more than once in *Kritische Studien* [54], and later on in *Stammler,* where Weber writes: "Nur der *Ausgangs*punkt des [kausalen] Regressus ... wird durch die "Relevanz" vom Standpunkt der "Norm" aus bestimmt" [55].

Between these passages, Weber seems to be caught in a dilemma: in *Objektivität,* he acknowledges the role of value relation even within the chains of causation, while in *Stammler* (and implicitly in *Kritische Studien*), he seems to deny it, since value relation is here restricted to the formation of the original historical concept.

5.2. The contradiction is however more apparent than real. Weber's point of view, as it emerges from a closer examination of the essays in question, may probably be put more or less as follows:

Any occurrence—in *Kritische Studien,* Weber takes the death of Caesar as an example [56]—is in itself impossible to grasp in every particular. In order to reduce it to the elements which appear significant to him, the historian performs the original value relation. If, for instance, he is writing the political history of Ancient Rome, it will be the political aspects of the event which will engage his attention. This selection introduces a subjective element into the process, since other scholars or scientists (e. g. surgeons or art historians) might have adopted a different aspect, and, under it, selected quite different features of the event as the important ones [57].

50. *Cf. supra,* pp. 98–99.
51. The discussion (above all in *Kritische Studien*) of the general problem of causation in the historical sciences is not directly relevant to the question treated here
52. GAW, p. 184.
53. For a fuller discussion of this point, *cf. infra,* pp. 131–37.
54. For instance GAW, pp. 261, 271.
55. GAW, p. 341.
56. GAW, pp. 272–73.
57. GAW, p. 272.

Now the factors which made the politically important features of the event "Caesar's death" politically important, i. e., roughly speaking, the causes of the *political* event "Caesar's death", may *in principle* [58] be objectively ascertained. In this sense, Weber is justified in saying that we may obtain "absolut und unbedingt gültige" [59] knowledge of the causes of a historical phenomenon. If the number of these causes is limited, it is just possible that the historian will list them all, although even here certain (mostly negatively defined) factors might well be left out (as, for instance, the fact that Caesar did not have a permanent bodyguard); but as these factors are pursued further, the scholar will find that the chains of causation which he unravels will to an increasing degree run outside his field of interest; accordingly, he will limit himself to a few such chains, which considerations of space will even prompt him to abandon beyond a certain point of the inquiry. The same process of selection will take place with regard to the *effects* of the event.

This process of selection again undoubtedly represents a *subjective* element; but this subjectivity does not render the conclusions reached any less objective, but only forces the historian to formulate them with greater caution. Instead of results of the form: "A was *the* cause of X", he must content himself with more limited statements, usually of the type: "A was a *necessary* condition of X". If we take the correctness of the intellectual operations on which such statements are based, as given, the conclusions which they embody are certainly *objectively* true; but they are also partial and *subjective* in that they only relate to certain aspects of an event (summed up in the term "the event X") and only state *certain* necessary conditions of this (partially defined) event (in this case, the cause A, which the historian regards as interesting) [60].

6.1. Although Weber by and large subscribes to Rickert's doctrine of value relation as the "forma formans" of the object of history, and consequently as the criterion for the formation of historical concepts, it is interesting to note that the concept of value which he employs is markedly weaker and less characteristic than the one discussed in the chapter on value freedom [61].

58. In *practice,* this causal analysis in the field of the social sciences poses a number of problems, which are, however, for the most part irrelevant to the present account (but *cf. infra,* p. 136).
59. GAW, p. 261.
60. Schelting (*Wissenschaftslehre,* 1934, p. 241) and Judith Janoska-Bendl (*Methodologische Aspekte des Idealtypus,* Berlin 1965, p. 50) come to the same conclusion, while Pietro Rossi (Stammer (ed.), *Weber,* 1965, pp. 91–92) seems to go rather too far when he asserts that Weber saw the subjective element as influencing not only the selection but also the results of scientific activity (*cf.* Loos, *Wertlehre,* 1970, p. 10n57).
61. *Cf. supra,* pp. 25–31.

In the discussion of the *occasion* of value relation and value interpretation, viz, the practical value judgment, the term "value" is obviously employed as the result of a conscious reflection on Weber's part: he sees practical valuation as important and positive as such. But as soon as the argument is transferred to the theoretical level, the "relation at a distance" of the scholar to his object, Weber only infrequently speaks of "theoretical value relation" and of "Wert" as being at the root of such value relation, and instead employs expressions of a less philosophical nature, like, for instance, "Interesse" and "Bedeutung". This wording apparently reflects a deliberate tendency in Weber's discussion: thus, we find him more than once claiming that the concept of "Wertbeziehung" is superfluous from a purely methodological point of view. In this connection, it is interesting to refer to a number of rough notes jotted down by Weber on his first reading the *Grenzen* [62]. Here he criticizes Rickert for employing the vague and ambiguous terms "Werth" and "Werthbeziehung" to denote ideas which can be expressed more simply:

"So sehr man Rs Begriff "Werth" ... schütteln mag, es fällt nichts Anderes heraus als die Bedeutung *wissens*werth u. also bedeutet die "Notwendigkeit" der Beziehung auf einen Werth nichts andres als der *scheinbar* recht triviale Satz: daß die Geschichte aus der empirischen *Wirklichkeit* das *Wissenswerthe* darstellen solle".

In *Knies* (which is probably in part based on these notes), the same point is made, but in weakened form and without the polemical thrust [63]. In *Kritische Studien,* we find a similar utterance, according to which the "strikt auf dem Boden der Methodik verweilende Betrachtung" has to content itself with the simple demonstration of "[das] *faktische* Vorhandensein eines ... Interesses" [64]. And as late as *Wertfreiheit,* the doctrine of value relation is summed up in the short statement that the term "value relation" represents "die philosophische Deutung desjenigen spezifisch wissenschaftlichen "*Interesses*" ... , welches die Auslese und Formung des Objektes einer empirischen Untersuchung beherrscht" [65]. Moreover, certain of Weber's own discussions seem to serve as a practical correlate to this theoretical doubt concerning the relevance to methodology of the concept of value [66].

6.2. Why, then, does Weber retain the concept of value, or, for that matter, introduce it at all? For Rickert, this was a necessity because his demonstration of the objectivity of the historical sciences depended on the assumption of general and objective values as criteria of selection. Whether this necessity

62. DZA II, Rep. 92, No. 31, Vol. 6.
63. See for instance GAW, p. 92n1.
64. GAW, p. 254.
65. GAW, p. 511.
66. For instance GAW, pp. 161–64, where the classification of phenomena as being "ökonomisch", "ökonomisch relevant" or "ökonomisch bedingt" is carried out without any reference to the concept of value.

118

was also incumbent on Weber is a question which will be discussed below [67]; but if we provisionally abstract from this point, it might seem legitimate and tempting to interpret the doctrine of theoretical value relation, as it appears in Weber's methodology, as referring simply to the choice of different *aspects:* the expression "value relation" would in that case have to be regarded as a linguistic remnant, and be taken to imply simply that reality may be viewed under many different aspects or points of view, and that different parts of reality become relevant under different aspects. This interpretation would in fact bring Weber into accordance with modern views of the fields and tasks of the social sciences.

6.3. Against this hypothesis must be set certain explicit denials by Weber himself. The most unequivocal of these denials is found in *Kritische Studien* [68]. Franz Eulenburg and others had criticized Rickert and claimed that his theoretical value relation was in fact nothing more than a subsumption under *general concepts,* "... dasselbe wie die gesonderte Behandlung der "chemischen", "physikalischen" usw. "Seite" der Vorgänge in den Naturwissenschaften" [69], that it was, in other words, an aspect theory trimmed with metaphysical value judgments. Weber angrily rejects this criticism: "Dies sind merkwürdige Mißverständnisse dessen, was unter einer "Wertbeziehung" verstanden ist und allein verstanden werden kann" [70]. As for practical *valuation* (which is relevant to the discussion, since it is a *practical* "value relation"), he—correctly—insists that it is something essentially different from subsumption under a general concept; but when it comes to theoretical value relation, the argument begins to waver. Weber claims that the value interpretation of a historical object consists in pointing out with precision the numerous different relations in which the object engages our interest, and that the object which in this way engages our interest to the maximum is that which is relevant under a large number of aspects; and he concludes from this that it is just as pointless to try to exhaust the whole complex of meaning and values which we find in such an object, by referring to *one* general concept, as it would be to try, for instance, to say the *whole* truth in one sentence [71]. But Eulenburg had no such ambitions, which do not in fact form part of his or later actual attempts to formulate an aspect theory: on the contrary, the idea of an aspect theory in Eulenburg's view implied that the reality and actual meaning of a phenomenon could only be rendered by a—possibly unending—listing of its meaning under different aspects [72].

67. Pp. 131–34.
68. GAW, pp. 252–54.
69. GAW, p. 252.
70. GAW, p. 252.
71. GAW, pp. 253–54.
72. "... wenn man von einem einzelnen Objekt wiederum *alle* Seiten—seine sog. "Wirklichkeit"—zu erfassen sucht, so muss man diesen Prozess in Teilprozesse

A more pertinent argument of Weber's is found in a letter, of March 28th, 1906, to Gottl-Ottlilienfeld [73], in which Weber writes:

"Übrigens ist *nicht* zuzugeben, daß "Werth" und "Interesse" oder "Wesentlich-keit" auf gleicher Stufe ... stehen ... "Werthen" führt unter *allen* Umständen in eine andere Welt hinein (die des "stellungnehmenden Subjektes" nach Münsterberg). Das "Interesse" und das "Wesentliche" als Leitseile gibt es auch in den *nomothe-tischen* Wissenschaften, die Verankerung an "Werthen" *nicht*".

Although this passage makes it quite clear that Weber is opposed to any "aspect interpretation" of the doctrine of value relation, it may be asked how far-reaching this opposition is. Two points become relevant here. First, Weber supports his retention of the value element by pointing to the necessity of distinguishing between the natural and the social sciences (as defined by their respective typical methods); in other words, the necessity adduced is rooted in a respect for *Rickert's* methodological problems and aims [74]. And secondly, it is worth noting that Weber elaborates his defence of the role of the concept of value by claiming that we should otherwise look in vain for "der letzte Grund" of scientific interest [75]: the latter is thus not *re-interpreted* as a value relation but *explained* by it; and this kind of seeking for "ultimate reasons" seems to belong to a sphere which embraces philosophy rather than mere methodology. Here again, what is defended is clearly the *Rickertian* position.

One is led to conclude that Weber normally actively defends the retention of the explicit value element in the theory of the constitution of scientific objects only when he argues on Rickert's behalf (in rejoinders to criticism, and thus in a context which is imposed upon him). In his own methodological constructions, the use of the concept of value is still *justified;* but because of Weber's exclusive interest in the social sciences, the concept does not carry its original weight; it becomes unproblematical—indeed, in purely method-ological discussions, unnecessary—and it comes to be employed tonelessly [76]. To close the gap between Weber's version of the theory of value relation and

zerlegen und *nacheinander* doch wieder *einzelne* Oberbegriffe zugrunde legen" (Franz Eulenburg, "Gesellschaft und Natur", *Archiv,* vol. XXI (1905), p. 526n18; this is the essay to which Weber refers).

73. DZA II, Rep. 92, No. 11.

74. This circumstance is explained by the fact that the primary target of both Eulen-burg and Gottl is Rickert, not Weber (*cf.* certain remarks in the letter of March 28th, 1906 to Gottl, and in letters to Eulenburg (April 16th, 1905) and v. Bort-kievicz (March 12th, 1906) (copies in DZA II, Rep. 92, No. 30, Vol. 4)).

75. DZA II, Rep. 92, No. 11.

76. One of the clearest expressions of this interpretation is found in Schulz, *Politisches Denken,* 1964, p. 340. A large number of other commentators (for instance Baum-garten, *Weber,* 1964, p. 592 and Loos, *Wertlehre,* 1970, p. 34) tacitly replace "value" by terms like "aspect" or "point of view" in their interpretations.

a modern aspect theory, all that is needed is the subsidence of the conflict between the natural and the social sciences [77].

6.4. In fact, only in two cases—if we still abstract from the problem of the objectivity of science—does Weber's discussion of the formation of historical concepts depend on the use of the concept of "value" rather than "aspect" or "point of view": first, as mentioned above, with regard to the *valuation* which is the *point of departure* of historical interest; and, secondly, in connection with his treatment of the implications of *value interpretation*. And on this last point, his analysis comes close to the general conceptual analysis of values which is primarily relevant not to the logic of history, but to the practice of social science [78].

7. Summing up, we can conclude that Weber's discussion of the relation between values and phenomena, without being actually different from Rickert's, implicitly diverges from it on the following points:

Rickert's careful distinction between the object level and the research level is blurred, mainly as a result of Weber's attacks on objectivism and intuitionism: since the investigator is allowed to assume, within limits, the role of practical valuation of the historical phenomena, the transition to his primary role of theoretical contemplation, although stressed by Weber as essential in principle, is not necessarily in practice identical with a complete shift from an (observed) historical valuation on the object level to an (experienced) value relation on the research level, but often simply amounts to an internal change of roles of the scholar.

The theory of value relation as applied merely to history as a type of scientific activity is elaborated by means of Weber's reflections on value interpretation as a practical aid to the scholar; partly because of his belief in the importance of brilliant and unusual valuations on the scholar's part, Weber discusses this practical aid almost as if it were a scientific technique.

Weber puts the number of possible aspects as very great, indeed as infinite in the case of the most important historical objects; he sees the discovery of new aspects as highly desirable.

The reflections on value interpretation as an *instrument* for the construction of historical concepts tends to be absorbed by the more concrete treatment of values as an *object* of social science.

Weber's discussion of theoretical value relation eliminates the need for a specific reference to value, and paves the way for a modern aspect theory.

77. *Cf. infra,* p. 137, for a discussion of the contribution made by Weber himself towards such a subsidence.
78. "*Der logische Sinn der axiologischen Klärung des praktischen Handelns und seiner gegenwärtigen konkreten Situation und der logische Sinn der historischen Objektformung stehen ... bei Max Weber in bezug auf wesentliche Pünkte in voller Parallelität zueinander*". (Schelting, *Wissenschaftslehre,* 1934, p. 206).

2.2.3. The origin of the values; the concept of culture

As in the account of Rickert's argument, it may now be asked *where* the scholar is to seek the values to which he relates historical phenomena, or, to formulate the question in accordance with a modern aspect theory, what are the criteria of his choice of aspects. The fundamental reason for this question is of course the need for a *justification* of the value or aspect chosen. As we have seen, the demand for such a justification was in Rickert's case extremely urgent, since the question of the origin of the values was identical with that of their validity, and consequently of the *objectivity* of the results of historical science.

1.1. In Weber's case, this problem of objectivity and validity is best approached by asking whether the scientific *material* has a decisive influence on the selection of values.

The answer to this question was already intimated in the discussion above of Weber's attack on objectivism and intuitionism. Obviously, a scholar whose basic premise is that history only has the meaning with which we provide it, will find it difficult to accept a view according to which this intrinsically "sinnlos" subject-matter has any material influence on the formation of historical concepts. Weber's work contains a profusion of positive statements to this effect. Thus, he writes in *Kritische Studien:* "[Es ist] ... unbedingt ... richtig, daß jede "Geschichte" vom Standpunkt der Wertinteressen der *Gegenwart* geschrieben wird ..." [1], and in *Objektivität:* "Wenn immer wieder die Meinung auftritt, jene Gesichtspunkte könnten dem "Stoff selbst entnommen" werden, so entspringt das der naiven Selbsttäuschung der Fachgelehrten ..." [2]. On the contrary, Weber points out that the view which he criticizes contains a logical circularity, since it assumes the historical object to be formed—that is, defined—by means of values which are to be taken from ... the object itself [3].

1.2. But even though these passages conclusively show that the values cannot *initially* be found in the historical subject-matter, Weber might still possibly accept the idea of a *subsequent* control, in the sense that the material, although not invested with a "value initiative", might, by virtue of its content, *prevent* certain value relations from being carried out. As mentioned above [4], this may even be the most accurate rendering of Rickert's

---

1. GAW, p. 259. See also GAW, p. 254.
2. GAW, p. 181. The opposition to Rickert, both in views and in their actual expression, is flagrant; *cf. Grenzen,* 1902, p. 567: "Die leitenden Werthe der Begriffsbildung sind von einer "objektiven" wissenschaftlichen Darstellung stets dem historischen Stoff selbst zu entnehmen"!
3. GAW, pp. 175–76.
4. P. 91.

thought. However, Weber explicitly rejects even this moderate version (whose logical structure is admittedly just as circular as that of the extreme one): for instance, he states in *Objektivität* that it is legitimate to classify an institution as "economic"—i. e., mainly interesting to the scholar in its economic aspect—even where its origin and function give no evidence of *deliberate* attempts to orientate it according to an economic point of view [5]. And in *Knies II,* Weber is quite explicit:

". . . [value interpretation] interpretiert . . . nicht, was die historisch an der Schaffung des "bewerteten" Objekts Beteiligten ihrerseits subjektiv "empfanden"—das ist ihr, soweit sie Selbstzweck ist, nur eventuell Hilfsmittel für unser eigenes, besseres "Verständnis" des Wertes—, sondern was *"wir"* in dem Objekt an Werten finden "können"—oder etwa auch: "sollen" " [6], [7].

The practical valuations found on the object level may at the most serve as useful signposts to the scholar and fire his imagination; but often, and particularly if the period investigated is one which has been discussed by scholars for a long time, the "object valuations" will be generally known, and have been used by generation after generation of unimaginative historians; they will be "Alltagswertungen". In such cases, Weber clearly expects scholars who are not methodologically "unconscious" to leap boldly to new and untried points of view.

2. It follows from this conclusion that the subject-matter of historical science may include more than culture in Rickert's normative sense of the word. This, however, only shifts the problems of the origin of the values, but does not solve it. In Weber's view, the values entering into theoretical value relation originate on the research level, they are chosen, that is, from among the views of the social scientist (or of his contemporaries) as to what is of interest; but is the scholar justified in regarding himself as quite free in this choice, so free that the aspect chosen may turn out to be interesting only to himself? Or is the choice restricted to values which are "general" in some sense, as was the case in Rickert's construction?

It is not possible to state Weber's position on this point unambiguously. The blurring (noted above) of the distinction between the object level and the research level is accompanied by a similar uncertainty in the distinction between the scholar and his contemporary public, his "times". Weber usually employs the term "we": "we" find a phenomenon interesting; "our" values have a decisive influence; and while this terminology emphasizes the

---

5. GAW, p. 162.
6. GAW, pp. 122–23.
7. Similarly Schelting, *Wissenschaftslehre,* 1934, p. 226 and Loos, *Wertlehre,* 1970, 11n60.

opposition to objectivist views [8], it does not tell us whether Weber addresses himself to, and by this expression refers to, his colleagues only, or whether he speaks to and of all those of his contemporaries who take an interest in scientific writings [9]. That Weber himself is conscious of the vagueness of his use of the term "we" is indicated by the inverted commas with which he quite often provides the pronoun [10].

2.1. A number of arguments can be marshalled to support the view that Weber did not see any necessity for the scholar to restrict himself to, or even to include, empirically or normatively general values as criteria of selection, that, in short, he saw theoretical value relation as the personal prerogative of the scholar. In this connection, the discussion of value interpretation (summarized above) seems important, since it was clearly marked by Weber's conviction that the ability to arrive at new and original value relations was a positive attribute of the scholar. A number of other passages also support this "subjective" interpretation. In *Objektivität*, for instance, Weber writes:

"... ohne Wertideen des Forschers gäbe es kein Prinzip der Stoffauswahl und keine sinnvolle Erkenntnis des individuell Wirklichen, und wie ohne den *Glauben* des Forschers an die *Bedeutung* irgendwelcher Kulturinhalte jede Arbeit an der Erkenntnis der *individuellen* Wirklichkeit schlechthin sinnlos ist, so wird die Richtung seines persönlichen Glaubens, die Farbenbrechung der Werte im Spiegel seiner Seele, seiner Arbeit die Richtung weisen. Und die Werte, auf welche der wissenschaftliche Genius die Objekte seiner Forschung bezieht, werden die "Auffassung" einer ganzen Epoche zu bestimmen ... vermögen ..." [11].

Here, Weber's view is clearly that the personal preferences of the scholar are important to the selection of value relations, so important, in fact, that these preferences may influence the way in which a whole generation formulates its problems. But the values arrived at in this way are not explicitly stated to be those of the scholar himself [12]; the beautiful expression "die Farbenbrechung der Werte im Spiegel seiner Seele" rather seems to imply that these values are shared by a number of people, and that they are only *modified*, varied, by the treatment which they receive at the hands of the imaginative scholar.

A more distinct "subjective" tendency is found in a passage in *Kritische Studien* where Weber concurs with the view of Ed. Meyer, according to which the historian draws the problems in terms of which he approaches his subject "aus sich selbst" [13]. And the "subjective" interpretation is most clearly

8. At least to the extent to which it is possible to state with certainty that Weber identifies himself with the *investigator*. This is usually the case in his methodological writings.
9. Instances of such neutral formulations are GAW, pp. 126, 175, 257.
10. For instance GAW, pp. 122, 123, 253.
11. GAW, p. 182.
12. As for the term "Kulturinhalt", *cf. infra*, pp. 125–31.
13. GAW, p. 254. This expression of Meyer's is particularly interesting since it is

supported by the footnote, quoted above, in *Knies II* in which he stresses the potentialities, with regard to value interpretation, of the "brilliant" historian, and then goes on to formulate his attitude as follows: "... in der Auswahl der leitenden Werte [of value relation] ... ist der Historiker "frei" " [14].

2.2.1. Against these passages supporting the "subjective" construction, we have to set a number of others which explicitly refer to the values of the contemporaries of the scholar as having an important influence on his value relation.

Thus, we find Weber talking of "allgemeine Kulturbedeutung" ("general cultural significance") [15], and, since he interprets "allgemein" in this connection as synonymous with "universell" [16], of "universelle "Kulturwerte" " and of "universell bedeutsame" phenomena [17]. Expressions like "die den Forscher und seine Zeit beherrschenden Wertideen" [18] are also relevant here.

2.2.2. Of course it is *possible* to see the contrast between the affirmation of the independent, subjective role of the scholar on the one hand and the importance of general or universal values on the other, as indicating an inconsistency in Weber's thought. This interpretation is not invalidated by the fact that the discrepancies which it would postulate must be reckoned among the "grobe Widersprüche" which Henrich refuses to find in Weber's work [19]; as mentioned in the introduction, the possibility of such discrepancies cannot *a priori* be excluded. However, it seems important to emphasize that Weber's construction is not in the same way as Rickert's dependent on the general validity of the values entering into the theoretical value relation. The complete chain of reasoning leading to this affirmation will be given at a later point [20]; but already at this stage, it seems useful to quote the most relevant passage in this connection, which is found GAW, pp. 183–84:

> "Ohne alle Frage sind nun jene Wertideen "subjektiv". Zwischen dem "historischen" Interesse an einer Familienchronik und demjenigen an der Entwicklung der denkbar größten Kulturerscheinungen, welche einer Nation oder der Menschheit in langen Epochen gemeinsam waren und sind, besteht eine unendliche Stufenleiter der "Bedeutungen", deren Staffeln für jeden einzelnen von uns eine andere Reihenfolge haben werden".

> intended as a *clarification* of an earlier statement, according to which the interests of "die Gegenwart" in general were decisive in the formation of historical concepts.

14. GAW, p. 124n1.
15. GAW, p. 178. Similarly GAW, p. 272: "allgemeine Bedeutung".
16. *Cf.* Rickert's essay "Die vier Arten des Allgemeinen in der Geschichte", reprinted in *Grenzen* [5], especially pp. 742–44, 751–52.
17. GAW, pp. 181 and 236n1 respectively.
18. GAW, p. 184.
19. Henrich, *Einheit*, 1952, p. 2.
20. Pp. 131–34.

This must surely be taken to mean that the values chosen may be of great importance to one person while commanding little or no interest in another. Consequently, these values need not always, and perhaps cannot ever, be *empirically* general, i. e., be regarded as interesting by *everyone*. However, the most essential part of the passage is the sequel:

"... Daraus folgt nun aber selbstverständlich *nicht*, daß auch die kulturwissen-schaftliche *Forschung* nur *Ergebnisse* haben könne, die "subjektiv" in *dem* Sinne seien, daß sie für den einen *gelten* und für den andern nicht. Was wechselt, ist viel-mehr der Grad, in dem sie den einen *interessieren* und den andern nicht".

In other words, the fact that values may lack empirical generality does not mean that a scientific work based on them in any way forfeits its validity or sees it restricted, but only that fewer, possibly very few, people are going to be *interested* in the work. This last consequence is of course serious enough from the scholar's personal point of view; but it is of no great *logical* impor-tance [21]. While it is therefore still *possible* to see the different passages quoted above as revealing an inconsistency in Weber's construction, it is not *necessary* to do so: the "subjective" and the "contemporary" point of view may be reconciled in an interpretation according to which the fundamental right of the scholar to choose his theoretical values freely is tempered by his interest in (but not duty of) choosing values whose empirically general incidence will ensure the necessary interest in his work. This not unreason-able construction is not contradicted elsewhere in the secondary literature on Weber and will be taken as the basis of subsequent discussions.

3. Much more important than the scattered references to "allgemeine" or "universelle" values is Weber's strikingly frequent use of the term "Kultur", by itself or in constructions like "Kulturwert" or "Kulturbedeutung" [22]. As mentioned above [23], Rickert defines a concept of culture which includes not only empirically but also normatively general validity. If Weber's use of the word can be shown to coincide with the Rickertian definition of the con-cept, the harmonizing conclusion arrived at above must be abandoned to make place for an interpretation which accords far more prominence to the general aspects of the values entering into value relation than to the subjective ones.

3.1. The concept of "Kultur" is analysed, explicitly or implicitly, by Weber, or at least given a closer definition by him, in various passages. Naturally,

21. Weber still reflects on the criteria for the selection of values, however, but for different reasons. *Cf. infra,* pp. 128–29.
22. For "Kulturwert", *cf.* GAW, pp. 54, 83, 178, 187, 257; for "Kulturbedeutung", *cf.* GAW, pp. 170, 175, 214, 232 (the term is mostly used in *Objektivität*).
23. Pp. 93–94.

these conceptual discussions must stand at the centre of the account given here.

The apparently most "Rickertian" statement is found in a footnote [24], in which Weber, in a context which includes theoretical value relation, laconically declares that "der hier verwendete "Kultur"-Begriff ist der Rickertsche" [25]. It should be noted, however, that Weber adds: "Absichtlich wird hier, vor der Auseinandersetzung mit Stammler"—that is, for polemical reasons rather than because of any fundamental necessity— "der Begriff "soziales Leben" vermieden", and that he refers to *Objektivität* and *Kritische Studien*.

If we turn to the latter essays, we find in *Objektivität* a thorough and interesting definition and analysis of the concept of "Kultur". Weber here writes: "Der Begriff der Kultur ist ein *Wertbegriff*. Die empirische Wirklichkeit *ist* für uns "Kultur", weil und sofern wir sie mit Wertideen in Beziehung setzen..." [26]. One notes the "subjective" approach which characterizes both the non-objectivist definition of culture (as something to which the *observer* ascribes importance) and, particularly, the complete vagueness as to what values are to be used as guidelines in this process. "Wertinteressen", is, as such, an expression which may refer to any value, from the solitary and subjective to the social and general ones.

GAW, p. 180, this definition is repeated in even more urgent form:

" "Kultur" ist ein vom Standpunkt des *Menschen* aus mit Sinn und Bedeutung bedachter endlicher Ausschnitt aus der sinnlosen Unendlichkeit des Weltgeschehens".

And shortly afterwards, in a passage on which Henrich, for instance, to a large extent bases his interpretation:

"Transzendentale Voraussetzung jeder *Kulturwissenschaft* ist *nicht* etwa, daß wir eine bestimmte oder überhaupt irgend eine "Kultur" *wertvoll* finden, sondern daß wir Kultur*menschen sind*, begabt mit der Fähigkeit und dem Willen, bewußt zur Welt *Stellung* zu nehmen und ihr einen *Sinn* zu verleihen" [27].

Here again, culture is defined *subjectively:* everything to which we ascribe meaning is, because and only because of this circumstance, culture; and any value which can be used in such a value relation may legitimately be called a cultural value. The latter part of the quotation should probably be inter-

24. GAW, p. 343n1.
25. A similar statement is found in the *Gutachten,* p. 103, where Weber, commenting on the term "Kulturwissenschaft", refers to Rickert. The quotation is not very important, though, since "Kulturwissenschaft" is obviously a purely formal reference without any attempt at closer discussion or definition. This formal character is emphasized by the fact that the reference to Rickert disappears in *Wertfreiheit* (GAW, p. 511), which now speaks of "empirische Disziplinen".
26. GAW, p. 175. Similarly in a letter of Oct. 10th, 1905 (DZA II, Rep. 92, No. 17) to Willy Hellpach.
27. GAW, p. 180. A perhaps not unimportant point of detail is the unusually great number of underlined words in this passage.

preted as a restatement of the argument without the special reference to the *theoretical* dimension: to a person moving in real life, culture is anything to which he takes a, practical or theoretical, valuational attitude. Nothing in the passage suggests that the values in question must fulfil certain conditions of generality.

In a number of other definitions or analytical passages, the same tendency is noticeable. GAW, p. 185, Weber records the following definition: " "Kultur", d. h. in ihrer Eigenart bedeutungsvoll". A similar, if implicit, reference is found in *Knies II* [28]. In *Kritische Studien,* too [29], "Beziehung auf Wertideen" is stated, without further specification, as constituting the essence of the concept of culture, an identification which is repeated in *Wertfreiheit* [30].
3.2. However, this array of, in themselves, unequivocal definitions does not completely solve the problem of the relation between Weber's and Rickert's concepts of culture. For one thing, they conflict with the footnote quoted above, which simply referred to Rickert; and moreover, it seems inexplicable that Weber, if "Kultur" to him meant *nothing* more than "the result of any value relation" should repeatedly go to the trouble of talking about "Beziehung auf *Kultur*wertideen", "*Kultur*bedeutung", etc. (my italics)— since the definition quoted would render such formulations purely tautological.

An interesting clue in this connection is provided by Emerich Francis, who points out that the term "Kultur" in Weber's work can often be replaced by "sozial" without any change of meaning in the given context [31]. Although this identification is not directly supported by the definitions of "Kultur" quoted above, it does seem to break through now and then. One instance of this is the footnote quoted above, GAW, p. 343nl, in which "Kultur" and "soziales Leben" are implicitly treated by Weber as synonyms; in other passages, the term "die Wissenschaften von der menschlichen Kultur" is placed in close conjunction with "die Wissenschaften vom sozialen Leben" or "die sozialwissenschaftliche Erkenntnis" [32]; and "die grundlegenden Komponenten der Kultur" are said to be the object of "die "Sozialwissenschaft" " [33]. This social aspect is even indirectly present in the definition, GAW, p. 180, quoted above, since the latter is accompanied by the remark: "Welches immer dieser Sinn sein mag, er wird dazu führen,

28. GAW, p. 83.
29. GAW, p. 262.
30. GAW, p. 512: "Kultur- und das heißt: *Wert*interessen . . ."
31. Emerich Francis, "Kultur und Gesellschaft in der Soziologie Max Webers", Karl Engisch, Bernh. Pfister, Joh. Winckelmann, *Max Weber. Gedächtnisschrift der Ludwig-Maximilians-Universität München* . . ., Berlin 1966, pp. 92, 98–99.
32. GAW, pp. 207 and 190 respectively.
33. GAW, p. 357.

daß wir im Leben bestimmte Erscheinungen des menschlichen Zusammen-
seins aus ihm heraus *beurteilen* . . ." [34].

Quite convincing reasons have been given to explain why Weber was somewhat wary of the term "sozial" in his early methodological work [35]; but
the passages quoted already seem to warrant the hypothesis that the term
"Kultur" indicates or evokes overtones of a *social* element; consequently,
the choice of the "Kulturwerte" which govern the value relation may be
similarly restricted to social values, the latter term being defined as values
which in their orientation reach beyond the isolated individual. It should
be noted, however, that all the passages supporting this hypothesis refer to
the *subject-matter* of history, while not explicitly setting limits to the *values*
which may be used as criteria of selection from this subject-matter.

3.3. If we compare the two possible definitions of culture sketched out
above: culture as meaningful reality, and culture as meaningful social life
(the latter concept defined as broadly and as formally as possible), with the
Rickertian one, we arrive at the following conclusions:

3.3.1. The first Weberian concept of culture contains no indications of the
nature of the values entering into the value relation. More especially, it
implies no need to keep to social values (as, for instance, politics, art, economics, religion, literature). Naturally, it is to be expected that the interest
of the scholar's contemporary public will be more readily awakened by work
based on such social criteria; but it is quite possible to conceive of scholarly
investigations where the criteria of selection are solitary rather than social
values, but which would nevertheless command considerable attention [36];
and even if works guided by such solitary values claimed the attention only
of a very narrow circle, perhaps only of the scholar himself, this deficiency
would not in Weber's eyes detract from the *validity* of the scholarly effort.
Consequently, the divergence from Rickert's concept of culture here seems
essential in a double sense: first, Weber nowhere excludes solitary values; and
secondly, the values chosen (whether solitary or social) do not have to be
empirically general in order to become logically acceptable.

3.3.2. The other possible, "social", Weberian concept of culture lies considerably closer to the Rickertian one. Although the social aspect is only in-

34. GAW, pp. 180–81.
35. Francis, *Kultur,* 1966, pp. 106–10.
36. The following may be a possible instance: In "Les caves du Vatican", André
    Gide introduces the idea of "le meurtre gratuit", i. e., murder motivated solely
    by the wish to commit it, and lacking any other "rational" motive. Such an act
    would be solitary in the sense that the murderer does not regard his victim under
    any specifically human aspect, but simply as a source of personal satisfaction,
    and, as such, as being on the same level as a number of non-human phenomena
    (food and drink, the delights of nature, etc). Nevertheless, an "histoire du meurtre
    gratuit" might be of considerable interest, for instance to psychologists.

troduced explicitly by Weber with regard to the subject-matter, this admittedly implies a similar limitation of the theoretical values, since under a solitary value aspect only those parts of the subject-matter would be considered important which interested the scholar because of their solitary, i. e., *non*-social, significance. Social life might of course serve as raw material for this scientific process; but its social aspects would not be incorporated into the concepts formed, so that the result could only in terms of a very formal interpretation qualify as part of "die Wissenschaften vom sozialen Leben".

It therefore seems reasonable to assume that Weber's second definition of culture contains the implicit demand that the scholar should only use *social* values as criteria of selection in his scientific work. But this is the narrowest construction which can be put on the passages in question in Weber's work: *any* social value must be considered as logically acceptable in his view. Whether it will also engage the *interest* of the public is a question without importance in this connection.

Rickert's concept of culture initially exhibits features which seem to permit a similar interpretation. Although he relates the "allgemeine Werthe", necessary to the objectivity of history, to the concept of "Gemeinschaft", the latter is defined very broadly: "allgemeine Werthe ... [kommen] nur bei solchen Menschen vor ..., die in irgend einer *Gemeinschaft* mit einander leben, also *soziale Wesen* im weitesten Sinne des Wortes sind", and the general values are accordingly referred to as "soziale Werthe" [37]. So far, Weber's "social" definition of culture is identical with the one proposed by Rickert.

Rickert's broad definition of "Gemeinschaft" is however only tenable as long as he does not bring up the question of the relation between empirical and normative generality. When this happens, a little later on in the argument [38], the result—which is necessary to Rickert's subsequent chain of reasoning—is that *normative* generality is seen as the major concept. In accordance with this conclusion, the formal definition of "community" is supplanted by a material one: Rickert now sees general values as those values which pertain to affairs or institutions common to "die Glieder einer Gemeinschaft" or "die Glieder einer Gesellschaft" [39]. "Gemeinschaft" becomes an objective *structure* embracing the persons or institutions who possess the "legitimate" (according to some higher principle) power of defining cultural values, as well as the persons of whom acceptance of these cultural values may "legitimately" (according to the same principle) be demanded.

37. *Grenzen,* 1902, p. 573.
38. *Cf. supra,* pp. 93–94.
39. *Grenzen,* 1902, pp. 576–77. The argument only deals directly with the historical *object;* but because of Rickert's doctrine of the interdependence of object and investigator, the conclusions are also valid for the "Gemeinschaft" of the scholar, a point which is made quite clear in the discussion *ibid.,* p. 629.

Nothing in Weber's work corresponds to this further limitation on Rickert's part of the number of value aspects in social ("cultural") science [40]. The scholar may often employ value criteria corresponding to those current among his contemporaries; but this is in no way a logical necessity in Weber's eyes. On the contrary, the scholar may base his work on social values which, although they are not normative from the point of view of his own "Gemeinschaft", his nation, may nevertheless claim a large measure of interest from his contemporaries (one instance of this would be a work concerning the history or sociology of religion, written in a society which, *qua* society, was quite indifferent to religion, but which tolerated religious interest and religious practice on the part of its citizens: this work might be considered very interesting, but would apparently not, according to Rickert's criterion, be based on cultural values). As mentioned above, Weber even expects that scholars who base their work on unusual value relations may *influence* their contemporaries: the fact that certain value criteria lack general validity may thus even endow them with a positive educational function.

3.3.3. A *third* concept of culture lies close to the surface in Rickert's work, without ever emerging completely, viz, the view of cultural values as embodying that which is normatively *valuable*. In this connection, one may point to the definition of "Kultur" [41] as "... alle die Güter ..., welche allen Gliedern einer Gesellschaft am Herzen liegen sollten, und deren Pflege von ihnen gefordert werden darf". This definition corresponds to a common-sense idea of culture frequently met with, and is indeed often used by Weber in this sense [42]. But this use of the word as a linguistic aid does not permit the conclusion that Weber deliberately defined "culture" as identical with the *positively* valuable part of social life. On the contrary, he sharply rejects "Mißverständnisse so grober Art, wie die Meinung, Kulturbedeutung solle nur *wertvollen* Erscheinungen zugesprochen werden", and adds: "Eine *Kultur*erscheinung ist die Prostitution so gut wie die Religion oder das Geld ..." [43]. If we substitute "prostitution" for "culture" in Rickert's "posi-

---

40. On the contrary, an early draft note from Weber's hand explicitly qualifies Rickert's view of culture as emanationist, perhaps even as wholly metaphysical: "... die konsequenten philosophischen Vertreter dieser [cultural] emanatistischen Ethik [werden] unweigerlich zu bestimmten metaphysischen Aufstellungen, mindestens zur Annahme der *Absolutheit* des Werthes jener Idealität in welche der Einzelne eingegliedert werden soll, gedrängt ...—so jetzt Rickert—..." (DZA II, Rep. 92, No. 31, Vol. 6). Before 1913, Weber only twice employs the term "Gemeinschaft", and in both cases (GAW, pp. 35n1, 141) in connection with a criticism of organic political theories. After 1913, the word acquires a technical meaning which is not far removed from the definition of "sozial" made above (*cf.* GAW, p. 441).

41. *Grenzen,* 1902, p. 577.

42. Francis, *Kultur,* 1966, pp. 94–98.

43. GAW, p. 181.

tive" definition of culture quoted above, we immediately see that Rickert cannot expect Weber to support this definition [44].

3.3.4. The discussion can be summed up as follows: Neither of Weber's two possible concepts of culture contains the normative element which is a prominent feature of the Rickertian definitions of culture. The first discussed and most explicitly defined of the two Weberian concepts also lacks the social element which is essential to "Kultur" in Rickert's sense. The provisional hypothesis according to which Weber allows the scholar a free choice of theoretical values may therefore be regarded as correct, subject to two modifications: the value chosen must permit the endowment of reality with *meaning;* and it must moreover, if the second of Weber's definitions of culture is adopted, allow the socially (in the widest sense of the word) relevant phenomena to stand out, i. e., it must be a social value. On the other hand, it should be stressed that a large number of the theoretical values *actually* employed by historians are probably covered *both* by one of Weber's *and* by Rickert's definitions of cultural values [45].

2.2.4. Objectivity

1. The next problem, in a certain sense decisive both to Weber and to Rickert, is that concerning the *objectivity* of the results of social science. First of all, it is necessary to provide a firm logical basis for the conclusion touched upon [1] and even pre-empted [2] in the account given above, according to which the question of the general validity of the value criteria in Weber's view, unlike that of Rickert, is irrelevant to the validity of the scientific results.

1.1. As we have seen, Rickert's conclusion was based on the following argument: since immediate reality is infinite in its multiplicity, any science

---

44. Probably, though, the definition in question results from the confusion between the "technical" and the common-sense concepts of culture; such a confusion is almost inevitable when technical terms lie close to everyday language, as they do in the *Grenzen.* Cf. on this last point Weber's criticism of Rickert's term "Naturwissenschaft", GAW, p. 126n1.

45. The interpretation adopted in the present work on this point is most clearly supported by Schulz (*Politisches Denken,* 1964, p. 340), who denies that the concept of "Kultur" in Weber's work carries any speculative connotations at all. The same position, if in a less explicit form, is taken up by Schelting (*Wissenschaftslehre,* 1934, pp. 226–27). Otherwise, most commentators seem to assume that Weber's acceptance of the Rickertian *term* of "Kultur" also implies an acceptance of Rickert's *definition* and *discussion* of this term. This assumption is not unnatural, considering the number of instances where Weber's vague and imprecise use of the term seems to cover a normative concept of the Rickertian kind.

1. Pp. 113, 117–18.

2. P. 124.

has to select its subject-matter from it. The objectivity of the scientific results therefore cannot reside in their correspondence with the *material* on which they are based, since this material is always the result of a prior selection and processing; instead, the objectivity of the results must depend on the *objectivity of the criteria* of this prior selection. Since the criteria of selection in the historical, "cultural" sciences are cultural values, we need a demonstration of the empirical objectivity of these cultural values; and Rickert carries out this demonstration by establishing empirically that the cultural values in question are *normatively* general.

1.2. This kind of demonstration is completely lacking in Weber's work. From the very beginning, on first reading *Grenzen,* he rejects the whole idea in a note (DZA II, Rep. 92, No. 31, Vol. 6), writing:

"Das *faktische* Bestehen *allgemeinen* Interesses an manchen Teilen der Wirklichkeit u. das *Fehlen,* auch das faktisch *allgemeine* Fehlen von solchem an dem überwiegenden andern Teil derselben ist als Thatsache *psychologisch* recht leicht zu erklären, ebenso wenigstens in ihren allgemeinen Zügen die *Grad*abstufung ... [,] der Versuch aber— *Normen* zu *formulieren* führt m. E. ... in die Metaphysik ... [unfinished]".

In *Knies I,* the question of the validity of the guiding theoretical values is relegated to the field of the philosophy of history [3]. In *Objektivität* [4], *Knies II* [5] and *Kritische Studien* [6], we find similar refusals of a discussion of the question. In the last of these essays, Weber illustrates his view by an example: it is not possible, he says, to *prove,* by logical or empirical argument, the value of a scientific interest in Marx' "Das Kapital", in modern political history, or in any other historical object [7].

1.3. These passages fully conform to the principle of value freedom, according to which it is illegitimate to deduce the normative *validity* of a value from empirical *facts;* but they do not seem to apply to Rickert's logical short-circuit, since the substance of the latter is rather the attempt to prove *empirical* objectivity by means of the demonstration of the existence of valid cultural *norms.* Actually, however, Rickert's argument does consist in a deduction of values from empirical fact, since the essential part of his concept of "empirical objectivity", i. e., the possibility of claiming that certain values are objectively valid inside a certain culture, can only be safeguarded by means of a *normative* element which prevents individuals from "opting out" of the culture and of the objective validity. Translated from philosophical into concrete terms Rickert's argument would run as follows: The persons or

3. GAW, p. 47n1. "Geschichtsphilosophie" should here probably be interpreted as "philosophy" in the non-scientific sense of the word adopted in the present work.
4. GAW, p. 213.
5. GAW, p. 122.
6. GAW, p. 261.
7. GAW, p. 251.

institutions who may, in my view, legitimately set norms for the culture in question have defined the values a, b and c as being cultural values; consequently, every single individual who is a member of the cultural community in question *ought* to acknowledge the cultural values a, b and c, i. e., ought to consider these values to be valid for himself. In terms of this, admittedly very concrete, interpretation of his position, Rickert turns the recording of an empirical fact (the "setting" of the norm) as *true* (valid) into a basis for the demonstration of the *normative* validity of a value; and this is precisely the kind of logical jump which Weber wants to avoid.

Thus, Weber severs the connection between empirically demonstrated and normatively valid values; at the most, his interest goes as far as the empirical generality of the latter, but this is not for logical reasons but because he sees it as *practically* desirable that the work of scholars should command interest among their contemporaries. In principle, Weber regards the theoretical values which guide the work of social science as purely subjective—except perhaps for a necessary social element, if we take his second definition of culture to be the important one—and not tied to any higher philosophical or logical necessity.

2.   This undoubtedly brings Weber into harmony with his own demand for the *value freedom* of science. But on the other hand, the question of the *objectivity* of science presents itself with renewed urgency: if the theoretical values which have a constitutive function in social science are completely subjective, how are we able to speak of "objective" knowledge in these disciplines at all? Has not the strict adherence to the principle of value freedom brought with it the logical disintegration of the "Sein" category? Have not *both* spheres, the sphere of scientific inquiry as well as the value sphere, been made optional, so that you *choose* scientific truth in the same way as you choose (indeed, *must* choose) a value?

The account given above showed that Weber certainly did not accept this interpretation. But the central problem is of course that of *defending* the objectivity of social science, and this problem grows more acute when Rickert's line of defence is rejected. In the light of this, Weber's own argument seems surprisingly brief. Even in *Objektivität*, the title of which indicates that the essay is above all meant to discuss the question of objectivity, the direct treatment of the problem is limited to a few pages and has an almost casual character [8].

2.1.   While Weber in *Roscher* keeps quite silent on this point, in *Knies I,* he breaks with "categorical" objectivity and introduces his own solution: "objective" reality is here defined as the reality which we find when we

8. The implications of this circumstance will be examined below, pp. 137–40.

abstract from all value judgments *and value relations,* i. e., as identical with immediate reality [9]. Consequently, this "objective" reality in itself has no settled value or interest; but the conclusion arrived at above still holds, according to which Weber regards immediate reality as consisting of something more than just an infinite number of fragmentary events and qualities, and in fact ascribes to it a common-sense structure. Weber believes that it is possible in this mass of material, which is structured and infinite at the same time, to record qualitative changes and unanalysed causal connections: "... das "objektivierte". ... [10] Geschehen kennt eben lediglich den Begriff der qualitativen Veränderung, und die objektivierte kausale Beobachtung dieser Veränderung denjenigen der Kausalungleichung" [11].

Consequently, questions of empirical fact and of causal connections must, *and can,* in Weber's view, be answered by reference to "objective" reality. Rickert was forced by his logical fragmentation of immediate reality, and led by his Kantian belief in "categorical" objectivity as fundamental, to try to demonstrate the objectivity of the guiding theoretical values of the historical sciences; but Weber's view of immediate reality as "objectified" and "structured" permits him to define "objective truth" by means of a *reference to reality* [12].

2.2. In *Knies I,* this definition of the objectivity of the scientific results is only implicit in the definition of the term "objective"; it is formulated once, but in a very tentative fashion [13]. In *Objektivität,* however, Weber approaches the problem of objectivity more directly, and devotes particular attention to the relation, in social science, between subjective value criteria and objectively true results.

The necessity of the former is emphasized just as strongly as the possibility of the latter: "Es *gibt*", Weber writes GAW, p. 170, "*keine* schlechthin "objektive" wissenschaftliche Analyse des Kulturlebens oder ... der "sozialen Erscheinungen" *unabhängig* von speziellen und "einseitigen" Gesichtspunkten ..."; and the *subjectivity* of these points of view is constantly stressed [14]. It is impossible to take the whole of reality as one's subject-

9. GAW, pp. 49, 53, 63, 65. *Cf. supra,* p. 107.
10. The concept "objektiviert" is here used by Weber in order to assure the distinction between the amorphous stream of consciousness postulated by intuitionism and the "structured" statements of empirical fact arrived at by means of "distant" investigation.
11. GAW, p. 63; see also GAW, p. 53.
12. Naturally, this does not mean that all the philosophical problems connected with the objectivity of statements of fact have been solved. But Weber's view at least seems to correspond closely to the "reference theory of truth" mentioned by Brecht (*Theory,* 1959, pp. 49–51), who believes this solution to be adequate from the point of view of Scientific Method.
13. GAW, p. 75n2(4).
14. GAW, pp. 182, 183, 213.

matter; no discipline provides us with the whole truth concerning any phenomenon, however minute. But within this subjective and partial framework, the results of scientific inquiry *can* attain the status of empirical truth, of objective validity: they are *not* subjective in the sense that they "für den einen *gelten* und für den andern nicht" [15]; on the contrary, they constitute "rein *kausale* Erkenntnis". And this assumption of the objectivity of truth in its turn means that the scholar is not allowed to proceed at will when performing a causal analysis: he is not allowed to stress, for purely subjective reasons, one cause rather than another; in his scholarly work, he is "selbstverständlich ... an die Normen unseres Denkens gebunden" [16].

2.3. Perhaps the best summary of his views with regard to the simultaneously subjective and objective character of the results of social science is given by Weber in *Kritische Studien:*

"Es ist ... auf der einen Seite unrichtig, wenn E. M. [Ed. Meyer] ... meint, wir vermöchten *"niemals"* zu einer "absoluten und unbedingt gültigen" Erkenntnis von etwas Historischem zu gelangen: das trifft für die "Ursachen" nicht zu;—ebenso unrichtig aber ist es, wenn alsdann gesagt wird, es stehe um die Geltung der naturwissenschaftlichen Erkenntnis "nicht anders" als um die historische: das trifft für ... die *Art,* in welcher "Werte" in der Geschichte eine Rolle spielen, und auf die Modalität dieser Werte nicht zu ..." [17].

Since the two parts of Weber's definition of "objectivity", the emphasis on the objective validity and on the subjective framework of social science, differ in their polemical tendency and actual importance, it may be useful to treat them and their implications separately.

3. As mentioned above, Weber ascribes *objective validity* to the "causal" analysis of social science, i. e., to the demonstration of the causes or consequences of a certain, individually important, phenomenon. This analysis of course by definition also includes the recording of individual facts, a point which in one case is made quite clear by Weber [18].

3.1. The concept of objectivity, as defined by Weber for the social sciences, is in principle identical with the one current in *natural science.* Causal analysis consists in the practical application of a knowledge of empirical

15. GAW, p. 184.
16. GAW, p. 184; see also GAW, p. 124n1. Already in letters from 1895 and—quite clearly—1897 (to Alfred Weber and L. Brentano respectively; copies in DZA II, Rep. 92. No. 30, Vol. 4), Weber insists that it is fundamentally impossible to arrive at more than one correct causal explanation of a particular phenomenon.
17. GAW, p. 261. In a note (DZA II, Rep. 92, No. 31, Vol. 6) from 1905, Weber records this same double aspect, but with a stronger emphasis on the claim that the results of scientific activity are *objective,* and that their claim to this objectivity is based on their correspondence with the *material.*
18. GAW, p. 271: "... ein rein kausales, durch bloße Feststellung "objektiv", durch Wahrnehmung und kausale Deutung, zu ermittelnder Tatsachen lösbares Problem ..."

regularities, and this knowledge is supplied by the natural sciences (in Rickert's—and Weber's—logical sense of the word) [19]. Consequently, it must be possible to claim for the causal explanation of historical phenomena the same degree and kind of validity as that possessed by the general laws by the aid of which the explanation is established. Weber of course realizes that most of the "laws" which the historian applies when carrying out a causal analysis are of an everyday kind and may even, if formulated with precision, appear slightly comical [20]. But this does not in the least weaken the logical principle.

On the other hand, Weber is perfectly aware that the possibilities open to natural science of controlling results by means of experiments and prognostic hypotheses cannot be extended to the social sciences, since the primary objects of the latter are, by definition, interesting by virtue of their individual characteristics, so that two or more of such objects are hardly ever alike in all essential respects. However, this circumstance does not lead Weber to abandon his claim that the results of social science are objective, but instead impels him to elaborate a specific theory of causation in the social sciences, the theory of the "objektive Möglichkeit" ("objective possibility") [21]. A complete discussion of this concept lies outside the scope of the present work. It must suffice to mention that the term refers to an intellectual operation by which the scholar attempts, by means of his knowledge of scientific or everyday empirical regularities, to ascertain whether a certain actual historical event would have been likely to occur if one or more of the causal factors actually present had been lacking; in other words, the scholar tries to establish whether a combination of causes which was altered or reduced (compared to the actual one) would still have been sufficient to bring about the actual result (that is, those of the elements of this result which seem important to the observer). In continuation of this, the scholar may try to imagine what *other* outcomes seem to be the "objectively possible" results of the altered or reduced combination of causal factors. The significance of this kind of analysis does not primarily reside in its concrete value to history or social science—in fact, it hardly amounts to more than a conveniently labelled, and perhaps rather more controlled, version of ordinary historical analysis—but rather in its purely theoretical, artificial, hypothetical character, what H. Stuart Hughes calls "the fictional approach" [22]. The full importance of this approach, and its connection with other problems in Weber's work, will become apparent in chapter 4 (on the ideal type).

19. *Cf. infra*, p. 168.
20. See for instance GAW, p. 112, where Weber describes the following rhyme by the German humorist Wilhelm Busch as a "ganz tadellos formuliertes "historisches Gesetz" ": "Wer sich freut, wenn wer betrübt/macht sich meistens unbeliebt".
21. See in particular GAW, pp. 266–90.
22. Hughes, *Consciousness*, 1958, p. 310.

3.2. In establishing the objectivity of the social scienses, Weber has accomplished his primary and short-term purpose, viz, the successful rejection of the pretensions of *posivism*. By defining this objectivity in such a way as to make it not only equal in dignity to, but in certain essential respects even identical with that claimed by natural science, he has at the same time repudiated the concept of spiritual intuition propagated by the *intuitionist* school and also—since objectivity is now rooted in the subject-matter and not in the categories—dissociated himself from *Rickert*'s neo-Kantian views of objectivity. But, moreover, he has in a sense rendered the conflict between natural and social science unimportant for the future. Rickert still bases his argument on the demonstration of two aims of scientific investigation which, even if they are of equal rank and equally "objective", are diametrically opposed to each other: this fundamental opposition form part of his proof. Weber's chain of reasoning, on the other hand, implies the fundamental *unity* of all empirical disciplines: the criteria of truth which are his tacit premises when he speaks of "causal validity" and of "truth which must hold even for a Chinese" [23], what he calls "die Regeln der Logik und Methodik" [24], in fact constitute an embryonic and unreflected form of Scientific Method in Arnold Brecht's sense. In this perspective, Weber's campaign against positivism is terminated not only by an armistice, but by an actual conclusion of peace [25].

4. This conclusion of peace with natural science is secured from degenerating into a capitulation, by means of the *subjective framework* into which the objective results of social science have to be inserted. It is significant that

23. *Cf. supra,* pp. 25, 48–50.
24. GAW, pp. 598–99.
25. Occasionally (for instance in Loos, *Wertlehre,* 1970, pp. 13, 22), one meets this last conclusion in the pointed form that Weber himself adhered to a *positivist* ideal of scientific inquiry. This is only correct if "positivism" is interpreted broadly, as roughly synonymous with "the ideal of scientific inqury usually accepted today in the field of natural science". Weber had no wish to be associated with positivism in its *classical* form, a fact that is clearly brought out in his letter to Hermann Kantorowicz of Oct. 10th, 1908 (DZA II, Rep. 92, No. 19), in which he dissociates himself from Kantorowicz' professed "positivism".

While it is correct to say that Weber "den transzendentalen Rationalismus des Neukantianismus . . . in eine methodologisch gezügelte Forschungsrationalität [überführt]" (Friedrich Jonas, *Geschichte der Soziologie, IV,* Reinbek 1969, p. 29), it is extremely important to emphasize that Weber's "Scientific Method" does not even remotely approach the status of a practical set of "instructions for scholars" or of a "logical chronology" like the one constructed by Brecht (*Theory,* 1959, pp. 27–29). It does not seem warranted to modernize Weber by dressing up his conclusions in Brechtian terminology, as when Jonas speaks of "intersubjektiv überprüfbares Wissen" (*Geschichte,* 1969, p. 37). The problem of how actually to *attain* objective knowledge is treated by Weber less as a problem of method than as one of ethics.

the discussion of this subjective aspect—as was the case with the discussion of the value element in the principle of value freedom—commands Weber's attention to a far greater degree than the objective one. This is obvious in *Objektivität*: Weber's treatment of the foundations of empirical objectivity is sparing, indirect, almost casual, whereas the apotheosis of the essay, the almost passionate last pages which culminate in a sweeping quotation from Goethe, are devoted to the problems of the theoretical values, the changing aspects[26].

4.1. The reason for this special interest may of course partly lie in the necessity of retaining the subjective element of social science as a bulwark against positivism and its involuntary helpmates, objectivism and intuitionism, in order to prevent the "Götterdämmerung aller Wertgesichtspunkte" which Weber sees as a grim possibility[27]. In the general subjective tendency of his approach, and in the definition of the spheres of the respective groups of sciences on grounds of method rather than according to some uncertain criterion applying to their subject-matter, Weber is completely at one with Rickert. But it is significant that Weber does not stop here, but elaborates those implications of the subjective point of view which are in fundamental conflict with Rickert's doctrine:

Rickert's foundation of the objectivity of social science in the objectivity of the essential methodological category, i. e., of the cultural values as criteria of selection, had forced him to take a static view of these value criteria. According to him, a correct and thorough review of the given historical material would once and for all bring to light all the value criteria which could claim to be legitimate in relation to this material; later changes, however radical, in the ranking and estimate of the cultural sciences would make no difference in this connection:

"Die Geschichtswissenschaft wird daher wohl auch niemals dazu kommen, alle ihre Darstellungen deswegen umzustossen, weil die Werthe, die sie benutzt hat, nicht mehr als normativ allgemein betrachtet werden, d. h. sie wird es nicht für nöthig halten, mit ganz neuen Kulturwerthen ihre Begriffe zu bilden, denn sie muss das menschliche Leben der Vergangenheit immer aus sich selbst [ɔ: das Leben] heraus verstehen ..."[28].

His rejection of the neo-Kantian categorical objectivity allows Weber to dispense with this static view of the theoretical values, and to emphasize to a far greater degree the importance and positive role of the personality of the scholar in the field of social science. Not only the value aspects in general, but even the practical valuations of the scholar, are given a central place in the scientific process.

4.2. The value aspects are justified by their usefulness and fruitfulness:

26. In view of this, Weber's choice of the *term* "Objektivität" for the title of the essay does not seem particularly apt. *Cf. supra,* p. 16n2.
27. GAW, p. 186.
28. *Grenzen,* 1902, pp. 638–39.

"[Die einseitige Analyse der Kulturwirklichkeit] ist so lange nicht "willkürlich", als der *Erfolg* für sie spricht, d. h. als sie Erkenntnis von Zusammenhängen liefert, welche für die kausale Zurechnung konkreter historischer Vorgänge sich als *wertvoll* erweisen" [29]. As mentioned above, Weber sometimes states this fruitfulness to be a direct consequence of the ability of the scholar to reach beyond ordinary points of view, in short, of his *personality*. Where Rickert saw the historical material as dictating its conditions to the scholar, the latter may, in Weber's view, by virtue of his value-oriented personality, fashion the views of right and wrong, of significance and insignificance, of a whole age [30].

5. But while Weber's elaboration of the subjective point of view permits the scholar to leave his imprint on an age, it also compels him to acknowledge that his work will by necessity grow obsolete and unimportant. This view of the constant change of scientific aspects is formulated by Weber with the urgency and literary passion which he often reserves for truths which run contrary to his personal preferences and which—perhaps *for this reason*— must be expressed with full respect for their status as true [31]. In *Objektivität*, the question is still formulated in close connection with problems of methodology:

"Endlos wälzt sich der Strom des unermeßlichen Geschehens der Ewigkeit entgegen. Immer neu und anders gefärbt bilden sich die Kulturprobleme, welche die Menschen bewegen, flüssig bleibt damit der Umkreis dessen, was aus jenem stets gleich unendlichen Strome des Individuellen Sinn und Bedeutung für uns erhält ... Es wechseln die Gedankenzusammenhänge, unter denen es betrachtet und wissenschaftlich erfaßt wird. Die Ausgangspunkte der Kulturwissenschaft bleiben damit wandelbar in die grenzenlose Zukunft hinein ..." [32].

Kritische Studien contains a laconic statement to the same effect [33]. It is only in *Wiss. Beruf* that the idea is taken up again, but now marked by a strong note of personal commitment which indicates that the problem occupies a central place in Weber's thought:

"Jeder von uns ... in der Wissenschaft weiß, daß das, was er gearbeitet hat, in 10, 20, 50 Jahren veraltet ist. Das ist das Schicksal, ja: das ist der *Sinn* der Arbeit der Wissenschaft, dem sie, in ganz spezifischem Sinne gegenüber allen anderen Kulturelementen, für die es sonst noch gilt, unterworfen und hingegeben ist: jede wissenschaftliche "Erfüllung" bedeutet neue "Fragen" und *will* "überboten" werden und veralten. Damit hat sich jeder abzufinden, der der Wissenschaft dienen will. [...]

29. GAW, p. 170.
30. GAW, p. 182.
31. For a similar view of Weber's emphasis on facts which are "uncomfortable" to himself, *cf.* Günter Abramowski, *Das Geschichtsbild Max Webers,* Stuttgart 1966, p. 181.
32. GAW, p. 184; see also GAW, pp. 213–14.
33. GAW, p. 262.

Wissenschaftlich ... überholt zu werden, ist—es sei wiederholt—nicht nur unser aller Schicksal, sondern unser aller Zweck" [34].

The literary quality of these last passages should not be allowed to obscure their real importance. Weber's view of aspects as ever-changing can be seen as part of a wider theoretical whole, which has a decisive influence on the principle of value freedom, on his reflections on values as an object of scientific inquiry, and on his views concerning the essential relation between science and politics [35]. More concretely it serves as an additional indication of the "fictional" tendency in Weber's theory of the concepts of social science: in itself, any true statement is partial and one-sided; and not even a constantly growing complex of such partial truths will ever be completely exhaustive [36, 37].

Appendix A. Henrich's and Tenbruck's discussion of Weber's concept of reality. The question of Weber's concept of reality has above all been discussed by Henrich and Tenbruck, with the paradoxical result that the sociologist Tenbruck implicitly assumes the existence of philosophical elements in Weber's thought, whereas the philosopher Henrich explicitly denies it [1].

Behind Weber's methodological argument, Tenbruck sees "entscheidende ontologische Voraussetzungen" [2], which he in turn identifies by reference to *positivism*, with its belief in a system of elementary and *essential* (physical, chemical, etc.) causal relations. He admits that Weber in practice limits himself to "die Erscheinungen aus dem Bereich der alltäglichen, sinnlichen Wahrnehmungen" [3]. But Tenbruck still maintains that there is no lower limit to these "Erscheinungen", that they can always be disintegrated even further by analysis, so that the boundless multiplicity of which Weber speaks must be regarded as completely amorphous, as a "nackte Tatsächlichkeit" [4]. And since Tenbruck tacitly equates this amorphous immediate reality with Weber's concept of reality altogether, he is still able to maintain his ontological assumption: in Tenbruck's view, Weber's concept of reality is quite unstructured; it contains no objects or events; in short, it implies that all perception is the result of a previous *processing* of reality, and as such artificial and unreal. In terms of this interpretation, "real" reality, the "nackte Tatsächlichkeit" is in principle more amorphous, lies "further down", than any given perception. To Tenbruck, Weber's "reality" is fundamentally non-empirical, and, in its metaphysical sense, ontological.

Henrich rejects this interpretation. To him, Weber's description of immediate

34. GAW, p. 592.
35. *Cf. infra,* pp. 178–79, 247–49.
36. This is probably the correct construction to put on the following passage in a letter from Weber to Gottl of March 28th, 1906 (DZA II, Rep. 92, No. 11): "Bei [den idiographischen Disziplinen] ist [die Einseitigkeit des Gesichtspunkts] stets Provisorium ..."
37. For a different interpretation of Weber's concept of science, *cf.* Appendix B of this chapter.
 1. Henrich, *Einheit,* 1952, pp. 11–15, 18–20; Tenbruck, *Genesis,* 1959, pp. 598–601.
 2. Tenbruck, *Genesis,* 1959, p. 598.
 3. *Ibid.,* p. 599.
 4. *Ibid.,* p. 600.

reality as boundless is a proposition which relates to "das Wirkliche *als solches*" [5], i. e., not to some philosophically (be it epistemologically or ontologically) defined "basic" reality, but to reality *as perceived,* naturally and unscientifically, by human beings. Webers assumption "... *enthält also lediglich eine empirische Aussage, die freilich von höchster empirischer Allgemeinheit und umfassender Geltung ist*" [6].

There seems to be no doubt that Weber's discussions always relate to reality in its perceiv*able* aspect. In these discussions in *Roscher,* he several times uses the term "anschaulich" [7], and in later essays the word "empirisch" [8]; and even when this is not the case, it is generally clear from the context that the level of discussion is that of reality *as it appears* to human beings [9]. Consequently, Tenbruck's assertion that Weber's argument contains ontological, fundamentally non-empirical, elements, cannot be accepted.

This does not solve the whole problem, however. Even if we modify Tenbruck's argument so that the empirical character of the elements of reality is preserved even when the latter are analysed into their component parts, we still have to consider his statement that Weber's concept refers to a totally unstructured reality: "In der [i. e., Weber's] Wirklichkeit gibt es keine Gegenstände" [10]. This in its turn means that all descriptions of objects are purely subjective and fortuitous, since reality itself does not provide any objective criterion for the construction of such objects: "... die Erkenntnis läßt sich nicht mehr von der Wirklichkeit her legitimieren" [11].

Compared with this position, Henrich's interpretation does not seem quite consistent. On the one hand, Weber, as he reads him, holds that reality in its immense multiplicity is not the reality which we normally perceive, but the result of an intellectual processing of this "normal" reality. On the other hand, Henrich supposes this processing to result only in the removal of the *scientific* structuring of immediate reality; consequently, reality viewed as an infinite multiplicity is the pre-scientific, and in this sense the *original,* one [12]. This construction is necessary in order to support Henrich's contention that Weber's statements concerning the "infinite multiplicity" are "empirical", i. e., refer to something which can be observed in practice. But in order to provide this "empirical", "pre-scientific" reality with a material *content,* so that it does not simply stand as an abstract link in the chain of reasoning, Henrich is also forced to ascribe a *structure* to it; and to preserve the consistency of his system, he must maintain that the elementary description of this structure does not amount to a scientific processing of it [13]. In this immediate, infinite multiplicity, we may even, he claims, find "Dinge",

5. Henrich, *Einheit,* 1952, p. 11.
6. *Ibid.,* p. 11.
7. ("intuitable"). GAW, pp. 6n6, 11, 14.
8. GAW, pp. 75n2(1), 120.
9. See for instance GAW, pp. 171, 231–32.
10. Tenbruck, *Genesis,* 1959, p. 600.
11. *Ibid.,* p. 600.
12. Henrich, *Einheit,* 1952, p. 12.
13. *Ibid.,* pp. 14, 18. Otherwise, Henrich would have to defend the untenable position that a reality which was supposedly original and pre-scientific could not in any way be subjected to description without becoming scientific and consequently "unoriginal" and artificial; reality would become a figment of abstract thought like Tenbruck's ontological, non-empirical reality.

for instance a "concrete act of barter" [14]. This view is in flagrant opposition to Rickert's assumption that *any* description (and consequently any description of qualities, especially of complex ones like "barter") presupposes *words,* i. e., concepts, if only of a very vague kind, and so goes beyond immediate perception [15]. Generally speaking, Henrich's interpretation is difficult to uphold in the face of Tenbruck's strict and consistent "disintegrating" argument.

When we take into account Weber's own treatment of the question, however, this judgment has to be revised or rather supplemented in important respects. In fact, Weber's lack of logical consistency throws light on both Henrich's and Tenbruck's interpretations and explains the apparent insufficiency of their solutions. Both of them see Weber's argument as logically consistent and therefore feel justified in assuming that any logically correct construction in connection with the problem, as for instance the points made by Rickert, must have been taken over by Weber. In Tenbruck's case, this leads to the—logically unassailable—conclusion from the concept of "infinite multiplicity" that reality is completely unstructured, and to the attribution of this conclusion to Weber. For Henrich, who keeps closer to Weber's text, the task is more difficult; on the one hand, he must acknowledge the logic of Tenbruck's construction, and has to suppose that Weber stayed within the bounds of logic; but he has to square this view with the logically deficient common-sense concept of reality which emerges from Weber's text. The result, not unsurprisingly, is the confusion and wavering between the text and the demands of logic which was described above.

Appendix B. Henrich's interpretation of Weber's concept of science. Dieter Henrich is the only important commentator who tries to deny that Weber's concept of science, of changing aspects, etc., reflects a fundamentally *subjective* attitude [16]. He mainly relies on the passage, GAW, p. 213, in which Weber writes:

"... der uns allen in irgendeiner Form innewohnende *Glaube* an die überempirische Geltung letzter und höchster Wertideen, an denen wir den Sinn unseres Daseins verankern, schließt die unausgesetzte Wandelbarkeit der konkreten Gesichtspunkte, unter denen die empirische Wirklichkeit Bedeutung erhält, nicht etwa aus, sondern ein: das Leben in seiner irrationalen Wirklichkeit und sein Gehalt an *möglichen* Bedeutungen sind unausschöpfbar, die *konkrete* Gestaltung der Wertbeziehung bleibt daher fließend, dem Wandel unterworfen in die dunkle Zukunft der menschlichen Kultur hinein".

This Henrich takes to mean that Weber acknowledges the constancy of the "letzte und höchste Wertideen". Henrich does agree, however, that it is justified to speak of changing *aspects,* but only because he sees the subject-matter of social science, "culture", as constantly developing and changing. Consequently, the *problems* defined by the investigation of cultural phenomena under the guidance of constant cultural values will also change [17]. For instance, under the (cultural)

14. Henrich, *Einheit,* 1952, p. 12. The example is probably taken from the passage GAW, p. 171 quoted above.
15. "Selbst in den einfachsten Urtheilen, in denen wir, wie man zu sagen pflegt, nichts weiter thun, als die Wirklichkeit *beschreiben,* nehmen wir immer bereits eine weitgehende Vereinfachung und ... eine logische Bearbeitung der Wirklichkeit vor". (*Grenzen,* 1902, pp. 44–45).
16. Henrich, *Einheit,* 1952, pp. 30–35.
17. *Ibid.,* pp. 32–33.

value of economics the age of, say, Thomas More saw the question of the enclosures as an economic problem of culture, whereas the same cultural value would, to Weber and his age, serve to define the problem of modern capitalism. Thus, while Thomas More chose to investigate other cultures (in the actual case, the fictional society of Utopia), at least partly, in relation to their solution of the enclosure problem, Weber tried to show the importance of a number of historical factors in the evolution of modern capitalism: the aspects change, but the guiding value of "economics" remains unchanged.

Against this argument, the following objections seem relevant: Henrich's examples of values which Weber regarded as "constant" are of the same kind as Rickert's cultural values: religion, art, science, economics, etc. Now this does not seem justified, since Weber's concept of culture and of cultural values was not, as we have seen [18], in principle identical with the Rickertian one (although the concepts would probably often coincide in practice). It may also be mentioned that not even Rickert regarded cultural values as being completely constant; for instance, he explains that primitive peoples may not have known the cultural value of "art" [19].

Finally, and most important, it should be emphasized that the scope of the passage adduced by Henrich is much more limited than he supposes. Above all, one may point to several passages in the same essay in which Weber explicitly, and in direct contradiction to Henrich's conclusion, speaks of the changes through time of the *guiding values:* GAW, p. 183, for instance, he writes: "Ohne alle Frage sind nun jene Wertideen [20] "subjektiv" ... Und ebenso sind sie natürlich wandelbar mit dem Charakter der Kultur und der die Menschen beherrschenden Gedanken selbst"; and GAW, p. 209, Weber quite clearly refers to "der unvermeidliche Wechsel der leitenden Wertideen" [21, 22].

On the other hand, the passage GAW, p. 213 does admittedly speak of constant *values* and changing *subject-matter.* Should this be taken to imply an inconsistency in Weber's thought, a hovering between the emphasis on the changing aspects and the importance of the evolution of the subject-matter?

If the passage in question is read in the wider context of Weber's argument, any possible major inconsistency seems to disappear:

If we base ourselves on the interpretation advanced above [23], Weber starts from

18. *Supra,* p. 131.
19. Heinrich Rickert, *Kulturwissenschaft und Naturwissenschaft,* Freiburg 1899, p. 59.
20. "Jene" refers to an earlier sentence which makes it clear that "Wertideen" should be interpreted as synonymous with "letzte Werte", i. e., with values of the kind which Henrich claims to be constant.
21. It is curious that Henrich bases his argument *solely* on the passage, GAW, p. 213, in spite of the fact that he in other connections quotes both of the passages contradicting his contention.
22. One may also refer to a letter from Weber to Willy Hellpach of Sept. 10th, 1905 (DZA II, Rep. 92, No. 17), in which he talks of "die Beziehung zu inhaltlich wandelbaren "Culturwerthen" "; a little later, he continues: "S. 71 [in Hellpach's work] verstehe ich dahin, daß ein über alle Culturwertungen hinweg *gleichartiges* Kriterium, welches jede historisch-subjektive Bedingtheit der Wertung [this should apparently be read as identical with "Wertbeziehung", *cf. supra,* pp. 104–06] *ausschließen* soll, von Ihnen in Aussicht gestellt wird. Ich vermisse aber—vorläufig— die Durchführung dieses ... Criteriums, und die Andeutung, *wie* es zu finden wäre". This at least seems to show that Weber himself did not in *Objektivität* (1904) claim to have found such a criterion.
23. P. 131.

the—not uncomplicated—assumption that a scholar committed to certain values will regard his own contemporary culture in the light of these ("primary") values and thereby form an opinion as to what the important parts of this culture are (in his eyes). For him, this position will determine the meaning and content of the concept of "contemporary culture". Now the scholar's investigation of *other* cultures (older or contemporary) will be guided *partly* by his primary values, and *partly* by his idea of contemporary culture; those parts of his raw subject-matter will become relevant to him which a) are important in relation to his primary values and b) have had or still have considerable causal influence on, or make an important contribution towards the understanding of, "contemporary culture", as he defines it.

GAW, p. 213, Weber starts by defining the objective validity of the results of social science without reference to the neo-Kantian objective categories. Instead, he reminds us that the categories, the "partial aspects", necessary to any scientific inquiry are *subjective* and essentially undemonstrable, and he repeats this view, which embodies his principal divergence from Rickert's concept of objectivity, in other passages: the empirical subject-matter selected as relevant under a particular aspect can never—and consequently never ought to—be made to prove the "objective" validity of the aspect in question.

Since the passage quoted by Henrich is directly connected with this chain of reasoning, it takes on a different complexion: Weber does not, as Henrich believes, claim that certain values are constant, but wishes to analyse critically a counter-argument to his own construction which runs as follows: if the scholar is committed to certain constant values, how then can we say that his points of view change? Weber rejects this counter-argument by pointing out that society is not static, but is involved in a process of constant change; consequently, different aspects of societal life are going to be selected as "contemporary culture" by the same scholar at different times, even if his own values remain constant; and since the aspects which he applies to his subject-matter are partly determined by his idea of contemporary culture, these aspects may change as a result of changes in the latter concept. A modern example which may help to elucidate Weber's position is the following: a scholar who, like Weber, is committed to the ideal of the politically responsible nation-state, might in 1920, in the light of this primary value, regard the bureaucratization of society as an essential phenomenon and problem of culture, and might take this as the starting-point of an inquiry into the history of Western rationalism, since this rationalism seemed to reach its culminating point in the development of modern bureaucracy; here, the concrete aspect is "rationalization"[24]. Under the guidance of the *same* primary value, this scholar might in our present culture find certain charismatic tendencies or "fascist" features far more important than bureaucratization, and the concrete aspect under which he would regard the "So-und-nicht-anders-Gewordensein" of modern culture, and consequently also those elements of the past which were the conditions of modern culture, viewed under this particular aspect, would therefore be "charisma" or "fascism" (defined in this or that concrete fashion), or perhaps generally "irrationalism". Presented in formalized terms, Weber's argument may be re-stated as follows: the concrete aspects a according to which the historian selects his subject-matter are a function of the primary value V and of contemporary culture c: $a = f(V, c)$; consequently, a may change not only with V but also with c (V remaining constant).

24. *Cf. infra*, pp. 275–78.

3. Values as an object of scientific inquiry: value analysis

1. The question of values as an object of scientific inquiry occupies a distinctive place in Max Weber's methodology and raises problems different from those concerning the principle of value freedom, theoretical value relation and the concept of the ideal type. The fundamental *susceptibility* of values to scientific investigation was no longer seriously contested by Weber's contemporaries; and consequently, the field of constructive argument was much more clearly defined than in the case of, for instance, the principle of value freedom.

The actual problems only presented themselves when it came to the question of the *ways* in which values could be treated as an object of scientific inquiry and, more particularly, the question of what results could *not* be achieved by means of such scientific treatment (which will be referred to below as *value analysis*). But in fact, these questions are nothing more than concrete versions of the problem of value freedom ("what methods and results should be invested with the predicate "scientific?"); both they and the answers which Webers supplies must be regarded as being of little independent interest.

It accords well with this conclusion that Weber himself, when reviewing (in *Wertfreiheit*) the errors and misconceptions of his critics [1], is particularly scathing about the claim that values could *not* be the object of value-free (in Weber's sense) science, a claim which he brands as a "fast unbegreiflich starkes Mißverständnis".

There are also indications that Weber had more support in this part of the debate on value freedom than elsewhere: at least, his own treatment of the question is less polemical and more detailed and constructive than his general arguments concerning the problems of value freedom [2].

While Weber's position with regard to the question of value analysis is

---

1. GAW, pp. 499–500.
2. This is only true, though, as far as his treatment of the positive *content* of the value analysis is concerned. His views on its *limitations* form part of his general position concerning the value freedom of the scientific results, and are formulated with corresponding polemical vigour.

not calculated to stir up methodological passions, it seems on the other hand to be far less important than his treatment of the other value problems. Unlike the idea of theoretical value relation, it does not involve the elaboration and restatement of complicated methodological arguments; nor does it contain definitions of new concepts which, like the ideal type, come to occupy a central place in later theoretical debates. The discussion of values as an object of scientific inquiry almost seems to be a detail in Weber's methodology, a special case presenting no great problems and possessing but little interest.

If Weber's treatment of the problem is still of considerable importance, and indeed on certain points essential to the further argument of the present work, the reasons lie not in the abstract methodological *premises* or *status* of scientific value analysis, but in the concrete *results* which Weber alleges that this value analysis yields or may be able to yield. His combination of "abstract" and "practical" value analysis forms the basis of the "methodological rationalism" which is a prominent feature of his theory of science and of his concrete research, and which in the present context helps us to understand both his concept of the ideal type and his view of the relation between science and politics. Moreover, scientific value analysis lays the foundations for Weber's theory of the fundamental value conflict, a theory which is closely connected with his demand for value freedom and which has a decisive influence on his theoretical and practical discussion of the nature of politics.

2. It may be seen as an indication of the fairly uncontroversial status of the question of values as an object of scientific inquiry that it is almost exclusively discussed by Weber in *Objektivität* and *Wertfreiheit* [3], that is, in the more general and positive "programmatic" essays. *Wiss. Beruf* and *Pol. Beruf* touch upon one aspect of the question (the value conflict); and in *Stammler,* Weber deals with problems which have a certain connection with those of value analysis, without however being directly relevant to the present account [4]. Weber also comments upon the questions of value analysis at the various sociological and social-political congresses in the years 1909–12 [5], but here, too, polemical overtones are largely absent.

Weber's position does not seem to have developed materially after its first statement in 1904. Certain points are only taken up in the later essays; other ones recede into the background; but by and large, Weber's attitude remains unchanged.

3. On this point, the *Gutachten* differs significantly from *Wertfreiheit;* these divergences will be taken into account in the course of the discussion below.
4. *Cf. supra*, p. 53.
5. Particularly of the *Verein* in Vienna 1909 and of the *Gesellschaft* in Frankfurt 1910.

3. As mentioned above, Weber is firmly convinced that values are in principle susceptible to scientific inquiry. He explicitly states this conviction in order to rebut the fallacious objection to the principle of value freedom that the latter also implies freedom from values on the *object level* of scientific inquiry. "Was folgt ...", he writes in *Objektivität,* "aus diesem Satz [the demand for value freedom]? Keineswegs, daß Werturteile deshalb, weil sie in letzter Instanz auf bestimmten Idealen fußen und daher "subjektiven" Ursprungs sind, der wissenschaftlichen Diskussion überhaupt *entzogen* seien". And, widening the concept of "Diskussion" [6], he continues: "Die Kritik macht vor den Werturteilen nicht halt" [7].

The question is rather how far this critical discussion may go without leaving the field of scientific inquiry. Weber gives one comprehensive answer to this question in his report to the first congress of the *Gesellschaft* in 1910: according to this, values are susceptible to scientific treatment concerning "... die *Tatsache ihrer Existenz,* ... die vermeintlichen oder wirklichen Gründe derselben, ... ihre Erfolge und Erfolgschancen, ... ihre "prinzipiellen" und "praktischen" Konsequenzen ..." [8] The part of the enumeration which is most important to the present account is that mentioning the "abstract" and "practical" consequences of values.

The "abstract" part of value analysis, consisting in a *"Durchleuchtung des ideellen Sinnes* unseres Wollens" [9], i. e., in the treatment of values in their theoretical aspect, as ideas, will be referred to in the following as *axiological* [10] *value analysis,* while the "practical" part, which is concerned with the empirical consequences of setting the value in question as a practical *goal,* will be called *teleological value analysis* [11].

The first of the following sections will deal with axiological value analysis, the second one with teleological value analysis. The "combined" value analysis, which brings together the two pure types, will be the subject of a third section [12]; the following section will be devoted to the discussion of the

6. *Cf. infra,* pp. 153–54.
7. GAW, p. 149. Similar passages are found GAW, pp. 499–500; GASS, p. 417.
8. GASS, p. 431.
9. Schelting, *Wissenschaftslehre,* 1934, p. 22.
10. The term is borrowed from Schelting (*Wissenschaftslehre,* 1934). Admittedly it is not a very happy one; but it seemed preferable to terms like "theoretical" which carry too many unspecifec connotations. French translators of Weber's work use "axiologique" to translate Weber's "Wert-"; and the English translators of *Wertfreiheit (cf.* Max Weber, *The Methodology of the Social Sciences* (transl., ed. Edward A. Shils & Henry A. Finch, intr. Edward A. Shils), Glencoe, Ill. 1949) would probably have avoided much vehement and justified criticism if they had used a similar technical term instead of the misleading expression "ethical neutrality".
11. The term "teleological" is meant to emphasize that the value is actually set as a goal, and that the focus of interest is its relations in *this* context.
12. As already noted by Schelting (*Wissenschaftslehre,* 1934, p. 20n1), axiological

analysis, referred to above, of the causes and consequences of the existence of certain values ("explanatory value analysis"); the fifth and last section will deal with Weber's views concerning the conflict of values.

3.1. Axiological value analysis

The concept of value with which Weber operates in his discussion of axiological value analysis is not unambiguous; instead, we find the same complex of "active" and "static" components, of value judgments and ultimate "ideals" which we met with above [1] in Weber's definition of the value elements which it was necessary to eliminate from the research level of scientific inquiry [2]. Weber is particularly fond of discussing value analysis, even in its axiological form, in terms of "Zwecke" [3], that is, in a pure means-end context. Below, this dual aspect of the terminology—which apparently does not indicate any material change in Weber's position [4]—will be retained. As far as the axiological value analysis is concerned, it is therefore sufficient to indicate that the value judgments, value axioms, goals, etc. analysed are all regarded as "ein rein ideelles, vom ... Forscher destilliertes Objekt begrifflicher Analyse" [5].

3.1.1. Content

1. When confronted with a given valuation or concrete goal, the scholar who conducts the axiological value analysis may first of all, in Weber's view, carry out an "Aufzeigung und logisch zusammenhängende Entwicklung der "Ideen", die dem konkreten Zweck zugrunde liegen oder liegen können" [6]. Weber's term "Ideen" probably is not meant to cover all the possible "ultimate" value axioms [7], but only those which are or have been pre-

and teleological value analysis will in practice always be applied together; but in view of the fact that Weber discusses the two forms separately, it seems justified to take over this analytical separation (which is also adopted by Schelting).
1. Pp. 26–31.
2. Among the "static" ones, we find, for instance, "Wert", "Idee" (GAW, p. 150) and "Ideal" (GAW, p. 151); among the "active" ones, "Werturteil" (GAW, p. 151) and "Wertung" (GAW, pp. 508, 510).
3. For instance GAW, pp. 150, 151, 508.
4. Cf. Schelting, Wissenschaftslehre, 1934, p. 22n4.
5. GAW, p. 346.
6. GAW, p. 150.
7. The term "higher" value axiom, goal, etc. will—in accordance with Weber's own usage, cf. GAW, p. 510, where he speaks of "höher aufsteigende" analysis—be used to denote the axioms and ends from which the value or goal in question may be deduced by conceptual logic. Similarly, the "highest" or "ultimate" values or goals are those which cannot be deduced by this means from any other axiom or goal. The word "general" has been purposely avoided in this connection, cf. infra, pp. 159–60.

sent as *conscious* motives if not to the person observed, at least to his age or to past generations, and which have been formulated with sufficient precision to become the legitimate object of empirical examination [8]. If, for instance, we were today to examine the political goal of referring the greatest possible number of legislative matters to decision by popular vote (referendum), we might as one possible ultimate "idea" behind this goal refer to and discuss Rousseau's theory of "la volonté générale".

To put it a little crudely, Weber seems to be referring to the scholarly presentation and systematic discussion of the various "isms", in the actual case (*Archiv*) of course mainly those connected with the theory of *social policy*. Weber himself sees this kind of analytical work as an "Aufgabe der Sozialphilosophie" [9].

It is characteristic of this kind of analysis that the immediate focus of scientific interest is not the concrete value or goal sparking off the investigations, but rather the systems and complexes of ideas to which this concrete value may, hypothetically, be traced back. When Weber sums up the general aim of axiological value analysis as the "*Kenntnis* der *Bedeutung* des Gewollten selbst" [10], this is in the present case only true in a hypothetical and limited sense. What the "analysis of ideas" can offer the persons who acts is a discussion of those *explicit* systems and complexes of ideas which *might* have been the ultimate premises of his concrete goal. *If* his goal was in fact derived from these ideas, such a discussion is naturally of value to him; but even then, its usefulness to the individual will often be limited by the fact that such systems or complexes belong on a rather low level of abstraction, so that the systematic "analysis of ideas" does not trace the concrete goal back to its abstract premises beyond a certain point. And possibly the actual motives for the setting of the goal were quite different from the "ideas" analysed, in which case the "analysis of ideas" has no real connection with the concrete goal which, in principle, formed its point of departure. Thus, the narrowing down of the object of the analysis to "Ideen" of a conscious and explicit kind, mostly stands in the way of a systematic and exhaustive axiological analysis of the motives leading to the setting of a concrete goal.

Actually, Weber's reason for introducing the "analysis of ideas" into the account of the possibilities of axiological value analysis must rather be sought in the *historical* importance of formulated and conscious ideas acting as driving forces of behaviour [11]. From this general point of view, it seems much

---

8. See a number of other passages, GAW, pp. 150, 151 and 195–96, where "Idee" is defined in the same way.
9. GAW, p. 151.
10. GAW, p. 150.
11. *Cf.* GAW, p. 151.

more reasonable to go into the detailed axiological structure of the various ideas, since this structure may have exercised great influence on the action *actually* motivated by the ideas. The differences between the Maoist and Soviet versions of Communism are certainly not without interest to those who wish to understand the behaviour of China and Soviet Russia in the world today. Viewed in this perspective, the "analysis of ideas" is an axiological *preliminary* to the "explanatory" value analysis discussed below.

While it is quite reasonable for Weber to include this kind of preliminary work among the tasks of the *Archiv,* and consequently to defend its role in *Objektivität,* the place of the "analysis of ideas" in the *general* scheme of axiological value analysis is more doubtful; and the secondary character of its role is probably confirmed by the fact that Weber does not raise this question in his later essays. Nevertheless, the point has its importance, since it gives an indication of the specific viewpoints and problems which dominate Weber's discussion (also in *Objektivität*) of the ideal type [12].

2. Far more thorough than Weber's discussion of the tracing back of concrete valuations to already explicit "ideas" is the treatment which he accords to the axiological value analysis concentrating on the concrete goal structures and on their, conscious *or unconscious,* premises.

2.1. The first task of such axiological value analysis is to enumerate the various *possible* ultimate axioms from which the concrete valuation in question may be deduced [13]. By means of this enumeration, the goal or valuation is placed in a systematic context of higher and ultimate axioms from which it *might* theoretically have been deduced: its "letzte sinnhafte Struktur", as Weber calls it [14], is uncovered: what we may refer to as the *vertical* structure of the valuation.

This process of uncovering may be useful in several ways. Generally speaking, it is of course valuable in cases where the individual in question has not thought at all about the "higher" premises on which his goal is based, where he has simply formulated an "unreflektiert sich aufdrängendes Werturteil" [15]. In that case, value analysis makes the very first contribution towards the understanding of the essential (axiological) basis of a concrete attitude.

Perhaps only one possible higher or ultimate axiom can be found; but it is also conceivable that *several* value axioms must be considered as possible premises of the concrete valuation. In this situation, which is given special attention by Weber [16], value analysis may be of use not only where the

12. *Cf. infra,* pp. 231–32.
13. See for instance GAW, pp. 151, 312–13, 510, 608; GASS, pp. 417, 435.
14. GAW, p. 508.
15. GAW, p. 153.
16. *Cf.* GAW, p. 500: "... [es] kann sich ergeben: daß der genau *gleiche* Zweck aus

valuation is totally unreflected, but also in cases where the acting person has correctly identified *one* of the possible ultimate axioms as a premise of his goal, without considering the other possible axioms. A last possibility is of course that the individual in question has made every conceivable effort to investigate the valuational basis of his action and goals, but that his analysis has simply been wrong on some point [17].

2.2. After working out in this way the vertical structure of the concrete valuation, the scholar may in Weber's view, within the framework of the axiological value analysis, go on to examine the relation between this vertical structure and *other* value axioms (and the concrete valuations deduced from the latter), "... ihnen [the valuations] ... den "Ort" innerhalb der Gesamtheit der überhaupt möglichen "letzten" Werte anweisen und ihre sinnhaften Geltungssphären abgrenzen" [18]. Such a theoretical localization of the concrete valuation and its higher axioms enables us to understand clearly what value systems we implicitly support and—above all—*reject* by committing ourselves to a particular valuational attitude. As Weber puts it in *Wiss. Beruf:* "Ihr dient, bildlich geredet, diesem Gott *und kränkt jenen anderen,* wenn Ihr Euch für diese Stellungnahme entschließt" [19].

This analysis, which we can call the horizontal value analysis, starts from an examination of the relevant ultimate value axioms, since the full extent of the opposition to other value systems only becomes apparent at a high level of abstraction. But Weber assumes that the analysis may then move downwards again in order to show the acting individual what other concrete attitudes are compatible or incompatible with his own value judgment or goal.

In *Wertfreiheit* and *Wiss. Beruf,* Weber particularly refers to a variant of this horizontal analysis, in which the starting-point is not a vertical value structure, but some phenomenon which can be judged according to a number of different value premises. Here the analysis in question is supposed to enumerate *all the value axioms* which may serve as the basis for a possible

---

sehr verschiedenen letzten Gründen gewollt wird ...". Direct or indirect (through the use of the plural "Axiome", etc.) references to the possibility of *a number of* ultimate value axioms are found GAW, pp. 151, 608; GASS, p. 417. The particular importance of this kind of situation to Weber's argument will be considered below, pp. 154–56.

17. This interpretation has to be taken into consideration when we meet with terms like "sich täuschen" (GAW, p. 510) and "sich irren" (GASS, p. 417). More probably, however, these passages refer to one of the first two categories: the wholly or mainly unreflecting valuation, or the imperfect analysis of a valuation which can be deduced from more than one ultimate value axiom. Thus, for instance, GASS, p. 417 speaks of value axioms "die du gar nicht gesehen hast", a phrase that indicates an unreflecting valuation.

18. GAW, p. 508; similar passages, GAW, pp. 511, 608.

19. GAW, p. 608.

value judgment concerning the phenomenon [20]; the analysis may even go so far as to try to list the concrete possible value judgments [21]. This kind of value analysis is of course simply an extension of the vertical and horizontal types, taking its point of departure among the higher rather than among the lower value premises. But at the same time, it corresponds exactly to the *value interpretation* discussed above [22], since the latter also tried to discover "Angriffspunkte für *mögliche* "wertende" Stellungnahmen" [23]; Weber himself acknowledges the parallel by remarking that value analysis of this kind may prepare or even supplant a value interpretation [24].

The interesting point about this function of axiological value analysis is that it confirms the possibility of constructing a clear and not too complicated framework for theoretical value relation. The somewhat intangible preconditions of inquiry in the social sciences become accessible to precise analysis. Rickert's philosophical and epistemological tours de force are transformed by Weber into ordinary, almost routine methods.

A further step in this direction is accomplished when the analysis not only reveals how a *particular* phenomenon is judged under different value axioms, but also tells us what concrete value judgments would result from the application of a certain value axiom or combination of such axioms to a whole series of phenomena (ideally, every possible relevant one). This amounts to the tracing *downwards* of the vertical structure of a value axiom. As Weber points out, this kind of investigation is not purely axiological, since it implies a "möglichst erschöpfende Kasuistik derjenigen empirischen Sachverhalte, welche für eine praktische Bewertung überhaupt in Betracht kommen *können*" [25]. On the other hand, the empirical element is supplied rather by the imagination and general faculty of combination of the scholar than by the empirical value analysis discussed below, so that it seemed more reasonable to deal with the point—which acquires a particular importance in the discussion of the ideal type—at this stage.

Naturally, horizontal value analysis is especially important in cases where the value judgment examined may be deduced from more than one axiom. In such cases, the demonstration of a *conflict* between these axioms is of immediate interest to the individual concerned, because it points to a latent

---

20. GAW, p. 499. The fact that Weber here speaks of "normative" sciences does not imply that the analysis is less binding than the other kinds of axiological value analysis or even than empirical analysis in general. *Cf. infra,* pp. 160–62.
21. GAW, p. 607. The "Stellung" referred to has the status of a concrete valuation rather than of a value axiom.
22. Pp. 109–14.
23. GAW, p. 253.
24. GAW, pp. 511–12.
25. GAW, p. 510.

inconsistency in the goal structure which may require solution in the form of some kind of choice or compromise [26].

3.1.2. Function

This leads us to the question of the *function* of axiological value analysis. In the passage from *Objektivität* quoted above, p. 147, this analysis is referred to as a "criticism" of value judgments, and in *Wertfreiheit*, too, Weber claims that such criticism is the essential purpose of axiological value analysis [1]. On the other hand, a closer examination is necessary to the proper understanding of the nature and scope of this criticism, as Weber sees it.

1.1. Criticism of this kind is of course most direct in cases where the horizontal value analysis is not restricted to the theoretical and hypothetical level, that is, if one or more of the values conflicting with the one examined is not only considered, but actually *held* by the scholar performing the analysis. This "positive" criticism, as Weber once calls it [2], may in his opinion be extremely useful to science, because it shows up the scope of the values criticized in a more effective way than the usual neutral discussion [3]. The parallel to the discussion of value interpretation, with its shift from the practical value judgments of the scholar to the neutral listing of possible valuational attitudes, is obvious, although Weber himself does not mention it. *1.2.* Certain passages even give the impression that Weber regards the scholar's *ability* to formulate practical value judgments concerning the object of the valuations or goals examined by him, or, more radically still, his *actual* formulation of such value judgments, as a *necessary* condition of at least horizontal value analysis [4]. While the former view is sufficiently moderate to present no special difficulties, the latter one certainly goes beyond Weber's conclusions concerning value interpretation, according to which the practical value judgments of the scholar were useful aids to, but not inevitable preconditions of analysis.

When the extreme view is considered, it is probably important to keep in mind that this view is found in a passage from *Objektivität,* i. e., from the earliest of the essays in which Weber deals with value analysis at all, and moreover from one which is to a certain degree marked by its status as a programmatic essay for a periodical called "Archiv für Sozialwissenschaft und Sozial*politik*" (my italics). Probably it is this latter consideration which

---

26. This point is implicit in the formulation, for instance, of GASS, p. 417.
 1. GAW, p. 501; see also GAW, p. 151.
 2. GAW, p. 157.
 3. GAW, p. 157.
 4. GASS, p. 477 and GAW, pp. 156–57 respectively.

leads Weber to discuss at all the question of the scientific status and value of the essays on social policy which the *Archiv* would be publishing. And the former circumstance, the place of *Objektivität* at the very beginning of Weber's methodological production, may serve to explain the apparently rather too pointed statement that practical valuations are "geboten" and "unvermeidlich" in axiological value analysis [5]. As the discussion [6] of theoretical value relation showed, Weber's distinction between practical valuation and theoretical value relation is still rather uncertain in *Knies I–II*, not in the sense that he shows an insufficient grasp of the fundamental difference between science and values, but because his attack on objectivism makes him take up a position from which the *difference* between value orientation and value relation seems less significant than their *common distance* from the intrinsically "meaningless" material. In the same way, Weber's emphasis in *Objektivität* on the fundamental possibility of value analysis may have overshadowed his wish and ability to transform the positive criticism of values into a *theory* of horizontal value analysis. In fact, *Objektivität* does not contain any attempt to formulate such a theory. However, Weber's fundamental position remains unshaken here, as in *Knies I–II*, a fact which is attested by the following passage: "... wir denken nicht daran, derartige Auseinandersetzungen ["positive" criticism based on the ideals of the scholar] für *Wissenschaft* auszugeben" [7].

2.   In fact, there is no doubt that the critical function with which Weber invests axiological analysis is not practical, but *scientific* [8], not positive, but what he calls "dialectical" criticism [9].

When it comes to the substance of this dialectical criticism, however, it turns out to be strangely intangible. When discussing the function of axiological analysis, Weber constantly emphasizes the possibility of uncovering the *consistent* vertical value structures of concrete valuations or goals, and of examining, by means of horizontal analysis, the mutual compatibility of these various consistent structures. It is not unreasonable for Weber to describe the critical function of this kind of analysis as "eine Prüfung der Ideale an dem Postulat der inneren *Widerspruchslosigkeit* des Gewollten" [10]. But what exactly is the meaning of the statement that a particular goal is or is not "non-contradictory"? And in what sense can a demonstration of inconsistency be said to possess a critical function *in relation to the concrete goals*

5. GAW, pp. 156 and 157 respectively.
6. Pp. 107–09.
7. GAW, p. 157.
8. See for instance GAW, pp. 151, 501.
9. GAW, p. 151; GASS, p. 417.
10. GAW, p. 151.

or valuations examined? If we take the enumeration above of the various possible results of axiological analysis as our starting-point, we may arrive at the following conclusions:

2.1. It is always possible to carry out a horizontal value analysis; and this form of analysis may be said to contain an element of criticism even in relation to the concrete goal or valuation under discussion, inasmuch as it makes the acting person conscious of certain fundamental value conflicts which may induce him to alter his concrete goal.

2.1.1. However, it is important to be aware of the nature and limits of such criticism. If we suppose that the analysis may sometimes bring about a change of attitude in the acting person, the implication is that the latter must already have regarded as positive (have "embraced") the value or values which are shown by the horizontal analysis to conflict with the ultimate value axiom of the primary concrete goal. Thus, value analysis confronts the concrete valuations of an individual with opposing value axioms *held by the same individual:* the resulting criticism has the form: "You are not acting in accordance with the value axioms which you have hitherto professed and/or been guided by" [11]. Undoubtedly, this criticism shows up an inconsistency in the individual, when all the values held by the latter are viewed as a whole [12]. Nevertheless, the "critical function" does not operate directly, but depends on a further condition, viz, that the individual accepts the positive value—ideally: the duty—of *acting consistently.* Particularly with respect to axiological analysis, it may be doubted whether this condition is fulfilled. The inconsistency demonstrated will be of a purely *theoretical* kind, and does not, in the context of an axiological argument, lead to any practical difficulty: both the opposing values may be implemented; indeed, it may be that they can only be implemented together. Viewed in isolation, axiological consistency by no means always appears to be necessary [13].

11. A good example of the actual use of this kind of criticism is found in Weber's letter to Robert Michels of May 12th, 1909 (copy in DZA II, Rep. 92, No. 30, Vol. 7), in which he writes: "Die "Streikethik"? Ja, lieber Freund, am Schluß Ihres Artikels heißt es doch: *Jeder* Streik ist gerecht weil er auf dem Wege zum Zukunftsziel liegt ... das [ist] doch *Erfolgsethik:* das Mittel ist "gerecht", weil der gehoffte Erfolg "gerecht" ist—Während doch der Syndikalismus ... eine *Gesinnungs-*Religion [ist], die auch dann zu Recht besteht, wenn es nie ein Zukunftsziel *giebt,* welches "erreicht" wird und wenn auch wissenschaftlich feststeht, daß dazu keinerlei Chance ist".

12. It is doubtful, however, whether this is the demonstration of "internal inconsistencies" which Weber has in mind. *Cf.* GAW, p. 151 (where Weber claims that dialectical criticism may lead to a heightened consciousness of "die letzten Maßstäbe, die sich *in dem konkreten Werturteil* manifestieren" (my italics)) and GAW, p. 511 (which speaks of "neue Wertaxiome").

13. *Cf.* Schelting, *Wissenschaftslehre,* 1934, p. 24: "Denn in der Welt, in der wir leben und handeln, ist in keiner Weise eine Garantie dafür gegeben, daß der realen

2.1.2. If we abstract from this condition of consistency, the only other possible critical function of the value analysis described here consists in denouncing cases where concrete valuations are described, in more or less good faith, in terms which are properly applicable to a conflicting value axiom. This problem is, however, as Schelting remarks [14], one of correct "labelling" which, although its importance is considerable in practical politics (where certain axiomatic labels like "democracy", "popular", "progressive", "liberal", etc. are much coveted because of their positive connotations) is of little theoretical interest [15].

2.2. If we turn to the possibility of uncovering inconsistencies within a *single* valuation or goal, we can distinguish between two cases:

2.2.1. It can be shown by vertical analysis that the valuation in question can only be deduced from *one* ultimate axiom. Here, the only critical functions possible are those described under *2.1.* above.

2.2.2. The valuation may be deduced from *several* conflicting ultimate value axioms. This is apparently the problem which occupies Weber most, at least in his early essays and speeches [16]. In what sense may the awareness of this conflict be said to possess a critical function? Certainly not with regard to the concrete value judgment in question, which not only cannot be called inconsistent, but which may even be said to be backed up by *several* legitimating value axioms. Only in relation to *subsequent* concrete valuations of *other* phenomena may the knowledge of this latent conflict acquire a critical potential, since the acting person must then, but only then, choose one of the several possible ultimate value positions as a basis for his *new* value judgment. This kind of criticism may therefore be said to be *hypothetical,* since it demonstrates the possible inconsistency of *future* actions, viewed in relation to the *present* one. And since this hypothetical criticism turns out to be a confrontation of *several* (hypothetical) goals pursued by the same person, it comes under the heading of *2.1.* above, and consequently also depends on the acceptance by the individual of the positive value of axiological consistency [17].

"Reibungslosigkeit" ideelle Widerspruchslosigkeit entsprechen muß, oder daß ideelle und reale "Harmonie" Hand in Hand gehen müssen".

14. *Ibid.,* pp. 24–25.
15. This is Weber's general view concerning terminological discussions; *cf.* GAW, p. 499: ". . . terminologischer, daher gänzlich steriler, Streit . . ."
16. *Cf.* GAW, p. 151 and, quite unambiguously, GASS, p. 417: ". . . ich nehme dein Werturteil und zergliedere es dir dialektisch, . . . um es auf seine letzten Axiome zurückzuführen, um dir zu zeigen, daß darin die und die "letzten" *möglichen* Werturteile stecken . . .". This category also includes the cases discussed by Schelting (*Wissenschaftslehre,* 1934, pp. 24–25) where one part of a value judgment may be deduced from a particular value axiom, and another part of it from a different axiom, which conflicts with the first one.
17. See also Appendix A of this chapter.

3. We can sum up the results reached above by saying that the axiological criticism of concrete valuations will always, if it is to go beyond mere terminological feuds, be conditional on the acknowledgement, by the individual whose valuations are being examined, of the positive value of logical *consistency* in one's valuations and actions. In the cases, which are apparently of particular importance to Weber, where more than one ultimate value axiom can be demonstrated as the possible theoretical basis of a concrete valuation, the intended criticism is further restricted in that it applies only to *future* valuations and goals, but not to the concrete attitude examined.

3.1. The latter element: the *potential* character of the value conflict, has a certain bearing on the question of the construction of the ideal type. But the former one: the acknowledgement of the value of axiological consistency, is of more immediate interest. The problem in this connection is whether Weber, as in the case of his discussion of value freedom, clearly indicates the hypothetical character of the criticism, the existence of an implicit "Sollen" premise, or whether he claims that criticism of an attitude as being axiologically inconsistent may be scientifically binding *in itself*.

The point is open to dispute. While Weber clearly denies science the right of telling the individual *which* of several possible ultimate axioms of a concrete valuation should be chosen [18], he at least once [19] demands, without any qualifying clauses, that the individual *should* choose between the conflicting axioms, i. e., *should* be consistent. The passage in question speaks of the various *possible* value axioms, "die vielleicht sich untereinander gar nicht oder nicht ohne Kompromisse vertragen und zwischen denen du also *wählen* mußt". Other passages, however, seem to support a different interpretation. At GAW, p. 151, for instance, Weber writes: "Ob sich das urteilende Subjekt zu diesen letzten Maßstäben bekennen *soll,* ist seine persönlichste Angelegenheit und eine Frage seines Wollens und Gewissens, nicht des Erfahrungswissens"; and this passage seems to refer not to the choice *between* value axioms (although this act of choice must, *a fortiori,* be regarded as lying within the exclusive province of the individual) but to the decision to choose between them *at all,* that is, the decision in favour of axiological consistency.

In *Wiss. Beruf,* too, Weber touches on the question: "... die und die praktische Stellungnahme läßt sich mit innerer Konsequenz und also: Ehrlichkeit ihrem *Sinn* nach ableiten aus der und der letzten weltanschauungsmäßigen Grundposition ..."; "... Ihr kommt notwendig zu diesen und diesen letzten inneren sinnhaften *Konsequenzen,* wenn Ihr Euch treu bleibt" [20]. Although it may sound paradoxical, these last passages also seem to support

18. For a more thorough account of Weber's argument in support of this position, *cf. infra,* pp. 178–79.
19. GASS, p. 417.
20. GAW, p. 607.

the hypothesis that Weber did not pretend to have *scientific* backing for a demand for axiological consistency [21]. The terms employed: "Ehrlichkeit", "treu", have significant ethical connotations. In *Wiss. Beruf,* Weber puts forward his view of the "ethic" of science, i. e., of the duties necessarily incumbent on anyone *who has chosen science as a vocation.* One of these duties was, as we have seen [22], "intellektuelle Rechtschaffenheit", the duty to follow truth wherever it leads. Towards the end of the lecture [23], Weber claims that the result of axiological value analysis is binding in this sense; but in the passage quoted, in which Weber clearly addresses himself to the members of the audience in their quality as practically value-oriented and goal-setting individuals, the demand, which is evidently a passionate and immensely charged absolute in Weber's personal ethic, is formulated in purely ethical terms. He who *wishes* to be true to himself, to be honest, must acknowledge that his concrete valuational attitude will always conflict with this or that ultimate value. But this demand for intellectual honesty is nowhere said to be *objectively* binding. If a person denies the value of scientific truth and in practice acts without regard for it, he is logically blind and deaf, "intellectually dishonest" and "untrue" to himself in the sense defined above; but Weber indicates no way of proving him wrong [24].

Against this array of passages, the solitary dissenting opinion from GASS seems to lose importance: it forms part of an uncorrected lecture, while *Objektivität* and *Wiss. Beruf* were, respectively, written and revised in written form before publication [25]. In view of this, it seems justified to conclude that Weber's demand for logical consistency is a premise which is often treated as self-evident, and invested with a strongly positive ethical value, but which Weber nevertheless regards as fundamentally undemonstrable by scientific means [26]. On the other hand, the apparent vagueness of Weber's

21. One indication of this is the fact that Weber does not here see the function of value analysis as one of criticism, possibly resulting in a change of behaviour, but as that of providing "Klarheit"—*knowledge.*
22. P. 65.
23. GAW, p. 613.
24. *Cf. supra,* pp. 32–34.
25. It may also be noted that Weber, in the passage from GASS quoted above, underlines "wählen" but not "muß"—an indication that he is rather thinking about the value conflict.
26. Both Schelting (*Wissenschaftslehre,* 1934, pp. 23, 350) and Löwith (*Weber u. Marx,* 1960, p. 15n23) come to the same conclusion; Henrich, on the other hand, seems implicitly to interpret Weber's demand for logical consistency as one for which Weber would claim scientific validity (Stammer (ed.), *Weber,* 1965, p. 84), but unfortunately quotes no passages from Weber's work in support of this contention. (It is possible, however, that Henrich is referring to the demand for "intellectual honesty" which Weber addresses specifically to the *scholar (cf. Einheit,* 1952, p. 111), a demand which Weber certainly believed to be demonstrable by scientific means (*cf. supra,* p. 65).

position is symptomatic of the difficulty which he found in separating his own value judgments from his scientific statements. As in his description of Mommsen and Treitschke [27], it is sometimes necessary, when reading Weber, to infer the location of the boundary between science and values from the variations of pitch of his literary passion rather than from his exact formulations.

3.2. Weber's emphasis on the *consistency* of the value structures elaborated by means of axiological value analysis has further interesting implications. Thus, the "tracing back" of concrete valuations to the ultimate value axioms from which they can be deduced with "inner consistency", logically, if it is to fulfil its critical function discussed above, presupposes that the ultimate value axioms are themselves defined in detail. In order to claim that an axiological conflict exists between certain value axioms, it is necessary to know the exact implications of these axioms; ideally, the value axiom should be formulated in such a way as to allow a precise indication of the concrete attitude implied by it—if any—towards any relevant empirical phenomenon. Valuations and goals are *practical* attitudes; and if the axiological analysis is to be of value to this intended practice, it must limit itself to the formulation and enumeration of the value axioms which may produce *unambiguous* concrete norms for action.

A number of passages indicate that Weber himself is aware of this point. Thus, it is significant that his repeated use of the terms "Konsequenz" and "konsequent" is not always restricted to the analysis of the relation between concrete valuations and ultimate values (where the terms might still, theoretically, refer to a vertical tracing back of value judgments to vague and nebulous ultimate values) [28], but comes to apply, in a central passage in *Wertfreiheit,* to the *axiom as such:* here, the first task of axiological value analysis is said to be "die Herausarbeitung der letzten, innerlich "konsequenten" Wertaxiome, von denen die ... Meinungen ausgehen" [29], a terminology which clearly indicates the demand for precise axioms. And Weber goes on to state as the second task of value analysis the "Deduktion der "Konsequenzen" für die *wertende* Stellungnahme, welche aus bestimmten letzten Wertaxiomen folgen würden, wenn man sie, und nur sie, der prak-

27. *Cf. supra,* pp. 72, 77.
28. Weber's own examples, however, even here make it quite clear that the ultimate axioms must be exactly defined. For instance, since he feels able to acknowledge (GAW, p. 514) the right of scientific analysis to conclude, on the basis of a vertical analysis "upwards" of syndicalist behaviour, that a pure "Gesinnungsethik" (*cf. infra,* pp. 183–84) is "die einzig innerlich folgerrichtige", this implies that the value analysis must have moved beyond the level on which syndicalism could be classified, for instance, both "democratic" and as "undemocratic".
29. GAW, p. 510.

tischen Bewertung von faktischen Sachverhalten zugrunde legte" [30]. Here, the direction of the analysis: *from* the axiom *towards* the concrete attitude, logically presupposes that the axiom is unambiguous.

We may sum up the discussion in the conclusion that Weber's view of axiological value analysis, and of its function as a potential criticism of practical goals and valuations, includes the demand for an exact definition of the ultimate value axioms. This demand implies that the vertical value structure is an unambiguous complex of related concepts: a valuation of a particular phenomenon may be traced back only to the value axiom or axioms included in the structure; and it is the only concrete valuation of the phenomenon in question which may be deduced from this axiom or these axioms [31].

In a general theoretical context, this conclusion is interesting because it would have been possible for Weber to define an axiological value analysis which obeyed different rules and served different ends; and in the context of the present work, the point has a certain importance for the understanding of Weber's concept of the ideal type [32].

3.1.3. Validity

1. The question of the validity, the binding force, of axiological value analysis presents certain difficulties. Above all, Weber now and then speaks of this kind of analysis as "philosophy" [1]; and although we were able to conclude [2], that a term like "Geschichtsphilosophie" *might* be used by Weber to denote a form of analysis possessing a validity equivalent to that of ordinary empirical science, a closer examination nevertheless seems to be required.

1.1. The results of such an examination, however, leave no doubt: as mentioned above [3], Weber describes the critical function of axiological analysis as "scientific", a term which must be taken to imply that he regards the

30. GAW, p. 510. GAW, pp. 311, 313, we find passages marked by the same "practical" tendency. The fact that Weber alters the expression "immer allgemeinere wertende Stellungnahmen" (*Gutachten,* p. 100) to "immer prinzipiellere wertende Stellungnahmen" (*Wertfreiheit,* GAW, p. 510) may also be seen as an indication of his wish to remove any overtones of vagueness suggested by the term "allgemein", as applied to ultimate values.
31. This unambiguousness may entail that the ultimate value axioms remain on a fairly low level of abstraction. The ultimate cultural values: religion, politics, etc., are far too vague to serve as axioms for practical valuations.
32. *Cf. infra,* p. 219.
1. GAW, pp. 508, 608; see also GAW, p. 151, which, however, only deals with the "analysis of ideas" discussed above (pp. 148–50).
2. Pp. 112–14.
3. P. 154.

results of axiological analysis as *binding*. In fact, Weber throughout employs the terms "Wissenschaft" and "wissenschaftlich" when speaking of this kind of value analysis [4]. In a passage from *Objektivität*, he even quite explicitly states that the binding force of axiological analysis is equivalent to that of empirical science:

"... daß ... auch die *logische* Analyse eines Ideals auf seinen Gehalt und auf seine letzten Axiome hin und die Aufzeigung der aus seiner Verfolgung sich logischer und praktischer Weise ergebenden Konsequenzen, wenn sie als gelungen gelten soll, auch für [einen Chinesen] gültig sein muß,–während ihm für unsere ethischen Imperative das "Gehör" fehlen kann, und während er das Ideal selbst und die daraus fließenden konkreten *Wertungen* ablehnen kann und sicherlich oft ablehnen wird, ohne dadurch dem wissenschaftlichen Wert jener denkenden *Analyse* irgend zu nahe zu treten" [5].

1.2. One apparently inexplicable departure from this assumption is found in *Wertfreiheit* [6]. Here, Weber enumerates two sets of questions, of which only the first one can be solved by scientific means, and includes among the "non-scientific" problems the following two: "... unter welchen Gesichtspunkten [eine konkrete] Situation praktisch erfreulich oder unerfreulich erscheinen könne?, ob es—wie immer geartete—allgemein formulierbare Sätze (Axiome) gebe, auf welche sich diese Gesichtspunkte reduzieren lassen? ..." The first of these questions obviously refers to the kind of value analysis which Weber calls "value interpretation", while the second one forms part of an ordinary vertical value analysis. Naturally, they differ from purely empirical questions in that they are *theoretical* and axiological; but Weber seems to range them with questions belonging *wholly* to the value sphere (such as: "...was man in einer konkreten Situation *tun* solle", etc.), an arrangement which does not seem to square with the discussion referred to above.

The fact that Weber's statements in *Wertfreiheit* concerning the possibilities of "philosophische Disziplinen" in the context of the value analysis [7] are not found in the *Gutachten,* seems to indicate that the curious grouping of questions in the passage quoted is not to be ascribed to mere chance. On the other hand, Weber's main account of the possibilities of value analysis is already substantially present in the earlier version [8]. In fact, the best explana-

---

4. See for instance GAW, pp. 150, 508 (where value analysis is described, albeit in a negative context, as "(rationales oder empirisches) wissenschaftliches Verfahren"), 608.
5. GAW, pp. 155–56. We find a similar passage GASS, p. 418.
6. GAW, p. 509.
7. GAW, p. 508.
8. GAW, pp. 510–11; *Gutachten,* pp. 100–01. It is *conceivable* that this account is only meant by Weber to cover the analysis of one's *own* values, while the analysis of the values of *others* is only dealt with GAW, p. 508. One point in favour of this interpretation is the insertion, GAW, p. 510 (*Gutachten,* p. 100): "[Der Sinn von Diskussionen über praktische Wertungen] (der an der Diskussion *Beteiligten* selbst) ..." On the other hand, there seem to be no rational grounds for a restriction of this kind: why should not the four main tasks of value analysis apply

162

tion which can be offered of the passage quoted is simply that Weber has confused the distinction between theoretical and empirical science with that existing between science and values. At any rate, the divergence does not seem to warrant a modification of the main conclusion concerning the validity of axiological value analysis.

2. Hans Albert has drawn attention to a development in Weber's thought on a point of detail [9]. In *Objektivität* (1904) [10], *Stammler* (1907) [11], at the congress of the *Verein* in Vienna (1909) [12] and as late as the *Gutachten* (1913) [13] Weber refers to axiological analysis as *logical* analysis, and in the *Gutachten* accordingly describes its validity in the words: "Sie "gilt" kraft der Geltung der Logik" [14]. In *Wertfreiheit,* however, "logisch" is consistently replaced by "dem Sinn nach", "sinnhaft" or similar expressions, or is removed completely [15]. Apparently, Weber wishes to correct his earlier, perhaps rather uncritical, classification of any kind of scientific philosophy, especially the philosophy of value, as "logic" [16], in favour of a more neutral terminology. The change does not, however, seem to affect the essential problem of validity [17]: thus, the passage in question now reads: "Sie "gilt" in gleicher Art wie die Logik" [18].

3.2. Teleological value analysis

While axiological value analysis considers its object under a conceptual and theoretical aspect, its complement, teleological value analysis, employs a more restricted concept of value. Values as an object of this kind of analysis are

also to the analysis of other people's values? Translators of Weber's works seem to have been baffled by this insertion. Thus, Freund (Max Weber, *Essais sur la théorie de la science* (transl. Julien Freund), Paris 1965, p. 431), without comment amplifies his translation by a—very reasonable—interpretation: "... (*y compris* celles des personnes qui y participent) ..." (my italics), while Shils and Finch (Weber (Shils, Finch), *Methodology,* p. 20) simply drop the troublesome passage from their translation (!).

9. Hans Albert, "Theorie und Praxis. Max Weber und das Problem der Wertfreiheit und der Rationalität", Ernst Oldemeyer (ed.), *Die Philosophie und die Wissenschaften (Simon Moser zum 65. Geburtstag)*, Meisenheim a/Glan 1967, p. 268n60; Albert, *Traktat,* 1968, p. 74n27.
10. GAW, pp. 151, 155.
11. GAW, p. 311.
12. GASS, pp. 417–18.
13. *Gutachten,* pp. 100–01.
14. *Ibid.,* p. 100.
15. Curiously enough, we find the word "Logik" in the "old" sense in an insertion from 1917 (GAW, p. 524).
16. *Cf.* Rickert, *Grenzen* [5], 1929, p. XXV: "... er [Weber] glaubte eigentlich nur an die "Logik" ..."
17. This is also the conclusion reached by Loos, *Wertlehre,* 1970, p. 58.
18. GAW, p. 510.

considered exclusively in their capacity as *goals* [1], the latter concept being interpreted in a strictly empirical sense, as the *empirical situation* which the individual tries to bring about, not the *psychological act* of setting the goal [2].

3.2.1. Content

1. Teleological value analysis invariably takes as its starting-point a situation in which the value in question functions as a fixed or hypothetical goal. In this connection, the first task of analysis, according to Weber, is to find out by what means this goal may be attained. Theoretically, such an analysis should at least try to list the *sufficient* and the *necessary* means of bringing about the desired state of affairs; and there seems to be no doubt that Weber is constantly aware of *both* of these possibilities. It is possible, however, to demonstrate a certain shift of emphasis in his treatment of this point. In *Objektivität*, Weber mostly dwells on the analysis of the relation to the goal of certain *given* means: "... [wir] können ... auf diesem Wege die Chancen, mit bestimmten zur Verfügung stehenden Mitteln einen bestimmten Zweck überhaupt zu erreichen, abwägen ..." [3] The problem seems to be defined in very concrete terms: is it possible, with the given means A, B and C, to attain the desired and previously fixed goal? In short, we are asking whether certain means are *sufficient*. A somewhat broader, but otherwise perfectly similar discussion is found in a couple of passages written during the years 1905–07; here, Weber simply refers to the examination of the means that lead to the goal at all: "... es wird ein x gesucht, dessen Herbeiführung y ... zur generellen Folge haben würde ..." [4] Again, what is asked for—in quite general terms—are the means *sufficient* to reach a given goal.

In interventions during the 1909 and 1910 congresses of the *Verein* and the *Gesellschaft* respectively, one notices a small but significant change: Weber now focuses his discussion on the means which *must* be employed if the given goal is to be attained: the *necessary* conditions [5]. In *Wertfreiheit*,

1. In *Objektivität*, and at the 1909 congress of the *Verein*, Weber explicitly speaks of "Zweck" (GAW, p. 149; GASS, p. 418). In *Wertfreiheit* and *Wiss. Beruf*, he tries to emphasize the relation to the object of axiological analysis by instead employing terms like "Durchführung einer praktischen Stellungnahme" (GAW, pp. 510–11, 607), "aus praktisch-politischen Wertungen abgeleitete Direktive für ein wertvolles Handeln" (GAW, p. 508), etc. But he everywhere reverts to the "Zweck" terminology, probably because of the lack of precision and the general unwieldiness of the alternative expressions.
2. This last conclusion is not explicitly stated by Weber, but lies implicit in his views concerning the questions which teleological value analysis may ask and answer. The "goal" may of course be negative (something which one strives to avoid) as well as positive (something striven for).
3. GAW, p. 149.
4. GAW, p. 312; see also GAW, p. 402.
5. GAW, p. 418; similarly GASS, p. 482.

this shift of emphasis becomes even more pronounced: here, Weber speaks of the need to know the "unvermeidliche Mittel" [6] of reaching the goal. Interest is now focussed on the *necessary* means.

2.1. When the scholar has enumerated the various (sufficient or necessary) means of attaining the goal, his next task within the framework of teleological value analysis is that of examining the causal side effects ("Nebenerfolge") of these means. On this point, the two groups of conditions distinguished above merge into a single one: Weber's discussion of the side effects of *sufficient* means seems to proceed on the assumption that these means have, in this connection, attained a status of *necessity* in relation to the goal [7]. *2.2.* It is important to make explicit the premise of Weber's analysis of the side effects of the means. This premise is, at one point, described by Weber as "der Allzusammenhang alles Geschehens" [8], and lies implicit in his general description of the side effects as "ungewollt" [9], and in fact even in the term "Nebenerfolg" as such. The premise may be stated as follows: *any action has consequences apart from those directly wanted and anticipated by the acting person.* This view, which Weber also expresses in *Roscher* and *Knies II* [10], is taken by him to be a special instance of the general theory, which he borrows from Rickert, of the infinite multiplicity of reality; and he consequently seems to regard it, like the main theory, as an indisputable axiom. In itself, it does not imply that the side effects are important from the point of view of the acting, or any other, person; nor does it indicate whether these effects should be regarded as positive or negative. But the idea as such is the first link in a long chain of reasoning which will be described below.

3. A third possible task of teleological value analysis, according to Weber, is that of establishing the actual consequences which would result from the attainment of the given goal. Although Weber's treatment of it is not very explicit, this kind of investigation is undoubtedly envisaged by him, at least in the later essays [11]. It forms a parallel to the vertical axiological analysis, but does not exhibit characteristic features apart from those noted in connection with the two first tasks of teleological analysis.

6. GAW, pp. 508, 510. Similarly GAW, p. 607 and in a letter to Marianne Weber of March 22nd, 1916 (copy in DZA II, Rep. 92, No. 30, Vol. 2).
7. *Cf.* GAW, pp. 149–50. GAW, p. 312 and GASS, p. 402 do not seem to go into the question.
8. GAW, p. 150.
9. For instance GAW, pp. 150, 508, 510.
10. GAW, pp. 34n1, 142.
11. *Cf.* GAW, pp. 312, 510–11.

3.2.2. *Function*

1. Weber ascribes to teleological value analysis, as to its axiological complement, a *critical* function. Just as the pure dialectical criticism tests the axiological consistency of concrete valuations, the "technical" [1] criticism is concerned with teleological consistency, i. e., with the actual empirical possibility of attaining the chosen goal. This means that the teleological criticism, and the analysis which gives it force, does not raise any problem of *validity*. Its binding force is identical with that of ordinary empirical science, since its propositions are simply inversions of (more or less exact and established) statements of cause and effect [2].

2.1. The first possibility of formulating teleological criticism occurs when the analysis of the potential means shows that there are *no* means (at the command of the acting person or at all at a given time, during a shorter or longer period or, marginally, anywhere at any time) capable of attaining the goal [3]. In less extreme cases, it may be that the desired result can only be brought about under more or less *improbable* circumstances [4].

2.2. Apart from such uncomplicated cases, which correspond to the first task of teleological analysis, the analysis of the side effects of the means forms the basis of a rather interesting kind of criticism: It is concivable that the means necessary, or chosen, to attain a given goal are burdened with side effects which, with certainty or with a greater or lesser degree of probability, preclude the goal from being attained [5]. Analogously to the well-known concept of the "self-defeating prophecy", one might here speak of a "self-defeating strategy" [6]. Naturally, this problem of the "self-defeating strategy" is particularly prominent with regard to situations involving complex relations of cause and effect, as for instance those relevant to political action. A striking example of a strategy which, in Weber's view, is self-defeating is discussed in his letter of Feb. 9th, 1908 to Robert Michels [7]: "Es kann Ihnen doch unmöglich entgehen", he writes, "daß ein *recht* erheblicher Teil aller Streiks (so der verlorene Hamburger Hafenstreik) nicht etwa nur die Gewerkschaften ... sondern *jedes* Fortschreiten der Klassenbewegung um Jahre, ja Jahrzehnte *zurück*werfen ..."

1. See GAW, p. 150, where the term, however, seems to include the "combined" criticism discussed below, pp. 170–71.
2. GAW, p. 517.
3. GAW, pp. 149, 510.
4. GAW, pp. 510–11.
5. GAW, p. 511.
6. As far as the *necessary* means are concerned, such a self-defeating strategy amounts to the complete impracticability of the goal.
7. Copy in DZA II, Rep. 92, No. 30, Vol. 7; see also the copy of a letter to Michels of May 12th, 1909, *ibid.*

3.1. Just as the acknowledgement of the positive value of axiological consistency was a necessary premise of the critical function of axiological analysis, teleological value analysis can only claim to possess a critical function if we presuppose that the person setting the goal actually *wants to* attain it. Of course, this condition is a matter of form to a far greater extent than that on which the axiological criticism depends: while no inner *necessity* prevents a person from acting in an axiologically inconsistent manner (as long as his behaviour does not result in teleological inconsistencies), he will almost by definition want to reach the goal which he has set for himself, at least in the sense that he will not lavish time, energy or money on trying to reach a goal which he knows in advance to be *un*attainable, and that his willingness to "invest" in the attempt will rise with the chances of success. Here, a "Sein" premise almost irresistibly slides towards a "Sollen" conclusion: one should not attempt what one knows to be impossible.

In *Objektivität,* Weber accordingly seems to tend towards the view that teleological criticism of this kind is not dependent on other conditions: the demonstration that a goal is unattainable seems to him to amount to an implicit criticism of the goal as such as "nach Lage der gegebenen Verhältnisse [praktisch] sinnlos" [8].

3.2. In view of this, it seems particularly interesting that Weber in *Wertfreiheit* clearly emphasizes the *hypothetical* nature of teleological criticism. Any new fact, he says—he himself discusses tendencies of development of some kind—may render the attainment of the goal "derart unwahrscheinlich ... daß seine [the acting person's] Arbeit daran, an der Chance des Erfolgs bewertet, als sterile "Donquixoterie" erscheinen müßte" [9]; and this will of course raise the problem whether to abandon the goal [10]. But this decision, this "Ausgleich zwischen Zweck und unvermeidlichem Mittel, gewolltem Ziel und unvermeidlichem Nebenerfolg", cannot be assumed by any scientific discipline, whether empirical or non-empirical [11]. To support this contention, Weber advances two arguments:

3.2.1. According to Weber's first argument, politics may be "the art of the possible", but the possible is often only attained by striving for the impossible. This opinion doubtlessly reflects central aspects of Weber's views on the

8. GAW, p. 149. The modification "praktisch", however, may be read as restricting the field of application of the criticism to the sphere dominated by *practical* values and goals, i. e., the value sphere. In any case, Weber does not speak of "demonstrably false" or "objectively absurd" valuations or goals.
9. GAW, p. 513.
10. Weber uses the expression: "die Hoffnung auf Realisierbarkeit seiner praktischen Wertungen aufzugeben habe", a phrase which may theoretically be interpreted as referring only to the *acknowledgement* of impossibility, not to the abandonment of the goal as such. However, the context seems to make it clear that the problem discussed is one af valuations and goals, and not simply of theoretical clarity.
11. GAW, p. 513.

nature of politics; but in the present context, its logic is not very convincing. If we suppose the teleological value analysis to have been thorough and skilful, one of its results will have been the knowledge (on which, in fact, Weber's contention is based) that a certain political goal may not be attainable, but that it is most nearly reached if it is retained as a goal *in spite of its being unattainable.* The knowledge of the feats of individuals serving unattainable ideals is a knowledge of empirical fact, and one which is extremely important, for instance, to political scientists; and in the present case it actually leads to the modification of the original goal. The retention of the original goal A, in spite of the fact that it is impossible to attain, can no longer be classified as the setting of a goal, but instead serves as the necessary means to a new end B ("a situation as close as possible to A").

3.2.2. Weber's second argument, however, completely dispenses with the idea of an "external" goal. Here he mentions that an individual (he himself discusses the case of syndicalists), although acting in a way which may theoretically be interpreted as contributing to some goal, in fact does not at all orient his behaviour according to its "external" results. He only acts in order to produce or affirm his "internal" conviction that his commitment is "genuine"; his actions are motivated only by their "Gesinnungswert", not by their "Erfolgswert" [12]. In Weber's view, it is absurd to submit behaviour of this kind to criticism based on teleological value analysis, since the latter can only state the chances of achieving "external" results [13]. The action can only be analysed *axiologically,* and this latter kind of analysis is in its turn limited to the statement that the behaviour in question can only, *if it is to be regarded as consistent,* be oriented towards some purely "internal", axiological goal, and that it consequently cannot be "proved wrong" by the results of teleological analysis [14].

3.3. Thus, Weber's discussion of unattainable goals leads to the conclusion that the retention of such goals indicates that the goals are now functioning

12. GAW, pp. 513–14; similarly in a letter to E. Lesser of Aug. 18th, 1913 (copy in DZA II, Rep. 92, No. 30, Vol. 11). For a discussion of the problems raised by these categories, *cf. infra,* pp. 183–84.
13. GAW, p. 514. One might of course construct an "internal" teleological analysis: on the basis of his previous knowledge of abortive attempts to strengthen the same commitment by means of the same actions, the scholar might warn the individual in question, and supplement his warning by an affirmation, based on his "intuition" of the *concrete* situation, that the actions would again this time fail to produce their desired "internal" effects. Both kinds of argument and "proof", however, are based on "evident" analogies which must always, according to Weber, be controlled by means of external observation; in themselves, they do not attain the "threshold of validity" of real teleological analysis.
14. This seems to be the most reasonable interpretation of the rather cryptic passage, GAW, p. 514: " "Wissenschaftlich" läßt sich lediglich feststellen, *daß* diese Auffassung seiner eigenen Ideale die einzig innerlich folgerichtige, durch äußere "Tatsachen" nicht widerlegbare ist".

as a means *either* to a modified "external" *or* to an "internal" end, and that teleological criticism is consequently never absolute, but always depends on the assumption that the acting person actually wishes to reach the "external" goal which he originally set himself, and to reach it completely.

4. A function of teleological value analysis which Weber particularly discusses in *Wertfreiheit* is that of defining certain vague concepts like "Fortschritt" and "Anpassung" more exactly [15]. To the extent that the situations to which these concepts refer are amenable to precise definition, it is possible, on the basis of a teleological value analysis which takes these situations as the fixed goal, to arrive at statements according to which the discovery or use of certain means marks a "progress" towards or a greater or lesser "adaptation" to the previously defined situation [16]. In other cases, too, Weber regards it as legitimate to designate certain means as more or less "correct", if the context is a purely teleological one, and the end given [17].

To designate this last category, Weber several times employs a term which, like other parts of Weber's terminology, almost invites misunderstanding, viz, "teleologische Wertung" [18]. Of course, this expression does not refer to a value judgment in the ordinary sense, and Weber emphasizes that such "teleological valuations" are nothing more than inversions of statements of cause and effect [19]. Moreover, he makes it clear that the objectively binding force which he—rightly—ascribes to these "valuations" depends on the acceptance of the same premise as that on which the critical function of teleological value analysis rests. For one thing, one must presuppose a wish to strive for the goal, i. e., that it is legitimate to regard the goal as fixed [20]; and since the means are not only described as sufficient or necessary in relation to the goal, but may in the "teleological valuations" be weighed against each other as being, teleologically, more or less acceptable, one must further presuppose a fixed order of priority concerning the various technical principles of rationality (speed, security, completeness, etc.) [21]. Finally, the validity of the teleological valuation is conditional on the wish to pursue the goal

15. *Cf. supra,* pp. 39–40.
16. Concerning "adaptation", *cf.* GAW, p. 517; concerning "progress", *cf.* GAW, pp. 520, 524–27, 529–30.
17. See for instance GAW, pp. 125n1, 603.
18. For instance GAW, pp. 125n1, 129. Weber's choice seems all the more curious since he himself, as early as 1897, criticizes Sombart (in a letter of Feb. 8th, 1897) for employing the term "Ideal" to designate the same concept as that covered by the term "teleologische Wertung" (copy in DZA II, Rep. 92, No. 30, Vol. 4).
19. GAW, pp. 129, 517, 529, 538.
20. For instance GAW, pp. 129, 517, 603.
21. For instance GAW, pp. 527, 529.

rationally; the acting person must acknowledge the teleological form of analysis as a relevant standard for the judging of his behaviour [22].

3.3. The combined value analysis

Viewed separately, axiological and teleological value analysis are only partial,
and their critical function is artificially restricted to their respective spheres:
axiological analysis allows us to demonstrate axiomatic inconsistencies; by
means of teleological analysis, we are informed of pragmatic conflicts. The
two forms only acquire their full weight and moment when they are combined; and even though Weber constantly emphasizes the distinction between
them (and between their various elements) his discussions are usually rounded
off by an examination of the most complex form of goal criticism.

Here, the basic analysis is teleological, while the intended criticism is
axiological: what value conflicts can be expected to result from the attempt
to reach a given goal [1]? In the same way, the concept of value analysed is
a compound of the conceptual/theoretical and the practical/goal-oriented ones
described above [2].

1. The substance of the combined value analysis is subdivided by Weber
according to the same principles as those governing the teleological examination of *attainable* goals.

1.1. In order to reach a certain goal, one must employ certain means. In
Weber's view, combined value analysis may initially elaborate the vertical
value structure of the means *as such,* and subsequently confront these value
structures with the ideals of the acting person.

This point is taken up by Weber at a remarkably late stage. It is first
mentioned in his speech at the congress of the *Verein* in 1909 [3], and is
elaborated in *Wertfreiheit* [4] and *Wiss. Beruf* [5]. The parallel to the late appearance in Weber's work of the problem of "Gesinnung" lies close at hand.
In order to judge means *by themselves,* without reference to their external
consequences, one needs a permanent internal standard of legitimate forms

---

22. This is expressed directly GAW, pp. 329, 529; indirectly, Weber reminds us of
these limits to the field of validity of the teleological valuations by always letting
the predicate "richtig" be accompanied by modifying words like "technisch"
for instance GAW, pp. 129, 520, 526).
1. The opposite problem: teleological criticism based on axiological analysis, would
depend on the assumption that the axiological starting-point (the value) had
empirical consequences, i. e., was set as a goal; but in that case, the analysis would
belong to the category discussed under *3.2.* above.
2. Thus Schelting, *Wissenschaftslehre,* 1934, p. 20n1.
3. GASS, p. 418.
4. GAW, pp. 508, 511, 513.
5. GAW, p. 607.

of behaviour. For instance, a democratic politician who refuses, for reasons of "principle", to negotiate with a dictator, even though he knows that the negotiation may result in the advancement of his democratic cause, will have to justify his refusal by means of arguments based on internal value axioms (questions of conscience, etc.) if he wants to shield himself from teleological criticism.

1.2. A second task of combined value analysis is that of working out the relations between the *side effects* of the necessary or chosen means and various value structures [6]. This analysis will show whether the side effects are ın accordance with the ideals of the acting person, or whether they conflict with these ideals to a greater or lesser degree [7].

2. Axiological criticism only applies to a goal which is isolated from the whole causal structure surrounding it, and is consequently only able to eliminate wholly inappropriate valuations. Teleological criticism, on the other hand, is concerned only with the practicability of the chosen goals. However important these forms of criticism may be in isolation, it is still reasonable to expect that the material on which actual criticism of goals (or of the means calculated to reach them) is based will in practice be furnished by the *combined* value analysis. The latter elaborates the vertical and horizontal value structure not only of the goal itself, but of the whole sequence of moves by which it is to be attained, and, in so doing, prepares our final verdict on it. In order to achieve this purpose, combined value analysis tries to furnish the answers to the two questions which may be said to define, in conjunction with the axiological and teleological questions ("What do we want?" and "What can we do?"), *the* central and fundamental political problem: "Does the end justify the means?" and "Does the end justify the side effects?".

As the above discussion concerning the binding force of teleological and axiological criticism showed us, it is not possible to *demonstrate* the necessity of answering these basic questions. In his methodological writings, Weber does not go into this problem as far as the combined analysis is concerned. But we find a significant passage in *Objektivität:* "... an der Abwägung von Zweck und Folgen des Handelns gegeneinander [kann] keine Selbstbesinnung verantwortlich handelnder Menschen vorbeigehen ..." [8] While *consistency* is the undemonstrable axiom of *axiological,* and orientation after

6. GAW, pp. 150, 508, 511, 513, 607; GASS, p. 418.
7. When Weber, GAW, p. 150, speaks of "ungewollte Folgen", the context shows this to refer to all *unforeseen* side effects, whether or not they are desirable. Consequently Brecht (Theory, 1959, p. 224n24) is right in describing the American translation of "ungewollt" by "undesirable" (Weber (Shils, Finch), *Methodology,* p. 53) as misleading.
8. GAW, p. 150.

external results that of *teleological,* criticism, Weber sees *responsibility* as the specific precondition on which the critical function of *combined* value analysis, the conclusive sifting of ends and means, is based. The aid which objective knowledge is able to render to subjective goals and actions depends on the assumption that the individual concerned is willing to act in a *responsible* manner [9]. This element of *responsibility* plays an important role in a part of Weber's argument which will be discussed towards the end of the present account [10].

3.1.1. A precondition of combined value analysis, and particularly of its critical function, is the acknowledgement of the fundamental "ethical irrationality" or "value irrationality" of the world [11]. Schelting, who strongly insists on the importance of this concept, explicates it as follows: "Wir stehen in unserem bewußten Leben und Handeln in zwei heterogenen "Gesetzesreihen", die sich völlig "indifferent" zueinander verhalten, und es gibt keine Gewähr dafür, daß die *kausal* notwendigen Mittel sich nach dem Wertgehalt der Zwecksetzung "richten" " [12]. In short, causal necessity and axiological consistency may run counter to each other.

If this assumption did not hold, it would be a waste of time to combine the axiological and teleological value analysis at all: in that case, empirical regularities would run absolutely parallel to the various axiological structures; the technically necessary or sufficient means to reach an ethically positive goal would always be equally positive from an ethical point of view, and would only have ethically positive side effects.

3.1.2. Although (or perhaps: because) it is quite clear from Weber's work, and in fact follows logically from his theory of the fundamental value conflict [13], that he himself regards the world as value-irrational, his explicit treatment of the point is limited to the discussion, in *Pol. Beruf,* of a special case, viz, *ethical* irrationality, which is of course of particular importance to the active politician [14]. However, the idea is based on a view [15] of causal

---

9. The importance of the idea of *responsibility* in this connection is strongly emphasized by Schelting (*Wissenschaftslehre,* 1934, pp. 13, 14, 16).
10. P. 263.
11. The first term is Weber's own (GPS, p. 541); the second one, which represents a generalization of the principle, is coined by Schelting (*Wissenschaftslehre,* 1934, p. 28).
12. Schelting, *Wissenschaftslehre,* 1934, p. 26.
13. Pp. 178–79. Reference may also be made to a note from 1903 (DZA II, Rep. 92, No. 31, Vol. 6) which contains the following passage: "Welt ist auch *darin* irrational, daß der *Campf* ewig ist, auch *im* Menschen, auch zwischen *Zweck* u. Mittel". Loos, *Wertlehre,* 1970, p. 56n173 rightly observes that the idea of "value irrationality" does not *necessarily* imply the existence of a value conflict: the world may be viewed as value-irrational even if only *one* value is assumed to be relevant.
14. GPS, pp. 542–44.
15. *Cf.* Schelting, *Wissenschaftslehre,* 1934, p. 28.

connections as being in themselves "wertindifferent", neutral with regard to values, which is closely connected with Weber's previously [16] discussed, reiterated doctrine according to which the material of social science only *possesses* such meaning as it is *given:* Weber's fight against objectivism and intuitionism is implicitly a fight to prevent the axiological and the teleological systems from being identified with each other.

3.1.3. In *Pol. Beruf,* Weber strongly emphasizes the ethical irrationality of the world. This irrationality is, in his view, demonstrated by "nicht nur der ganze Verlauf der Weltgeschichte, sondern jede rückhaltlose Prüfung der Alltagserfahrung" [17], and it is the active factor behind the rise of the various religions, although the solutions of the problem provided by the latter have of course varied widely.

It will be noticed that the argument is partly based on empirical facts which may serve as an indication, but by no means as a verification, of its correctness [18]. The rise of religion may perfectly well result from the prevalence of logical fallacies, and the "course of world history" is also a somewhat shaky standard of measurement, if one considers Weber's own warning that the subject-matter of history possesses no intrinsic meaning. Strictly speaking, we are left only with "die rückhaltlose Prüfung der Alltagserfahrung", but the latter is in fact amply sufficient. As soon as a person has established by this means (which in practice amounts to a combined value analysis *en miniature*) the existence of just one discrepancy between the teleological and the axiological system, he is compelled to acknowledge that only a combined value analysis can help him to a full awareness of his various goals and values.

3.1.4. It should be stressed that the assumption of the value irrationality of the world does not imply that the axiological and the teleological systems run counter to each other at *every* point, that, for instance, *only* evil means lead to good results. Such an interpretation would mean that the assumption of value irrationality could never be conclusively verified, since any future instance of concordance between the axiological and the teleological systems would suffice to disprove it.

3.2.1. The idea of the value irrationality of the world becomes especially significant when viewed in conjunction with the assumption, discussed above [19], of the "Allzusammenhang alles Geschehens". To repeat a metaphor of Schopenhauer's, which Weber uses [20], causation is not a cab which can be hailed and made to pull up at will. The first consequence of this is that behaviour

16. P. 106.
17. GPS, p. 542.
18. *Cf. supra,* pp. 45–46 and *infra,* pp. 184–85.
19. P. 164.
20. GAW, p. 77.

does not only have calculated and desired consequences: means, even when viewed in an isolated context of cause and effect, are not "causally neutral"; this circumstance raises the whole problem of the teleological "side effects". But moreover, the causal effects of behaviour not only reach beyond what is *desired,* but also, in principle, beyond the realm of *prediction:* an individual who acts should be aware of the fact that he will never be able to enumerate or predict all the consequences of his actions. If the world were value-*rational,* this would not matter greatly, since all the consequences, predictable or unpredictable, of, for instance, ethically positive actions would be ethically positive in their turn. But the fundamental value *irrationality* of the world means that the consequences of a given action cannot be guaranteed to take over its axiological status; and in the present case, where we deal with unpredictable consequences, no combined value analysis, however thorough, would be able to reveal *what* the axiological status of these unpredictable consequences would be. Any person acting with the intention of attaining a certain goal should realize that the final result of his action may be absolutely contrary to his original intention, and that he has no means of preventing this development, or even of predicting its precise direction. This is what Schelting in his careful analysis, keeping close to Weber's own terminology, refers to as "die Paradoxie der Folgen" [21], *the paradox of consequences.*

3.2.2. Apparently, Weber himself only once, in *Pol. Beruf,* discusses this question explicitly, and then in close connection with the problems of political action [22]. However, the concept of a "paradox of consequences" is rooted in Weber's view of theoretical value relation. According to the latter, the values which have guided human behaviour during a certain period or in a certain culture may be absolutely different from those which guide the judgment or investigation by posterity of this behaviour. This idea of a theoretical "Bedeutungswandel" is quite parallel to the assumption of a paradox of consequences. But whereas the phenomenon of "Bedeutungswandel", which is viewed in a theoretical context, primarily engages our neutral *interest,* its practical correlate, the paradox of consequences, defines a situation which Weber sees as deeply *tragic,* when he speaks of "das Wissen um die Tragik, in die alles Tun ... in Wahrheit verflochten ist" [23, 24].

21. Schelting, *Wissenschaftslehre,* 1934, pp. 42–52.
22. GPS, p. 535.
23. GPS, p. 535.
24. Judith Janoska-Bendl (*Idealtypus,* 1965, p. 11) claims that Weber's "Überzeugung von der prinzipiellen *Irrationalität* der an sich seienden Wirklichkeit" acted as a (philosophical) ontological premise in his methodology. If the statement is meant to refer to the value irrationality discussed above, the choice of terms is unfortunate: what Weber sees as irrational is not reality *in itself* (since the category of irrationality is not inherent *in,* but applied *to* the subject–matter) but reality *in*

4.1. As we have seen, Weber regarded both axiological, teleological and combined value analysis as necessary to the complete understanding of the premises and consequences of action in a given situation. But in *Wiss. Beruf* [25], he interestingly enough ranks these three kinds of scientific investigation of values not only according to their content or function, but also according to the inherent *dignity* which they possess in his eyes. He accords the lowest place to the empirical analysis (including teleological value analysis) "... wie man das Leben, die äußeren Dinge sowohl wie das Handeln der Menschen, durch Berechnung beherrscht ..." [26]. This is *technical* knowledge, which can be regarded as a transferable *commodity*, fundamentally no different from the vegetables bought at the greengrocer's [27]. Combined analysis, of course, goes further, but is still seen by Weber as restricted to the field of technical knowledge in the sense that the situations of choice are defined according to the empirical relations of the means, ends and side effects to each other. The purpose of this kind of analysis is finally to sanction or reject a concrete goal; the intention is practical [28]. Consequently, the highest rank in Weber's hierarchy is assumed by the purely axiological analysis of values, by means of which the goal is not criticized on grounds of empirical impossibility or because striving for it has undesirable consequences, but simply as the concrete embodiment of a certain *value*. Weber sees this kind of analysis, and this kind only, as yielding purely *theoretical* knowledge: "... *Rechenschaft ... über den letzten Sinn seines* [the acting person's] *eigenen Tuns*" [29]. Whereas technical knowledge (in the broad sense of the word), and consequently the results of teleological and combined value analysis, *may* be defined as valuable solely on account of the material advantages which its possession affords, axiological analysis, being completely theoretical, yields knowledge the value of which cannot be deduced from its practical advantages, and which Weber therefore sees as having an *ethical* function. And it is significant that Weber believes one of the results of this ethical function to be a heightened sense of *responsibility* of the acting person [30], the quality, that is, which this person needs in order to acknowledge teleological and combined value analysis as legitimate not only when they offer him material advantages, *but also in cases where the criticism which they imply*

its relation to (and, in Weber's view, fundamental discrepancy from) any axiological structure. Nor is it accurate to claim that Weber's theory of value irrationality depends on or hides ontological and philosophical premises. Weber's argument is based on a combination of axiological and teleological value analysis, both of which he regards as objectively valid.

25. GAW, pp. 607–08.
26. GAW, p. 607.
27. The simile is Weber's.
28. GAW, pp. 607–08.
29. GAW, p. 608.
30. GAW, p. 608.

conflicts with his material interests. An individual who entirely keeps within a "technical" universe—in the broad sense—will not get sufficient opportunity to exercise his sense of responsibility. Only by submitting to the abstract and theoretical demands of axiology will he learn how to withstand the concrete temptations of teleology [31].

4.2. This part of Weber's argument seems to have evolved gradually in his mind and to have received its clear formulation at a rather late stage of his methodological production. Apart from the date of *Wiss. Beruf* (1919), another circumstance, which was already touched upon above, points in the same direction. While Weber in the *Objektivität* and *Stammler* essays [32] bases his discussion on the question whether the available, or any other, means are *sufficient* to reach a goal, and what would be the side effects of such sufficient means, in his later essays [33] he instead takes as his starting-point the problem of the *necessary* means and their side effects. In its shortest form, the question of the early essays runs: "Is it possible for me to reach the goal A with the means at my disposal and without too heavy a "cost" to other ideals and goals to which I am committed?"; while Weber later asks: "What does my acceptance of the goal A entail?" The shift of emphasis is small but significant: in the former case, the goal *as a concrete goal* is given. Although it may be dropped as a result of the criticism implicit in the value analysis, this criticism is basically directed at the means: "I cannot reach my goal A by the means available without paying too high a price. That is: the means are unsuitable; therefore I must modify the goal". In the latter case, the goal is given only in a hypothetical sense, not absolutely fixed, and serves as the direct target for the criticism resulting from the value analysis: "The achievement of the goal is tied to the employment of means the "cost" of which is unacceptable. That is: the goal is unacceptable". There seems to be a definite shift here away from a technical towards an "axiological" *starting-point,* a closer attention to the ultimate value axioms. This shift of emphasis does not amount to a change of attitude, but rather indicates a greater awareness of the consequences of an already drawn conclusion. The problem changes, but not the solution.

3.4. *The "explanatory" value analysis*

1. The forms of value analysis dealt with above do not exhaust all the possibilities of scientific treatment of values: we still have to consider the analysis

---

31. This train of thought is not made explicit in Wiss. Beruf, but seems to lie close to the surface of Weber's argument.
32. GAW, pp. 149, 312; see also GASS, p. 402.
33. GAW, pp. 508, 510, 607.

of how values come to be held, and of the consequences of their existence. Although it may be tempting to ignore these relations, they are independent of the teleo- and axiological problems: the *causes* of a commitment to a valuation (say, the rejection by a die-hard Conservative of a liberalization of the Penal Code) are seldom restricted to the relevant ultimate value axioms (principles of law and order, of responsibility, etc.), but may originate in, for instance, traumatic personal experiences (in this case perhaps authoritarian education, personal losses in connection with crimes of violence or burglary, etc.); in the same way, the *actual* consequences of committing oneself to a certain value or course of action are by no means identical with the *logical* ones (thus, the fact that the West German government abandons the Hallstein doctrine has political effects apart from the logical one that the Federal Republic will no longer automatically break off diplomatic relations with countries according diplomatic recognition to the GDR).

On the other hand, one might regard these last points as less important inasmuch as the values are here treated as what the Germans call "reine Faktizitäten", i. e., without any regard for their specific axiological or goal-character, but simply as empirical facts.

2. In fact, Weber's methodological work seems to contain only infrequent references to these empirical relations [1]. With regard to the question of the *causes* of valuational commitment we find only one explicit discussion, in *Wertfreiheit;* but in the light of the conclusions drawn above, the passage in question seems so difficult to interpret that it is necessary to quote it in full:

"Durch empirisch-psychologische und historische Untersuchung eines bestimmten Wertungsstandpunktes auf seine individuelle, soziale, historische Bedingtheit hin gelangt man nun und nimmer je zu irgend etwas anderem, als dazu: ihn *verstehend zu erklären*. Das ... ist ... wissenschaftlich höchst wichtig 1. für den Zweck einer empirischen Kausalbetrachtung menschlichen Handelns, um dessen *wirkliche* letzte *Motive* kennen zu lernen, 2. aber, wenn man mit einem (wirklich oder scheinbar) abweichend Wertenden diskutiert, für die Ermittlung der wirklichen gegenseitigen Wertungsstandpunkte" [2].

Both the passage and the context [3] make it plain that the kind of scientific inquiry described here by Weber goes beyond teleological, axiological and combined value analysis and enters the field of causal explanation. Moreover, the term "verstehend zu erklären" seems to suggest that the causal analysis

1. The question discussed above, p. 53, of the empirical consequences of judicial norms will not be considered in this connection.
2. GAW, p. 503.
3. Weber has been discussing "realistic" normative sciences (ethics, mathematics), i. e., disciplines which causally explain the formulation of ethical or mathematical (normative) statements (GAW, pp. 502–03).

in question is of a special kind, by which the value judgment is not only explained but also, and apparently as an integral part of the explanation, somehow "understood" or "intuited", the former term carrying a meaning which may be more or less distant from that of ordinary language. And this kind of "intuitive" causal explanation should apparently, according to the wording of the passage, be seen as having a function which not only *supplements* that of the other kinds of value analysis, but which actually *competes* with them since it is supposed (like teleological value analysis) to explain human behaviour and (like axiological value analysis) to uncover the "actual" valuation. This opens new perspectives of interpretation; and although the present account should not pursue the theme of human action beyond the point at which it loses contact with the problem of values as an object of scientific inquiry, it seems necessary to clarify the implications of the passage quoted by placing it in a broader context.

3. In order to achieve this purpose, it may be useful to reconsider Weber's view that axiological and teleological value analysis, combined or in isolation, possess a *critical* function. This criticism is based on the examination of a number of conceptual or empirical facts which, *if the individual in question had not yet taken them into account,* might impel him to a change of attitude. In other words, the critical function of the value analysis presupposes a certain measure of empirical and/or conceptual *ignorance* in the person whose value judgment is submitted to criticism. And in actual fact, behaviour which is axiologically fully elaborated and at the same time teleologically faultless must be regarded as a limiting case. If we are therefore to *understand* values, i. e., realize *why* people commit themselves to this or that position, axiological and teleological value analysis is not sufficient. One must try to supplement their *logically* and *empirically* correct constructions by a correct *psychological* explanation [4].

4.1. Such an explanation may have a certain *derivative* importance as a condition of effective axiological analysis. An axiological discussion of values may be completely unfruitful if the scholar restricts himself to telling the participants what their value judgments "really" mean, and that if they think differently, they are wrong. It will be far more effective to look for the ultimate axioms which *actually* guide these persons, (i. e., from which they (wrongly) believe that their concrete valuations may be deduced), and to

4. The "historical" and "social" aspects mentioned by Weber are not taken into account here, not because they are less important, but because their axiological importance is only *indirect;* values do not, in Weber's view, exist independently of human beings; and consequently, the fact that a value is subject to "historical influence" is to be classified as an external factor of the psychological development of the value structure of the individual concerned.

continue the discussion on this level by demonstrating the incompatibility of such axioms with other ones, etc.

4.2 The most important function of psychological explanation, however, is an *independent* one: if we examine human behaviour, we are not usually able to explain it—to decide, that is, *why* people act as they do—simply by reference to a faultless teleological construction. Instead, we have to attempt a *psychological* explanation of the kind mentioned: since the latter is based on more or less certain knowledge of the probable axiological or teleological "fallacies" which may operate in the concrete case, and of the circumstances in which they are particularly liable to flourish, it may, at least, provide the scholar with hypotheses which he may even be able to test. In other words, if we wish, as Weber says GAW, p. 503, to carry out "eine empirische Kausalbetrachtung menschlichen Handelns, um dessen *wirkliche* letzte *Motive* kennen zu lernen", psychological explanation of this kind, "verstehende Erklärung", is usually unavoidable.

The "explanatory" value analysis plays a very large part in Weber's own sociology. In the context of the present work, it becomes important in connection with the discussion of the ideal type.

3.5. The value conflict

Weber's discussion of the *possibilities* of value analysis, as set out above, frequently includes a further point, viz, the claim that ultimate values are in axiological conflict with each other, what we may call the doctrine of the *fundamental value conflict* [1].

3.5.1. Formulation

1. The theory of the collision of values is put forward as early as *Objektivität*:

"Das Schicksal einer Kulturepoche, die vom Baum der Erkenntnis gegessen hat, ist es, wissen zu müssen, daß ... die höchsten Ideale, die uns am mächtigsten bewegen, für alle Zeit nur im Kampf mit anderen Idealen sich auswirken, die anderen ebenso heilig sind, wie uns die unseren" [2].

The nature and consequences of this view are obviously not regarded by Weber as being of an everyday nature, a point which is emphasized by his expression "der gewaltige Ernst dieser Sachlage" [3]. The emotional tension seems to be greater still in the later essays: here, the conflict of values and

1. Weber himself in one case (GAW, p. 508) uses the term "Wertkollision", but also speaks of a "Konflikt" between values (for instance GAW, pp. 504, 508).
2. GAW, p. 154.
3. GAW, p. 154.

ideals is interpreted as a fight between the different "gods"[4], and in *Wertfreiheit*, even more radically, as an "unüberbrückbar tödlicher Kampf, so wie zwischen "Gott" und "Teufel" "[5]. *Wiss. Beruf* contains similar phrases [6].

The exact meaning of passages like the ones quoted is a matter of some difficulty: their precision is blurred by their literary pathos. Read in the context of axiological and combined value analysis, they can probably be interpreted as follows: For any value axiom or valuation, the proposition holds that it is possible to define another such value axiom or valuation, on the same level of abstraction, with which it conflicts axiologically (in the sense that the value judgment of a concrete phenomenon deduced from the former axiom would be different from that deduced from the latter one). And since Weber emphasizes that ultimate value axioms must be *unambiguous,* this means that he regards all value systems as being "open" upwards [7], i. e., that no empirical or theoretical science is able to demonstrate, whether in a concrete case or generally, the existence of only one single ultimate value axiom: on any level of abstraction, it will always be possible to find two or more conflicting axioms [8].

2. Weber does not limit himself to the general assertion of the existence of a fundamental axiological value conflict, but frequently goes into closer detail concerning the nature of the conflict and the values involved.
2.1. The more detailed treatment of these problems occurs rather late in Weber's production, though. In *Objektivität,* where the basic idea of a value conflict is already propounded with much weight, Weber's only concrete example is that of the conflict between ethical norms and "Kulturwerte" [9]. This conflict, which forms a parallel to Weber's claim [10] that it is impossible to deduce ethical norms of behaviour from empirical cultural values, is quite general. Either side may accommodate a number of materially different

4. The first instance of this is found in *Zwei Ges.* (GPS, p. 142).
5. GAW, p. 507; the passage in question is not found in the *Gutachten,* but is an addition from 1917.
6. GAW, pp. 603, 608.
7. If we discard the assumption that the ultimate value axioms are unambiguous, this means that an axiological conflict on a lower level of abstraction need not persist on a higher level: for instance, if the term "democracy" is not defined in precise terms, it is possible to deduce from it totally opposed concrete value judgments.
8. This does not, of course, imply that *all* imaginable ultimative value axioms conflict with each other in each given case. Such an implication could only be supported by a philosophical theory of the structure of the value sphere, and this theory could not be regarded as scientific in the sense of the term adopted by Weber, and in the present account.
9. GAW, p. 154.
10. *Supra,* pp. 44–45.

value systems, so that the opposition expressed seems to be simply the fundamental one between society and the individual.

2.2. Letters and fragments quoted by Baumgarten [11] contain slight indications of the value spheres which Weber has in mind; but it is not until *Wertfreiheit,* and a political essay from 1916 bearing the significant title "Zwischen zwei Gesetzen" (*Zwei Ges.*), that we find explicit discussions of this point, which is later taken up in *Wiss. Beruf* and *Pol. Beruf.*

It is clear from these essays that Weber mostly remains within a well-established and traditional framework. As examples of the values involved in the value conflict, he mentions the *erotic* [12] and the *aesthetic* [13] sphere, and values like intellect (truth) and religion [14].

2.3.1. Occasionally, Weber treats the *ethical* sphere in quite the same way as the other "traditional" value spheres. Thus, he writes in *Wiss. Beruf:* "... eine Alltagsweisheit ist es, daß etwas wahr sein kann, obwohl und indem es nicht schön und nicht heilig und nicht gut ist" [15]. In the same passage, the Good is opposed to the True. But closer scrutiny reveals that Weber experiences difficulty in treating the ethical value sphere as being on the same level as those of religion, aesthetics, etc.

2.3.2. In this connection, the problem seems to have been that the Kantian categorical imperative of ethics, which was regarded by Weber as the natural basis for a definition of a distinctive ethical value sphere, was of an extremely *abstract* and correspondingly formal nature [16]. This led certain thinkers to claim that the categorical imperative was *completely* formal, i. e., that it could not serve as a basis for practical value judgments at all.

If this extreme interpretation were accepted, Weber's doctrine of the fundamental conflict of values would be seriously weakened: *every* value, *qua* value implies that a person committed to it acknowledges the legitimacy of the demand for value orientation, i. e., accepts the value of ethics (defined in this

11. Baumgarten, *Weber,* 1964, pp. 400–01 (fragment from c. 1912), 645 (letter to E. Jaffé 1907), 670n1 (letter to Toennies 1908).
12. GAW, p. 507; see also GARS, pp. 554, 556–63.
13. This value sphere is opposed to that of religion (GAW, pp. 603–04; GPS, p. 142; GARS, pp. 554–56), of ethics (GAW, pp. 603–04; Baumgarten, *Weber,* 1964, p. 652) and of truth (GAW, pp. 603–04).
14. Concerning the tension between intellect and religion, *cf.* GAW, pp. 504, 603, 604; GARS, pp. 564–66; Baumgarten, *Weber,* 1964, p. 670n1. Concerning the tension between intellect and ethics, *cf.* GAW, pp. 504, 604.
15. GAW, p. 604. In a letter to Mina Tobler from 1915 (Baumgarten, *Weber,* 1964, p. 652) we find a similar contrast between the "sittlich" and the "schön".
16. Apparently, Weber concentrates on one of the two parts of the Kantian imperative, viz, the statement according to which other human beings may not be used exclusively as *means,* but should also invariably be the *end* of action, a statement which in Weber's discussion seems to be interpreted as follows: To qualify as ethical, an action must be oriented towards *some* value. *Cf.* GAW, p. 506 and Schelting, *Wissenschaftslehre,* 1934, p. 46.

completely formal manner); consequently, formal ethics must be regarded as standing outside or aloof from the general conflict of values. Naturally, such a special status of ethics, while extremely welcome to the "ethical" school of economics, was not acceptable to Weber [17]. An article by the leader of the "ethicists", Schmoller, in the *Handwörterbuch der Staatswissenschaften* [18], in which the "formal" view of ethical norms was used as an argument against Weber, made evident the need for an explicit defence on the latter's part [19]. Accordingly, the *Gutachten* contains a brief rejection of Schmoller's view [20]; and in *Wertfreiheit,* this summary denial is underpinned by a detailed argument [21], which for the first time gives a clear indication of Weber's solution of the problem concerning the status of ethics relative to the other traditional value spheres, and at the same time reaffirms his doctrine of the conflict of *all* value spheres.

3.1. Weber is perfectly aware, however, that the "traditional" examples are by no means exhaustive, but only represent "die elementarsten Fälle dieses Kampfes der Götter der einzelnen Ordnungen und Werte" [22].

For one thing, the conflict between the "traditional" value spheres may manifest itself on all levels of abstraction: since it is impossible to demonstrate scientifically that only *one* particular value is relevant to a concrete phenomenon, the fundamental value conflict may flare up in connection with quite insignificant details: the tension beteeen "God" and "the Devil" communicates itself, in its full logical force, to the problems of everyday life.

Although it seems justified to ascribe this view to Weber, it usually remains implicit in his work. But he gives a number of instances of value conflicts *apart from* the "traditional" ones mentioned above.

Occasionally, the definition of such "non-traditional" conflicts seems to indicate that Weber finds the "traditional" antagonisms too vague and ambiguous. In *Wiss. Beruf,* he writes: "Wie man es machen will, "wissenschaftlich" zu entscheiden zwischen dem *Wert* der französischen und deutschen Kultur, weiß ich nicht" [23]. *Zwei Ges.,* too, contains a strong reminder

---

17. *Cf. supra,* pp. 80–81.
18. Reprinted as Schmoller, *Volkswirtschaftslehre,* 1949.
19. Notes of Weber's (DZA II, Rep. 92, No. 31, Vol. 6) show that he was probably convinced of the inadequacy of the radically "formal" position as early as 1903.
20. *Gutachten,* pp. 97–98.
21. GAW, pp. 505–06. Here Weber, reversing Schmoller's argument, claims that "jene Sphären von Werten, welche die Behandlung des andern "nur als Mittel" gestatten oder vorschreiben, der Ethik gegenüber heterogen [sind]" (GAW, p. 506).
22. GAW, p. 604.
23. GAW, p. 604. Naturally enough, Aron (*Introduction,* 1963, p. 48) concentrates on this example, and even regards it as the (in his view, insufficient) *basis* of Weber's general theory of the fundamental value conflict (Raymond Aron, "Max Weber und die Machtpolitik", Stammer (ed.), *Weber,* 1965, p. 116). The singling

that "Kleinvolk-Kulturwerte" conflict with the duties and possibilities of the "power state" [24]. In these cases, the general value sphere of "culture" (with which Weber contrasted that of the individual: cultural values vs. individual ethics) is not differentiated according to material fields of activity —i. e., into various "cultural values", such as politics, literature, art, etc.— but along "formal" geographical lines. Although other "formal" distinctions (e. g. chronological ones) are conceivable [25], Weber seems to be particularly interested in the geographical one [26].

3.2. As far as the "non-traditional" conflicts are concerned, Weber's main attention seems to centre on the problems of the *ethical* sphere. True, he assumes (as we have seen) that Kantian ethics *may* serve as a basis for certain practical value judgments. But, on the other hand, he emphasizes that this assumption in no wise amounts to the claim that the categorical imperative, as he interprets it, offers a basis for unambiguous value judgments of *every* phenomenon and event. In other words, certain groups of problems are ethically neutral, if "ethics" is defined in the narrow Kantian sense adopted by Weber. Consequently, value judgments concerning these problems may only lay claim to the predicate "ethical" if they are based on a new and more "material" definition of ethics.

A number of passages seem to indicate that Weber expects such problems to be of a *practical* nature, to be relevant to the sphere of action. In *Wertfreiheit,* for instance, he writes: "Die Möglichkeit einer normativen Ethik wird allerdings dadurch nicht in Frage gestellt, daß es Probleme *praktischer* Art gibt, für welche sie aus sich selbst heraus keine eindeutigen Weisungen geben kann . . ." [27]

3.2.1. The concrete example given by Weber in this connection is also, as he himself points out, a practical one: that of "justice" and "just distribution" in the field of social policy [28]. Here, he outlines two diametrically opposed definitions of "just distribution": according to the first one, benefits should be distributed in *direct* proportion to effort (the latter being, of course, in part a product of the physical and intellectual *ability* of the individual); according to the second one, benefits should be distributed in *inverse* proportion to effort (in order to *neutralize* differences of intellect and strength) [29].

out of the purely political motives of Weber's thought seems a little excessive; as we shall see, Weber argues his theory and gives instances of it with respect to many other fields than the political one.

24. GPS, pp. 139–41.
25. GAW, p. 246, Weber points to a possible chronological conflict in the field of aesthetics.
26. *Cf. infra,* pp. 253–55.
27. GAW, p. 504.
28. GAW, p. 505.
29. The example is becoming increasingly important: where Weber had to go back

Both of these principles, he claims, are "ethical" in the Kantian sense; consequently, the question of the just distribution of benefits in society cannot be finally resolved by recourse to Kantian ethics.

3.2.2 The problem of justice showed the difficulty of deciding *what* should be the end of practical (here: political) action. But Weber goes still further and raises a fundamental question on which the whole of his subsequent discussion of politics and of its relation to the ethical and other value spheres is based: should action be deliberately guided by the wish to attain certain goals *at all?* This question is put in an important passage:

> "... die Grundfrage: ob der Eigenwert des ethischen Handelns—der "reine Wille" oder die "Gesinnung", pflegt man das auszudrücken—allein zu seiner Rechtfertigung genügen soll, nach der Maxime: "der Christ handelt recht und stellt den Erfolg Gott anheim", wie christliche Ethiker sie formuliert haben. Oder ob die Verantwortung für die als möglich oder wahrscheinlich vorauszusehenden *Folgen* des Handelns, wie sie dessen Verflochtenheit in die ethisch irrationale Welt bedingt, mit in Betracht zu ziehen ist.
> ... diese Maximen liegen untereinander in ewigem Zwist, der mit den Mitteln einer rein in sich selbst beruhenden Ethik schlechthin unaustragbar ist" [30].

3.3. Alongside of the theory of the fundamental conflict of values, it is this special antagonism which will be the focus of the discussion in the rest of this chapter. Even though its full weight and importance will only become apparent later on, an introductory treatment and definition is necessary at this stage.

The essence of the dichotomy, as described in the passage quoted above [31], is the rejection or acceptance by the acting person of the principle of letting his actions be guided by their predicted *consequences* and by the positive or negative value with which the person invests these consequences. Though contradictory, both attitudes are "ethical" in the narrow Kantian sense, so that it is justified to qualify them both as "ethics", and, as Weber does a little later, to define them respectively as the *ethic of conviction* ("Gesinnungsethik"), and the *ethic of consequences* ("Erfolgsethik") [32].

to Babeuf for his "neutralizing" definition, we may now point to works like Michael Young's *The Rise of the Meritocracy.*

30. GAW, p. 505. This passage is not found in the *Gutachten,* which, however, already contains a number of other observations concerning the fundamental conflict described (*Gutachten,* pp. 104–06, *cf.* GAW, pp. 513–15). The latter is definitely present in Weber's mind as early as 1912, in the "fragment on ethics" quoted above (Baumgarten, *Weber,* 1964, pp. 399–400), which appears to be his first statement of the problem. Another early account of the dichotomy is found GARS, pp. 552–53.

31. Weber's views are not modified through time, so that the passage quoted may legitimately serve as a paradigm.

32. The term "Gesinnungsethik" is Weber's own, whereas "Erfolgsethik" is not found in GAW, but constructed by Baumgarten (*Weber,* 1964, p. 655) in close

Obviously, the two sides of the antagonism find their complete parallels in aspects of Weber's thought discussed above. Thus, the ethic of conviction is by definition guided by the wish to conform to the ethical rationality inherent in any axiologically consistent system [33]. On the other hand, the ethic of consequences is based on the *combination* of ethical and causal rationality reflected in the combined value analysis.

The fact that the two alternatives are neutral in relation to Kantian ethics means that they *cut across* the traditional value distinctions forming the framework of Kantian ethics. The ethic of conviction may legitimately operate in connection with any consistent axiological system which in some way rejects the "world", i. e., which denies the relevance of the category of physical causation to problems of action [34]. Accordingly, the fact that ethics and religion, the Good and the Sacred, are described by Weber as separate spheres when he discusses the value conflict, does not prevent him from defining a *religious ethic of conviction*. Quite on the contrary: Weber may even without contradicting himself regard the radical commitment to religious values as the most extreme instance of an ethic of conviction. The dichotomy between the ethic of conviction and the ethic of consequences merges with the fundamental tension between the "spirit" and the "world" [35].

3.5.2. *Logical status*

3.5.2.1. *Validity*

1. Naturally, a crucial question is that concerning the kind of validity which Weber claims for his theory of the fundamental conflict of values. Does he see the latter as demonstrable by scientific means? as an undemonstrable, speculative conclusion? or simply as an (absolute or relative) subjective preference?

1.1. In *Objektivität* (in which, as we have seen, the theory is stated in a fairly undifferentiated form) Weber occasionally employs modified formula-

connection with Weber's thought and terminology (see for instance the contrast between "Gesinnungswert" and "Erfolgswert", GAW, p. 514).

33. *Cf. supra,* p. 171.
34. This is the gist of Weber's statement concerning the consistent syndicalist: "Im übrigen ist ... sein Reich, wie das Reich jeder Gesinnungsethik, nicht von dieser Welt" (GAW, p. 514).
35. In *Zw. betr.,* where Weber describes the development of the tension between the religions of salvation and the "world", the amalgamation mentioned in the text is clearly noticeable. This, Weber speaks of "Gesinnungsreligiosität", as opposed to the "innere Eigengesetzlichkeiten" of the world (all of the latter being connected with rational systems apart from that of religious conviction); *cf.* GARS, p. 552. For Schelting's interpretation of the dichotomy, see Appendix B of this chapter.

tions which suggest that he only regards it as (more or less) *probable* that an axiological conflict can be demonstrated to exist between the value chosen and one or more other values. For instance, we find a passage like: "Da in der großen Ueberzahl aller Fälle jeder erstrebte Zweck ... etwas "kostet" oder doch kosten kann ..." [1], and, a little later: "... wenn wir ... die Konflikte, in welche der Versuch der praktischen Durchführung [of a goal] alsbald hinein führt, für rein technische Fragen der Zweckmäßigkeit ansehen wollten—was recht oft irrig wäre ..." [2]. The first of these passages, however, deals not with the *fundamental* value conflict but with the weighing, in the course of a combined value analysis, of undesirable side effects against the desired goal, a situation which in certain respects differs from that with regard to which the value conflict is defined [3]. As for the second passage, it only seems to emphasize the fundamental truth that means cannot be expected to be value neutral: because of the value irrationality of the world, a value analysis is insufficient if it does not go beyond a teleological examination.

The only indication of a genuine hesitation on Weber's part with regard to the absolute validity of the principle is also found in *Objektivität*, GAW, p. 150, where Weber uses the expression that any kind of behaviour "in seinen Konsequenzen eine *Parteinahme* zugunsten bestimmter Werte bedeutet, und damit ... regelmäßig *gegen andere*". Strictly speaking, the term "regelmäßig", with its exclusive *empirical* reference, is incompatible with the postulate of *logical* truth.

1.2. On the other hand, Weber constantly, and particularly in his later essays, claims that the value conflict is *eternal* and *absolute*. As we have seen, he is fond of the metaphor of an *eternal* conflict between "gods", "God" and "the Devil", etc: "Es handelt sich ... zwischen den Werten letztlich überall und immer wieder ... um unüberbrückbar tödlichen Kampf ..." [4]; and this terminology which, although expressive, is not altogether precise with regard to the question of validity, is supplemented by references to the *absolute* nature of the conflict, its "Unaustragbarkeit" in terms of scientific demonstration [5]. These two characteristics are even explicitly linked together in a passage in *Wiss. Beruf* where Weber speaks of "der ewige Kampf [der] ... Götter miteinander ...—unbildlich gesprochen: die Unvereinbarkeit und also die Unaustragbarkeit des Kampfes der letzten überhaupt *möglichen* Standpunkte zum Leben ..." [6]

1. GAW, p. 150.
2. GAW, p. 153.
3. *Cf. infra*, pp. 194–97.
4. GAW, p. 507; similar formulations GAW, pp. 154, 604, 605, 608.
5. See for instance GAW, pp. 603, 609.
6. GAW, p. 608.

All in all, it seems justified to conclude that Weber regards his theory of the fundamental conflict of values as the expression of a "Grundsach-verhalt" [7], as a *logically true statement*.

2. This positive conclusion has a number of negative implications:
2.1. First of all, the *logical* validity of Weber's theory stands in sharp contrast to its definite lack of *actual empirical acceptance*. This is pointed out by Weber himself in *Wertfreiheit*: "In fast jeder einzelnen wichtigen Stellungnahme realer Menschen kreuzen und verschlingen sich ... die Wertsphären" [8]: in other words, the principle of axiological consistency is not observed in practice. One reason for this intermingling of the value spheres *may* be the wish for material gain: the confusion may be "pragmatisch bedingt" [9]; but, as in the case of his discussion of pseudo-value freedom [10] (which runs parallel to the present one), Weber often points to the part played by purely psychological and unconscious factors. The grim consciousness of the antagonism of values is worn down and fades away into the "routine" of everyday life, the "Alltag", absorbed by its toil ("das stumpfe Geschehenlassen") or neutralized by the unconscious and steady tendency to bring about a comfortable harmonization of opposites [11, 12].

Weber's discussion of the question of the empirical awareness (or lack of awareness) of the value conflict, and of the connected problem concerning the actual axiological consistency of action, has strong ethical overtones. But it is worth noting that his treatment of the problem of the "Alltag" is not restricted to the ethical and axiological field, but includes reflections on the very *fact* of the unconscious harmonization of conflicts, and on its

7. GAW, p. 608.
8. GAW, p. 507.
9. GAW, p. 507.
10. *Cf. supra*, pp. 66–67.
11. GAW, pp. 154–55, 507, 517.
12. Occasionally (for the first time in *Zwei Ges.*), Weber employs a phrase borrowed from John Stuart Mill, according to which all purely empirical views of the world lead to polytheism (GPS, p. 142; GAW, pp. 507, 603, see also GPS, p. 542). However, the scope of this assertion remains somewhat hazy. Sometimes (GAW, p. 507), Mill's "polytheism" seems to be interpreted as the *actual* "Verschlingung der Wertsphären". But elsewhere, for instance in *Zwei Ges.* (GPS, p. 142), and most clearly in *Wiss. Beruf* (GAW, pp. 603–04), Weber extends the argument and makes the "polytheism" in question function almost as a synonym for the value conflict *itself*.

The latter construction does not appear justified. The polytheism of the Greeks, the fact, in Weber's own words, that they "einmal der Aphrodite opferte[n] und dann dem Apollon und vor allem jeder den Göttern seiner Stadt" (GAW, p. 604), definitely seems to imply a conception of *harmony*. In *Pol. Beruf* (which is delivered a few weeks after *Wiss. Beruf*), Weber apparently reverts to a less radical interpretation, according to which the gods of the Greeks were worshipped side by side, although they "quite often" fought among themselves.

consequences. As was the case with a previous example of this kind of dispassionate analysis of ethically loaded problems, viz, Weber's criticism of the vague concepts of the Schmoller school of economics [13], Weber here points out that the axiological confusion may be "folgenreich", and that its consequences become the more dangerous for not being clearly perceived [14].

He gives a concrete example of this by pointing out that any kind of society gives certain types of people a particularly good chance of arriving at the levers of influence. Consequently, the acceptance of a particular kind of societal organization, even one which seems to guarantee peace and harmony under all conditions, represents a regular *choice,* one result of which is to create better conditions for the growth of certain characteristics, and to retard or hinder the flowering of others [15].

This view of the causal connection between the macro-analysis of society and the micro-analysis of the individual is important in connection with questions discussed towards the end of the present work [16]. Moreover, it should be mentioned that Weber in the theoretical framework of his sociology accords an important place to the phenomenon of "Veralltäglichung" which, in the concrete instance, is responsible for the tension between the axiological and the empirical validity of the theory of value conflict. In a number of sections of WG, the problem is discussed with particular reference to the *charismatic* type of political legitimacy [17].

2.2. Although the doctrine of the fundamental conflict of values is axiological, i. e., based on a conceptual analysis and undemonstrable by *direct* empirical observation, its truth, its logical *validity* cannot be doubted.

2.2.1. It is easy to understand, though, how such doubts have arisen in spite of Weber's assertions that it is impossible to draw theoretical conclusions from empirical premises. The language used by Weber in his discussion is so charged, and seems to invest conflict with a positive and peace with a negative emotional value to such an extent, that commentators have had good grounds for assuming that the field of scientific inquiry has been left behind. On closer examination, however, Weber everywhere turns out to regard the value conflict not only as a passionate preference, but also as a scientific truth. For instance, one may point to his metaphor of the "Kulturepoche, die vom Baum der Erkenntnis gegessen hat" [18] and to his prominent use of words

13. *Supra,* p. 43.
14. GAW, p. 517.
15. GAW, p. 517.
16. *Cf. infra,* pp. 280–81.
17. See part 1, chap. 3 and chap. 5 (§§ 11, 12, 12 a) and part 2, chap. 9, sect. 5, § 2 (WG, pp. 182–88, 841–66). The "traditional" type of behaviour defined by Weber also seems to contain elements connected with the concept (see for instance GAW, pp. 565, 580 (WG, part 1, chap. 1, §§ 2, 7)).
18. GAW, p. 154; see also GAW, p. 507.

like "wissen", "bewußt", etc. when speaking of our knowledge of the value conflict [19, 20].

2.2.2. The fact that the definition of scientific knowledge adopted here only evolved slowly from a metaphysical and religious unitary conception of the world does not detract from the truth of the theory of value conflict (although it may of course have had an influence on the *value* of this truth, i. e., on the interest which it commanded at various times) [21]. Especially in *Zw. betr.*, Weber gives detailed accounts of the historical developments by which the various "worldly" spheres were differentiated according to their different "worldly" internal laws ("Eigengesetzlichkeiten") [22]. But here, as in *Wiss. Beruf,* his conclusion contains the additional assertion of normative *validity:* "Schicksal unserer Kultur ... ist, daß wir uns dessen [the value conflict] wieder deutlicher bewußt werden, nachdem durch ein Jahrtausend die ... ausschließliche Orientierung an dem großartigen Pathos der christlichen Ethik die Augen dafür geblendet hatte" [23], he writes in *Wiss. Beruf;* and in GARS, the tension between intellect and religion is traced back, beyond the multitude of its historical incarnations, to "die unvermeidliche

19. GAW, p. 507; GARS, p. 542. See also GAW, p. 605. Strauss (*Nat. Right,* 1953, p. 67) and Mommsen (*Weber,* 1959, pp. 53, 129; "Universalgeschichtliches und politisches Denken bei Max Weber", *Historische Zeitschrift,* Vol. 201 (1965), pp. 606, 608) use language which strongly suggests that they see Weber's view of the fundamental conflict of values as being based solely on personal preference; this interpretation does not seem to take sufficient account of Weber's formulations, as quoted above.
20. In their discussion and criticism of Weber's ideas concerning the function of value analysis, Voegelin and—in a more moderate form—Runciman, Baumgarten and Albert interpret Weber along the same lines as those followed by Mommsen and Strauss (*cf. supra,* n19). Voegelin apparently attaches great importance to the word "Dämon" used by Weber to describe man's innermost convictions (for instance GAW, p. 613); from this, he concludes that Weber regarded valuational attitudes as "demonic", in the sense that they could not (and perhaps ought not to) be modified as a result of discussion and analysis (Voegelin, *Politics,* 1952, pp. 14–16). Runciman initially adopts an almost identical interpretation, although he expresses it in rather more homely terms ("A political philosophy, to Weber ..., is like a taste for ice-cream. One can only state one's taste and go away—there is no point in arguing" (W. G. Runciman, *Social Science and Political Theory,* Cambridge 1963, p. 156)), but later on modifies his view. Baumgarten (in Stammer (ed.), *Weber,* 1965, p. 150) and Albert (*Th. und Prax.,* 1967, pp. 267–68) rather read Weber to mean that value analysis cannot *in practice* expect to do much apart from confirming people in their prejudice.
   In fact, Weber seems simply to emphasize that values are fundamentally undemonstrable, and that value analysis may have the useful function of shattering a vague and conventional harmony by showing where the various opinions diverge (GAW, pp. 503, 602). He nowhere denies the possibility or the desirability of discussing values, or of changing them as a result of such discussions.
21. See the parallel discussion above, pp. 46–48.
22. GARS, pp. 540–73.
23. GAW, p. 605.

Disparatheit der letzten Formungen des Weltbildes" [24]. Thus, Weber always observes his own principle of value freedom in this connection. He carries out the empirical investigation of the growing awareness through time of the antagonism of values in the manner of the "sociology of knowledge" (the term is only coined later); but this does not weaken his claim that his assertion of this antagonism is true and, as such, objectively valid.

2.3.1. On the other hand, passages like the one quoted above on "die letzten Formungen des Weltbildes" seem to suggest that Weber's theory has a philosophical and speculative basis. Other formulations superficially seem to support this "philosophical" interpretation, as for instance the identification of an "echte Wertphilosophie" or "die Fachdisziplin der Philosophie und die dem Wesen nach philosophischen prinzipiellen Erörterungen der Einzeldisziplinen" [25] as sources of the theory of value conflict. On closer scrutiny, however, this interpretation cannot be retained as the only binding one [26]: if we accept the results of the discussion above [27], the existence of a fundamental value conflict can be proved by the concrete demonstration that it is possible to define alternative value axioms at any level of abstraction. The dichotomy ethic of conviction/ethic of consequences and, especially, its extension in the opposition between the "spirit" and the "world" defines a universal dilemma which, being based on the fundamental logical principle of contradiction (teleological action—non-teleological action; consequence—nonsequence) can be described as scientific and non-philosophical in the sense of the word used in the present account.

2.3.2. Certain commentators, notably Dieter Henrich, who draw special attention to Weber's passionate description of the "Veralltäglichung" of the value conflict, have felt able to infer from this passionate commitment the existence of a *normative theory of ethics* in Weber's work. Here again, it seems possible, even without a detailed discussion of the arguments advanced, to dismiss the idea that this "ethical dimension" was a *necessary* part of Weber's thought. As we have seen, Weber's theory of value conflict is based on the same premises as axiological value analysis and shares the normative validity of the latter. The claim that normative ethics is the (implicit) necessary basis of axiological value analysis seems to rest on the assumption that Weber regarded the demand for axiological consistency as *objective,* the *duty* of observing it being somehow *demonstrable* by scientific means. As we have seen [28], this assumption cannot be regarded as correct.

24. GARS, p. 565.
25. GAW, pp. 507 and 608 respectively.
26. The question whether it is at all *possible* does not concern us here.
27. Pp. 178–79.
28. Pp. 157–59.

3.5.2.2. Relation to the principle of value freedom

1. In the discussion of the value conflict, parallels have several times been drawn to the principle of value freedom. It may therefore be useful to try to clarify the relation between the theory that the sphere of scientific inquiry and the value sphere are logically heterogeneous (the theory forming the logical *basis* of the principle of value freedom) and Weber's thoughts concerning the axiological value conflict.

2.1. Weber himself does not go much into this question. Apart from a fleeting reference in *Objektivität* [1], he only once, in *Wiss. Beruf*, explicitly links up the two principles with each other: "Die Unmöglichkeit "wissenschaftlicher" Vertretung von praktischen Stellungnahmen ... ist prinzipiell deshalb sinnlos, weil die verschiedenen Wertordnungen der Welt in unlöslichem Kampf untereinander stehen" [2]. Here the principle of value freedom is *deduced* from the theory of value conflict.

On the face of it, this construction seems unacceptable: the theory of value conflict is not methodologically on the same level as the discussion of value freedom or of axiological and teleological value analysis, since it is only a *result*—albeit a very general and important one—of an axiological analysis. And since the validity of the latter in its turn depends on its value freedom, it seems logically impossible to *deduce* the view of the heterogeneous nature of the spheres from the theory of value conflict.

2.2. This chain of reasoning rather seems to point in the opposite direction, to the deduction *of* the theory of value conflict *from* the principle of value freedom. But although value freedom is a *necessary* condition of objective knowledge concerning the relationship of values to each other, it cannot pretend to be a *sufficient* condition of objectivity.

2.3. In fact, however, the objection set out above to Weber's argument in *Wiss. Beruf* is inadequate: The theory of value conflict is the result of an axiological value analysis claiming scientific *validity*. But the same applies to the view that the sphere of scientific inquiry is logically heterogeneous from the value sphere; and this view was the only argument advanced by Weber to support his demand for value freedom. Thus, *both* principles, value freedom and value conflict, are based on logic or conceptual analysis and, in the last instance, are derived from a common premise, viz, a certain conception of the conditions defining knowledge as objectively true. The science to which the theory of value conflict denies the right of mediating between ultimate value axioms is defined in the same way as the science which, according to

1. GAW, p. 154: "... und daß *also* die höchsten Ideale ..." (my italics).
2. GAW, p. 603.

the principle of value freedom, is incapable of demonstrating the objective truth of values.

3.1. In fact, a closer examination reveals that the two principles coincide. On the one hand, this is true in a *negative* sense. In a situation in which one of them does not hold, the other one cannot be maintained either. For instance, the theory of a fundamental value conflict is false if the truth of one of the following two propositions can be demonstrated by scientific means: 1) Any value or valuation can be traced back to one and the same ultimate value axiom; 2) although we can find more than one ultimate value axiom, one and only one of them can be shown to occupy an objectively higher rank than the others, or, alternatively, they all have their place in some objectively fixed hierarchy.

If 1) holds, any valuation would be demonstrably equivalent to any other one, all preferences would be equally true (or false). The principle of value freedom would lose all meaning. Probably this is the situation which Weber refers to as *genuine* "relativism", which is "nur auf dem Boden einer sehr besonders gearteten ("organischen") Metaphysik sinnvoll durchführbar"[3]. It seems justified to interpret the term " "organic" metaphysics" as referring to a theory according to which valuations have a natural function in an "organic" whole embracing them all; in such a system, all valuations would be equivalent, and relativism in the strict sense of the word would reign, as in the situation defined under 1)[4].

If 2) holds, value conflicts would be possible but not insoluble. Their solution would be provided by scientific analysis, which would eo ipso be able to decide whether a particular valuation was objectively warranted in the situation analysed. Consequently, the principle of value freedom would not be applicable. The passage, GAW, p. 509, which speaks of "eine durch *kirchliche* Dogmen [i. e., religion or metaphysics] eindeutig vorgeschriebene Rangfolge der Werte"[5], probably refers to this kind of system.

From an opposite angle, too, the effects of the two principles are identical: a science which was able to demonstrate the objective truth of *one* value would thereby lay the foundation for a scientific hierarchy of values; and a science which was able to demonstrate the objective truth of *all* values would make nonsense of the theory of the fundamental conflict of values[6].

3. GAW, p. 508.
4. It seems reasonable to connect these reflections on "organic" metaphysics with Weber's discussion, mentioned above (pp. 38–40), of various kinds of "organic" or "emanationist" theories of the state, the more so as these discussions are always concluded by a rejection of the theories in question.
5. GAW, p. 509.
6. Schelting (*Wissenschaftslehre,* 1934, pp. 59–63) is the only commentator who tries to show that the assumption of a fundamental value conflict is compatible with the

3.2. The two principles may on the other hand be shown also to coincide in a *positive* sense: the basis of the principle of value freedom, according to which it is impossible to deduce an objective valuation from an empirical fact, finds its sufficient reason in the theory of the value conflict, which lays down that any valuation may be confronted with another one on the same level of abstraction, without any chance of scientific mediation. And inversely, the theory of value conflict may be said to follow from the heterogeneity of the spheres, since the impossibility of demonstrating the superiority of one value over another is only a special instance of the general impossibility of proving the objective validity of *any* value.

4. If the two principles are thus to be regarded as, so to speak, coexistent formulations of the same fundamental theory (that of the logical gap between Is and Ought), one may ask why they are kept separate in Weber's work.

The nature of this question precludes an exhaustive or binding answer. But a *contribution* may be made by pointing out that the principles are on the whole relevant to different groups and to different situations.

The idea of value freedom is relevant to *scientific inquiry;* without going into the motives of its formulation and propagation, we may describe it as being above all a caveat addressed to the *scholar,* enjoining him to acknowledge the limits of his activity and the dangers to its objective character.

The theory of value conflict, on the other hand, has a far more direct relevance to human *action.* The impossibility of choosing objectively between two values only presents a real dilemma to persons who wish to choose them both, i. e., whose situation is not that of theoretical inquiry, but that of practical valuation and, often, goal-setting. As Weber himself admits, the essential framework for the discussion and application of this principle is that of *the weighing against each other of ends and means.*

existence of *objective* valuations. However, the lack of references to Weber's work indicates that Schelting's reasoning, at least in part, goes further than Weber did himself. Moreover, it should be noted that Schelting's use of the term "objectivity" rather seems to cover the notion of *normatively absolute* validity (see for instance *ibid.,* pp. 60–61: ". . . unbedingte, normativ allgemeine, objektive Gültigkeit . . ."), i. e., of a value which does not allow compromises with other values, but which is not claimed to be the *only* absolute value: in terms of this interpretation, one might be able to demonstrate the existence of a number of different value spheres which all possessed absolute validity for the individual concerned.

Apart from this, there are indications that Schelting's argument is motivated by the desire to defend the objectivity of *truth* against the onslaughts of the sociology of knowledge. And since he adopts a definition of truth which is still near to that of the neo-Kantians (*cf.* the formulation "Wertungen des Wahrheitsgehalts theoretischer Sätze" *(Wissenschaftslehre,* 1934, p. 61)), his defence leads him into the difficulties described above.

3.5.3. *Relation to the value analysis*

1. As we have seen [1], combined value analysis can show us in what cases the achievement of a goal has negative consequences for *other* goals and values; that is, it uncovers the value conflicts implied by the realization of a certain goal. In itself, value analysis, as Weber describes it, cannot go beyond this point. But the most important *result* of axiological value analysis: the theory of the fundamental conflict of values, adds to this abstract set of possibilities the concrete demonstration that value conflicts uncovered by combined value analysis are *insoluble* by scientific means. Weber, who otherwise does not devote much space to the theoretical possibilities or actual results of value analysis, strongly emphasizes this element and links it up with his general discussion of value analysis.

1.1. Occasionally, Weber quite explicitly claims that it is impossible to weigh the values involved in a value analysis against each other in a scientifically binding manner: "... [die] Abwägung selbst ... zur Entscheidung zu bringen", he writes in *Objektivität* [2], "ist freilich *nicht* mehr eine mögliche Aufgabe der Wissenschaft, sondern des wollenden Menschen"; and in later essays, we find similar formulations [3]. The main point is everywhere the same: "... [es] handelt ... sich um den unaustragbaren *Ausgleich* von Zweck, Mittel und Nebenerfolg" [4].

1.2. Often, though, Weber states this view in *positive* terms [5]: the individual must *choose* between the values in question: "Er [the individual] hat zu *wählen*, welchem dieser Götter, oder wann er dem einen und wann dem anderen dienen will und soll" [6]. This might lead one to think that Weber always demands a *radical* decision, that his ideal of human behaviour is of the "all or nothing" variety. This assumption is supported by the fact that in one instance, referring to the issue of the use of physical force [7], Weber undoubtedly takes this radical position, which indeed seems to correspond to a general polarizing trend in his thought. In Weber's writings on value analysis, however, he is anxious to dismiss this assumption. The necessity of *choice* between the values entering into the value analysis is absolute, in the sense that science can provide us with no objective decision in this matter;

---

1. Pp. 169–70.
2. GAW, p. 150.
3. See for instance GAW, pp. 508, 607; GPS, p. 540; GASS, p. 482; Baumgarten, *Weber*, 1964, p. 399.
4. GAW, pp. 516–17.
5. This is another small but significant indication of Weber's positive attitude to the value sphere: the affirmation of the *limits* of science is transformed by him into an emphasis on the *possibilities* open to human valuation.
6. GPS, p. 142; similarly, GAW, pp. 150, 312, 508, 608; GPS, p. 536; GASS, p. 417.
7. *Cf. infra*, pp. 249–53.

but the choice may lead to a compromise as well as to an extreme position. This conclusion is already implicit in Weber's use of the word "Abwägung" [8]; but more than once, he directly proclaims the legitimacy of trying to reach some middle position in a given situation [9].

However, Weber usually relegates his discussion of the possibility of taking up a mediating and harmonizing attitude to a secondary place. This may be seen as symptomatic of the polarizing trend of his thought; but he himself provides a more explicit explanation—or at least rationalization—of the low priority given to the positions of compromise: although a compromise may be the result of a choice no less deliberate than that leading to a radical position, the *danger* that "middle-of-the-road" valuations will be regarded as "scientific" is far greater than in the case of "consistent" ideals [10]. Since moderate positions will usually *in fact* command a greater following than extreme ones, Weber's warning can also be seen as referring to the danger of facts (in this case: the views of the great majority) exercising a normative function in politics: the "self-evidence" of a view, resulting from its actual dominant position, is not a valid argument. This attitude of Weber's is parallel to his explicit relativation of the *"objective"* value of scientific inquiry and of its results [11].

2.   The reflections made above, concerning the lack of scientific criteria for decisions in situations where ends conflict with means, seem to represent nothing more than the application of a general rule to a concrete, and particularly relevant, instance. However, the means-ends relation exhibits peculiarities which on certain points weaken the relevance of the theory of the fundamental conflict of values and which consequently merit closer attention.

This question is never discussed thoroughly by Weber. But at various points of his argument, we find statements which indicate that he has been aware of the problem and that his thoughts must have run roughly along the lines followed below. Nevertheless, the systematic account given here clearly rests on the undemonstrable premise that Weber actually drew the conclusions implied by these statements. This premise is rendered more

---

8. GAW, p. 150.
9. For instance GAW, pp. 402n1, 508; GPS, p. 142. GASS, p. 417, Weber even links together the two possibilities: "... [Werturteile], die sich vielleicht untereinander gar nicht oder nicht ohne Kompromisse vertragen und zwischen denen du also *wählen* mußt". The acknowledgement of the legitimate role of compromise is very clear in a letter of April 2nd, 1913 to Rud. Wilbrandt (DZA II, Rep. 92, No. 27), in which Weber writes: "Ich halte den unausgleichbaren *Conflikt,* also die Notwendigkeit steter Compromisse, für das die Wertsphäre beherrschende ..."
10. GAW, pp. 154–55. This opinion is borne out by the frequent attempts to describe political movements of the Centre as being more "objective" than those of the Left or the Right.
11. *Supra,* pp. 33–34.

plausible by the fact that Weber continues his discussion *as if* he had tacitly drawn the conclusions in question. But it is still necessary to emphasize that parts of the account given below can only claim the status of *hypotheses* which harmonize with Weber's own remarks, and which are not *contradicted* by other passages, but which nevertheless cannot be *verified* by reference to explicit statements in Weber's work.

2.1. If a structure of ends and means is submitted to combined value analysis, it is by no means certain that the analysis will be able to reveal any axiological conflict between the goal, the sufficient or necessary means, and the side effects of these means. In limiting cases, this lack of conflict may be due to the fact that the person concerned has taken the goal as his only value axiom, and that neither the means nor their side effects conflict with this single goal. But even when the person is committed to a number of different (ethical, political, aesthetical, etc.) values, it is not inconceivable that the goal, as well as the means and their side effects, is considered as positive in relation to all these values. In both cases, we may speak of an *absolute harmony* of ends and means.

One passage in *Objektivität* seems to refer to this kind of absolute harmony: "Da in der großen Ueberzahl aller Fälle jeder erstrebte Zweck ... etwas "kostet" oder doch kosten kann ..." [12]: the modification "in der großen Ueberzahl aller Fälle" introduces the possibility of goals which "cost" *nothing*, i. e., which do not involve action standing in a negative relationship to any of the values of the acting person. In such situations of absolute harmony, the fundamental value conflict has no relevance for the acting person.

2.2. Even in cases where absolute harmony cannot be demonstrated to reign, i. e., where the realization of a goal depends on or leads to situations or phenomena standing in a negative relationship to values held by the acting person, where, in short, the goal is "axiologically controversial", we still find that a kind of axiological harmony exists within the means–ends relation.

The basis for this harmony is the following: science may not be able to define objective criteria for the solution of the axiological conflict between ends and means or between ends and side effects; but *the relevant group of values is restricted to those held by the acting person*. Thus, even if a value conflict is uncovered, it is not necessarily insoluble or eternal: *each* individual may, consciously or unconsciously, construct for himself a hierarchy of the values involved, and accept or reject the goal in question through reference to this subjective hierarchy. True, other individuals will always be able to define and hold values conflicting with that implicit in the decision taken; but these alternative values can be given no binding force in relation to

12. GAW, p. 150.

the acting person, since the latter, before taking his decision, examined all the values to which he was committed, and cannot logically be compelled to take any other value into consideration. We may say that the relation of ends and means for each individual on his own is one of *relative harmony:* as long as the only question is whether the goal "costs" more than it "yields", the number of potentially conflicting values is *limited,* and the fundamental value conflict does not operate. This is expressed by Weber in *Wiss. Beruf,* where he describes the situation of the "technician" (who is precisely defined as making this calculation of "cost") in the following words: "Nur daß für ihn eins, die Hauptsache, gegeben zu sein pflegt: der *Zweck"* [13]. If "der Zweck" is changed to "die Zwecke" (viz, the whole value system of the individual)—a modification which seems to lie implicit in Weber's thought—this quotation expresses the heart of the matter: where ends and means are weighed against each other, the relevant system of values is defined and limited in advance. Of course, value analysis may also demonstrate the relation of the goal, the means and the side effects to any *other* value; but this demonstration does not affect the concrete decision to be taken [14].

2.3. In this sense, any analysis of ends and means is the expression of a "technical" attitude. But it is based on the condition that the value analysis only includes *one* set of values, i. e., the values held by one person (or one hierarchy of values constructed hypothetically or according to convention), in its terms of reference. As soon as the decision affects more than one person or hierarchy of values, the fundamental value conflict is revived and assumes its full, eternal and insoluble character. Since the value analysis of any given structure of ends and means may always, according to the theory of value conflict, lead to the uncovering of value axioms conflicting with the fixed goal, or with some other value held by the acting person, it is always theoretically possible that some *other* person will be committed to these conflicting axioms; and science cannot mediate in the conflict. The principle of non-contradiction which can be applied to one person at a time (since this person, if he is committed to two contradictory values, cannot define an unequivocal goal at all in the relevant areas), loses its entire force when applied to more than one individual. Thus, *the theoretical value conflict is by definition an essential part of any situation involving more than one individual or more than one fixed hierarchy of values.*

2.4. Naturally, this acknowledgement of the limitations of the analysis of ends and means usually only becomes relevant on a high level of abstraction.

13. GAW, p. 608.
14. The idea of absolute and relative harmony—but not the terms—is present in Schelting, *Wissenschaftslehre,* 1934, pp. 25, 33.

The excluded alternatives will normally [15] have to belong to a level as high as the highest of the axioms involved in the decision. Even when the antagonism of the values involved can be *illustrated* by means of concrete examples (e. g. whether an officer should blow up himself and his fort or surrender) [16], its nature as a genuine dilemma is derived from the conflict of ultimate values (in this case, the conflict between the ethic of conviction and the ethic of consequences). This is probably why Weber usually lays special stress on the inevitability of conflicts between *ultimate* value axioms [17]. Apart from this, Weber does not explicitly discuss the problem. However, the shift of his interest from the "technical" to the "axiological" aspect of value analysis [18] seems to point to a growing awareness of the limitations of the ends-means analysis: a person asking questions about the *sufficient* means is primarily interested in the attainment of the goal as such; whereas a person asking questions about the *inescapable* means has transferred his interest to the side effects, the possible violation of other norms. The fixed goal is seen in a context extended to embrace at least *all* the values held by the acting person, and theoretically going farther still.

3. As we saw, any situation involving more than one set of value axioms, i. e., primarily any situation involving more than one person, results in a "loosening" of the fixed goals, which are now exposed to the full fury of the value conflict, and which consequently lose any trace of "self-evidence" or "inescapability". This also applies to the ethic of conviction and the ethic of consequences.

Combined value analysis, based on the results of axiological and teleological analysis, examines the relation between the various values and goals in the system subjected to analysis (and, theoretically, outside the system as well), and also the means, both in themselves and with respect to their side effects. Weber usually seems to regard the status of the means as being absolutely identical in the two respects [19]; but a closer analysis shows that the status of means-in-themselves is quite different from that of means-as-causes.

3.1. When Weber asserts that means may be rejected out of hand, "schon an sich" [20], this means that their status in the weighing of ends and means against each other is determined *solely by its place in some axiological system*. For instance, certain means, like murder and lies, normally lie under

15. Not invariably: an axiom may belong on a fairly "low" level of abstraction without being subsumable under any "higher" or "ultimate" value.
16. The example is Weber's (GAW, p. 515).
17. Thus for instance GAW, pp. 507, 608.
18. P. 175.
19. For instance GAW, pp. 511, 607; GASS, p. 418.
20. GAW, p. 607.

interdict, so to speak, in a "narrow" ethical system, that is, they are judged negatively whatever their possible desirable consequences. A number of other value systems (religion, aesthetics, etc.) *may* also be defined in such a way that they deny the "world", refusing to compromise with causation, and striving instead for the "pure" religious conviction, the immediately beautiful act, etc. Clearly, the existence of this kind of value among those which are to be taken into account in the analysis will result in the rejection out of hand, as such, of means judged to be negative in terms of these values. Strictly speaking, their means status is purely hypothetical; instead, they should be regarded as actions or objects possessing a negative intrinsic ethical (religious, etc.) value which debars them in advance from being taken into account as teleological means.

Inversely, this kind of analysis is unacceptable to the ethic of consequences. Here, the weighing of values against each other *must* include *both* a causal *and* an axiological element. Means must also be judged by their effects (as far as they can be predicted) and by the axiological value of these effects.

3.2.   In a sense, the complete examination of an ends–means structure, as described by Weber in his discussion of value analysis (particularly *combined* value analysis) implies a fundamental decision in favour of the ethic of *consequences*. The very setting of a goal at all, and the subsequent attempt to reach it by certain means, represents a compromise with causation, with the "world"; actions are viewed not only according to their intrinsic axiological value but also in the context of their causal *consequences,* which may bring about situations possessing a (perhaps radically) different intrinsic axiological value.

Consequently, the situation discussed above, where the premises of the ends–means structure are "loosened" because of the inclusion of more than one set of value axioms in the analysis, contains at least a latent possibility of conflict between the ethic of conviction and the ethic of consequences as fundamental guides of human behaviour. To put the matter shortly: by removing the premise that only *one* particular set of goals is relevant, we raise the theoretical question whether *any* kind of external goal is legitimate.

3.3.   Weber does not explicitly deal with this aspect of the discussion of values; but it seems justified in this connection to refer to a point made earlier [21], viz, that the question of the intrinsic axiological status of values, and the importance of this element in the combined value analysis, is not discussed by Weber until 1909. As we have seen, means considered according to their intrinsic axiological value are thereby deprived of their natural "means status" and included in a system of pure convictions. The inclusion of this element in the value analysis will consequently reduce the character

21. P. 169.

of *combined* value analysis of the latter and correspondingly increase its likeness to a purely axiological investigation: the implied bias of combined value analysis in favour of the ethic of consequences is counteracted. The emergence of this tendency in Weber's work in 1909 [22], and its later development, may indicate a heightened awareness of the dichotomy between the ethic of conviction and the ethic of consequences, a dichotomy which is normally masked by the bias of the ends–means analysis in favour of the latter ethical orientation.

4. The discussion above has tried to show that Weber's view of combined value analysis and of its possibilities rests on certain implicit conditions: the condition of fixed goals; and that of the acknowledgement of teleological considerations as legitimate. The complex of problems leading to the open discussion of this latent restriction of the value conflict is that defined by the nature of *politics* and the role of the *politician*.

Appendix A. Myrdal's criticism of Weber's reflections on axiological consistency. In his book "The Political Element in the Development of Economic Theory" [1], Gunnar Myrdal criticizes Weber's reflections on axiological consistency for their lack of clarity. He takes as his starting-point a passage from GASS [2], where Weber refers to a vertical axiological value analysis which results in the demonstration of a number of possible ultimate value axioms which conflict with each other, and between which one must consequently, in Weber's opinion, *choose*. In this connection, Myrdal claims that Weber does not make it sufficiently clear whether this act of choice is to be regarded as "merely a particular application of the value axiom ... inferred" or as "a new and independent valuation" [3].

While it must be admitted that the passage in question needs interpretation, the meaning of Myrdal's own reading seems difficult to unravel. It is not clear how an act of choice *between* a number of value axioms can be described as "a particular application *of* the value axiom [4] ... inferred" (my italics); nor does the term "independent valuation" appear adequate, if we consider that the axioms subject to the act of choice are already implicit in the concrete valuation. Part of the explanation of the obscurity of Myrdal's "criticism" may lie in his unfortunate translation of the passage from GASS: the phrases "... um es auf seine letzten Axiome zurückzuführen, um dir zu zeigen, daß darin die und die "letzten" *möglichen* Werturteile stecken ...", which should probably be read as co-ordinate, the latter phrase simply elaborating on the former one, in Myrdal's translation read as follows: "if I show you the ultimate axioms on which it rests, we may discover that they imply certain possible ultimate value judgments ...". Here, the second

---

22. For the first time, GASS, p. 418.
 1. London 1953.
 2. GASS, pp. 417–18.
 3. Myrdal, *Pol. Element,* 1953, p. 203.
 4. The German re-translation (Gunnar Myrdal, *Das politische Element in der nationalökonomischen Doktrinbildung* (2. ed.), Hannover 1963, p. 196), here has "Wertaxiome" (in the plural), a variant which is closer to Weber's text but which does not elucidate Myrdal's interpretation.

phrase is seen as a *consequence* of the first one, a construction which leads to "ultimate value judgments" being interpreted as independent of and different from "ultimate axioms". The insertion, a few words later, of the words "or with your explicit valuation" has no foundation in the German original. The confusion is not lessened when Myrdal, in the new German translation of his book [5], prints Weber's original text, but at the same time retains the discussion which relates to the incorrect English translation [6].

Appendix B. Schelting on the dichotomy between the ethic of conviction and the ethic of consequences. Schelting [7] goes thoroughly into the question of the fundamental antagonism between the ethic of conviction and the ethic of consequences, an antagonism which he re-interprets as the opposition of "das ... *in der Immanenz oder in der Transzendenz* sich erfüllende ... "Heilsziel" der eigenen "Seele" " to "die Weiterentwicklung [der] objektiven, den einzelnen überdauernden sozialen Lebensgebilde ..." [8]. Although the results of his discussion do not often diverge from those arrived at above and developed later on [9] with relation to the sphere of politics, his claim that the dichotomy in question can be demonstrated independently *both* of the value conflict *and* of the assumption of the value irrationality of the world, does not appear to be well founded [10].

Schelting bases his claim on the fact that resources are scarce: "... die beiden Sphären der Wertrealisierung [konkurrieren] ... um *dasselbe faktische* Individiuum mit seinen faktischen Mitteln und Kräften ..." [11]. In order to assess the validity of this contention, we may distinguish two groups of cases. In case a) (which Schelting appears to regard as the principally relevant one), the "internal" and "external" values striven for differ from each other; in case b) (which seems to be the focus of Weber's interest), the two values are *identical,* so that a conflict between them would not relate to their content but only to the mode of their realization.

In case a), the assumption that the value conflict does not exist would imply that the employment of (scarce) resources to reach one of the goals must at the same time further the realization of the other one; and in case b), the freedom from value irrationality would mean that the employment of resources to further a goal in its "internal" form must always at the same time be conducive to the attainment of the "external" goal. In neither case does the postulated scarcity of resources turn out to be fundamental.

5. *Ibid.,* pp. 195–96.
6. *Cf. ibid.,* p. 196: "oder zwischen den letzteren und den expliziten Wertprämissen", referring to the phrase inserted by the English translator.
7. *Wissenschaftslehre,* 1934, pp. 36–42.
8. *Ibid.,* p. 37.
9. Pp. 255–67.
10. Schelting himself admits (*Wissenschaftslehre,* 1934, p. 38) that he is making an "erweiternde und etwas modifizierende Interpretation" of Weber's position; but apparently, the "development" is chiefly supposed to refer to the fact that Schelting goes beyond the conflict between ethics and politics.
11. *Ibid.,* p. 42.

4. Values as an instrument of scientific inquiry: the ideal type

As we have seen, the question of the *formation of concepts* occupies a central place in Weber's methodology[1]. Apart from his *general* discussion of the construction of the concepts of social science, Weber's interest in this problem is evident from his exhaustive treatment of a *specific* kind of concept, which he calls the *ideal type*.

The fullest and most inclusive account given by Weber of the concept of the ideal type, its nature and function, is found in *Objektivität*[2]. In the essays published before 1909[3], his thought is developed at various points. Later, the problem is discussed in *Kategorien*, (briefly) in *Wertfreiheit*, and in the theoretical introduction to WG[4], which is the last finished work from his pen. Thus, the problems of the ideal type seem to have occupied him during the whole of the period marked by his interest in methodology.

Contrary to our findings concerning the other complexes of problems treated in the present work, Weber's ideas on this matter seem to have varied considerably. Above all, one may point to the pronounced change in favour of generalizing and sociological formulations found in *Kategorien* and WG, when compared with the earlier essays (particularly *Objektivität*); but other disparities, too, may be demonstrated, even within one and the same essay.

This circumstance has been noted by many commentators. Some of them, such as Schelting[5], explicitly draw the conclusion that Weber's concept of the ideal type was methodologically unclear and full of contradictions[6]; others, for instance Oppenheimer[7] and Weippert[8], implicitly concur with

1. *Cf. supra*, pp. 100–01.
2. Above all GAW, pp. 190–212.
3. Particularly in *Knies II, Kritische Studien* and *Stammler*.
4. WG, pp. 3–16. In the rest of WG, the theoretical 1. part as well as the more concrete 2. part, Weber *makes use of* a large number of ideal types.
5. *Theorie*, 1922 and *Wissenschaftslehre*, 1934.
6. "Alle Versuche, die darin [in the concept of the ideal type] steckenden Unklarheiten, Widersprüche und Zwiespältigkeiten wirklich zu beheben, müssen fruchtlos bleiben" (Schelting, *Wissenschaftslehre*, 1934, p. 329).
7. Hans Oppenheimer, *Die Logik der soziologischen Begriffsbildung*, Tübingen 1925.
8. Georg Weippert, "Die idealtypische Sinn- und Wesenserfassung und die Denkge-

this opinion by concentrating on *parts* of Weber's definitions, and neglecting other aspects [9].

On the other hand, it should be stressed that Weber himself apparently does not see his own use of the term "ideal type" as contradictory, and that he refers to his first discussion of the concept, in *Objektivität,* as late as WG [10]. It therefore seems reasonable to start, unlike the scholars named, from the hypothesis that it is possible to understand Weber's various discussions of the ideal type without assuming the existence of any major breaks in his thought, the central principle remaining fairly unchanged from its first formulation in *Objektivität,* but being later developed in various directions without, however, losing its essential inner consistency. More concretely, an attempt will be made to show the fruitfulness of viewing the concept of the ideal type in the light of Weber's reflections on *value relation* and *value analysis.*

The problems surrounding the ideal type quickly lead one into complicated discussions concerning, for instance, Weber's definition of an "intuitive method" ("Verstehen") in social science, and his concepts of causation and rationality. These questions will be referred to now and then; but they will only be discussed in their substance insofar as they are naturally related to the two main aspects mentioned above: value relation and value analysis. The reference to the two latter aspects also has the function of preserving the connection between the general problems treated in the present work and the discussions in this chapter.

4.1. The central principle

As mentioned above, Weber discusses the concept of the ideal type most thoroughly in *Objektivität.* This essay also contains the most complete enumeration of the central elements of the concept. At the very beginning of his discussion, Weber characterizes the ideal type as follows:

"Dieses Gedankenbild vereinigt bestimmte Beziehungen und Vorgänge des historischen Lebens zu einem in sich widerspruchslosen Kosmos *gedachter* Zusammenhänge. Inhaltlich trägt diese Konstruktion den Charakter einer *Utopie* an sich, die durch *gedankliche* Steigerung bestimmter Elemente der Wirklichkeit gewonnen ist" [11].

Shortly afterwards, the expression "gedankliche Steigerung" is defined more precisely, when Weber speaks of

bilde der formalen Theorie", *Zeitschrift für die gesamte Staatswissenschaft,* Vol. 100 (1940), pp. 257–308.
9. Oppenheimer emphasizes the *historical* aspect, whereas Weippert tries to interpret Weber along *objectivist* lines.
10. WG, p. 15. Similar references are found in *Knies II* and *Stammler* (GAW, pp. 131n1 and 330n1, respectively).
11. GAW, p. 190.

203

"einseitige *Steigerung eines* oder *einiger* Gesichtspunkte und ... Zusammenschluß einer Fülle von diffus und diskret, hier mehr, dort weniger, stellenweise gar nicht, vorhandenen *Einzel*erscheinungen, die sich jenen einseitig herausgehobenen Gesichtspunkten fügen, zu einem in sich einheitlichen *Gedanken*bilde" [12].

"Utopie" is explained in the same passage as follows:

"In seiner begrifflichen Reinheit ist dieses Gedankenbild nirgends in der Wirklichkeit empirisch vorfindbar ..." [13]

These enumerations from *Objektivität,* which are clearly meant as introductory summaries guiding the subsequent discussion, seem to include all the essential attributes of the ideal type. According to them, the ideal type is an *intellectual abstraction* ("Gedankenbild") constructed by means of theoretical *intensification* ("Steigerung") of certain selected, one-sided ("einseitige") *aspects* of reality [14], and consequently *unreal* ("Utopie") [15], as well as being characterized by *internal consistency* ("widerspruchslos").

The discussion below will be guided by the double intention of showing how the concept of the ideal type, as described, can be related to and be seen as evolving from other methodological chains of reasoning in Weber's work, and how it is further developed in various directions without being modified in its essence.

4.2. The conceptual aspect: ideal type and value relation.

4.2.1. The premises: the relation to the "controversy over method" and to Rickert.

The treatment of the ideal type in *Objektivität* opens with the description of it as "eine Form der Begriffsbildung, welche den Wissenschaften von der menschlichen Kultur eigentümlich und in gewissem Umfang unentbehrlich ist" [16]. This must be read as indicating that the previous discussion of the methodological peculiarities of the social sciences [17] may contribute to our understanding of the nature of the ideal type.

12. GAW, p. 191.
13. GAW, p. 191.
14. The exact meaning of the expression "intensification of selected, one-sided aspects" will be made clear later on (pp. 219–20). The translation of "Steigerung" by "intensification", which is not a very happy one, has been adopted in order to keep as close as possible to Weber's own terminology. The expression "one-sided aspect" admittedly sounds pleonastic; but each of its two components has a separate function.
15. In Weber's view, an intellectual abstraction, a concept, is of course always unreal in the sense that it cannot *reproduce* reality; but the unreality referred to here is so to speak, of the second degree, in that the concept has no actual correlate in empirical reality: it is a *construction*.
16. GAW, pp. 189–90.
17. Concerning the interpretation of Weber's expression "Wissenschaft von der menschlichen Kultur" as "social science" in this connection, *cf. supra,* pp. 127–28.

Predictably, the great majority of the passages in Weber's work relevant to this question are found in *Objektivität,* where the connection with the "controversy over method" in economics, and with Rickert's theory of science, is most immediate.

1. The first statement of Weber's, and the most generally worded, is to the effect that the concept of the ideal type is "eigentümlich", i. e., *specific,* to the social sciences. This assertion makes it natural, when looking for the elements of the concept which determine this specific function, to consider the characteristics which in Weber's view (as derived from Rickert) define the historical sciences as different from the natural sciences (in the logical sense of the word). As shown above [18], the most prominent of these characteristics was the theoretical *value relation* by which certain significant or interesting elements were selected from infinite reality.

1.1. In fact, Weber constantly emphasizes the power of the ideal type to select and express *significant* aspects of reality; thus, he writes that

> "der Historiker, sobald er den Versuch unternimmt, über das bloße Konstatieren konkreter Zusammenhänge hinaus die *Kulturbedeutung* eines noch so einfachen individuellen Vorgangs festzustellen ..., mit Begriffen arbeitet und arbeiten *muß*, welche regelmäßig nur in Idealtypen scharf und eindeutig bestimmbar sind" [19].

At one point, this parallel between the ideal type and the value relation is extended, the necessity of a *large number* of ideal types being stressed precisely with regard to those cases in which Weber usually emphasizes the importance of *value interpretation* [20].

Apparently, this ability to capture and express, unlike the ordinary average or general concepts, what is *interesting* to social science in a given phenomenon, is also central to the understanding of the rather obscure expressions "genetischer Begriff" and "genetische Definition" which are now and then employed by Weber in this connection [21]. This is seen most clearly in a discussion GAW, p. 194, where the "genetic" concept is distinguished from the "schildernde Auflösung" of a phenomenon into its separate components, since this latter disintegrating process is not guided by any criterion of *significance.*

1.2. The close connection of the ideal type with the theoretical value relation essential to the historical sciences permits us to explain a number of the elements of the concepts as described by Weber in the introductory summaries quoted above. Thus, the fact that the ideal type only includes those

18. Pp. 104–06.
19. GAW, p. 193. Similar formulations, GAW, pp. 192, 194.
20. GAW, p. 198; *cf. supra,* p. 112.
21. GAW, pp. 191, 194, 202, 208, 243. Another essential element of the concepts will be discussed below, p. 213.

parts of reality which become relevant under a certain aspect, makes it reasonable to describe it as an *intellectual abstraction* [22]; and the introduction of the idea of aspects implies a narrowness in the individual ideal type which justifies Weber's emphasis on the *one-sidedness* of the concept [23]. *1.3.* By linking up the concept of the ideal type so closely with the doctrine of the theoretical value relation, Weber clearly repudiates the position of the "younger historical school" in the "controversy over method" [24]. Weber himself points out, in more or less veiled terms, that his defence of the ideal type brings him into conflict with the views of Schmoller, the leader of the school, whom he never mentions by name in this connection, however.

1.3.1. This is already true with regard to the view of theoretical value relation as a starting-point for analysis. This view squares badly with Schmoller's idea of a historical "induction" and of a subsequent "deduction" of actual reality from the concepts formed by "induction"; and Weber expressly notes this discrepancy. He defines the nature and the extent of the latter more clearly by pointing out that the "inductive" theory is based on the assumption that it is possible to *reproduce* the whole of reality in a concept, an assumption which stands in obvious contradiction to the abstract view of concepts which he took over from the neo-Kantians [25]. This contradiction also expresses itself in Schmoller's dislike of the precise and one-sided concepts which Weber regards as quite necessary to social science [26].

Finally, Weber points to the fact that the younger historical school regards concepts as the *end* of scientific inquiry, whereas the ideal type is clearly meant to be an *instrument* at the service of other scientific purposes. He appears to attach great importance to this point, which is made not only in *Objektivität* [27] but also in *Stammler* [28], and as late as 1917 in *Wertfreiheit,* where Weber writes: "... die theoretischen Konstruktionen stehen durchaus nur im Dienst der von ihnen selbst keineswegs gelieferten Erkenntnis der Realitäten ..." [29]

1.3.2. Weber not only *records* his disagreement with Schmoller and his school, but directly *criticizes* the latter. Apart from his claim that the view of concepts as reproductions of reality is logically *untenable* [30], he points out

22. *Cf.* GAW, p. 192 ("... Auswahl der in einen Idealtypus einer bestimmten Kultur aufzunehmenden Zusammenhänge ..."), 193 ("... abstrakte Idealtypen ..."). In both cases, the element of significance is explicitly present in the context.
23. This quality is frequently mentioned by Weber in subsequent discussions: see for instance GAW, pp. 196, 208, 209.
24. *Cf. supra*, pp. 79–82.
25. GAW, p. 208, see also GAW, p. 192.
26. GAW, pp. 193, 205, 208.
27. GAW, pp. 193, 208–09.
28. GAW, p. 357n1.
29. GAW, p. 537. This passage is not found in the *Gutachten.*
30. For instance GAW, pp. 192–93, 208.

that the rejection by the historicists of value relation as a methodological guide means *either* that they have to restrict themselves to purely formal aspects, like those of the history of law, a restriction which implies the identification of the formally normative with the actually significant [31]; *or* that they run the risk of letting themselves be guided by obscure and unconscious criteria of selection [32].

2. Thus, there seem to be strong indications that the specific importance of the ideal type to social science is derived from its close connection with methodological principles which were already formulated by Rickert in his *Grenzen*. In view of this, it is interesting to note that Weber goes beyond Rickert's theory of science by claiming that the ideal type—a logical category which, as such, is *not* borrowed from Rickert—is *necessary* to social science. Unless Weber is simply exaggerating his independent and original contribution to methodology—a *prima facie* not very likely hypothesis—the ideal type must be supposed to contain elements which conflict with or at least go beyond Rickert's theory of science.

2.1. Formal considerations seem to invest this assumption with a certain plausibility. Thus, Weber, who is normally generous with his references to Rickert's methodology, completely avoids such references in his discussion of the ideal type. In a letter to G. von Below of July 17th, 1904 [33], he even explicitly excepts "der mir allerdings wichtigste letzte Drittel" of *Objektivität* (i. e., the discussion of the ideal type) from his modest statement that this essay is nothing more than an application of Rickert's ideas. Inversely, the references in *Grenzen* [34] (2nd and later editions) to the ideal type are extremely cursory, in spite of the claim advanced by Rickert himself [35] that Weber found the elements of the concept in the *Grenzen*.

2.2. These formal considerations are supported by a closer examination of the relevant portions of Rickert's theory of science, an examination which makes it clear that Weber's position differs from Rickert's *even with regard to the conflict with Schmoller* discussed above.

For one thing, there is *no* parallel in Rickert's theory to Weber's demand that the aspects considered by the scholar to be significant should be made *explicit* by means of ideal types. This is not surprising, since Rickert is interested in history as a *type* of scientific inquiry, whereas Weber's discussion

31. GAW, p. 195. This argument is akin to, for instance, Woodrow Wilson's "realist" criticism of traditional political science.
32. GAW, pp. 195, 196, 209. This obscurity and lack of conscious reflection may have serious consequences; *cf.* Weber's criticism of the Schmoller school (on a concrete point), *supra,* p. 43.
33. Copy in DZA II, Rep. 92, No. 30, Vol. 4.
34. See the account in *Grenzen* [2], 1913, pp. 322–23, 431–32.
35. Rickert, *Grenzen* [5], 1929, p. 758. Rickert in part seems to argue from a letter of Weber's of June 14th, 1904, which will be discussed below.

of methodological questions is rooted in and focusses on the concrete problems of the science of economics [36]; but it is worth noting that Rickert, by ignoring the need for explicit definition of the aspects, in principle runs the same danger as the younger historicists: the obscurity of the aspects increases the danger of an unwitting violation of the principle of value freedom.

To this must be added another consideration. As we have seen [37], Rickert, unlike Weber, assumes that the group of values to which a given historical material may legitimately be related is limited to the values which have demonstrably served as guides to human behaviour in this material.

This means that Rickert, although his neo-Kantianism of course prevents him from embracing a "reproduction theory", finds it difficult to subscribe to the idea of the *one-sidedness* of the ideal type which Weber emphasizes so strongly: the maximum number of legitimate aspects is fixed once and for all, so that the historical material in question can be summed up in, if not one, at least a finite number of concepts, the totality of which must be said ot exhaust the scientific importance of the material [38]; such a complex of concepts would have some claim to represent a *complete* rather than a one-sided view, and might even, when elaborated, turn out to be not unlike the historicist concepts supposed to contain *all* the historically significant material, and denounced so frequently by Weber [39].

2.3. While the discrepancies noted above may be said only to represent differences of *tendency,* we can establish the existence of an *actual* divergence between Rickert and Weber on a third point, viz, the relation between valuation and value relation. A letter from Weber to Rickert of June 14th, 1904 [40] offers important evidence in this respect. In the letter, Weber writes: "Ihre Zustimmung zu dem Gedanken des "Idealtypus" erfreut mich sehr. In der That halte ich eine ähnliche Categorie für notwendig, um "werthendes" und "werthbeziehendes" Urteil scheiden zu können".

As we have seen [41], Rickert apparently takes this statement to mean that Weber found the elements of his theory of the ideal type in Rickert's logical

---

36. *Cf. supra,* pp. 97–98.
37. Pp. 92–93, 121.
38. Rickert, *Grenzen,* 1902, pp. 638–39.
39. See the passage *ibid.,* pp. 408–09: "Die Begriffe der Geschichte ... müssen, je umfassender sie werden und um so grösser ihr Umfang ist, auch um so mehr Wirklichkeit enthalten und also einen um so reicheren Inhalt haben. Man kann dann geradezu sagen, dass ... der umfassendste historische Begriff ... die ganze Mannigfaltigkeit einer Universal- oder Weltgeschichte in sich aufnehmen müsste", contrasted with GAW, p. 198: "Je umfassender die Zusammenhänge sind, um deren Darstellung es sich handelt, und je vielseitiger ihre Kultur*bedeutung* gewesen ist ..., desto *weniger* ist es möglich, mit *einem* derartigen Begriffe auszukommen ..."
40. DZA II, Rep. 92, No. 25. See also a later letter to Rickert of April 18th, 1905 (*ibid.*), in which the ideal type is described as "sachlich gefordert".
41. P. 206n35.

distinction between valuation and value relation. But when the letter is read in a wider context, it seems to suggest quite a different interpretation.

The crucial problem in this connection is that of explaining why Weber found it necessary to develop a separate concept in order to distinguish valuation from value relation, while Rickert, who otherwise lays great stress on this distinction, does not seem to have experienced the same necessity. What can be the reason of this new development?

The answer to this question may perhaps be found in Rickert's normative concept of cultural values [42]. In Rickert's view, as we have seen, only certain kinds of human interaction qualify as "communities", i. e., as frameworks for the definition or adoption of cultural values. This restriction conceals an objectivist conception: certain patterns of interaction (the family, the nation, etc.) *are* "communities", while other ones (probably, for instance, classes) *are not* "communities" in Rickert's sense, whatever the subjective interests of the scholars concerned. This objectivism in its turn implies the existence of a *valuational* element in the historical concepts, as Rickert defines them: the cultural values on which the study of a given "community" and its history may be based are fixed in advance, since the historian is only allowed to regard certain setters of cultural norms as legitimate.

As mentioned above [43], Weber dissociates himself from this normative concept of culture and, with minor modifications, leaves the scholar free to choose his aspects as he pleases. In so doing, Weber has *in principle* disengaged his theory of the formation of historical concepts from the implicit objectivism and from the consequent valuational bias of Rickert's theory of science; but *in practice,* Weber's continued use of the Rickertian terminology may tempt the reader to ignore the repudiation of objectivism and to reintroduce the normative concept of culture into his interpretation of Weber. Consequently, Weber has to make certain that the concepts of social science are defined so that *they do not correspond to any any particular phenomenon in the reality from which their elements are taken.* Only in this way is it possible to translate the repudiation of objectivism into practice; a concept which is unreal in this sense, which is, in Weber's words, an "Utopie", cannot be suspected of latent objectivism [44]. This seems to be one of the main reasons for Weber's emphatic assertion that the ideal type is specifically *unreal,* that it is an "Utopie"; and this assertion at the same time constitutes a tacit, but unambiguous, dissociation from Rickert's theory of science [45].

42. *Cf. supra,* pp. 93–94.
43. P. 130.
44. *Cf.* Weber's warning against emanationist concepts, for instance GAW, pp. 195, 204, 205, and against the belief that scientific and objective criteria of selection and valuation may be found in the subject-matter as such, GAW, p. 199.
45. Naturally, this conclusion is not meant to imply that Weber, while deliberately dissociating himself from Rickert's thought, maintained a façade of fictitious

3. Weber's open criticism of Schmoller, and his implicit modification of Rickert, may be seen as important reasons for his characterization of the ideal type as being *abstract, one-sided* and *unreal;* they also explain his emphasis on its *instrumental* function in scientific research. But thus defined, Weber's position is in fact identical with the moderate one taken up by *Menger* in the "controversy over method" [46]: in Menger's view, the doctrines of theoretical economics were precisely characterized by their one-sidedness and abstraction [47]; and he believed that no "realistic", i. e., historical, science of economics could dispense with the help afforded by such abstract propositions. In fact therefore, Weber, in his discussion of the *nature* and general *function* of concepts, sides *with* the abstract school and *against* the historical one.

4.1. Weber repeatedly stresses the fact that the ideal *type* should not be confused with practical *ideals:* "... der Gedanke des Sein*sollenden,* "Vorbildlichen" [ist] von diesen in rein *logischem* Sinn "idealen" Gedankengebilden [...] sorgsam fernzuhalten..." [48]; indeed, the opposite view would violate Weber's general demand for the value freedom of the scientific process, and destroy the distinction between value judgments and theoretical value relation which he sees as necessary for the construction of historical concepts.
4.2. Viewed in this perspective, the choice of the *term* "ideal type" seems somewhat inapt, since the word must evoke exactly those connotations which Weber tried to avoid. In the letter (quoted above) to Rickert of June 14th, 1904, Weber gives the following reasons for his choice: "Ich nannte sie [the category of the ideal type] so, wie der Sprachgebrauch von "idealem Grenzfall", "idealer Reinheit" eines typischen Vorganges, "idealer Construktion" etc. spricht, *ohne* damit ein Sein-*sollendes* zu meinen, ferner wie das, was *Jellinek* (Allg. Staatslehre) "Idealtypus" nennt, als nur im logischen Sinn perfekt gedacht ist, nicht als *Vorbild*". In this passage, we find a number of the characteristics of the concept: the "ideale Grenzfall" invokes its *abstraction* and *unreality,* while the term "logisch perfekt" must be supposed to have some connection with the *internal consistency* of the ideal type. Nevertheless, the choice of the word "ideal type" seems to owe much to the

agreement with Rickert in his letters to him; more probably, Weber defined and developed the concept of the ideal type without realizing the extent of the divergence from Rickert which it implied.
46. *Cf. supra,* p. 82. See the general arguments in favour of Menger, GAW, pp. 187, 537.
47. It is open to discussion whether Menger regarded the propositions of theoretical economics as unreal in Weber's definite sense of that word; but his arguments naturally tend in this direction.
48. GAW, p. 192; similarly, GAW, pp. 199, 200.

more or less deliberate preference on Weber's part for terms from which the meaning almost has to be wrested [49, 50].

This apart, Weber seems to have attached little importance to the *term* "Idealtypus". Thus, in the letter of June 14th, 1904 quoted above, he writes: "Wie man sie nennt, ist ja Nebensache" [51], and in *Wertfreiheit,* he exhibits a similar indifference to the question of terminology [52]. The term is used less frequently in the later essays.

4.2.2. *The ideal type as an aid to the presentation of scientific results*

Above, an attempt was made to show how the one-sided, abstract and—especially—*constructed and unreal* character of the ideal type might be explained by its relation to previous methodological doctrines. The ideal type, thus defined, is now stated by Weber to have as its first function that of being a "Darstellungsmittel", an *aid to the presentation of scientific results.*

This function is above all discussed in *Objektivität* [1], i. e., alongside of the discussion of the conceptual element of the ideal type. But although Weber states that it is in principle linked with the latter element, his actual treatment of the function is curiously vague and ambiguous, and opens up new aspects of the problem.

49. A possible further explanation of the term is found in Weber's letter to Rickert of April 28th, 1905 (DZA II, Rep. 92, No. 25), in which he places the ideal type between "Ideal" and "Gattungstypus"; the term "ideal type" represents a linguistic amalgamation of these two latter terms.

50. The letter of June 14th, 1904 quoted in the text sheds new light on the question of the relation between Weber's and Jellinek's concepts of "Idealtypus". Marianne Weber (*Lebensbild,* 1950, p. 356) and a number of later commentators maintain that Weber not only borrowed the *word* from Jellinek, but that the *concept* to which it referred was the same in Jellinek's case as in Weber's. This has been strongly denied by Tenbruck (*Genesis,* 1959, p. 620), who, correctly, points out that Jellinek's ideal type is defined as a normative *ideal.* The letter to Rickert now permits us to explain how Marianne Weber came to make such an elementary mistake, since it demonstrates that Weber himself was apparently equally mistaken on the point, at least at that time. The text is quite unambiguous: "wie das, was *Jellinek* (Allg. Staatslehre) "Idealtypus" *nennt* ..." (last italics mine): not the terms, but their material reference are the object of the comparison. The possible variant readings of the (handwritten) letter ("weil" for "wie", "also nur" for "als nur") do not seem to permit any alternative interpretation, either. Since we know for a fact that Marianne Weber made use of her husband's letters, this one among them, when writing his biography, the error may in this way have slipped in, to be repeated by later commentators. At any rate, this example lends added strength to the warning that it may be dangerous to base one's interpretation of Weber on the assumption that his own thought was free from logical inconsistencies.

51. See for a similar statement the letter (DZA II, Rep. 92, No. 25) of April 28th, 1905.

52. GAW, p. 535.

1. Now and then (GAW, pp. 397, 536) he makes a brief reference to it in his later essays.

1. Weber seems to lay great stress on the usefulness of the ideal type as an aid to the presentation of results. Thus, he writes:

"Unsere Phantasie kann ihre [the concept formation's] ausdrückliche begriffliche Formulierung sicherlich oft als Mittel der *Forschung* entbehren,—für die *Darstellung* ist, soweit sie eindeutig sein will, ihre Verwendung auf dem Boden der Kulturanalyse in zahlreichen Fällen ganz unvermeidlich" [2].

While a tacit *notion* of the implications of the concepts which he employs is often sufficient for the purposes of the *scholar,* the passage above points to the necessity, which is already implicit in the demand for the value freedom of the scientific process [3], of furnishing the *reader* with an *explicit* definition of the concepts. Such an explicit definition is provided by the ideal type.

What apparently makes the ideal types particularly useful, in Weber's view, to the presentation of scientific results is their ability to retain and reproduce the *significant* parts of reality [4], the parts, that is, which are of special interest to the historical sciences (in the logical sense of the word). Moreover, Weber clearly assumes that this ability is a function of the *unreality* of the ideal type, of its status as a limiting case: "... [die] praktische *Bedeutung* ist es, mit der die Arbeit der Sozialwissenschaft in unserem Sinn zu tun hat. Diese Bedeutung aber ist sehr oft nur durch Beziehung des empirisch Gegebenen auf einen idealen Grenzfall eindeutig zum Bewußtsein zu bringen" [5]. This assumption is easy to understand: Weber's concern for the concrete problems of scientific inquiry leads him to operate with aspects possessing a far lower degree of abstraction, and consequently a far higher degree of complexity, than Rickert's cultural values [6]; and since the significance of the phenomena which are selected under those aspects is derived from their relation to the concrete and complex implications of the latter, these implications must be made perfectly clear if we are fully to understand the particular interest of the phenomena selected.

2. However, the use of ideal types to render the significance of phenomena intelligible to the reader leads to important changes in the character of the scientific account as such. Instead of a number of concepts deriving their significance from a relation to one or more aspects ("values"), but nevertheless described and analysed as individual units, we now get a group of constructed ideal types, to which the rest of the concepts are compared and in relation to which they are classified. The "classical" historical account,

2. GAW, p. 195.
3. *Cf. supra,* p. 42.
4. GAW, pp. 190, 193, 194.
5. GAW, p. 195; *cf.* GAW, pp. 190, 191.
6. See for instance GAW, p. 193, where we find examples like "individualism", "imperialism", "feudalism", etc.

which Rickert no doubt regarded as his paradigm, is superseded by the *systematic* treatment of the material.

In fact, the existence of this systematic element, which is directly acknowledged by Weber himself[7], means that the bounds of historical science, as defined by Rickert, are *overstepped*. Weber demands that history, as a "Wirklichkeitswissenschaft" characterized by concepts which are "close" to reality (in the sense that they represent a selection but not an abstraction from immediate reality) should be made to include elements of pure theory in the shape of types which are in a specific sense "remote from" reality. "The science of reality" is confronted with the necessity of having recourse to unreal concepts.

3.1. There are indications, however, that Weber does not regard the necessity of employing ideal types in the presentation of scientific results as equally pressing in all fields. "In unendlich vielen Fällen," he writes, "zumal auf dem Gebiet der darstellenden politischen Geschichte, tut nun die Unbestimmtheit ihres Inhaltes [of the concepts] der Klarheit der Darstellung sicherlich keinen Eintrag"[8]. Weber's reason for allowing the "darstellende politische Geschichte" in particular to dispense with ideal types may of course be that the major aspect, politics, is in this case so clear and well-defined that the reader does not require any comparisons with constructed limiting cases. A more important point, however, seems to be raised by the expression "darstellend". Since *all* kinds of history are based on "accounts", the word should probably be taken as an indication that the political history referred to is *merely* an account of events succeeding each other, unlike other kinds of history which go further than the simple recording of facts. It is not difficult to determine what is the additional element distinguishing the latter disciplines, since it will be remembered that Weber regarded *causal explanation* as the essential task of historical science[9]; in the field of economics in particular, the need to *explain* facts will probably be considerably greater than that of simply *describing* them.

3.2.1. Consequently, we may formulate the hypothesis that the usefulness (or even the necessity) of the ideal type as an aid to the presentation of scientific results is limited to, or at least especially prominent in, those cases where it is also able to fulfil some function in connection with the causal explanation of the material from which it has been abstracted. If, in the light of this hypothesis, we reexamine the reason given above for employing the ideal type in the presentation of scientific results, viz, that it brings out

7. *Cf.* GAW, pp. 198–99: "... von ... hohem systematischem Wert für die Darstellung ..."
8. GAW, p. 193.
9. *Cf. supra,* p. 114.

the "Bedeutung" of the phenomena, we notice that the expression "Bedeutung" often seems to refer not only to the interest and significance of phenomena, but also to their causal effects, their *consequences*. This is true of the term "praktische Bedeutung" [10], which is in fact contrasted with that of the purely formal legal "validity" in relation to a given community; and of a previous discussion of the relevance of the ideal type for instance "in bezug auf gewisse wichtige Kulturbedeutungen, die der "Sektengeist" für die moderne Kultur gehabt hat"; here, the causal element *coexists* with the element of significance ("wichtig") [11].

3.2.2. The term "genetischer Begriff" discussed above has a similar double reference. As we have seen, it indicates that the concept in question is historical, i. e., that it has been formed according to a criterion of theoretical value, of interest. But its etymology alone at the same time connects it with notions of development or of causation, and this element is noticeable in a number of the passages in which the concept is used. Thus, the passage from GAW, p. 194 quoted above is an exemplification of the term "genetischer Begriff", and later on, "genetisch" refers to a concept which "wie *jeder* logisch voll entwickelte Begriff, ein *Urteil* über die "typischen" *Bedingungen* ... [of the material reference of the concept, in this case the phenomenon of barter] in sich [enthält]" [12].

4. Thus, both the origin and the consequences of the function of the ideal type as an aid to the presentation of scientific results go beyond its immediate basis, Rickert's theory of science, and indicate the existence of a separate function connected with the causal explanation of historical phenomena. This function will be discussed and analysed in the following section.

4.3. The motivational aspect: ideal type and value analysis

While the connection between the conceptual and the causal aspect of the ideal type is not always made very clear by Weber, both *Objektivität* and the later essays make it perfectly obvious that a central purpose of the ideal type is to function as an aid to the causal explanation of social phenomena. At the very beginning of his discussion in *Objektivität*, Weber mentions the

10. GAW, p. 195.
11. GAW, p. 194. In an early note of Weber's (probably from 1903), a similar distinction is made between the "historische" (causal) and "persönliche" significance of individuals (DZA II, Rep. 92, No. 31, Vol. 6). The category of "persönliche" significance results from a relation to values which Weber identifies as a *practical* one ("*Messen an ethischen* u. a. Maßstäben"), a position characteristic of his early heitation between valuation and value relation (*cf. supra*, pp. 104–05).
12. GAW, p. 202.

function of the ideal type as an aid to "das Zurechnungsurteil" [1]; and a little later, he states that its value depends on its ability to aid "die Erkenntnis konkreter Kulturerscheinungen in ihrem Zusammenhang, ihrer ursächlichen Bedingtheit und ihrer *Bedeutung*" [2]. In this passage, the value-related and the causal component seem to be present side by side; and similar parallel discussions are found elsewhere [3]. The account given below will try to establish the premises of Weber's thought concerning the relevance of the ideal type to causal analysis, to demonstrate the relation between this part of his thought and the rest of his methodology, and to present a more detailed picture of the function of the ideal type in this connection.

4.3.1. The premise: value orientation

1. As mentioned above, Weber regards the ideal type as being specific to "die Wissenschaften von der menschlichen Kultur" [4]. This expression was interpreted as an indication of the fairly close connection with Rickert's theory of science; but even when read in isolation, the passage must at least be supposed to imply that the disciplines which are to make use of the ideal type, have as their object "Kultur", i. e., *the practical or theoretical valuational attitudes of human beings to the world in which they live* [5]. Consequently, causal explanation in these disciplines will always consist in the explanation *of* human behaviour (or of the results of such behaviour), and this subject-matter will be explained *by* factors peculiar to human behaviour rather than by non-human factors, of whatever kind. Thus, the ideal type is used as an aid to the causal explanation of phenomena characterized by human value orientation (in the broad sense of the term) [6].

1.1. This point is often explicitly made by Weber. In *Knies I–II,* his arguments are still marked by his dependence on Rickert (to whom the definition of *human* action as the essential object of historical science was beyond dispute) [7]: the concept of "history" is linked to the function of "... kulturhistorische Tatsachen kausal zu erklären", and Weber elaborates on this by claiming that this function

"infolge des begrifflichen Wesens der "Kultur" *stets* [bedeutet], daß sie [history] darin gipfelt, uns zur Erkenntnis eines Zusammenhanges hinzuleiten, in welchen *ver-*

1. GAW, p. 190.
2. GAW, p. 193.
3. For instance GAW, pp. 191, 397, 536.
4. GAW, p. 190.
5. *Cf. supra,* pp. 127–30.
6. "Broad" value orientation must be supposed to include any more or less clear subjective feeling of purpose.
7. *Cf. supra,* p. 91.

ständliches menschliches Handeln oder, allgemeiner, "Verhalten" eingeschaltet und als beeinflußt gedacht ist, da hieran sich das "historische" *Interesse* heftet" [8].

In *Knies II*, Weber follows up his argument, referring directly to Rickert, by stating that the object of history, viewed "geschichtsphilosophisch", is the human "Verwirklichung von Werten" [9].

1.2. As early as *Stammler,* though, Weber abandons the abstract methodological level of argument, concentrating instead on the empirical fact that norms of various kinds *may* motivate human behaviour, acting as a "reales Agens des Handelns" [10]. In *Kategorien,* this process of liberation from the philosophy of history is completed; here, Weber's discussion is carried on within the framework of a discipline the objects and aims of which are *defined* in advance. This discipline, the "verstehende Soziologie", takes as its object "Handeln", that is, the "durch irgendeinen ... "gehabten" oder "gemeinten" ... *Sinn* spezifiziertes Sichverhalten zu "Objekten" " [11], and the sociologist (in this sense) tries to *explain* behaviour by reference to this "Sinn" or supposed *motivation.* Weber does not in principle exclude the possibility of *different* approaches, even to the same material [12]; his definition of the field of activity of sociology is simply based on the assumption that the criteria adopted will prove to be *fruitful* [13].

4.3.2. The relation to the value analysis

1. The ideal type is constructed as an aid to the causal analysis and explanation of behaviour which is *value-oriented* in the broadest sense of the term; and, as we shall see, the principles of its construction are closely connected with the value analysis discussed above, both in its axiological and teleological form. Although Weber does not explicitly link up the ideal type with the value analysis [1], he frequently discusses the concept of the ideal type in terms indicative of the connection between the axiological and the teleological, the motivational and the causal aspect.

This is the case, for instance, with the definition, in *Objektivität,* of the ideal type as "die Konstruktion von Zusammenhängen, welche unserer *Phantasie* als zulänglich motiviert ..., unserem nomologischen Wissen als

8. GAW, p. 83; *cf.* GAW, p. 99.
9. GAW, p. 116.
10. GAW, p. 329; see also for instance GAW, pp. 335, 342.
11. GAW, p. 429; *cf.* WG, p. 3.
12. GAW, pp. 430–31; *cf.* WG, p. 9.
13. For a discussion of the view that Weber's definition of the object of social science relies on a philosophical anthropology, *cf.* Appendix A of this chapter.
1. He most nearly seems to do so GAW, p. 535, where the rational ideal type is described as "eine in möglichst rationale Form gebrachte "Wertung" welcher Art immer".

216

adäquat erscheinen" [2]. This vague alliance of "Phantasie" and "nomolo-
gisches Wissen", linked up by means of the term "adäquat", is developed
and clarified in the course of Weber's methodological production, to reach
its final form in WG[3] as the conceptual pair "sinnhaft adäquat"—"kausal
adäquat", which precisely corresponds to the distinction between axiological
and teleological value analysis. In *Stammler,* similar considerations lead
Weber to combine the elaboration of a "Sinn", an inner meaning, with the
empirical behaviour corresponding to this meaning [4]. In *Wertfreiheit,* too,
"empirisch-technische" and "logische" constructions are juxtaposed, but
the emphasis here seems rather to be laid on the possibility of constructing
and employing the two forms *separately* [5].

1.1. Occasionally, Weber discusses ideal types which apparently contain only
one of the two elements: the axiological/motivational and the teleological/
empirical one.

As far as the *axiological* aspect is concerned, this is true of the discussion
in *Objektivität* of certain ideal types like "medieval Christianity" and
"liberalism" which synthetize ideas, dogmas, principles, maxims, etc. [6]
These ideal types seem to contain no reference to empirical facts, and above
all not to the observable behaviour which the ideal type was supposed to
help to explain. Possibly the discussion of the concept of "Stadtwirtschaft" [7]
can be seen as marked by a similar one-sidedness. The passage from *Wertfreiheit* referred to immediately above also comes into this category.

As for the *teleological* aspect, it may similarly be said to occur by itself in
cases where the concepts discussed by Weber can be classified as ideal types
only because they refer to completely *rational* behaviour, while the actual
goal of this rational behaviour is not defined explicitly. Such types of
"isolated rationality" are now and then mentioned by Weber, and always
in the field of *economics* [8].

1.2. In the great majority of cases, however, the axiological and the teleological element are *jointly* present in the ideal types; the latter include *both*
motivation by ideas or values *and* the corresponding empirical (possibly rational) behaviour.

This is most clearly seen in the detailed discussion of various examples in
Objektivität. Here, Weber for instance describes how "die Idee" des
"Handwerks" " can be constructed as an axiological ideal type, and con-

2. GAW, p. 192. A somewhat differently worded but, as it seems, materially identical passage is found a couple of pages later, GAW, p. 194.
3. WG, pp. 8–9.
4. GAW, p. 333.
5. GAW, pp. 534–35.
6. GAW, pp. 197–98.
7. GAW, p. 191.
8. Thus for instance GAW, pp. 190, 394, 397.

tinues: "Man kann dann ferner den Versuch machen, eine Gesellschaft zu zeichnen, in der alle Zweige wirtschaftlicher, ja selbst geistiger Tätigkeit von Maximen beherrscht werden, die uns als Anwendung des gleichen Prinzips erscheinen, welches dem zum Idealtypus erhobenen "Handwerk" charakteristisch ist" [9]. *The idea embodied in the ideal type is assumed to be the constant motive of behaviour, the latter being described in similar ideal-typical terms.*

Another thorough discussion in *Objektivität* of such a complete ideal type is of particular interest in our context, since it concerns the possibility of constructing the ideal type of the "state" [10]. Here the "dual aspect" of the ideal type is especially prominent and bears an interesting relation to concrete reality. Empirically, Weber says, the "state" consists of an immense number of human actions of all kinds, "zusammengehalten durch eine Idee, den Glauben an tatsächlich geltende oder gelten sollende Normen und Herrschaftsverhältnisse von Menschen über Menschen" [11]: *behaviour* characterized by a particular, central *motivation*. This motive, however, can only be made intelligible by means of ideal types; and Weber sees such ideal types as extremely important motives of "state" behaviour [12].

In the later essays, the examples grow less detailed; but the complementary relation of the axiological and teleological aspects can still be clearly perceived, for instance, in the ideal type of "the rational economic behaviour of Robinson Crusoe" [13], and in the treatment, in minute details, in *Stammler* of the logical structure of card games(!) [14].

1.3.1. As mentioned above, the complementary relation of the axiological and the teleological value structures may, in certain of Weber's discussions of the ideal type, recede into the background to such an extent that one is tempted to define two *kinds of* ideal type (or even three, if the "complete" type counts separately); but if we relate Weber's description of the ideal type to the theoretical value analysis, the distinction between different kinds of

---

9. GAW, p. 191. Parallel to this, Weber outlines a "capitalist" principle and the corresponding "capitalist" society, GAW, pp. 191–92.

10. GAW, pp. 200–01.

11. GAW, p. 200. See also a note from 1903 (DZA II, Rep. 92, No. 31, Vol. 6) in which Weber, commenting on the concept of "state", says that "das Prius ist der gesetzte *Zweck*, der *Gedanke* der Institution".

12. Weber does not go more deeply into the construction of the *teleological* side of the ideal type of the state, and instead examines the fact—which is interesting from other points of view (*cf. infra,* p. 231)—that *actual* behaviour may be motivated by more or less correctly perceived axiological ideal types of the "principle of the state". There is no doubt, however, that 'his argument also implies an ideal-typical construction as a teleological correlate of this "principle of the state" (*cf. infra,* p. 223).

13. GAW, p. 333.

14. GAW, pp. 337–43, in particular p. 342. The game of Skat is used by Weber as a down-to-earth paradigm of all situations governed by judicial norms.

ideal types no longer seems justified: teleological value analysis, and the rational ideal type into which it may be transformed, can only be elaborated if the value or goal striven for are known in advance; and on the other hand, although it is possible to work out the axiological structure of a value without referring directly to empirical actions, this empirical element remains latent in the axiological analysis, since the latter always implies the possibility of defining practical attitudes to concrete phenomena in concrete situations [15].

1.3.2. If the "one-sided" ideal types mentioned above are re-examined in the light of this conclusion, and in a more general context, they are found to lose their one-sidedness and to exhibit features which can be related *both* to axiologically defined structures *and* to empirical behaviour. Thus, the syntheses of ideas referred to GAW, p. 197 are stated by Weber himself to include "die Menschen einer Epoche beherrschenden, d. h. diffus in ihnen wirksamen "Ideen" " [16], i. e., the (presumed) motives of behaviour of historical persons; similarly, Weber points out that the concept of "Stadtwirtschaft" is closely connected with certain *normative ideas* which served as a code of behaviour in the economic life of medieval cities [17]. The example of an apparently purely axiological type in *Wertfreiheit* also turns out, on closer examination, to be meant as an instrument for the analysis of human behaviour [18].

As for the "isolated rational" ideal types of economic behaviour, their apparent one-sidedness is due to the fact that the economic goal: (subjectively) optimal satisfaction of needs, remains *implicit*. In a number of passages, partly in connection with his discussion of the "one-sided" ideal types [19], Weber makes these goals and purposes explicit and thus supplies the types with the element of value which they apparently lacked.

15. *Cf. supra*, p. 152. Oppenheimer (*Logik*, 1925, p. 47) strongly emphasizes the *axiological* aspect of the ideal type. Thus, he claims that "die Idealtypen ... Begriffe von Sinn-, nicht von Seinszusammenhängen [sind] "(*ibid.*, p. 47); and even if the ideal types have been constructed with regard to the "Verwirklichung im historischen oder alltäglichen Kulturleben" (*ibid.*, p. 47) of these "relations of meaning", this "realization" is obviously regarded by Oppenheimer as non-causal, and consequently excludes a teleological element from entering into the type to complement the axiological one. Oppenheimer's "axiologization" of the ideal type can undoubtedly be explained by his dependence on Rickert's theory of historical science, with its dominant interest in the role of *values*. In fact, Oppenheimer's essay is written as a contribution to a *philosophical* essay competition set by Rickert; and the interpretation of Weber openly relies on Rickert (*cf. ibid.*, p. V).
    For a discussion of Schelting's emphasis on empirically oriented ideal types, *cf.* Appendix B of this chapter.
16. GAW, p. 197; similarly, GAW, p. 198.
17. GAW, p. 196, *cf.* GAW, p. 191.
18. GAW, p. 535.
19. For instance GAW, pp. 202, 391, 536. In the last passage in particular, Weber insists that the satisfaction of economic needs is a *point of view*, selected among other possible ends and motives.

2. The relation between the concept of the ideal type and Weber's theory of value analysis seems to explain some of the central characteristics of the ideal type which have not yet been discussed.

2.1. Above all, this is true of the *internal consistency* of the ideal type. Although Weber constantly, with insignificant variations, emphasizes the need for such consistency [20], this demand has not received more than a perfunctory analysis in the literature on Weber's methodology. However, the demand is by no means self-evident: it would be possible to construct concepts which referred to some kind of normative idea, but which contained internal contradictions, even in cases where these norms were regarded as motives of behaviour [21]. But if we view the premise of consistency in the light of the connection with the theory of value analysis, its necessity on the other hand becomes immediately apparent: as mentioned earlier [22], the unambiguousness and internal consistency of the ultimate value axioms were regarded by Weber as preconditions both of axiological and of teleological value analysis. As far as the axiological analysis is concerned, this unambiguousness is needed in order to permit the construction of a system of practical value judgments, and consequently the hypothetical pattern of behaviour motivated by an ethic of conviction, derived from any particular value axiom; and to teleological analysis, it is simply a *conditio sine qua non:* the appropriateness of means to reach a given end can only be demonstrated if the end is defined with complete precision.

2.2. The description of the ideal type as the result of a *theoretical intensification* of certain *one-sided aspects* also takes on a natural meaning if it is connected with the theory of value analysis: since Weber employs the terms "Gesichtspunkt" and "Wert" as synonyms, it seems justified to substitute the latter for the former one; and while to speak of a *point of view* being "intensified" seems obscure [23], the formulation "intensification of a *value*" is far easier to understand, as an indication that a value may be given added weight *in relation to other values.* The *theoretical* intensification of a value would accordingly mean the existence of an added *interest* in certain value aspects, and therefore indicate a tendency to regard reality *only* under these aspects. The claim that the ideal type represents a theoretical intensification of certain aspects in fact seems to imply that these aspects are

20. "Widerspruchslos", GAW, pp. 190, 191, 192, 197, 333, 535; "in sich einheitlich", GAW, pp. 191, 192; "Eindeutigkeit", GAW, pp. 206, 536.
21. Weber himself implicitly acknowledges this fact by referring, in one case, to the ideas of Christianity entertained by individual persons in the Middle Ages as "ein Chaos unendlich differenzierter und höchst widerspruchsvoller Gedanken- und Gefühlszusammenhänge aller Art" (GAW, p. 197).
22. *Supra,* pp. 159–60, 168.
23. GAW, p. 191. Even more obscure to a natural reading is the expression "Steigerung bestimmter Elemente der Wirklichkeit" (GAW, p. 190).

the *only ones* which are taken into consideration when the concept is constructed, and that they may, therefore, legitimately be described as *selected* and *one-sided*. This interpretation is supported by a passage in *Objektivität* where Weber employs the expressions "einseitig herausgehobene Gesichtspunkte" and "einseitige *Steigerung eines* ... [Gesichtspunkts]" alternately [24] but with what appears to be the same material reference.

Like so many other of Weber's concepts, that of "Steigerung" seems to have a dual aspect. Apart from indicating the "intensification" (i. e., the isolation) of the theoretical value, it also seems to cover that elaboration of the value in all its logical consequences which is the substance of axiological value analysis. This reading is suggested, for instance, by the expression "einseitig in ihren Konsequenzen gesteigert", which is used by Weber in the same discussion as that containing the terms referred to immediately above [25]; and the interpretation generally seems to render the curious idea of an abstract "Steigerung" of elements of *reality* more intelligible. The connection of the *unreality* of the ideal type with its "intensified" nature also becomes quite clear by this interpretation.

Thus, the "intensification" of a *valuational point of view,* in its axiological aspect, means that it is *isolated* and *worked out* in its last consequences. As for the ideal type of *rational* behaviour, the interpretation of the term "Steigerung" is less complicated: the principle of rationality includes the assumption of an absolute optimum, the attainment of or approximation to which (in relation to actual, purely non-rational behaviour) may naturally be described as an "intensification" of the rationality of the behaviour, a "Steigerung ins Rationale" [26].

3.   Up to this point, we have been concerned with those aspects of the ideal type which were connected with axiological and teleological value analysis, i. e., with those forms of analysis which operate on the assumption of either a logically or an empirically *correct* orientation of behaviour. It is interesting to note, though, that Weber follows up his earlier acknowledgement of the necessity of a *subjective,* "explanatory" value analysis by pointing out that the important element of motivation is *psychological* rather than purely *logical,* a circumstance which leads to certain difficulties in the analysis of motivation.

Weber touches on the idea as early as *Objektivität* [27]; but the greater part of his reflections on this point is found in *Kategorien* and later essays. Here, the ideal types as such, and their construction, play a minor role; the focus

24. GAW, p. 191.
25. GAW, p. 191.
26. GAW, p. 397 (slightly modified).
27. GAW, p. 198.

of discussion is Weber's claim that the deduction of hypothetical motives from observed behaviour cannot limit itself to the correctly deduced goals or axioms. Weber has apparently been impressed by the results of psycho-analysis and related disciplines, and he once dwells on the circumstance that it is possible to see behaviour as teleologically correct, in relation to a goal which is not clear to the acting person [28]; in such cases, we may be said to uncover the correct goal orientation of the subconscious. This line of thought is dangerous, however—a fact which Weber fully realizes—because it tends towards the assumption that the subjectively subconscious goals are *actual* goals; this assumption comes close to a violation of the principle of value freedom. Normally, therefore, Weber constructs his examples from the opposite point of view, and tries to demonstrate the possibility that behaviour which "from the outside", empirically, seems oriented towards a certain value or goal, may "from the inside", with regard to its actual, subjective motivation, turn out to be dependent on quite different motives [29]. In this connection, he refers to the particularly prominent case (which he examines in PE I) of the puritans, whose belief in religious predestination acted as a psychological motive for intense worldly activity, the results of which were regarded as indications of the future religious status of the persons concerned [30]. The intellectual connection between axiom and behaviour is in this case "understandable", and consequently amenable to "explanatory" value analysis; but it is not *logical,* and cannot be uncovered by means of axiological analysis.

4. We may now proceed to define the following variants of ideal types, according to the nature of their relation with the theory of value analysis [31]: 1) The type of *teleological rationality.* Here, the premises are: a) one or more goals striven for; b) the wish to attain this goal or these goals by means of causally adequate, "external" means. The elements entering into the construction of this type are provided by *teleological* value analysis, to the extent that the person concerned is presumed to possess and apply objectively

28. GAW, pp. 434–35. See also WG, p. 7.
29. For instance GAW, pp. 434–36; WG, p. 7.
30. GAW, pp. 435, 436.
31. On the whole, the types enumerated below are based on Weber's discussion of value analysis, and on previous sections of the present chapter. The types are closely linked with Weber's definitions, particularly in *Kategorien* and WG, of various types of behaviour and their meaningfulness; but since the types enumerated below are mainly constructed as an aid to the subsequent discussion of the heuristic function of the ideal type, whereas Weber's types of behaviour raise difficult sociological problems, the two sets of concepts will not be compared with each other. However, a few references to Weber's work have been inserted for the convenience of the reader.

correct knowledge of teleological relations (objective teleological rationality); if, on the other hand, the person is presumed to have applied wholly or partly *incorrect* teleological knowledge in his attempt to reach the goal by rational means (subjective teleological rationality), it is necessary in addition to make use of the results of *explanatory* value analysis [32].

2) The type of *axiological rationality*. Here, the premises are: a) one or more values to which a person is committed; b) the wish to act in immediate accordance with these values, i. e., to orient behaviour so that its *intrinsic* axiological value is always positive in relation to the value or values adopted. This type depends on the results of *axiological* value analysis, to the extent that the person concerned is supposed to perform correctly the logical calculation of the axiological status of his actions (objective axiological rationality); if we assume, on the other hand, that the axiological deduction, in spite of subjective *bona fides,* is more or less erroneous (subjective axiological rationality), *explanatory* value analysis will have to be brought in as well [33].

3) The type of *comprehensible, non-rational* behaviour. This includes, for instance, the behaviour (mentioned above) motivated by a belief in religious predestination; affective ("typically" angry, jealous, etc.) behaviour also comes under this heading. In the former case, the type is constructed exclusively on the basis of the results of *explanatory* value analysis, whereas in the second one it can only be said to be indirectly connected with value analysis at all, since the motive is not *value* orientation, but a comparatively uncontrolled *emotion* [34].

4) The type of *incomprehensible* behaviour. This type embodies the "typical" traits of observed behaviour the motivation of which remains obscure to the observer. It does not rely on the results of value analysis [35].

32. The objective type of teleological rationality corresponds to Weber's concept of "Richtigkeitsrationalität", which is only defined in the *Kategorien* essay (for instance GAW, p. 432); the subjective type of teleological rationality is identical with Weber's concept of "(subjektive) Zweckrationalität" (see for instance GAW, p. 432; WG, pp. 17–18).

33. The type of axiological rationality corresponds to the category of "Wertrationalität" in Weber's sociology (for instance WG, pp. 17–18). Although the distinction between the objective and the subjective variant is not made by Weber, it seems to bear a natural relation to his thought.

34. Neither of the two variants of this type is referred to by Weber as an *ideal type;* as for their role as *actual* motives of behaviour, *cf.* GAW, p. 436 and WG, p. 18 respectively.

35. This type is mentioned by Weber at GAW, p. 438. He claims that its lack of an "internal" axiological component does not preclude its classification as an ideal type. This point of view does not conflict with the characterization of the central principle of the ideal type set out at the beginning of the present chapter. However, the fact that Weber does not elsewhere deal with the non-comprehensible types seems to indicate that he regards them as limiting cases.

4.3.3. The ideal type as a heuristic aid

Apart from the function of the ideal type as an aid to the presentation of scientific results, Weber mentions its role as a *heuristic* instrument of causal analysis [1]. This function does not in itself present any special difficulty; but certain aspects of Weber's treatment of it require a more thorough discussion.

1. A brief account of the heuristic role of the ideal type is found in *Knies II:* "... [der idealtypische Begriff dient] dazu ..., die empirisch gültige Deutung dadurch zu erleichtern, daß die gegebenen Tatsachen mit einer Deutungs-möglichkeit—einem *Deutungsschema*—verglichen werden ..." [2]. Thus, observed behaviour is compared with models of behaviour *constructed* from certain explicit premises, and the distance between construction and reality is assessed. If this distance is small, we can assume that the motives of the actual behaviour were roughly the same as the premises of the constructed type; if, on the other hand, the distance is great, the comparison may at least serve as an indication of the *im*probability of the premises of the constructed behaviour, and perhaps also as a guide to the points at which *different* actual motives have been operative [3]. Since the ideal type is a deliberately *unrealistic* abstraction, the comparison will usually end in an invalidation of the latter kind.

2. The greater or smaller discrepancy existing between the ideal type and empirical reality may—depending on the kind of type concerned—be defined according to two different criteria. On the one hand, it may result from the fact that the persons observed were actually committed to other *values,* as teleological goals or as axiological norms, than the ones used as premises for the construction of the ideal type. The types of *teleological* or *axiological* rationality, or of value-oriented, *comprehensible, non-rational* behaviour, may be used to demonstrate this kind of discrepancy. On the other hand, the discrepancy may be the result of the fact that the persons observed exhibit a lower degree of *teleological rationality* than that assumed to be present in the ideal type [4]. By definition, this latter discrepancy can only be demonstrated by means of an ideal type of *teleological rationality.*
2.1. In view of this, it is highly significant that Weber almost completely ignores the purely axiological aspect in his discussion, and instead everywhere concentrates on differences in the degree of rationality.

1. Thus for instance GAW, pp. 130, 190, 205, 342; WG, p. 15.
2. GAW, p. 130.
3. See for instance GAW, p. 203; GARS, pp. 536–37.
4. Only *teleological* rationality is a point of view *independent* of the chosen value or goal. *Axiological* rationality turns out to be identical with the elaboration of the consequences of the value, i. e., with the "intensification" of the chosen value.

2.1.1. In fact, Weber only once [5] seems to mention that the comparison with an ideal type may possibly point to goals or *values* which were not incorporated into the type. This happens in the only detailed discussion in *Objektivität* of the heuristic function of ideal types, where Weber outlines an ideal-typical development, under certain conditions, from an "artisan" to a "capitalist" culture, and continues: "War der Idealtypus "richtig" konstruiert und entspricht der tatsächliche Verlauf dem idealtypischen *nicht,* so wäre damit der Beweis geliefert, daß die mittelalterliche Gesellschaft eben in bestimmten Beziehungen *keine* streng "handwerksmäßige" war". He adds that an "ideally" constructed ideal type would also indicate what *other* significant value orientations might be examined [6]. Since the ideal type of the "culture of the artisan", as defined by Weber, must be counted among the types of objective axiological rationality [7], the demonstration that the Middle Ages lacked this "artisan" character is a (partial) invalidation of the theory that this particular value acted as a norm for the historical persons concerned.

2.1.2. On the other hand, we find a very large number of instances, especially in *Stammler, Kategorien* and WG, where the function of the ideal type as a heuristic aid consists in the demonstration of a lack of *teleological rationality* in real life. For one thing, this dominating teleological interest is reflected in the fact that the ideal types discussed in all these essays are ideal types of teleological rationality, often even of *objective* teleological rationality, i. e., constructions based on the assumption that the conditions of behaviour are fully known by the acting person. This is the case, for instance, with the abstract economic "laws" [8], and elsewhere [9]. In other places, Weber refers to types of *subjective* teleological rationality [10].

To this must be added that the discrepancies noted by means of the ideal types usually relate to the teleological and rational aspect, while the axiological and motivational elements of the types are only included to a very minor degree. This is especially clear with regard to the objective types, since Weber, when discussing their heuristic function, interprets actual divergences from

5. GAW, p. 203. See also GAW, p. 535, where Weber denies that types of objective rationality possess any kind of heuristic monopoly, and refers to ideal types of axiological rationality without, however, discussing the *result* of working with such types.
6. GAW, p. 203.
7. *Cf.* GAW, p. 191, where expressions like "Prinzip" and "Maxime" are used to indicate both economic and inner, spiritual activity.
8. GAW, pp. 130, 429, 534.
9. For instance GAW, pp. 129, 432, 534; WG, pp. 5, 15. In WG, Weber in this connection speaks of "zweckrational" behaviour, a term which rather seems to refer to *subjective* teleological rationality. This is explained, however, by the fact that the term "richtigkeitsrational" is only found in *Kategorien.* The *objective* element in the examples is clear from the context.
10. For instance GAW, pp. 130, 430, 432; WG, pp. 5, 15.

them as indicating that the *actual* teleological rationality of the observed behaviour is only *subjective*[11]. As for the ideal types of subjective teleological rationality, Weber often claims that divergences from them indicate the presence of "non-rational" elements in the actual motivation of the observed behaviour [12]; and this expression, which *might* be interpreted as including what we have called axiological rationality, i. e., *value*-oriented behaviour, is explained by reference to comprehensible but non-rational [13], affective [14] or even incomprehensible [15] types of behaviour. Only once, in WG [16], the fact that the actual goals do not correspond to those included in the type is mentioned as a possible reason for the divergence of actual behaviour from that defined by the type; but only in passing, and at the very end of the list of possible factors.

2.1.3. It is possible to advance more than one explanation of this early and significant shift of interest from the axiological towards the teleological and rational elements of (assumed or actual) motivation. First, it may be noted that the examples quoted by Weber in *Objektivität* are remote from us in time, a circumstance which gives the question of the values guiding the observed behaviour a greater relevance than in the case of his later illustrations, which are of a more contemporary nature. This argument may be supplemented by the further observation that the *recent,* "rational" examples quoted by Weber often refer to situations in which the goals (for instance economic, strategic and political motives) must be taken as given *a priori.*

2.2. Both these arguments, however, seem to rest on a third, and more fundamental, circumstance: the shift in Weber's interest is the visible sign that Weber, in the years 1904–07, is liberating himself from the "static" theory of history implied by Schmoller's "historical induction" and still perceptible in Rickert's description of historical concepts as "charged with meaning" [17].

2.2.1. The conditions of this emancipation are of course present as early as *Objektivität,* in the sense that Weber in that essay elevates concepts characterized by deliberate *unreality* and *abstraction* to the status of indispensable aids to the historical sciences. But Weber's views concerning the heuristic function of the ideal type are in this essay still marked by a certain dependence on the static view. As long as the ideal type is supposed to transmit knowledge of the values to be found in a given historical object, and not directly of the actual consequences of these values (as motives) for the behaviour of the object, the focus of interest is the valuational significance, the

11. GAW, pp. 129, 432, 534; WG, pp. 5, 15.
12. For instance GAW, pp. 130, 430; WG, p. 5.
13. GAW, p. 432.
14. WG, p. 15.
15. GAW, p. 432.
16. WG, p. 15.
17. *Cf. supra,* p. 207.

"Wertbedeutung", of the object *as such*. Another indication of this is the fact that the role of the ideal type as an aid to the *presentation* of results is far more prominent in *Objektivität* than the description of its *heuristic* function.

2.2.2. Already in *Knies II,* however, the picture changes: Weber now concentrates on rational types and on divergences from such types, and the heuristic function is discussed more concretely. What is particularly interesting in this connection is Weber's distinction between "purely individual" concepts and general ideal types [18]. The former, but not the latter, in his view function as causal *hypotheses* in connection with *unique* historical phenomena and events. The fact that the two types are contrasted is in itself significant, because it testifies to Weber's growing interest in general types of behaviour. But a point of special interest is Weber's treatment of the "individual" concepts.

The latter are immediately afterwards classified as ideal types [19], and consequently belong to the same category as the *general* types mentioned. Moreover, their "individual" character on closer examination turns out to be less prominent than might be expected. True, their *function* is restricted to the causal analysis of unique historical objects (as, for instance, the foreign policy of Fr. Wilhelm IV.); but the same restriction applies to *any* attempt to employ the ideal type heuristically in causal research, even when the type is a *general* one [20]. And the "individual" *type* is in itself partly constructed in accordance with a general principle, viz, that of teleological *rationality*. Thus, the difference between the "individual" type and the ones described as general by Weber resides exclusively in the (presumed) uniqueness of the *goals* included in it; but even where these goals are formulated quite concretely, analysis may often show that they represent the application of general value axioms to unique conditions [21]; and moreover, Weber is obviously far less interested in the unique characteristics of the goal than in the greater or lesser degree of rationality with which it is pursued [22].

18. GAW, p. 130, *cf.* GAW, p. 115.
19. GAW, p. 130: "In allen Fällen [i. e., both in the case of the individual and of the general concepts] ... ist das Verhältnis solcher rationalen teleologischen Konstruktionen [zur] ... Wirklichkeit ... das eines idealtypischen Begriffs".
20. One example supporting this contention is the way in which Weber, in *Stammler* (GAW, pp. 329–30), applies the general ideal types discussed in *Knies II* (the propositions of economics) in an analysis of unique behaviour (the foreign policy of Fr. Wilhelm IV).
21. Thus, Weber himself introduces the constellation of the Great Powers into the type as a condition, alongside of the aims of Fr. Wilhelm IV.
22. GAW, p. 131, "Zweck" probably covers what Weber has earlier (GAW, p. 129) referres to as "rationales Motiv", a concept which embraces *both* the axiological *and* the teleological element.

   For a discussion of Schelting's aversion to the concept of individual ideal types, *cf.* Appendix B of this chapter.

2.3. In fact, the tendency towards *generalization* resulting from the inclusion (at least after 1904) of teleological rationality as a constant feature of Weber's ideal types, is in *Knies II* only kept in check by the function of the ideal type as an aid to the causal analysis of *unique* historical phenomena and events. And just as the rational element in the construction and function of the type quickly overshadows the "static" value element, the importance of the element of generality seems to increase with time: the ideal type is freed from its former association with historical science, and grows to be the basis of a general *sociology*. Here, too, the change is gradual: four years after the foundation of the *Gesellschaft* (in 1909), in *Kategorien*, Weber still places history and sociology side by side with regard to the utilization of the heuristic function of the ideal type[23]; in *Wertfreiheit*, "kausale Zurechnung" is seen as a major reason for the construction of types[24]. But in WG, the break is complete: "Die Soziologie bildet ... *Typen*-Begriffe und sucht *generelle* Regeln des Geschehens. Im Gegensatz zur Geschichte, welche die kausale Analyse und Zurechnung *individueller, kultur*wichtiger, Handlungen, Gebilde, Persönlichkeiten erstrebt"[25]. The *material* of sociology, Weber maintains, is largely, but not exclusively, selected according to the values relevant to historical science; its *results* are largely, but not exclusively, framed so as to be useful to the work of the historian. In short: although they may collaborate, sociology and history are two separate and independent disciplines.

This distinction has been interpreted as the symptom of a radical change in Weber's thought; but it seems quite legitimate rather to regard it as the natural consequence of the instability of the alliance achieved by Weber in *Objektivität* between ideal types and historical science, an alliance in which the type, the potentially sociological element, which is dominant from the beginning, grows quite supreme in its teleological and rational form. Weber's sociology is deeply rooted in his theory of historical science.

3.1. The fact that Weber in this connection describes the function of ideal types as *heuristic* already seems to indicate that such types are *not* to be regarded as hypotheses in the usual sense of the word. The terminology instead suggests a more indirect role: the ideal type may help us to *formulate* hypotheses. Weber's emphasis on the *un*reality of the ideal type gives strong substantive support to this interpretation.

As early as *Objektivität*, Weber explicitly stresses the fact that the relation of the ideal type to causal hypotheses is an indirect one: "... [der idealtypische Begriff] *ist* keine "Hypothese", aber er will der Hypothesenbildung

23. GAW, p. 433.
24. GAW, pp. 535–36. The passage is taken over from the *Gutachten* without any major changes.
25. WG, p. 14.

die Richtung weisen" [26]. In the light of this, one is surprised by his uncertainty in *Knies II,* where the individual, objective type of teleological rationality is more than once described as a "Hypothese" or "Deutungs-*Hypothese*" [27]. However, the subsequent discussion makes it clear that Weber, who is discussing the relation between ideal types and ordinary hypotheses, probably, as is his wont, adopts a doubtful terminology in order to point out the problems connected with the concepts which it denotes. In his discussion of the passage quoted from *Knies II,* Weber repeats that ideal types are constructed from abstract and unrealistic premises; their origin disqualifies them from attaining the status of hypotheses. But "sie können als Hypothesen bei der heuristischen Verwendung der Deutung konkreter Vorgänge *fungieren*" [28]; they may in some sense function as hypotheses. But whenever they are invalidated in this function—as they usually will be, because of their basic unreality—they are again separated from "normal" hypotheses; since the types are constructed on the basis of unrealistic assumptions, their validity is not affected by the empirical invalidation; they can be used afresh [29].

In later essays, the element of unreality grows more pronounced; Weber does not describe the ideal types as hypotheses, even in a qualified sense, but rather stresses their unreal character. In *Wertfreiheit,* this tendency leads him to denote ideal types by the term "Fiktion" [30]. This open acknowledgement of the fictional character of the concepts is a symbol of their emancipation from the framework of historical science: the concern for the contact with empirical reality recedes *pari passu* with the development of sociology as a discipline distinct from history.

3.2. The view of the ideal type as purely fictional naturally suggests that what is significant and fruitful about the concept is its *divergence* from reality. This is openly acknowledged by Weber in WG: "Je schärfer und eindeutiger konstruiert die Idealtypen sind: je welt*fremder* sie also, in diesem Sinne, sind, desto besser leisten sie ihren Dienst, terminologisch und klassifikatorisch sowohl wie heuristisch" [31]. Consequently, although all the ideal types concerned are types of teleological rationality, this does not imply the existence in Weber's work of a "rationalistic prejudice", i. e., a theory according to which the persons observed are *in fact* acting in a rational manner: the rationality of the ideal types rather, if anything, points to Weber's interest in the *irrational* elements of motivation.

26. GAW, p. 190.
27. GAW, pp. 115, 130.
28. GAW, p. 131.
29. GAW, p. 131.
30. GAW, pp. 529, 537. Both these passages are additions from 1917; the word does not occur earlier in Weber's work in this sense.
31. WG, p. 15.

In accordance with his own warning [32] against investing scientific approaches with the dignity of a philosophy of life, Weber takes pains to deny any suggestion that his types reflect a "rationalistic prejudice". Both in *Kategorien* [33] and in WG [34], he stresses the importance of *irrational* factors. But he does admit that the danger of rationalistic misconceptions of his types is very great [35]; and although he theoretically rejects any such misconception regarding his own work, it cannot be denied that his system of predominantly rational sociological concepts, the application of which must result in the labelling of irrational elements of motivation as "deviations", constitutes a fertile *basis* for misunderstanding. This does not invalidate Weber's theoretical position, but it does suggest that *psychological* factors may be stronger than the purely *logical* ones.

3.3.1. Weber's constant use of rational ideal types, in spite of his own warnings, may be ascribed to a number of factors. For one thing, it should be remembered that he regarded the wish to act rationally as a very significant component of modern occidental culture [36]. Although the rational types cannot, and ought not to, function as hypotheses, let alone as part of a *philosophy* of history [37], their basic premises conform to what Weber believes to be a rationalistic *tendency* in the subject-matter. Consequently, they are particularly well suited to the demonstration of the actual, greater *or lesser*, degree of rationality exhibited by this subject-matter.

3.3.2. A further explanation of the, above all objectively, rational character of the ideal type may be found in the circumstance that an ideal type constructed from a premise of objective rationality possesses a maximum of *objective validity*. Since the objectively rational type is nothing more than the embodiment of the results of an (axiological or teleological) value analysis, its only subjective element is the choice of the hypothetical goal or value. Consequently, it is theoretically possible to eliminate all sources of error from it. This circumstance has immense importance for the intersubjectivity of the scientific results: other scholars may always dispute the correctness of the more or less "explanatory" (subjective rational, comprehensible non-rational or affective) types, not only with regard to the choice of one rather than another type in the concrete case, but also with regard to the concrete elaboration of this type, since it will always to a certain extent depend on the subjective "intuition" of the scholar. A correctly

32. *Cf. supra,* pp. 41–42.
33. GAW, pp. 429, 430.
34. WG, p. 5.
35. WG, p. 5.
36. *Cf. infra,* pp. 276–77.
37. Weber explicitly and repeatedly rejects any attempt to interpret the concept of the ideal type as implying a philosophy of history. See for instance GAW, pp. 195, 205, 335.

constructed type of objective rationality, on the other hand, possesses inter-subjective validity (if we take the choice of the hypothetical goal or value as given); it is objectively *true*. Although the *fruitfulness* of such objective types is still open to legitimate doubt, they do, when actually applied, facili-tate the discussion of the scientific results attained by means of ideal-typical analysis.

Weber usually does not mention this aspect of the problem, perhaps because of his unwillingness to regard concepts as fixed once and for all [38]. His own defence of the rational type instead relies on their "comprehensible" nature [39], which however, as far as *intellectual* comprehension is concerned, seems to correspond exactly to the knowledge yielded by axiological and teleological value analysis [40].

4.3.4. *The origin of the values*

Since the rational ideal types are always constructed around a value acting as a hypothetical purpose or norm, one may ask where Weber believes these values to be found: is the scholar free to construct an ideal type around any value, or does he have to consider the subject-matter to which the type is to be applied? Although this question is in a sense parallel to the one discussed above [1] concerning the origin of the values entering into historical concepts in general, it differs from it on two counts: first, because the ideal types are presumably applied to a material which already possesses a conceptual struc-ture; and secondly, because the ideal type is usually meant to be a direct aid to the uncovering of the motivations by which the observed persons have actually been guided. The first point removes the logical circularity of the contention that the value premises should be taken from the material itself; and the second one establishes a very close connection between the values present in the material and those selected by the scholar for his construction of ideal types. Both of them seem to suggest a *diminution* of the almost unlimited subjectivity of choice conceded by Weber in his discussion of the theoretical value relation.

In view of this, it is interesting that the freedom of choice is seen by Weber as equally great with regard to the construction of ideal types. This is quite explicitly stated in *Objektivität*, where the discussion centres round

38. *Cf. infra*, pp. 233–34.
39. See for instance GAW, p. 432; WG, pp. 4–5.
40. WG, pp. 4–5. In this connection, Judith Janoska-Bendl (*Idealtypus,* 1965, p. 53) points to Weber's critical attitude to psychology. It should be borne in mind, however, that Weber's dislike was mainly directed against the pretensions of *generalizing* psychology, a discipline of *natural* science; "intuitive" psychology, on the other hand, was part of the basis of his own sociology.
1. Pp. 121–31.

the axiological types; and the same conclusion seems to be implicit in the later essays and in WG with respect to the teleological ideal types.

1. In *Objektivität* [2], Weber presents his view of the relation between the value premises of the ideal type on the one hand and reality on the other one; but this view, though fundamentally clear, is quite complicated in its details. The main line of the argument is the following:

1.1. On the basis of a given part of empirical reality, one or more ideal types may be constructed [3]. The value element entering into such constructions is arrived at by a process by which the scholar abstracts from the individual empirical phenomena "einen *Gedanken*ausdruck ..., den ... [the scholar] darin manifestiert findet" [4]. Thus, the influence of the subject-matter is decisive, in the sense that it must be possible for the value resulting from the process of abstraction to be "read into" the phenomena in question: the value must be *one possible* motive of the behaviour constituting or causing the observed phenomena. On the other hand, Weber does not demand that the "Idee" abstracted should have any connection with the *actual* motivation causing the phenomena; in fact, he seems to suppose that it is very difficult, if not impossible, to arrive at these actual motives at this stage of the analysis.

1.2. Now it is possible that the substance of these ideal types was present, if only in a more primitive and inchoate form, in the minds of those individuals whose behaviour constituted or caused the historical object on which the ideal type was based [5]. It is tempting to regard this identity of an ideal type abstracted *from* reality with an ideal motivating behaviour *in* this same reality as something more than a coincidence; but Weber carefully stresses that the causal relations between ideals, reality and ideal types may take many different forms: "Festzuhalten ist prinzipiell nur, daß beides [ideal and ideal type] selbstverständlich grundverschiedene Dinge sind" [6].

1.3. This intricate balance between norm and theory, concept and reality, is now complicated even further by the circumstance that the actually operative ideals, as mentioned above, are found in numerous, more or less articulate, deliberate and consistent variants in the minds of the historical in-

---

2. GAW, pp. 190–92, 195–98, 200–01.
3. GAW, p. 190. Weber refers to such ideal types as " "Ideen" historischer Erscheinungen". This expression exposes the concept to the danger of being confused with *actual* motivating ideas or of being hypostatized as the "essence" of history. Weber warns against both of these misconceptions (GAW, pp. 195–96, 336), but, characteristically, does not remove their cause.
4. GAW, p. 191, *cf.* GAW, p. 192.
5. GAW, pp. 195–96. Weber describes these ideals, too, as "Ideen". They are probably the ideals referred to in the opening discussion of value analysis (GAW, p. 150, *cf. supra,* pp. 148–50).
6. GAW, pp. 196–97.

dividuals concerned. If the scholar is therefore to arrive at a clear understanding of the significance of such an ideal in its various forms, he has to construct an *ideal type of the ideal* [7].

In principle, this process of construction does not differ from the abstraction from concrete phenomena of an inherent "Gedankenausdruck", as discussed above. In this case, however, the phenomena belong to the "internal" reality of the observed individuals, to the world of their ideas as it is revealed (usually through art and literature) to the scholar; and the abstraction of the "Gedankenausdruck" incorporated in these phenomena consists in tracing the ideal back to the ultimate principle on which it is based.

If this principle has been sufficiently clear and easy to grasp to be assimilated and applied without distortion by the observed individuals, it is of course easy to trace and to include, as found, in the ideal type [8]. In such cases, the material may properly be said to control the value basis of the ideal type. Very often, however, the principle has disappeared in its original form and has to be *reconstructed* from the various existing ideals which it has inspired; and since the relation of these ideals to the principle may be quite obscure, the independent role of the scholar, who "reads" hypothetical value orientations "into" the material, is re-activated. The status of the concepts constructed by the scholar as "eine "Idee", die *wir* [the scholars] schaffen" becomes even clearer in cases where the principle on which the ideal type is to be based has *never* been explicitly formulated. Here the "internal" material is just as inaccessible, and the role of the scholar as a source of value premises just as crucial, as in the case, discussed initially, of ideal types abstracted from empirical reality [9]. Wherever the analysis of actual motives is problematical, the subjective component of the value basis of the ideal type becomes an unavoidable necessity [10].

7. GAW, p. 197.
8. GAW, pp. 197–98.
9. GAW, p. 198.
10. Henrich's conclusion—which is apparently in accordance with the one reached above—is that "die Bildung des Idealtypus ... von einer jeweils vorgängig vollzogenen Kenntnisnahme des Inhaltes der Wirklichkeit [abhängig ist]" (*Einheit,* 1952, p. 92). However, his subsequent restriction of the number of values on which an ideal type may legitimately be based is hardly justified. He here describes the ideal type as a concept which "sagt, *welche Bedeutungen wirkende Kraft hätten sein müssen, wenn das bedeutungsbezogene Subjekt sich über seine eigenen Sinnorientierungen klar geworden wäre" (ibid.,* p. 94). In so doing, he alters the whole interpretation, substituting an "objectively necessary", if only latent, axiological orientation, constructed from within, i. e., through the elaboration of certain (postulated) essential ideas, for an "objectively possible" axiological orientation, constructed from without, i. e., by an abstraction from empirical reality. The plainly *fictional* nature of the ideal type is ignored, and replaced by a concept which is rooted in normative essentialism.

2. In his later essays, Weber is more concerned with teleological types, in which the value element is less prominent and often wholly straightforward (the fixed economic goal of the optimal satisfaction of needs, etc.). The problem which now comes to occupy him is that of distinguishing between *objective* and *subjective* types of teleological rationality. He applies himself to this task with great thoroughness, both in *Stammler* [11], *Kategorien* [12] and WG [13]. In the course of his discussion, he repeatedly emphasizes that the purpose of social science is the uncovering of the "subjektiv gemeinte Sinn" [14]. The significance of this expression, however, seems to lie in its negative, not in its positive content. This point is made very clearly in the commentary to Weber's fundamental definition in WG:

> " "Sinn" ist hier entweder a) der tatsächlich [vom Handelnden] ... oder b) in einem begrifflich konstruierten *reinen* Typus von dem oder den als Typus *gedachten* Handelnden subjektiv *gemeinte* Sinn. Nicht etwa irgendein objektiv "richtiger" oder ein metaphysisch ergründeter "wahrer" Sinn. Darin liegt der Unterschied der empirischen Wissenschaften vom Handeln ... gegenüber allen dogmatischen ..." [15]

Here the claims of *actual* and of *hypothetical and typical* value orientation to the description "subjektiv gemeint" are seen as equally justified: the fact that actual motivation is often difficult to unravel [16] means that the scholar retains his fundamental freedom of choice with respect to the value premise of the ideal type.

3. Weber's assertion of the subjectivity of the values on which the ideal type is based seems to reflect the connection between the ideal type and Weber's version of the theory of value relation; and this connection manifests itself in the subsequent discussion as well. Thus, in *Objektivität* (where the contact to the problems of history is most direct) he emphasizes that the ideal type depends on "one-sided aspects" [17], so that many *different* types are needed in order to characterize the central and significant historical phenomena [18]. In view of this, the explicit inclusion of *one-sidedness* as a constitutive element of the ideal type seems particularly justified. This one-

11. For instance GAW, pp. 333–34.
12. For instance GAW, p. 433.
13. For instance WG, p. 4.
14. As far as *Kategorien* is concerned, the introductory footnote introduces this aspect: "Die pedantische Umständlichkeit der Formulierung entspricht dem Wunsch, den *subjektiv* gemeinten Sinn von dem objektiv gültigen scharf zu scheiden ..." (GAW, p. 427n1). In WG, the fundamental definition of "soziales Handeln" contains the same emphasis (WG, p. 3).
15. WG, p. 4.
16. One reason for this may be that the acting person himself is not conscious of the motivation. *Cf.* WG, p. 15.
17. GAW, p. 192.
18. GAW, p. 148.

sidedness even (as in the case of theoretical value relation [19]) persist through time: in Weber's view, any single ideal type must be regarded as *transitory*. It is impossible for a complex of ideal types to exhaust the significance of a given object, even if new ideal types are added to this complex as time goes on [20]. The practical interest of the scholar changes with the development of his culture: new aspects of the historical material catch his attention, while older ones are discarded. Weber sums up this view as follows: "Die weittragendsten Fortschritte auf dem Gebiet der Sozialwissenschaften knüpfen sich *sachlich* an die Verschiebung der praktischen Kulturprobleme und kleiden sich in die *Form* einer Kritik der Begriffsbildung" [21].

4.4. The prognostic aspect: ideal type and politics

1. By elaborating the logical significance of the ideal type, Weber creates new possibilities of *prognosis* in the social sciences. The view of the ideal type as a one-sided, fictional course of action to which it is often possible to ascribe objective validity (as long as certain hypothetical premises are regarded as given) makes it possible to escape from the traditional position, according to which the object of historical science is unique, "unmittelbar zu Gott", and consequently unsuitable as a basis for predictions. On the other hand, the retention of the individual *significance* of historical phenomena as an integrated part of the ideal type means that any regularities arrived at avoid the emptiness of positivistic laws and preserve a natural relation with concrete cultural problems.

1.1. To certain disciplines in the field of social science, and to their practical counterparts, these new perspectives were of but slight importance. This was the case, for instance, of theoretical economics which, being based on the assumption that "economic man" was motivated solely by certain well-defined and constant purposes, was less interested in the axiological possibilities of the Weberian ideal type.

1.2. On the other hand, ideal types seemed particularly well suited to the world of *politics,* since the work of politicians was marked by the necessity of predicting, with a fair degree of certainty, the probable behaviour and the probable reactions of individuals acting from the most diverse motives. In view of the wealth of possible political attitudes, the axiological flexibility of the ideal type constituted a special advantage [1].

The main value of the ideal type from a political point of view, however, is derived not only from its flexibility, i. e., the possibility of introducing

19. *Cf. supra*, pp. 139–40.
20. GAW, pp. 206–07.
21. GAW, p. 208.
 1. Weber's general view of the nature of politics is described below, pp. 245–46.

into it a large number of different values and purposes, but also—and perhaps even primarily—from the fact that it is constructed in connection with, and is consequently able to transmit knowledge of, *motives of behaviour*. Since politicians seek to translate their values into practice, in constant conflict with other individuals committed to *different* values, they are often less concerned with the predictability of empirical behaviour than with the possibility of *revealing, understanding,* and *entering into the spirit of* the values motivating this conflicting behaviour. For this purpose the ideal type, which is rooted in axiological and explanatory value analysis, becomes a precious instrument. A particularly useful feature in this connection is its *internal consistency:* this characteristic endows the selected values—particularly those included in types of axiological rationality, as in *Objektivität*— with a unity and a resulting immediate *self-evidence* which is far greater than that possessed by ordinary models of behaviour and motivation. Another fruitful aspect of the concept is the possibility, directly mentioned by Weber (who makes lavish use of it in his own sociological work), of rendering the ideal type more graphic by the inclusion of elements of reality in it.

2. All the reasons named make the ideal type, particularly in its axiological form, an extremely useful instrument of political analysis. It should be noted, however, that the features referred to: axiological flexibility, internal consistency of the basic values, and graphic impressiveness, at the same time constitute the main danger to the correct utilization of this first-rate analytical instrument. The reasons for this are the following:

2.1. Naturally, the prognostic function of the ideal type is of a *hypothetical* nature: if the conditions embodied in the type are present in real life, *then* we may expect to find an actual course of behaviour corresponding to the "typical" one; or, since the ideal type is by definition *unreal:* to the extent that the conditions isolated in the type are met with in real life, we may expect real behaviour to conform more closely to the type. Since a great many conditions of behaviour *other* than those included in the type may be of importance to the actual chain of events, any such prognosis is *partial.* Now the danger of the ideal type (especially in its axiological form) is its tendency to make one forget this hypothetical restriction. Its plasticity, inner consistency and graphic self-evidence give it a power of psychological penetration which in practice sweeps aside any number of theoretical safeguards (warnings against universalization, generalization, etc.). The ideal type is, so to speak, by nature an *expansive* concept.

2.2. A good illustration of this is afforded by Weber's brilliant application of the ideal-typical method to the analysis of the Protestant Ethic and the possible importance of this ethic for the distinctive spirit of modern capitalism. Weber himself expressly denies that he has any other intention than that

of examining "ob und wieweit religiöse Einflüsse bei der qualitativen Prä-
gung und quantitativen Expansion jenes "[kapitalistischen] Geistes" über
die Welt hin *mit*beteiligt gewesen sind und welche konkreten *Seiten* der auf
kapitalistischer Basis ruhenden *Kultur* auf sie zurückgehen" [2], i. e., a one-
sided and partial examination of the relation between two aspects of concrete
reality (embodied in their respective ideal types). Nevertheless, Weber's thesis
has often been discussed as if he claimed the existence of a proper relation of
cause and effect between two sections of historical reality in their entirety.
It would be quite unjustified merely to ascribe this development to superficial
reading and unwarranted inferences on the part of the critics: the tendency
described should probably in part be put down to the "expanding" nature
of the ideal type, its ability to captivate and fill the imagination.

2.3.1. The same danger exists in the field of political analysis, where we possess an even clearer example of its reality: in his political writings of 1917–18,
Weber undoubtedly reads unreal and intensified features of ideal types
like "legal authority", "charismatic authority" and "bureaucracy" into the
concrete reality of German political life, and from his analysis draws conclusions which are meant as guidance for political practice after the War.
The actual developments in the Weimar Republic contradicted the chains of
reasoning supporting these conclusions in the most flagrant manner.

2.3.2. Of course, the danger of employing the "expansive" ideal type as
an instrument of political analysis is matched by the particular suitability of
the ideal type as a vehicle for political *propaganda*. The "expansiveness"
which clouds the clear vision of reality at the same time heightens the suggest-
ibility of the imagination. Although Weber occasionally employs ideal types
to this end [3], he is probably unaware of their absolutistic tendencies.

---

2. PE I, p. 77.
3. See for instance his passionate outburst against the Allied powers and their
   treatment of Germany after World War I: "Wir sind gleich den Juden zu einem
   Pariavolk geworden ..." (according to a contemporary report, copy in DZA II,
   Rep. 92, No. 30, Vol. 5). "Pariavolk" is defined as an ideal type WG, p. 386.
   The fact that the sentence formed part of a political speech made by Weber in
   front of his students (of economics and sociology) in Munich of course increases
   the impressiveness of the expression even further.

*Appendix A. Does Weber's definition of the object of sociology depend on a philoso-
phical anthropology?* Weber's definition of the object of social science (of sociology)
on the basis of the assumed existence of value orientation (in the broad sense) has
been taken by a number of commentators as evidence of a *philosophical-anthropologi-
cal* element in his thought, of an idea according to which man only becomes "real" by
virtue of his value orientation. This interpretation is vigorously advanced by Henrich [1],
as well as by Wegener [2] and by Tenbruck [3].

It will not be disputed here that such a philosophical interpretation is *possible;*
but is it a *necessary* premise of Weber's thought? The investigation of this problem
is facilitated by the fact that all the three commentators rely on one and the same
passage from *Objektivität:* "Tranzendentale Voraussetzung jeder *Kulturwissenschaft*
ist *nicht* etwa, daß wir eine bestimmte oder überhaupt irgend eine "Kultur" *wertvoll*
finden, sondern daß wir Kultur*menschen sind,* begabt mit der Fähigkeit und dem
Willen, bewußt zur Welt *Stellung* zu nehmen und ihr einen *Sinn* zu verleihen" [4].

The "philosophical" interpretations of this passage seem to be the result of an
unwarranted isolation of it; read in its context, it functions as an extension of
Weber's argument that the concept of "culture" presupposes a *value relation* but
not any *positive* valuation, and should consequently be interpreted in a formal and
theoretical way. This is quite obvious from the opening sentence (*"nicht* etwa",
etc.); but since both Henrich, Tenbruck and Wegener cut out this part of the passage [5], they view the "transzendentale Voraussetzung" in isolation. And since
they do not otherwise indicate the context of the passage, the expression "trans-
zendental" is over-emphasized and displaced, so that what is interpreted as transcendental, and accordingly as an essential characteristic of the "true" human being,
is his ability to endow reality with meaning, to be a "cultural individual".

It seems more reasonable, however, to regard the "transcendental" element as
connected with "Voraussetzung", and to interpret it along far less philosophical
and ontological lines, as the simple indication that the "science of culture" depends
on certain methodological conditions. This reading is supported by Weber's own
explanation, in *Stammler,* of the concept of "transzendentale "Form"" as *"logische Voraussetzung* der Erfahrung" [6]. Under this interpretation, the passage in
dispute is meant to emphasize that history (in the logical sense) is dependent on two
conditions: 1) that the historian is a human being, and thus presumed to be able
to define a value aspect, to take an interest in his subject; and 2) that the subject-
matter includes human beings presumed to be capable of value orientation in the
world which surrounds them. (Only this second condition, by defining the historical
object as "culture", justifies the employment of the term "Kulturwissenschaft"
synonymously with "Wissenschaft von der menschlichen Kultur", etc.). The fact
that the two conditions merge into one in Weber's "wir" accords well with Weber's
reluctance, noted above, to distinguish between the object level and the research
level [7].

1. *Einheit,* 1952, pp. 82–83.
2. *Wissenschaftsauffassung,* 1962, pp. 117, 270.
3. *Genesis,* 1959, p. 592.
4. GAW, p. 180.
5. In one place, Wegener does, however, retain it (*Wissenschaftsauffassung,* 1962,
   p. 117).
6. This is the only other instance in GAW of Weber employing the term "transzen-
   dental" at all, a fact which points to a certain wish on his part to dispense with
   such blatantly Kantian terminology.
7. *Cf. supra,* pp. 104–05.

In fact, Weber's reflections on man's motivation by an orientation after values, ideas, norms, etc., may be regarded as a *hypothesis,* which admittedly serves as a firm basis for a number of scientific disciplines, in the sense that they would lose their relevance if *nobody* acted according to the hypothesis, but which in *concrete* research is primarily justified by its *fruitfulness* as a guide to causal analysis. This *hypothetical* element strongly emerges in *Stammler,* where Weber argues that it is reasonable to regard judicial norms as important motives of behaviour because "die empirischen Menschen normalerweise "vernünftige", d. h. (empirisch betrachtet) der Erfassung und Befolgung von "Zweckmaximen" und des Besitzes von "Normvorstellungen" fähige Wesen sind" [8]. This kind of reflection marks a complete shift from any possible earlier "ontological" interpretation of value orientation as the "essence" of humanity, towards considerations of chance and probability.

A similar kind of hypothetical construction may be put on Weber's use of the vague and dangerous concept of "Verstehen", a category which H. Stuart Hughes not unjustifiably calls "the murkiest of many dark corners in the labyrinth of German social-science method" [9]. This concept may be regarded as tied to the assumption that the scholar is *essentially* similar to his human object; but this ontological interpretation is never raised by Weber above the status of a *supposition* that "intuition" on the scholar's part may be of heuristic value; and the hypothetical nature of this supposition is emphasized by Weber's frequent and undeviating demand that *empirical verification* should be regarded as the necessary complement of the "intuitive" grasping of the motives of the human object [10].

Appendix B. Schelting's restrictive interpretation of the concept of the ideal type. On two main points, Schelting applies a very restrictive interpretation to Weber's concept of the ideal type.

First, he wishes to reserve the term "ideal type" for empirically (above all teleologically and causally) oriented concepts, and is consequently critical of Weber's extension of the term to cover the axiological types as well [11]. The reason for Schelting's restriction of the concept, and for his criticism, seems to be his view that the axiological types serve no particular purpose in the causal analysis [12]. But on the one hand, he seems to ignore the existence, in purely axiological ideal types, of a latent description of behaviour (which is made manifest, for instance, in the construction of the ideal type of the "society of artisans"); and on the other hand, he pays no attention to the fact that the fixed goal of a causal ideal type may always be regarded as the practical correlate of a particular value [13].

In the second place, Schelting [14] maintains that only concepts of an "abstrakt-genereller Charakter" [15] can in principle lay claim to being ideal types; concepts which, although they conform to the ideal-typical principles of unreality, unambiguousness, etc., are constructed *ad hoc* in order to serve as aids to the causal analysis of *one* particular historical situation, seem to him to lie outside the sphere

8. GAW, p. 355; see also for instance the passages referred to above, GAW, pp. 329, 335, 342.
9. Hughes, *Consciousness,* 1958, p. 187.
10. See for instance GAW, pp. 115, 428; WG, p. 7.
11. Schelting, *Wissenschaftslehre,* 1934, pp. 332–33, 356–60.
12. *Ibid.,* p. 359.
13. *Ibid.,* p. 360.
14. *Ibid.,* pp. 330, 355.
15. *Ibid.,* p. 330.

of ideal types. However, he is forced to admit that Weber occasionally, "curiously", as for instance in the passage from *Knies II* discussed above [16], does not respect this restriction [17]; and he does not quote any passages from Weber's work to support his own view.

Schelting's interpretation is probably based on his fear that the individual ideal types, as defined by Weber, lie too close to the historian's intellectual constructions of "objectively possible" courses of events; such constructions, Schelting points out, are *not* ideal types, since they do not involve any proper *intensification* of the points of view selected [18]. However, Schelting's criticism on this point seems largely unfounded, since Weber's *ad hoc* individual ideal types are everywhere carefully labelled as objective types of teleological rationality. Moreover, the goals included in these types are often quite general ones (victory in a battle, maximum satisfaction of needs, etc.) or may, as mentioned above, be traced back to such general aims, so that the only unique element of the type is represented by the *conditions* under which the ideal type is meant to be applied; and such unique conditions must also be taken into account in the case of causal analysis aided by *general* ideal types.

16. GAW, p. 130. Schelting might have referred to other "curious" ideal types in Weber's work, for instance GAW, p. 534 and WG, p. 15.
17. Schelting, *Wissenschaftslehre*, 1934, p. 330.
18. *Ibid.*, p. 331.

5. The complementary relation of values and scientific inquiry: politics and science

Weber's reflections on politics have been discussed often, and from several different approaches. Authors working from a *historical* or *practical political* point of view [1] have concentrated on Weber's role as a publicist, as a politically—above all nationally—committed scholar, and accordingly on the essays and articles in GPS; from a *politico-ethical* [2] aspect, discussion has centred on Weber's view of politics as a vocation, as it emerges from *Pol. Beruf* contrasted with *Wiss. Beruf;* and *sociologists* [3] have mainly worked on Weber's systematic, empirical "Herrschaftssoziologie" and the rudiments of a "Staatssoziologie", and consequently directed their chief attention to WG. Under each of these three approaches, although the accents have been set differently, the results have been roughly the same: *conflict* and *power* are, in Weber's view, the fundamental conditions of political activity.

As far as I can see, however, most of the commentators have been content with *demonstrating* the existence of these two central features of Weber's thought and, having done so, perhaps showing the connections of these concepts with other sociological concepts, or evaluating them and their implications—usually in a negative fashion— from the point of view of the ideals of the commentators themselves. The elements of conflict and power in Weber's thought are so to speak viewed "from above", isolated from his theory of scientific inquiry. Attempts to regard them "from below" usually amount only to tracing back the elements to Weber's alleged abstract or "personal" philosophical attitude. As far as I know, no serious attempt has yet been made to study the question in the light of the hypothesis that the concepts of conflict and power, which indisputably constitute the central core of Weber's conception of the essence of politics, *may* be contained within the frame of reference defined by his various methodological reflections, and may consequently claim to have the same scientific validity as the rest of his theory of scientific inquiry. This attempt will be made in the present chapter;

1. For instance Mommsen, *Weber,* 1959; Aron, *Machtpolitik,* 1965, pp. 103–20.
2. For instance Aron, *Introduction,* 1963.
3. For instance Winckelmann, *Legitimität,* 1952; Manfred Hättich, "Der Begriff des Politischen bei Max Weber", *Politische Vierteljahresschrift,* Vol. 8 (1967), pp. 40–50.

but it is necessary to emphasize that the fundamental approach of this study has not been abandoned and that consequently the interpretations proposed do not pretend to detract from, let alone to disprove, the conclusions arrived at by scholars belonging to other schools of thought.

5.1. The premises

In the account given above (ch. 3) of Weber's thoughts concerning values as an object of scientific inquiry, one of the chief conclusions was that Weber claimed the existence of a fundamental, *theoretical value conflict*. The first explicit premise of his reflections on the essential qualities of politics is the idea of a *concrete struggle* between different political parties, camps, nations, and so on. The transition from the thought of a theoretical to that of a practical conflict may seem short and self-evident; and this is perhaps the reason why Weber himself does not comment on the relation between the two ideas. On the other hand, Weber's silence on the point has the consequence that a commentator who wishes to complete the chain of argument by inserting the missing link may find difficulty in ensuring that his interpretation is legitimate. If the attempt is nevertheless made in the present case, it is because the arguments lending an indirect support to the interpretation adopted are exceptionally good. First of all, it is implied by sporadic passages in Weber's work; and these passages are not contradicted on the relevant points by other ones. Second, the line of thought inserted stands as a natural continuation of the ideas discussed in the chapter on Weber's views on values as an object of scientific inquiry, and it serves, as will become apparent, as an equally natural and logical foundation for Weber's further reflections; it also stands in a natural relation to the ideas treated in other chapters of the present work and to what might be taken to be the fundamental characteristics of Weber's theory of scientific inquiry. Lastly, the premises inserted by means of the construction seem to me of such a kind that they could hardly be absent from any modern political theory, whether normative or empirical; it may even be asked whether a category of "politics" which did *not* accord with the interpretation could be regarded as anything but absurd.

Nevertheless, the implicit premises in question should only be taken as hypothetical, in the sense that there are not sufficient grounds for maintaining that they represent *the* correct construction of Weber's thought. For purely stylistic reasons, however, I have not retained the hypothetical *wording* of the argument: instead, I refer to the interpretation *as if* its correctness were established, and feel justified in doing so because of the probability that the construction points to something central in Weber's thought. But the stylistic transition does not pretend to advance any claim to final correctness for the interpretation itself.

5.1.1. The implicit premises

1. The fundamental conception of the essence of politics latent in Weber's works, as I see it, can be formulated as follows: Politics, in the broadest sense of the term, is characterized by *the attempt to attain one or more supra-individual goals* (i. e., goals the attainment of which does not solely depend on the person setting them). Politics, according to this characterization, is so to speak the essence of *behaviour whose intended consequences involve or are conditional on a certain behaviour of other persons than the acting person himself.*

2.1.1. The first part of the description, the element of *goal-setting,* is touched upon more than once in GPS and WG. Thus, in WG, Weber writes: "... es [das "parteimäßige" Gemeinschaftshandeln] ist stets auf ein planvoll erstrebtes Ziel, sei es ein "sachliches": die Durchsetzung eines Programms um ideeller oder materieller Zwecke willen, sei es ein "persönliches" ... gerichtet" [4]. The same element of "Ziel" and "Zweck" emerges in *Parl. u. Reg.:* "Der politische Betrieb ist *Interessenten*betrieb. (Unter "Interessenten" sind dabei ... jene politischen Interessenten [gemeint], welche politische Macht und Verantwortung zum Zweck der Realisierung bestimmter politischer Gedanken erstreben)" [5]. Similar views are expressed implicitly by Weber in other passages [6].

2.1.2. The *supra-individual* element is perhaps less explicit in Weber's work; still, it is possible to point to scattered hints, for instance in the passage from WG quoted above, which speaks of "Parteien" in the following way: "Ihr Handeln ist auf soziale "Macht" und das heißt: Einfluß auf ein Gemeinschaftshandeln ... ausgerichtet" [7], just as it may not be unjustified to maintain that the definition of politics by means of the concept of leadership, quoted from *Pol. Beruf* (n6), implies not only the setting of goals, as discussed above, but also seems to involve the idea of the leader leading one or more *other* persons towards the goal or purpose in question. Moreover, one may point to the fact that Weber's scientific interest was generally con-

4. WG, p. 688.
5. GPS, p. 389. GPS, pp. 516–17, the idea of "Interessenten" is again advanced, but this time without the element of goal-setting; this may be due to the fact that Weber is more interested (at this point) in the methods by which politicians try to obtain power.
6. GPS, p. 493, at the beginning of *Pol. Beruf,* politics in the broadest sense is defined as "jede Art von selbständig *leitender* Tätigkeit". It would seem impossible to speak of "leadership" without implying at the same time the idea that particular people are being led towards or away from some goal, so that the leader, in this sense, "sets goals" by his activity.
7. WG, p. 688.

centrated on social phenomena, although it should be added that his definition of "social" is wider than that of supra-individuality offered above [8].
2.2. It is easy to see that the element of goal-setting in the characterization
proposed above lies in direct continuation of Weber's thoughts on the problem
of value freedom and values as an object of scientific inquiry. In fact, it is
nothing more than a concrete formulation of the essentially valuational element which Weber is so careful to distinguish from the sphere of scientific
inquiry, and which, in the discussion of value freedom and, more explicitly,
of the teleological part of value analysis, he identifies with a practical role
of positive *action*. The supra-individual element in the characterization may
in the same way be linked to the discussion of the influence of social factors
on Weber's doctrine of value relation [9].
2.3. Finally, it seems fair to say that some kind of attainment of goals in
some kind of supra-individual setting is almost a necessary element of any
definition of politics. As a concrete example, we can take David Easton's
well-known definition of "political science" as "the study of the authorita-
tive allocation of values for a society" [10]. Here, both the goal-setting ("allocation") and the supra-individual ("for a society") element are present.
That the characterization hypothetically ascribed to Weber is a central element of *any* definition of politics is of course a statement which escapes
verification; but we can show it to be a reasonable one if we examine the
kind of behaviour which the characterization would *not* fit. This behaviour
would not include any attempt to attain or implement supra-individual
goals; supra-individual behaviour would lack all sense of purpose, and pur-
posive behaviour would exclusively affect the behaving person himself. Only
a meditative or chaotic-affective society seems to fulfil these conditions completely; and in such societies, the category of "politics" would be similarly
out of place.

3. It should be emphasized that the characterization does not claim to
exhaust Weber's definition of politics (and consequently has not been called
a definition). What it purports to give are the (hypothetical) *necessary* but

8. *Cf.* Weber's definition of "Soziologie" (WG, p. 3), where "soziales Handeln" is
   described as "ein solches Handeln ...., welches seinem von dem oder den
   Handelnden gemeinten Sinn nach auf das Verhalten *anderer* bezogen wird und
   daran in seinem Ablauf orientiert ist". Behaviour may very well be "social" in
   this sense without being directed to some purpose involving a particular behaviour
   on the part of other persons. This is the reason why I have preferred the cumber-
   some and unlovely term "supra-individual", when referring to Weber's implicit
   description, instead of using the more obvious term "social": the danger of misunderstanding would otherwise have been too great.
9. *Cf. supra*, pp. 127–30.
10. David Easton, *The Political System*, New York 1953, p. 129.

not necessarily *sufficient* conditions for classifying phenomena as "political" (politics in the broad sense of the term). This is obvious if one compares the characterization with the introduction to *Pol. Beruf,* where Weber defines the concept of politics more closely. But an implication which can be shown to be derived from the characterization, also holds for any narrower definition of politics based on the characterization: the qualities of the major term are always valid for the minor term. In the concrete situation, it therefore seems legitimate to relate any discussion by Weber of the special tasks, possibilities and duties of politics or politicians to the fundamental characteristics of *attainment of goals* and *supra-individual context.*

4. It may not be out of place to discuss the question of the logical status which can be claimed for the characterization proposed above. Is it a purely subjective category, or is the concept binding in some sense?

4.1. In the last instance, of course, any conceptual grouping of reality is subjective and optional. The meaning of even the most commonly used words is rooted in a *convention,* which only remains tacit because it is not questioned in practice: in relation to a large number of phenomena, nearly everybody uses a given language according to the same rules. The criterion for distinguishing conventional meanings from (more or less) subjective definitions is thus essentially an empirical one: definitions accepted by everybody without question or criticism are "objective", i. e., conventionally accepted meanings, while definitions which are discussed and subject to doubt retain the status of subjective and hypothetical delimitations. The borderline is vague and uncertain and shifts in the course of time, as particular phenomena disappear from or enter the focus of interest of conceptual criticism.

4.2.1. Weber's discussion and definition of the concept of "empirical knowledge" should be viewed in this context. His definition is, as mentioned above [11], linked to a particular quality, viz, that of being transmissible from one person to another *qua* knowledge, regardless of the valuational preferences of the person receiving it. The term "science" is thus in Weber's eyes reserved for what Arnold Brecht calls "intersubjectively transmissible knowledge" [12] and for the activity aiming at supplying such knowledge. As we have seen, Weber himself acknowledges the fundamentally undemonstrable character of such a definition of "science" and declares himself willing to surrender the *term* [13]. But the *content* of the concept does not change with the possible change of name; and however termed, the "denkende Ordnung der empirischen Wirklichkeit", the formulation of intersubjectively transmis-

11. P. 25.
12. Brecht, *Theory,* 1959, p. 114.
13. GASS, p. 482.

sible knowledge, must be supposed to retain its *interest*. In fact, Weber's definition of "science" is a conjunction of an objectively demonstrable *category* and a subjective *term*. If this term, "science", still cannot be regarded as quite arbitrary, the reason is that it corresponds to a widespread—although by no means universal—terminological convention covering the category in question. In relation to persons accepting the convention, Weber's definition can claim to represent the "essence of science", while opponents of the convention need only accept it as valid for the material category "the phenomena which Weber calls "science" ".

4.2.2. The characterization of politics proposed above should be interpreted in the same way. A material category with the objective content "behaviour with intended consequences involving a certain behaviour on the part of other persons" is said to be a necessary part of that which we refer to when we *speak of* "politics". The conclusions drawn by Weber concerning "politics" in this sense are thus derived not from the *term* but from the material *reference*. The fact that Weber's terminology can be expected, as in the case of "science", to receive broad approval does not alter the status of his results, but of course makes the discussion easier: the context of the argument is clearer when almost anyone calling himself a "politician" can be expected to accept Weber's characterization of the essence of politics as correct.

Weber's actual *definitions* of politics, like the one from *Pol. Beruf* quoted above, may in principle be regarded in the same way; but the category referred to is so much narrower that the arbitrary element in the terminology becomes more explicit.

5.1.2. The explicit premises

1. The proposed characterization of the essence of politics, in Weber's eyes, allows us to draw the negative conclusion that politics, at least in the broadest sense of the term, is *not* seen by him as being distinguished from other categories of behaviour or phenomena by the concrete *character* of the goals whose attainment or implementation is attempted. *What* is the aim of the supra-individual striving is a question to which no definite answer can be given.

2.1. This conclusion, however, leads us from the uncovering of the hypothetical and implicit foundations of Weber's thought to arguments which are directly expressed and explicitly present in his work. Already the introduction to *Pol. Beruf* suggests that the concept of "politics" cannot be given any *concrete* definition as to the goals pursued: here, Weber refuses to discuss "welche *Inhalte* ... man seinem politischen Tun geben *soll*. Denn das hat mit der allgemeinen Frage: was Politik als Beruf ist und bedeuten kann, nichts zu tun" [1]. This preliminary delimitation of the subject of the lecture is of course, as mentioned earlier, partly motivated by Weber's wish to counter the temptation to mix up "Sein" questions with "Sollen" questions, a temptation which was under the concrete circumstances particularly hard to withstand. But it also brings the question of the *means* of politics into focus and pushes that of its concrete *goals* into the background. As quoted above, Weber continues by characterizing politics in the broad sense as "jede Art selbständig *leitender* Tätigkeit" [2], a formulation which leaves the question of the goals pursued similarly open.

2.2. However, Weber immediately narrows down his characterization of politics by defining the concept as "die Leitung oder die Beeinflussung der Leitung eines *politischen* Verbandes, heute also: eines *Staates*" [3]. This definition carries certain difficulties with it: while a *positive* characterization of a major concept will always, according to the rules of logic, be valid also for the minor concepts, the same is not necessarily true of arguments *per contra*, like the one describing politics as "neutral with regard to concrete aims". Thus, it is necessary to examine separately the problem whether Weber maintains his condition of "goal neutrality" with respect to his narrower definition.

This question, however, can easily be answered in the affirmative. Apparently, Weber is anxious to emphasize quickly and strongly that the definition (in the true sense of the word) of politics which he employs (both in *Pol. Beruf* and in WG) does not contain any concrete reference to or exclusion of certain political goals. A "politischer Verband", particularly (but not, according to the wording, exclusively) a state, "läßt sich soziologisch nicht definieren aus dem Inhalt dessen, was er tut", as Weber conclusively remarks a few sentences later [4]. In WG, similar passages can be found [5]. Perhaps it is not even unjustified to see the passage in the *Antrittsrede* where Weber denies the existence of independent ideals of economic or social policy [6] as an early variant of the same idea: his purpose is of course in this early lecture to a much greater extent the defence of the freedom of the value sphere from allegations of scientific demonstrability; but the point of view adopted implies the rejection of *all* ideals claiming to be supported by disciplines working with value-free concepts, including also hypothetical "political" ideals derived from the definition of politics quoted above.

1. GPS, p. 493.
2. GPS, p. 493.
3. GPS, p. 493.
4. GPS, pp. 493–94.
5. WG, p. 658; see also the more indirect reference to the goals of political parties WG, p. 688.
6. GPS, pp. 16, 24.

5.2. *Politics as conflict*

The partly implicit (and insofar hypothetical), partly explicit premises
sketched out above: politics as the attempt to attain or implement supra-
individual, but otherwise undefined, goals, permit us to draw a number of
conclusions.

1.1. The statement that the attainment of a goal depends on the behaviour
of others means that these other persons are in principle able to *prevent* the
goal from being attained by refusing, deliberately or unconsciously, to act as
required.

In itself, this condition only constitutes an added *difficulty* in the elaboration of goals: the latter must be acceptable to the persons affected by it.
This presupposes that balances must be struck and compromises worked out
in the same way as in the case of fundamental conflict between different
value axioms held by the same person; but the condition *as such* does not
theoretically prevent an acceptable compromise from being worked out, nor
does it even exclude the possibility that hard and patient research into social
problems and into the psychology of human beings, their wants and needs,
may one day have yielded such a fund of knowledge that acceptable compromises can *always* be worked out.

1.2. This theoretical chance of political harmony is however definitely
dismissed by Weber, since his theory of the fundamental conflict of values
implies that it will always be possible to define a view in opposition to any
given and accepted social compromise. In other words, he regards it as an
objective fact that a harmonization of views will always carry with it an
antagonism in relation to one or more other ideals and values: " "Friede"
bedeutet Verschiebung der Kampfformen oder der Kampfgegner oder der
Kampfgegenstände oder endlich der Auslesechancen und nichts anderes" [1].
For the individual, this implies only the necessity of an *inner* weighing of
different values and ends against each other; and such a procedure may
theoretically result in an individual harmony [2]. This possibility disappears,
however, in a supra-individual context; the ends are no longer given: in a
political context, it is only possible to carry out the technical and teleological
weighing of ends and means against each other if one is conscious of the
fact that the basis of the operation, the group of ends and values regarded
as given points of reference, may change from one moment to the next, so
that the preliminary balance struck is upset. Science can point to no *theoretically* binding way of forcing another person to accept a political compromise

1. GAW, p. 517.
2. *Cf. supra,* pp. 195–96.

as valid. The theoretical conflict of values thus always entails a fundamental —even if perhaps only a latent—conflict between value positions and between the individuals committed to them.

2.1. This element of conflict is strongly brought out in Weber's work; as early as *Objektivität,* he writes: "Das Kennzeichen des sozial*politischen* Charakters eines Problems ist es ja geradezu, daß es *nicht* auf Grund bloß technischer Erwägungen aus feststehenden Zwecken heraus zu erledigen ist, daß um die regulativen Wertmaßstäbe selbst *gestritten* werden kann und *muß,* weil das Problem in die Region der allgemeinen *Kultur*fragen hinein-ragt" [3]. This methodological position is, as may be expected, hammered out again and again in Weber's *political* writings: "Politik ist: *Kampf",* he declares in *Parl. u. Reg.* [4]; and the status of this view as more than a sub-jective preference is emphasized by the fact that it is repeated in *Pol. Beruf:* ". . . Parteinahme, Kampf, Leidenschaft—ira et studium—sind das Element des Politikers" [5].

2.2.1. These pithy formulations should not be construed as implying that Weber regards politics as a continual actual conflict, or, at least, that he *wishes* it to take on this character. For instance, as shown by the quotation given above from *Objektivität,* he is perfectly aware that the actual potential-ities of conflict increase with the number of persons affected, i. e., as the problems grow more "general" [6]. He expresses the same view when he continues: "Und es wird gestritten nicht nur, wie wir heute so gern glau-ben, zwischen "Klasseninteressen", *sondern auch zwischen Weltanschauun-gen* ..." [7] The old dream of the ethical and utilitarian school of social policy: the uniting of all classes under the banner of nation-wide justice, is a naiveté: antagonistic views of life clash in this field; the nation as a general, harmonious value must capitulate in the face of more fundamental conflicts.

2.2.2. When speaking of the relation between ends and means, Weber in the same way emphasizes that it is justified to seek and accept *political*

3. GAW, p. 153. The term "Kulturfragen" should probably be interpreted as "soziale Fragen", i. e., questions concerning more than one person (*cf. supra,* pp. 127–28).
4. GPS, p. 317n1; see also the almost identical formulations GPS, pp. 335, 380. An early statement of the same kind, made at the 1896 congress of the "national-social" party, is quoted by Mommsen, *Weber,* 1959, p. 46.
5. GPS, p. 512.
6. In the passage quoted, Weber states that conflicts *must (will)* occur; however, this should probably only be seen as a realistic assessment of the chances of arriving at an all-embracing compromise for a "Kultur", a society.
7. GAW, p. 153. See also Weber's rejection of Schmoller's supposition that we are witness to a growing "Einmütigkeit aller Konfessionen und Menschen" (GAW, pp. 501–02).

compromises. We find this view, too, as early as in *Objektivität* [8], and find traces of it later in, for instance, *Wahlr. u. Dem.* [9] But the actual possibility, especially in smaller groups, and the understandable wish on the part of politicians to make compromises with the other side cannot disguise or remove the basic fact: that no compromise, no harmonious order, is "better" or more "objective", measured with the standards of science, than its opposite: "Der Politiker *muß* Kompromisse machen ...—der *Gelehrte darf* sie nicht decken", as Weber puts it in a letter from 1920 [10].

From the point of view of theory, this conviction is a result of the application of the principles of value freedom and value conflict to the sphere of politics. And in relation to political practice it means that conflict becomes the unalterable condition and fundamental element of politics, sometimes latent, sometimes manifest, never *completely* exorcised [11].

5.3. *Politics as power conflict*

1.1. Since it is to be expected that any striving to realize purposes in any supra-individual context may meet with opposition, and that such opposition cannot be removed by means of scientifically binding arguments, the attainment of such goals, i. e., any political act, depends on the ability to *surmount* the opposition if necessary. If the politician, as defined by Weber in the broad or narrow sense, is to carry out his policy, it is in theory always necessary for him to possess the means of *forcing other persons to bow to his will.* *1.2.* In Weber's terminology, this means that the politician must possess or control *power.* "Unter "Macht" wollen wir ... hier ganz allgemein die Chance eines Menschen oder einer Mehrzahl solcher verstehen, den eigenen Willen in einem Gemeinschaftshandeln auch gegen den Widerstand anderer daran beteiligten durchzusetzen", the definition runs in WG [1], and we find

8. GAW, p. 154.
9. GPS, p. 249, where "Kampf" and "Kompromiß" are put on the same level and both underlined.
10. Letter to Klara Mommsen, (probably) of April 12th, 1920 (DZA II, Rep. 92, No. 23).
11. Aron (*Machtpolitik*, 1965, p. 105), who stresses the element of conflict in Weber's thought regarding politics, seems to underplay the idea of the logical connection between the conception of a theoretical conflict of values and the view of politics as conflict (*cf. ibid.*, p. 117: "... lassen wir den Streit der Götter, der nur indirekt mit unserem Thema, der Machtpolitik, zu tun hat ...". As I shall try to show, it is possible to draw an extremely *direct* line from Weber's conception of "Machtpolitik" to his theory of a fundamental value conflict). Mommsen, who also dwells too much on the *subjective* aspects of Weber's thought in this respect, goes further than Aron in his conclusion and does not hesitate to see Weber's emphasis on the element of conflict as a "Bejahung des Kampfes" (*Pol. Denken,* 1965, p. 608, *cf. ibid.,* p. 606), a formulation which is at any rate inaccurate.
1. WG, p. 678; a somewhat shorter, but in all essential respects similar definition is found WG, p. 692.

an echo of this definition *Wertfreiheit,* where Weber speaks of the power of the state as "Zwangsmittel gegen Widerstände" [2]. If we base ourselves on this definition, politics is consequently a struggle with other persons, which in the last instance may have to be waged by means of *power:* it is a conflict involving power as an instrument, and therefore (already in this sense) essentially a *power conflict.*

That this view is only, in its general form, made explicit in *Pol. Beruf* does not indicate that it was not held by Weber earlier on. On the contrary, we already find it, as mentioned above [3], in the *Antrittsrede,* albeit rather more indirectly. Here Weber several times connects the terms "politisch" and "Macht" in a single sentence [4]; the two concepts seem to possess some kind of affinity in his thought; and in one instance, he comes near to identifying one with the other: "*Macht*kämpfe sind in letzter Linie auch die ökonomischen Entwicklungsprozesse, die *Macht*interessen der Nation sind ... die letzten und entscheidenden Interessen, in deren Dienst ihre Wirtschaftspolitik sich zu stellen hat; die Wissenschaft von der Volkswirtschaftspolitik ist eine *politische* Wissenschaft" [5].

In *Pol. Beruf,* this conceptual identification is complete: "[Der Politiker] arbeitet mit dem Streben nach *Macht* als unvermeidlichem Mittel" [6], as it is said in Weber's introduction to the discussion of politics as an inner vocation and of the qualities which it demands; and the stress laid on power as an unavoidable and specific instrument of politics recurs frequently throughout the lecture [7].

We also find Weber emphasizing the special link between politics and power in the special discussions of his *definition* of politics with its emphasis on the political *structure,* particularly the *state.* Thus, the "politische Gemeinschaft" is in WG partly defined by its "Bereitschaft zu physischer Gewalt" [8]; and Weber's characterizations of the "politische Verband" in later works strongly bring out the same element. In *Pol. Beruf,* Weber writes: "Man kann ... den modernen Staat letztlich nur definieren aus einem spezifischen *Mittel,* das ihm, wie jedem politischen Verband, eignet: der

2. GAW, p. 540. The passage—which was probably inserted on account of the conditions during the war—is not found in the *Gutachten.*
3. P. 61.
4. For instance GPS, pp. 18, 23.
5. GPS, p. 14.
6. GPS, p. 534.
7. For instance GPS, pp. 538, 542, 546. Chr. v. Ferber, *Die Gewalt in der Politik,* Stuttgart 1970, p. 55, qualifies Weber's identification of politics with power as a "definitorische Entscheidung", a choice, which is of an essentially *arbitrary* ("willkürliche") nature. This view does not seem tenable in the light of the passages from Weber quoted above and their relation to Weber's theory of science.
8. WG, p. 657; see also WG, p. 664.

physischen Gewaltsamkeit" [9]; and in GARS, the wording is still more pointed, the essence of politics being described as "der Appell an die nackte Gewaltsamkeit der Zwangsmittel" [10].

1.3. A characteristic trait of the "politische Verband", in particular of its modern variety: the state, is its monopolization of the means of physical violence which serve as instruments of politics (in the narrower sense), at least to the extent that concentrations of the means of violence are only regarded as legitimate if they are authorized by the state [11]. In practice, this means that persons who wish to engage in politics—and who consequently need power with which to wage the political struggle—at first have to fight others *for* this power. Politics in Weber's narrow definition thus in practice often becomes a power conflict in the sense of: struggle *for* power. This is directly pointed out in formulations like the definition in *Pol. Beruf* of politics as "Streben nach Machtanteil oder nach Beeinflussung der Machtverteilung" [12], and hinted at indirectly in the various analyses of the behaviour of *political parties,* which is seen as the striving for a share in the political power [13].

This shift of the problem of power in practice from the conflict *by means of* to the conflict *concerning* power does not in itself result in any major modification of Weber's views of the special demands of politics and the specific ethic of the political sphere; but it does form the background of an important, and often somewhat neglected, aspect of the political "ethic", as elaborated by Weber [14, 15].

9. GPS, p. 494.
10. GARS, p. 547.
11. The problem of legitimacy is central to Weber's political sociology, but will not be treated here. Indirectly, though, it has a certain bearing on some of the discussions below, for instance pp. 253–54, 275, 287.
12. GPS, p. 494.
13. See for instance the formal definition, WG, p. 211 and the chronologically earlier and rather more vague passages WG, p. 688; GPS, pp. 329, 335.
14. *Cf. infra,* pp. 272–82.
15. Both Mommsen and Aron emphasize the element of power in Weber's thought, and both, quite explicitly, take a negative view of it (Mommsen, *Weber,* 1959, p. 45; Aron, *Machtpolitik,* 1965, pp. 103–04). Their point of view is one-sided, however, in that they seem to interpret Weber's concept of "Machtpolitik" as the fight *for* power, i. e., as the conflict having political power as its *aim.* This interpretation does not, in my opinion, pay sufficient justice to the professed "goal neutrality" of Weber's concept of politics, and therefore cannot be regarded as correct; on the other hand, it may serve to explain why the two authors take such a negative view of Weber's definition: a policy whose final *goal* was by definition the accumulation of power would be much more terrible than one which simply had to accept power as a *means* of implementing freely chosen political goals.

We find a more balanced view of this problem in the works of, for instance, Günter Abramowski and Manfred Hättich (Abramowski, *Geschichtsbild,* 1966, p. 155n31; Hättich, *Politische,* 1967, pp. 41–42).

2. In a number of the quotations given above [16], Weber replaces the vague and moderate term "Macht" by the more precise and radical "Gewalt". Should this be taken to mean that "power" as a political instrument is always *physical* power, some form of physical *violence?*

2.1. Some other passages may give the impression that Weber actually identifies power with physical violence. The whole discussion subsequent to the definition given WG, p. 657 is carried out with the aid of terms like "Gewalt" and "Gewaltsamkeit" [17]. In *Pol. Beruf,* we find similar signs of an identification of the two concepts [18], particularly in the introduction, where Weber with approval quotes Trotski's statement that "Jeder Staat wird auf Gewalt gegründet" [19], a quotation which he himself has apparently elaborated and sharpened to the definition: "Alle politischen Gebilde sind Gewaltgebilde" [20].

The identification of the concepts of power and physical violence may, if we take the argument of the preceding sections as our point of departure, be seen as justified inasmuch as political power, in order to fulfil the need defined by Weber's implicit characterization, must include the ability to prevail against *any* kind of opposition. Naturally, the politician has a broad spectrum of formally non-violent means at his disposal, ranging from the utilization of positions of prestige and reputation, over cunning and lies, to downright psychological pressure. But there is always the risk that the persons on whose behaviour the attainment of the goal depends will be impervious to this pressure, and that they may even without provocation make use of physical means of violence in their resistance. In this case, only physical violence can break down the opposition [21], and just as the attainment of a goal in a superindividual context may always *in the last resort* come to depend on the use of power, the need for the use of such power may always *in the last resort* become a need for the exercise of physical violence.

2.2. Under this construction, power and physical violence are not *identical;* but the acceptance of political power implies the acceptance of the risk of having to use violence. Richelieu expressed this in epigrammatic form when he had the words "Ultima ratio regum" engraved upon the French cannon. And Weber does at one point emphasize that this is what he has in mind when defining the state as a "Gewaltgebilde". In continuation of such a definition, he writes in *Pol. Beruf:* "Gewaltsamkeit ist natürlich nicht etwa das normale oder

16. WG, p. 657, and particularly GARS, p. 547.
17. WG, pp. 657–60.
18. GPS, pp. 544, 546.
19. GPS, p. 494.
20. WG, p. 664.
21. Weber himself sketches out a similar spectrum of instruments of power and means of violence in connection with his treatment of the struggle of the political parties *for* power (*cf.* WG, p. 689).

einzige Mittel des Staates: – davon ist keine Rede –, wohl aber: das ihm spezifische" [22]. Physical violence is the backbone of political power, but not necessarily its visage [23].

3. In Weber's work, one notes a certain—more or less implicit—tendency to stress the violent element in the concept of power when the subject under discussion belongs to the field of *foreign* policy, whereas Weber's treatment of *domestic* political matters quickly concentrates on the various principles of legitimacy, their relation to one another, their development, etc. An explicit distinction between the external and the internal aspects of politics is found in GARS, where "der Selbstzweck der Erhaltung (oder Umgestaltung) der inneren und äußeren Gewaltverteilung" is stated as being a dominant principle of all politics, but more particularly of *foreign policy* [24]. This special emphasis on the reliance of foreign policy on physical violence seems to me closely bound up with Weber's thoughts on power conflict and on legitimacy.

3.1. According to Weber's definition, the legitimate use of physical violence is in a state limited to the organs of the state itself. This means, as noted earlier, that persons wishing to go in for politics in this state must in the great majority of cases start by attempting to get possession of the legitimate

22. GPS, p. 494. See also GPS, p. 538: " ... Macht, hinter der *Gewaltsamkeit* steht". It is of particular interest to note the importance accorded by Weber to the spoken and written *word,* and to the knowledge and insight which it represents, as an instrument of political power (See for instance GPS, p. 342). This has a certain bearing on the discussion below, p. 275.
23. Mommsen (*Weber,* 1959, p. 45), Aron (*Machtpolitik,* 1965, p. 114) and others (for instance Ferber, *Gewalt,* 1970, p. 56) on this point tend towards a more radical interpretation of Weber's concept of power, identifying it with "force of arms", "violence" or similar concepts. Against this interpretation, one may point to the passages in Weber's work on which the more moderate conclusions of the present account are based; (Mommsen's treatment of Weber's text is, in one instance at least, less than impeccable: he backs up an assertion by a quotation from *Wertfreiheit* (GAW, p. 517), but only retains the passages having a martial ring, while carefully leaving out Weber's more concrete, but much less warlike, formulations, which in fact point precisely to the theoretical and fundamental perspectives in Weber's reflections on conflict and power). As further evidence against the "radical" line of interpretation, one may point to the theoretical first part of WG, where Weber elaborates his concept of "Kampf" (WG, pp. 27–29). Although his definition quickly leads him to acknowledge *power,* as defined above, as the instrument of conflict, Weber includes under the concept of "Kampf" a long list of "peaceful" social competitive relationships, right down to erotic and artistic rivalry.
The tendency in Mommsen and Aron to concentrate on the element of physical violence and subsequently using it as *pars pro toto* in their argument may be regarded as a result of their interpretation of Weber, in which power is seen as the *end* of politics. "Power", as an *instrument,* may be defined abstractly as the *chance* of carrying out some purpose, while power as a *goal* is easily reified.
24. GARS, p. 547.

means of physical violence; their political activity *by means of* physical power is dependent on a preliminary struggle with others *for* power. In this preliminary power conflict, the participants *may* resort to physical violence [25]; but since this would constitute an act of provocation in relation to the state (which precisely possesses and tries to uphold a monopoly of legitimate use of physical force), the struggle will usually be of a non-violent kind. The state may even intervene in order to provide the power conflict with a fixed framework (electoral laws, etc.). The element of violence thus recedes into the background in this phase. When a group comes into possession of legitimate power, by whatever means, it may of course exercise it in its physical and violent form within the state. The legitimate character of the power may however make it possible to avoid the actual exercise of violence, since legitimacy is defined by Weber in such a way that legitimate power (order, etc.) "als irgendwie *für* das Handeln geltend: verbindlich oder vorbildlich, angesehen ... [wird]" [26]. The legitimacy of the political power will often express itself in a tendency on the part of the persons affected to anticipate and adjust themselves to the goals which the power is meant to back up if necessary. The element of violence, and in many cases also of power, is replaced by relations of legitimacy.

3.2. When it comes to relations *between* states, to international politics, conditions are quite different. Above all, each actor, or state, by definition possesses in advance a greater or smaller amount of control over means of physical violence. The latter may of course be quite modest compared to those of other states (frontier guards, police, small armed forces); but a number of states, by reason of their size and/or historical tradition, have very considerable amounts of physical force at their disposal; they are, in Weber's terminology, "Machtstaaten" [27].

The states, particularly of course the "power states", as actors in international politics, consequently have the specific instrument of political activity at their disposal; in principle, therefore, they are able to conduct a foreign policy (in Weber's sense of the word). On the other hand, the possession of this ability does not compel them to make use of it; a state may remain "unpolitical" in the field of foreign policy, concentrate exclusively on the attainment of domestic goals or at least in its foreign relations only back up its initiatives by non-violent means [28]. This introversion, however, has as its condition that no *other* state wishes to expand at the expense of the "passive" state, or at least does not see its way to realizing such ambi-

25. *Cf.* WG, p. 689.
26. WG, p. 22.
27. GAW, pp. 139–41.
28. As examples of such "introverted" states which "auf Politik in der Welt *verzichten*" (GPS, p. 277), Weber mentions Switzerland, with its neutralist ideology (GPS, pp. 140–41, 277), Denmark, Holland and Norway (GPS, p. 277).

tions. The first possibility: the lack of even the threat to a given state, *may* exist [29]; but often the factor permitting the state to turn inwards, remain passive in the field of foreign affairs, will be some sort of balance of power among the surrounding *power* states [30]. On the other hand, such a balance of power implies a *willingness* on the part of the states participating in it to take positive political action, if required, in international politics, in the sense discussed, i. e., to make use of their means of violence to the full; and to this willingness must, as Weber points out, be added the fact that a power state, in its capacity of power state, represents an obstacle and a danger in the eyes of other power states, and may consequently, simply because of its *potential* ability to play a role in foreign affairs, be drawn into the manoeuvres of international politics as a possible object of the exercise of power [31].

3.3. Thus, Weber sees strong inherent forces in the international political system (to use a modern term) pushing power states into the field of active foreign policy. Furthermore, in international conflicts, one power state participating can claim no greater legitimacy than another: on the contrary, *each* power state will claim a legitimacy based on national or national-cultural values [32]; as mentioned above [33], the values of different national cultures are, in Weber's eyes, axiologically incommensurable [34]. If we add to these reflections the fact that *each* power state taking part in a conflict will often have enormous physical means of violence at its disposal, whereas the state in its domestic relations with the person or persons who are to be influenced possesses a decisive *margin of strength,* it is not difficult to see why Weber found it necessary to stress the violent aspect of foreign, rather than of domestic, policy.

Concerning the relation of the concepts of power and "Herrschaft", see Appendix A.

5.4. The ethic of conviction and the ethic of responsibility

5.4.1. The ethic of conviction

1. Although the characterization of politics as a power conflict is linked to certain implicit premises, it is as such explicit in Weber's work. Since Weber's

29. Weber here points to Norway and, partly, Switzerland (WG, p. 664).
30. This, according to Weber, is the case of Switzerland (GPS, p. 140; WG, p. 664).
31. GPS, p. 140.
32. WG, pp. 674–75. The paragraph in question is a striking example of Weber's capacity for value-free analysis; he carries through a discussion of one of the highest and most passionately defended of his own ideals, the belief in the nation as a supreme value, without flinching from any of the consequences.
33. Pp. 181–82.
34. GAW, p. 604.

further reflections on politics as a vocation are to a large extent based exclusively on this characterization, and independent of the connection between the latter and the rest of his methodology, it follows that the question of the validity of the account given in the following does not depend on the acceptance of the hypothetical and implicit premises, although reference will be made to the latter at certain points of the discussion.

2. The characterization of politics as a conflict, as made above, implies that political goals can never, in principle, be regarded as fixed once and for all—let alone as demonstrated by scientific means—but that on the contrary the conflict between different goals is a distinctive feature of politics. In the last instance, this means that the fundamental problem may arise whether human activity should be guided by the wish to attain "outer" goals at all, i. e., whether the interest in the *teleological* component of values is at all legitimate, or whether behaviour should be motivated only by *axiological* considerations. In short, the fundamental conflict inherent in the concept of politics also includes the dichotomy between the ethic of conviction and the ethic of consequences.

2.1. This dichotomy acquires a special poignancy with respect to political questions. The ethic of conviction manifests itself, among other things, in that means to a given end are judged according to their intrinsic value and are rejected regardless of their teleological, means, status if this intrinsic value turns out to be a negative one. Now, politics is characterized by its distinctive instrument, power, which has an extremely negative value in the ethical system within which Weber usually operates. This ethically negative character is above all due to the fact that *physical violence* is the extreme manifestation of power. Weber is quite conscious of this and brings it out clearly: "Das spezifische Mittel der *legitimen Gewaltsamkeit* rein als solches in der Hand menschlicher Verbände ist es, was die Besonderheit aller ethischen Probleme der Politik bedingt"[1]. But it should not be overlooked that other forms of power, as for instance *lies,* may also carry a strongly negative ethical load[2]. So much at least is certain that the function of power as an instrument of politics is at the root of a fundamental axiological conflict between the political and the ethical sphere.

2.2. Moreover, in Weber's view the element of power is responsible for the carrying over of the fundamental tension between politics and ethics onto the plane of empirical reality: the extreme manifestation of power, war, creates among the participants on either side a feeling of inner solidarity,

1. GPS, p. 544. See also GPS, pp. 538, 540–41, 545.
2. *Cf. per contra* Weber's discussion of the demand for unconditional truth made by *absolute* ethics (GPS, p. 539).

of essential brotherhood, which is the only sentiment strong enough to rival effectively the ethical and religious feelings of brotherhood and solidarity [3].

Accordingly, Weber mainly discusses and elaborates the dichotomy: ethics of conviction—ethics of effect in the light of his knowledge of the ethically negative value of the political sphere. When confronted with the political sphere, marked inescapably by its specific element of power, one may, according to Weber, choose either of two fundamental attitudes: that of the *ethic of conviction* or that of the *ethic of responsibility* [4].

3. A person who accepts the ethic of conviction will reject any other criterion for judging his actions than that based on their intrinsic axiological (in this case: ethical) value [5]. If forced to choose between ethically "clean hands" and the attainment of political goals—a choice which he cannot hope to escape permanently if he engages in any kind of politics—he will always sacrifice the goal in order to preserve the ethically correct character of his conduct.

It may be useful to give a brief account of Weber's treatment of variants of action motivated by an ethic of conviction and their relevance to political problems in particular. These variants may be termed the *religious-acosmistic,* the *pacifist-political,* and the *radical-revolutionary* attitude respectively.

3.1. If a person committed to an ethic of conviction finds himself in a political situation where power, particularly physical violence, is being employed *against* him, he will, according to Weber, solve the problem of the ethically correct behaviour along the lines of the simple formula: "Widerstehe nicht dem Uebel mit Gewalt" [6]. By completely abstaining from the use of force, and by respecting instead in practice the injunction of the Sermon on the Mount to "turn the other cheek", the person committed to an ethic of conviction wholly escapes what Weber calls "das unentrinnbare Gewaltsamkeitspragma" [7]: he avoids the, theoretically, infinite quantitative escalation of physical compulsion by taking refuge on a qualitatively different level of reaction: the violence necessitated by politics is intercepted by a passivity legitimated by ethics.

3. GARS, pp. 548–49. It should be emphasized, however, that this empirical circumstance is of no consequence with regard to the question of the *logical* incompatibility of politics and ethics.
4. These attitudes are only given their definitive names in *Pol. Beruf* (1919). Materially, however, we find them defined, in their essentials, as early as 1912 (1908 in the case of the ethics of conviction), and they are referred to in printed works already in 1916 (Weber's sociology of religion).
5. GAW, p. 505; GPS, p. 539.
6. GARS, p. 547; similarly GARS, p. 549; GPS, p. 538; GAW, p. 604.
7. GARS, p. 549; *cf. infra,* pp. 265–66.

If this attempt to break down barriers between human beings is carried to its last conclusion, it involves more than simply the rejection of a particular *means:* power, and culminates in a complete *religious acosmicity,* the absolute rejection of the "world" and of all worldly things.

This attitude, which corresponds to a complete fulfilment of the demands of the Sermon on the Mount [8], stands in an absolute contrast to the essence of worldly activity, political action. All teleological considerations are rejected en bloc: "[Die Evangelien] stehen im Gegensatz nicht etwa gerade nur zum Krieg—den sie gar nicht besonders erwähnen—, sondern letztlich zu allen und jeden Gesetzlichkeiten der sozialen Welt, wenn diese *eine Welt der diesseitigen "Kultur",* also der Schönheit, Würde, Ehre und Größe der "Kreatur" sein will" [9]. The kingdom of the religious-acosmistic ethic of conviction "is not of this world".

3.2. In my opinion, however, one sometimes finds in Weber a tendency, albeit an implicit one, to limit the discussion to the question of the rejection or acceptance of certain means *in a context which otherwise remains wordly* [10]. The position defined in these cases, if still marked by the rejection of force as a political instrument, does not extend the rejection to the whole sphere of political activity in general, as long as the political ends are striven for only by non-violent means. Thus, the attitude can be seen as a commitment to a *policy of pacifism.* Such a policy is not opposed to all dealings with the "world", nor does it put a negative value on teleological considerations as such [11]; rather, it operates on the assumption that the axiological and teleological systems are *identical,* that "aus Gutem ... nur Gutes, aus Bösem nur Böses folgen [kann]", a view for which Weber criticizes his pacifist colleague F. W. Foerster [12].

3.3. The *radical-revolutionary* protagonists of an ethic of conviction, as described by Weber, exhibit a similar tendency to ignore the teolological system or to identify it with the axiological one. Here, the situation is a little more complicated, though, and in certain respects differs from that of the two other variants.

3.3.1. Unlike the religious-acosmistic variant of the ethic of conviction, but like the pacifist-political one, the radical-revolutionary tendency accepts the

8. GPS, pp. 538–39.
9. GPS, p. 142.
10. For instance, one may compare the passage GPS, p. 539 ("Wer nach der Ethik des Evangeliums handeln will, der enthalte sich der Streiks—denn sie sind: Zwang—und gehe in die gelben Gewerkschaften") with GPS, pp. 141–42, where Weber maintains that the Gospels condemn *any* participation in or connection with economic activity.
11. *Cf.* Loos, *Wertlehre,* 1970, p. 54, who arrives at substantially the same conclusion.
12. GPS, pp. 541–42. Such a reflection on the *consequences* of a certain kind of behaviour is already in itself a violation of the demands of religious acosmicity.

"world" and regards activity directed towards worldly ends as legitimate. The attitude is described in *Wertfreiheit* as "radikal revolutionäre politische Haltung", and illustrated by the example of consistent syndicalism [13]; in other discussions, too, Weber constantly brings in examples relevant to politics [14]. Unlike *both* the other variants, it must furthermore be supposed that radical revolutionaries do not condemn the use of physical violence on the grounds of its ethically negative value, but rather have a predilection for employing it themselves [15]. Here, unlike the case of the other variants, the problem of power is not negative but *positive:* what Weber sees as the problem is not the rejection, but the *use* of force according to this conception of the ethics of conviction.

In *Wertfreiheit,* the chain of reasoning, with the modifications set out above, is more or less parallel to the one concerning the religious-acosmistic variant; the syndicalist's goal is exclusively *internal,* viz, to demonstrate and prove again and again by his actions the sincerity of his convictions. The teleological system is ignored in the sense that the syndicalist completely abstracts from the *external* practical effects of his action [16].

3.3.2. In *Pol. Beruf*, Weber, probably under the influence of the current political chaos [17], discusses a different kind of radical revolutionary attitude, that involving an *external* goal. The radical revolutionaries in question strive to attain this goal, however, on the basis of "teleological" premises of the same crypto-axiological kind as those demonstrated in the case of the pacifists described above. Where Professor Foerster believed that evil means can only lead to evil results, the radical revolutionaries described in *Pol. Beruf,* the prophets of the milennium—often pacifists who have been unable to stand up to the test of patience which a consistent pacifist policy imposed upon them—act on the supposition that evil means employed in a good cause will, by virtue of the character of the latter, be cleansed of their bad side effects [18]. In the view of these people, a war waged in the cause of peace has the quality

---

13. GAW, pp. 505, 514–15. The same example is found in Weber's letters to Robert Michels of Aug. 4th, 1908 and May 12th, 1909 (copies in DZA II, Rep. 92, no. 30, Vol. 7) and to E. J. Lesser of Aug. 18th, 1913 (copy in DZA II, Rep. 92, No. 30, Vol. 11).

14. GPS, pp. 538, 540–41; GARS, p. 549.

15. This is most clearly brought out in the passages from GPS and GARS referred to.

16. Weber's treatment of this example introduces a further complication, in that the syndicalist is provided with an *internal* goal. As mentioned above (p. 167n13), however, the internal character of such a goal probably prevents it from being subjected to teleological analysis; and in light of this, it seems justified to assimilate this example to those of purely axiological orientation.

17. The lecture *Pol. Beruf* was given in Munich in the winter of 1918–19, at a time when Bavaria was in the midst of revolution. It may be added, though, that Weber had considered, as early as 1916 (in *Zw. betr.*), the similar case of religious movements which want to remedy the evils of this world by its own evil means.

18. GPS, p. 541.

of being final, "the war to end all wars". The consistent pacifist politician assumes that the intrinsic axiological value of the means communicates itself to the effects and consequently to the end; the consistent radical revolutionary, on the other hand, believes that the intrinsic axiological value of the end will also colour the means conducive to it and their side effects. In both cases, the teleological system is merged with the axiological one.

3.4. Common to these three tendencies, however, is their sceptical view of teleological considerations. Either they regard them as quite illegitimate, and reject them absolutely; or they replace the real teleological value analysis, the computation of the chance of reaching a given goal, by some kind of axiological consideration, not so much in the belief that causation does not function in the world, but rather on the basis of the view that they have no right, or at least no duty, to justify their actions by their consequences. The logical complement to this view is the denial by such persons of any responsibility for the *consequences* which might result from their actions. According to the ethic of conviction, responsibility is purely axiological [19].

5.4.2. The ethic of responsibility

In opposition to the ethic of conviction, it is possible, particularly in relation to problems of politics, to define an attitude corresponding to the "ethic of consequences" [1]. Weber normally [2] uses the name "verantwortungsethisch" for this attitude, which will consequently be termed the *ethic of responsibility*.

1. From a formal point of view, Weber's terminology here is—as is the case with so many other of Weber's important terms—an unfortunate one, since it does not adequately indicate where the difference from the ethic of conviction lies. A person committed to the latter also feels responsible in a certain sense, viz, to an "inner" goal or an "inner" axiological principle. Weber clearly sees this: "Nicht daß Gesinnungsethik mit Verantwortungslosigkeit ... identisch wäre", as he writes in *Pol. Beruf* [3]. But what matters to him is the fact that the individual accepting the ethic of responsibility

19. Loos, *Wertlehre*, 1970, p. 56n177, is probably right in claiming that Weber does not establish a satisfactory logical connection (GPS, p. 542) between the ethic of conviction and a positive solution of the problem of the theodicy.
1. Pp. 183–84.
2. For instance GPS, pp. 539–40. That the term itself is formulated very late (later than the term "ethic of conviction" which can be found as early as the *Gutachten*, p. 105) is obvious from GAW, p. 505 and GARS, p. 552, where "Verantwortung" is used, but not in conjunction with "Ethik". There can be no doubt, though, that the concept, however termed, is the same in *Wertfreiheit*, GARS and GPS.
3. GPS, p. 539; see also GPS, p. 540.

acknowledges a responsibility for the *consequences* of his actions; this every-where forms the core of his definition of the ethic of responsibility [4].

1.1. It is possible to interpret this ethic of responsibility as purely "passive", i. e., as giving no indication as to the *behaviour* which can be expected from persons committed to this attitude. In this case, the scope of the ethic is limited to the acceptance in theory of the right of others to judge one's actions according to their "external", "worldly" consequences; the teleolog-ical system is acknowledged, in principle, to be relevant to the act of judgment.

In this "passive" sense, the model of the ethic of responsibility is not in practice opposed to all the variants of the ethic of conviction discussed above. It is theoretically possible that a person accepting a "passive" ethic of responsibility does not act at all, but agrees to having his passivity judged on the basis of its consequences. From a teleological point of view, he would seem to have an attitude parallel to the religious-acosmistic ethic of convic-tion, or to the revolutionary one insofar as it is only, as is the case in *Wert-freiheit,* guided by an *inner* goal [5].

1.2. Certain of Weber's formulations seem, on the face of it, to be limited to this "passive" aspect [6]. The acknowledgement of a *passive* "external" responsibility of the kind referred to, however, quickly seems to lead to the acceptance of an *active* "external" responsibility, i. e., a responsibility for the state of the "world" (to the extent that it is possible to influence it). This active aspect is quite regularly included in Weber's formulations, some-times even in explicit conjunction with the passive one: "Nicht die Dänen, Schweizer, Holländer, Norweger werden künftige Geschlechter ... verant-wortlich machen ... *Sondern uns* ... deshalb eben liegt auf uns, und nicht auf jenen, die verdammte Pflicht und Schuldigkeit vor der Geschichte ... [7] The responsibility to *history* and to the future generations for the world which one leaves behind, is continually stressed [8].

The active ethic of responsibility thus implies a demand for action, guided by knowledge of external consequences. In the political field, this, as we have seen, involves a willingness to include force, possibly even physical violence, among the means to be employed if necessary (for instance, when force is used against oneself). In this case, therefore, the maxim applied is quite the opposite one to that of the religious ethic of conviction: "Du *sollst* dem Recht auch mit *Gewalt* zum Siege verhelfen,—bei eigener Verantwor-

---

4. GPS, pp. 539–40; GAW, p. 505; GARS, p. 552.
5. This partial identity between the passive ethic of responsibility and aspects of the ethic of conviction acquires importance below, p. 284.
6. For instance GPS, p. 540: "... daß man für die (voraussehbaren) *Folgen* seines Handelns aufzukommen hat".
7. GPS, p. 140.
8. GPS, pp. 139, 142, 537.

tung für das Unrecht" [9]. The teleological system is acknowledged to be relevant not only for judging one's actions, but also for the planning of these actions: the ethic of responsibility carries with it the duty of striving for the goals which one has set oneself, making use of all means adequate to the given end, and moreover *taking into account the actual consequences of the means and the relation of these consequences to the end.* What is repudiated here is not only the principle of acosmicity, but also the identification of the teleological with the axiological system performed by the pacifist and the crusading revolutionary. The active ethic of responsibility and the ethic of conviction are absolute contrasts [10].

2. Since the active ethic of responsibility involves a duty to attain external goals, while taking into account the actual consequences of the means, i. e., to perform teleological calculations before acting, this in turn implies that a politician committed to the ethic of responsibility needs *knowledge.* This is emphasized by Weber in the terse, repeated phrase: "Politik wird mit dem Kopfe gemacht ..." [11]. Consequently, it may be useful to examine the points on which such a politician must, according to Weber, be quite clear, the *knowledge* which he must possess in order to act.

2.1. Unlike persons committed to the ethic of conviction, those accepting the ethic of responsibility need to know facts as they are, since they may have an influence on their decisions. To quote Weber's own simple and at the same time curiously weighty phrase, they need to know "was *ist*" [12].

In the most elementary sense, this of course means that the ethic of

9. GARS, p. 547; similarly, GAW, p. 604.
10. This is probably the reason for an interesting correction, first noted by Baumgarten (*Weber,* 1964, p. 614n1), in the manuscript notes of *Pol. Beruf.* Here, Weber originally contrasts "Gesinnungs-" with "Machtpolitik" (Baumgarten's reading "Politik der *Macht*" (see the list of errata in his book) is wrong: the manuscript (reproduced on fig. 16 of Baumgarten's work; now in the archives of the Max-Weber-Institute, Munich) clearly in the first version reads "Gesinnungs–Machtpolitik"), but changes the latter to "Verantwortungspolitik". Baumgarten sees this as an indication of Weber's fear of the *abuse* of power. It seems more reasonable, however, to view the correction as motivated by the fact that the term "Machtpolitik", while indicating a definite contrast to the pacifist-political and religious ethic of conviction, does not explicitly exclude the ethic of conviction of the radical revolutionary who wishes to confirm the true faith in himself, or to propagate it to others, with fire and sword. The term "Verantwortungspolitik" more clearly conveys the double emphasis: on the responsibility for the state of the "world", i. e., the fundamental agreement to act "politically"; and on the responsibility for the means (including force) which the acceptance of the first responsibility forces one to employ.
11. GPS, p. 534; *cf.* GPS, p. 546.
12. See for instance GASS, p. 482 ("das *sind* die Tatsachen ...") and the letters to Naumann (Oct. 12th, 1908, GPS [1], p. 455) and to Frau Gnauck-Kühne (July 15th, 1909; DZA II, Rep. 92, No. 28): "Mein entscheidendes inneres Bedürfnis ist "intellektuelle Aufrichtigkeit": ich sage, "was ist" ".

responsibility imposes a duty to know the circumstances surrounding the intended action, and to assess their actual weight correctly, unmoved by hopes or fears. This not only refers to isolated facts, but involves a complete, and correct, teleological value analysis, absolutely certain knowledge concerning the appropriate means to reach a given end and the side effects of these means.

2.2. What gives this kind of knowledge its special significance is the fact that it does not only include empirical facts and the chain of causation relevant to a particular goal, but also an acknowledgement of the relationship between such facts, i. e., the empirico-teleological system, and the axiological one. In short, the teleological value analysis must be integrated into a complete value analysis. The value premise of the latter is precisely, as demonstrated above [13], the value of *responsibility*. And the combined value analysis implies a recognition of the tension between the empirical sphere and a given value sphere, what we called [14] the *value irrationality* of the world. While the ethic of conviction refuses to acknowledge the teleological system or assimilates it to the axiological structure, the ethic of responsibility accepts empirical knowledge as true, and accordingly as relevant to political action. "Der Gesinnungsethiker erträgt die ethische Irrationalität der Welt nicht" [15], and consequently suppresses it, whereas it is accepted for what it is, as a fact, by those who have committed themselves to the ethic of responsibility.

In itself, the recognition of the value irrationality of the world only implies a theoretical willingness to acknowledge the possibility of tensions arising between the attainment of political goals, i. e., the political sphere, and other value spheres, particularly that of ethics. Concretely, it may carry with it a number of different consequences.

2.2.1. Thus, under the ethic of responsibility, one must refrain from *identifying* an actual, e. g. a political, advance or defeat with an ethical one. In this connection, Weber, inspired no doubt by the situation in Germany immediately after the war, mentions the tendency of the victorious side to ascribe its victory to the justice of its cause, and the parallel trend among the defeated to search for ethical culprits in the hour of defeat [16]. This view of Weber's, however, is not simply a reflection of current events, but is found in the same form already in GARS: "... der *Erfolg* der Gewalt oder Gewaltandrohung ... hängt natürlich letztlich von Machtverhältnissen und *nicht* vom ethischen "Recht" ab ..." [17]

13. P. 171.
14. *Ibid.*
15. GPS, p. 541.
16. GPS, pp. 536–37.
17. GARS, p. 547. See also Weber's letter (of Oct. 17th, 1918) to Naumann (GPS [1],

2.2.2. On the other hand, this means that persons acting according to the ethic of responsibility should recognize that the teleological and the axiological analysis of ends and means may conflict. Thus, Weber mentions that ethically *good* means may have ethically bad consequences: pacifism may, he points out, allow the side using physical force to get the upper hand [18]. The main part of his discussion in this connection, though, is, naturally enough, devoted to the complementary fact that the use of ethically *negative* means may have ethically *positive* results.

In *Pol. Beruf,* the emphasis is on the *negative* component, the ethical "costs" of implementing a goal by all necessary means: here, the contrast is most pronounced with respect to the radical revolutionaries who believe that the end justifies the means. For instance, Weber mentions that revolutionaries committed to the ethic of conviction, "Glaubenskämpfer", need an "apparatus", an *organization* at their disposal, and that such an organization must be kept loyal by means of concessions which may conflict with the fundamental ideals propagated: to a large extent, the behaviour of the leader, which is theoretically oriented after ethically positive goals, is in fact guided by the—often ethically reprehensible—wishes of his followers [19]. More concretely and directly, Weber criticizes the revolutionary socialists for having preferred continuing the war, and the resulting possibility of Germany being made ripe for revolution, to making peace, even though the latter course of action might have led to the conservation of the existing political system [20]. Here again, according to Weber, the factual *knowledge* concerning the consequences of continuing the war, and the ethically negative character of these consequences, have been pushed aside.

Weber's reflections on the good effects of evil means sometimes appear with a different emphasis, viz, on the positive *goal*. In this connection, one may for instance quote an interesting letter of May 8th, 1917 from Weber to Naumann, in which Weber quite deliberately, so to speak in a "Machiavellian" way, points out the lesson of history: that it may be wiser to lie than to tell the truth. Formally, of course, the letter only has scant value as a source, compared to the printed essays; but it contains reflections of a sufficiently general interest to warrant the passage in question being quoted *in extenso:*

"Lord Salisbury sagte seinerzeit im Burenkrieg: "Wir wollen *keine* Diamantfelder und Goldgruben". Die Erklärung wirkte sehr vorteilhaft. Als dann die militärisch-

p. 479), where Weber, while calling for the abdication of the Kaiser, carefully distinguishes between the *political* blame and the—hypothetical—*ethical* guilt attaching to Wilhelm II.

18. *Cf.* GAW, p. 604: "Widerstehe dem Uebel—sonst bist du für seine Uebergewalt mitverantwortlich".

19. GPS, pp. 544–45.

20. GPS, pp. 540–41.

diplomatische Lage endgültig so war, daß er sie *hatte* und gefahrlos behalten *konnte, behielt* er sie. Wir machen es bisher genau umgekehrt. Das halten wir für "ehrlich". Aber es mußte doch auch den Militärs und den verständigen Führern des Zentrums und der Rechten klar zu machen sein, daß Lord Salisburys Verfahren das *klügere* von den beiden ist" [21].

What is important here is not Weber's positive political *suggestion*—which belongs to his political activity—but his demonstration of a *fact* which must be taken into account by politicians acting under the ethic of responsibility. 2.2.3. A special circumstance connected with political activity, which is pointed out by Weber, is the so-called "Machtpragma" mentioned above [22]: "Gewalt und Bedrohung mit Gewalt gebiert ... nach einem unentrinnbaren Pragma alles Handelns unvermeidlich stets erneut Gewaltsamkeit" [23]. This view, which is stressed both in *Zwei Ges.* and in *Pol. Beruf* [24], apparently in Weber's opinion has the status of objective *knowledge* of empirical regularities [25]. One may, however, ask whether it is compatible with Weber's emphasis on value irrationality as an eternal condition of political activity. Since power is the ethically negative instrument which is normally seen as being at the root of the tension between the political and the ethical sphere, the theory that "force always breeds force" is apparently identical with the thought, which Weber normally rejects, that "evil means can only lead to evil results"; this identity seems particularly prominent in cases where Weber, as in *Pol. Beruf*, employs the language of the Bible to express the "power pragma": "Wer zum Schwert greift wird durch das Schwert umkommen" [26].

Weber *himself* does not appear to have found any inconsistency between the "power pragma" and the theory of value irrationality, since he links the two concepts closely together in *Pol. Beruf*. In one instance, he even emphasizes *in the same sentence* the "diabolical" nature of power as an instrument (a view which seems to point to the actual consequences of using power, and particularly to the "power pragma") and the possibility of reaching good ends by evil means [27].

It is, however, possible logically to separate the two concepts, as defined by Weber, from each other in such a way that the apparent inconsistency is removed: the proposition denied by Weber's theory of value irrationality is that evil means can *only* have evil results [28]; the idea of "power pragma"

21. GPS [1], pp. 471–72.
22. P. 257.
23. GARS, p. 547; *cf.* GARS, p. 553.
24. GPS, pp. 142, 538, 542.
25. Cf. GARS, p. 553, where the "power pragma" is called a "dauernde Qualität alles Kreatürlichen".
26. GPS, p. 538.
27. GPS, p. 542. *Cf.* GPS, p. 545, where the two concepts are also used in close connection with each other.
28. GPS, p. 542.

in fact only completes the thesis by pointing out that evil means will always have *some* evil results.

Another question is whether Weber's theory of the "power pragma" is *correct*; but a falsification of it would not weaken his fundamental view of the value irrationality of the world.

2.3. The knowledge demanded by the ethic of responsibility of those who respect it seems, according to the account given above, to be twofold: first, it includes empirical facts, knowledge of the existence of things and of causal connections relevant to the goal which one is trying to attain; and, secondly, it involves knowledge of the axiological structure of the empirical facts, i. e., the way in which the means, their side effects and the goal itself will be judged according to different value axioms. Accordingly, both these categories seem to be limited to the *predictable* consequences of political actions. Apparently, Weber, as might be expected considering his legal training, sees responsibility as similarly limited [29]: what a person cannot reasonably predict, he cannot reasonably be held responsible for. Thus it would seem that a politician committed to the ethic of responsibility, who has carried out the necessary analysis and who has found the unpleasant (to him or to others whose values he concerns himself with in a positive way) side effects and consequences of the intended behaviour to be minimal compared to the positive value of the activity, might with a good conscience set about implementing his goal.

In a sense, this conclusion is correct; but a thesis mentioned in an earlier chapter [30]: Weber's theory of the *paradox of consequences,* affects the political act still further. According to this theory, every action stands at the beginning of an infinite chain of consequences which can never be properly foreseen; and it follows *a fortiori* that it is even more impossible to assess the positive or negative relation of these consequences to the *intended* effects. Thus, the fund of knowledge required of those respecting the ethic of responsibility necessarily includes the recognition that any action will have consequences *beyond the limits of predictability.*

In itself, this recognition remains a general condition which might be ignored precisely because it is so general and indeterminate. But the problem grows acute because it is possible *ex post* to assess, provisionally, the actual unpredictable chains of causation and their axiological value. According to Weber, such *ex-post* examinations will often show that "das schließliche Resultat politischen Handelns oft, nein: geradezu regelmäßig, in völlig unadäquatem, oft in geradezu paradoxem Verhältnis zu seinem ursprünglichen Sinn steht" [31]. The paradox of consequences means that any person com-

29. GAW, p. 505, and a similar limitation GPS, p. 540.
30. P. 173.
31. GPS, p. 535.

mitted to the ethic of responsibility must realise that his action may, without his knowledge and against his wish, set in motion chains of causation destroying the possibility of attaining the very goal which his action was calculated to achieve.

5.5. The ethic of conviction, the ethic of responsibility and the ethic of politics

1.1. As Weber sees it, the antagonism between the ethic of conviction and the ethic of responsibility is fundamentally insoluble by scientific means; only an act of personal *choice* leads to the acceptance of one rather than of the other as a standard of concrete behaviour. On the other hand, there are strong indications that Weber, in discussing the alternative between the two ethical orientations in the field of *politics,* accords a special prominence to the ethic of responsibility. It may therefore be of interest to examine to what extent, in what sense, and with what justification the ethic of responsibility is claimed by Weber to be the specific standard of political behaviour, the *ethic of politics.*

1.2. The essential, if not the only, source for the examination of this problem is *Pol. Beruf,* particularly the last fifteen pages of the lecture, where Weber turns from a discussion, in terms of political sociology, of the *external* conditions of work of politicians in older and modern times to the *internal* component of "Politik als Beruf", to politics as an *inner vocation.*

A difficulty in relation to the general aim of the present study is the fact that Weber in this lecture oscillates between the level of scientific discourse and the level of personal (political or ethical) commitment. The methodologically relevant passages in it are formulated in terms of personal commitment and subjective ethical judgment from which it is almost impossible to abstract fully. Consequently, the following sections will undoubtedly, to a larger extent than elsewhere, bear witness to the unity between Weber's work and his personality.

2. At the first glance, many passages in Weber's work seem to support the claim that the ethic of responsibility is the correct or legitimate norm of political behaviour. For instance, the concept of "Verantwortung" is often used in the first part of *Pol. Beruf* to distinguish the politician from the administrator[1]; and in his later characterization of the necessary inner qualities of the politician, Weber puts "Verantwortungsgefühl" between "Leidenschaft" and "Augenmaß", and in his subsequent treatment of the three

---

1. For instance GPS, pp. 512–13, 515. This contrast will be the subject of further discussion below, pp. 275–82.

concepts makes it clear that the sense of responsibility is in his view not only a central point of reference for the two other qualities, but represents a kind of *synthesis* of them and in that sense constitutes the true ethic of politics [2].

However, the term "Verantwortung" is as such and without further specification rather a vague one. More particularly, as mentioned earlier, Weber admits that *both* the ethic of conviction *and* the ethic of responsibility contain an element of responsibility, with the difference that the responsibility implied by the ethic of conviction is purely axiological, whereas that involved in the ethic of responsibility is also in some sense teleological and extends to the *consequences* of the action. In the following, I shall try to show how the concept of "Verantwortung" as a specific quality of the ethic of politics should be interpreted, and particularly to what extent it shares its characteristics with the ethic of conviction and the ethic of responsibility.

5.5.1. The "power responsibility": the politician's responsibility for the result of his actions

1. A first hypothetical interpretation of the "Verantwortung" of the politician would of course be one which saw this "Verantwortung" as identical with the essential element distinguishing the ethic of responsibility from the ethic of conviction. The core of the concept in terms of this interpretation is the inclusion of the *teleological* system in the process of planning political actions: the responsibility becomes the responsibility for the empirical calculation of the possibility of reaching a given goal, for the means *as means,* as *causal* elements.

1.1. A reading of *Pol. Beruf* makes it quite clear that this interpretation covers essential aspects of the problem as Weber sees it. As we saw, Weber describes "Verantwortungsgefühl" as the synthesis of the complementary qualities "Leidenschaft" and "Augenmaß" (which will be translated as "commitment" and "sense of realities"); but although the two qualities are formally equal, to a considerable extent the sense of realities in fact seems to be the dominating one: it is described as "die entscheidende psychologische Qualität des Politikers'" [3]; and a major part of the ensuing discussion is devoted to the discussion of the importance to the politician of precisely this quality: "Distanz", the ability to assimilate knowledge of the situation in which one is acting, is in Weber's view a political necessity, and "Distanzlosigkeit" accordingly "eine der Todsünden jedes Politikers" [4].

2. GPS, pp. 533–34.
3. GPS, p. 534.
4. GPS, p. 534.

1.2. In itself, the "reality" which the politician must have a "sense" of, i. e., the knowledge which he must be able to assimilate with a sufficient degree of objectivity, need not be only empirical and teleological; it may, as we have seen, include axiological relations as well. However, a number of instances in Weber's work seem to indicate that his idea of this "reality" is dominated by the teleological and causal aspects of the situation. This becomes particularly clear when Weber criticizes the politicians whose love of the influence and prestige bestowed by the semblance of power leads them to confuse apparent with real power[5]. This kind of vanity testifies to the absence of any ability coolly to estimate phenomena connected with power. Weber later directs a similar criticism of a missing sense of realities at those politicians who refuse to or are not able to calculate the effects of their political actions, i. e., actions backed up by force:

"Wenn ihm [the political goal] ... mit reiner Gesinnungsethik im Glaubenskampf nachgejagt wird, dann kann es [the goal] Schaden leiden und diskreditiert werden auf Generationen hinaus, weil die Verantwortung für die *Folgen* fehlt. Denn dann bleiben dem Handelnden jene diabolischen Mächte, die im Spiel sind, unbewußt. Sie sind unerbittlich und schaffen Konsequenzen für sein Handeln .. denen er hilflos preisgegeben ist, wenn er sie nicht sieht"[6].

Both the teleological elements described above: the *situation as such* and the *predictable consequences,* can be identified in Weber's concrete description of the "sense of realities".

2. It is important to realise *to what extent* Weber is able to maintain—more or less explicitly—that the ethic of responsibility is *the* legitimate ethic of politics. As long as the principle of value freedom is to be respected, Weber cannot *demand* that the politician should accept this and no other ethic. In fact, he nowhere formulates such a demand[7], but on the contrary writes that "Ob man ... als Gesinnungsethiker oder als Verantwortungsethiker handeln *soll* ... darüber kann man niemandem Vorschriften machen"[8]. The reason for the apparent dominance of the ethic of responsibility in Weber's thoughts on politics should in my opinion rather be sought in his (hypothetical) implicit characterization of politics and in the theoretical consequences of this characterization.

5. GPS, p. 535. See also GPS, p. 327, where Wilhelm II. is implicitly criticized for his lacking sense of the realities of power (in a letter, GPS[1], p. 456, the criticism is perfectly explicit). GASS, p. 515, Weber, from similar premises, criticizes Trotski's attempt to start a revolution in Germany.
6. GPS, p. 546.
7. Ferber, *Gewalt,* 1970, p. 53, claims that Weber elaborates his idea of the ethic of politics "unbekümmert um das Postulat der Werturteilsfreiheit". This points, at the very least, to an inadequate analysis on Ferber's part.
8. GPS, p. 546. The scope of this passage is not quite clear; it will be discussed further below, pp. 283–86.

2.1. According to Weber, science cannot legitimate choices between goals, values or standards of behaviour. But it does have the right and ability to clarify the actual causal relations connected with such values and standards. In cases where the goal implied by the value constituting a value sphere is defined by the existence of or the striving for some situation of fact, scientific inquiry can decide, with general validity, whether a certain kind of behaviour fulfils the conditions of belonging to this sphere. This procedure is a variant of the "teleological valuations" discussed in an earlier chapter [9], which can describe a situation, act, etc., as more or less "correct" *in relation to an unambiguous and given goal* (and on the condition that a wish actually exists to try to achieve this goal in a technically rational way). In this sense, science may define the "ethic" of different value spheres. Hermann Lübbe formulates this view clearly in an article on *Wiss. Beruf:* "Jede Praxis ... kennt eine Moral, die ihr zugehört. Die Moral ist, als Lehre, im Verhältnis zur Praxis jeweils der Ort, wo das Ziel dieser Praxis erörtert und die Wege, die zu ihm hinführen, vorgezeichnet werden" [10].

In the first chapter, we saw how it was possible for Weber to establish the principle of value freedom as the ethic of scientific inquiry: nobody can be forced to respect the principle in practice, or even to acknowledge in theory the value of value-free scientific inquiry and of its results. But *if* we acknowledge the value of, and consequently wish for, a certain *kind* of knowledge, *objective truth,* "denkende Ordnung der empirischen Wirklichkeit", *then* the principle of value freedom is the ethic of the sphere of objectively true knowledge.

2.2. In a similar sense, one may talk of the ethic of responsibility, as described above, as being the ethic of the *political* sphere.

In its broadest form, politics was characterized by the attempt to attain supra-individual goals, i. e., roughly, goals which involved a certain kind of behaviour on the part of others. Thus, what Lübbe calls "das Ziel dieser Praxis" is outside the person acting, and "die Wege, die zu ihm hinführen" must therefore also run outside the person and his axiological principles: the road to a political goal by definition passes through the "world" and is conditioned by its regularities. Consequently, the politician's attainment of the goal is dependent on a knowledge of the teleological structure and a wish to let his actions be guided by this knowledge. The possibility of reaching the goal he has set himself, by an act of non-scientific choice, depends on his ability to recognize and make use of the facts established through the teleological value analysis.

9. Pp. 168–69.
10. Hermann Lübbe, "Die Freiheit der Theorie", *Archiv für Rechts- und Sozialphilosophie,* Vol. 48 (1962), p. 345. Similarly Aron, *Introduction,* 1963, p. 23.

3. This demand for intellectual discipline in the service of the will may in a larger context be seen as parallel to the demand for the value freedom of scientific inquiry. If the teleological value analysis by which political action is guided is to claim objective validity, all other practical valuations than those constituting scientific inquiry as a value sphere must be excluded from the scientific process and the scientific results. We can in fact draw the paradoxical general conclusion that *the implementation of science-free values is dependent on the existence of a value-free science.* The latter may thus acquire a legitimation for its own ascetic ethic by virtue of the fact that it is a necessary basis for practical (here: political) action [11]. The duty of the politician to make use of or accept this knowledge cannot be *demonstrated* scientifically; but science may show that the possibilities of attaining the desired goal are lessened by a lack of "Distanz". In *this* sense, the ethic of responsibility may be said to be the ethic of the political sphere.

4. The emphasis laid in *Pol. Beruf* on the "technical", teleological aspects of the politician's responsibility normally appears as, and always implies, a rejection of the ethic of conviction, which either ignores the teleological value analysis or identifies it with the axiological one. Under the interpretation adopted above, a person committed to the ethic of conviction would consequently be a bad politician, or at any rate a worse one than if he acted according to the ethic of responsibility.

4.1. It is natural that this view was especially strong in Weber's mind when he wrote *Pol. Beruf.* To the painful consciousness of the dilettantism of Wilhelm II. had been added the experience of the Russian Revolution and the revolutionary agitation in Germany after the abdication of the Kaiser. The fact that Weber *gave* the lecture at all should probably be ascribed to his ingrained dislike of politicians committed to the ethic of conviction: according to the testimony of one of the organisers of the meeting in question, Weber for a long time refused to speak on the subject, and only—but then immediately—changed his mind when he was informed that the students' association was considering passing on the invitation to the leader of the provisional Bavarian National Council, Kurt Eisner, who was an idealistic but extremely unrealistic left-wing intellectual [12].

11. In his interpretation of Weber on this point, Ferber, *Gewalt,* 1970, pp. 12–13, 33, 45, 50, also stresses the dependence of politics on the existence of a sphere of scientific inquiry, but, in doing so, seems to degrade the latter to a mere handmaiden of the former, a point of view which does not do justice to the specific dignity with which Weber undoubtedly invests the sphere of scientific inquiry.
12. Immanuel Birnbaum in René König, Johannes Winckelmann (eds.), *Max Weber zum Gedächtnis,* Cologne/Opladen 1963, pp. 20–21. The ethic of conviction practised by Kurt Eisner seems to have made a strong impression on Weber: in the first part of WG (written 1918–20), Eisner's name is included in a list of "improperly"

The very fact that Weber's attack in *Pol. Beruf* seems to owe so much to the concrete historical and political situation in which it was delivered, seems to call for a certain caution and to stand as a warning against the often adopted interpretation, which without further ado, on the basis of *Pol. Beruf*, proclaims the ethic of responsibility as Weber's ethic of politics.

4.2. This caution is all the more warranted since Weber in *Pol. Beruf* in fact only to a comparatively small degree emphasizes the teleological aspect. The treatment of the importance of the "sense of realities" quickly grows rather blurred; and out of the somewhat hazy discussion rises a *second* concept of "Verantwortung" which is no longer exclusively linked with the "sense of realities".

5.5.2. The "goal responsibility": the politician's responsibility for the maintenance of the goal

The two duties of the politician: "commitment" and a "sense of realities" are in Weber's view matched by two "deadly sins" of polititics. One of these, "Distanzlosigkeit", is mentioned almost at the outset [1], and is obviously a violation of the demand for a "sense of realities". A little later, Weber mentions *both* the "deadly sins" together, and here describes them as "Unsachlichkeit" and "Verantwortungslosigkeit" respectively [2]. Since the political commitment has been explicated by Weber as *"Sachlichkeit: leidenschaftliche Hingabe an eine "Sache" "* [3], it would seem evident that "Unsachlichkeit" must be interpreted as "lack of commitment" and "Verantwortungslosigkeit"—in accordance with the ethic of responsibility discussed above—as "lack of a sense of realities". This is not the case, however. On the contrary, Weber amplifies the concepts as follows: "Seine [the politician's] Unsachlichkeit legt ihm nahe, den glänzenden Schein der Macht statt der wirklichen Macht zu erstreben, seine Verantwortungslosigkeit aber: die Macht lediglich um ihrer selbst willen, ohne inhaltlichen Zweck, zu genießen" [4]. In terms of this interpretation, "Unsachlichkeit" seems to be distinguished by a neglect of means *as means*, an absence of respect for realities; whereas "Verantwortungslosigkeit" characterizes the complementary neglect of "der inhaltliche Zweck", of that which the means were supposed to bring about or attain. While the quotations given earlier stressed the politician's responsibility for the *teleological* elements in the chain of means and ends, this is now com-

charismatic personalities (WG, p. 179); *cf.* the similar, but several years older, list, WG, pp. 832–33.
1. GPS, p. 534.
2. GPS, p. 535.
3. GPS, p. 533.
4. GPS, p. 535.

pleted by a responsibility for the end pursued, i. e., for the nexus between the axiological and the teleological system: what we might call a "goal responsibility" [5].

Whereas the "power responsibility" was specific to the ethic of responsibility, the "goal responsibility", as defined here, is *common* to the ethic of conviction and the ethic of responsibility: the attainment of the goal is defined differently in the two ethics; but both of them have in common the idea of a goal which the individual seeks to reach. Consequently, the emphasis on the "goal responsibility" does not, as in the case of the "power responsibility", serve to contrast the ethic of responsibility with the ethic of conviction, or to attack the latter; instead, it is theoretically aimed against the extreme form of "realpolitik", i. e., the political attitude which completely overrates the importance of the means and, in concentrating on them, neglects the end which they are supposed to serve.

5.5.2.1. The danger of "power politics"

Weber's interest in the "goal responsibility" is most obvious in his discussion of what he calls "absolute power politics" [6].

As mentioned above [7], the phenomenon of legitimacy means that domestic politics often turn into a fight *for* power as a prelude to political action *by means of* power; the *means* of politics in many cases becomes the *goal* of the politician.

1. Of course, Weber must accept the fundamental necessity of this change of focus; he mentions, in a neutral tone, "Machtgefühl" as the first "inner joy" which politics may afford those engaged in it [8], and "Machtinstinkt" as a quality necessary to politicians [9]. But he is also conscious of the possible consequences of the actual and theoretical predominance of the concept of power: the original goal, the attainment of which is the politician's first motive for seeking to obtain power, recedes into the background, while the acquisition and expansion of power becomes an increasingly long-term goal for the politician.

2.1. In *Pol. Beruf,* Weber describes this as an empirical tendency: "Wer

---

5. Hättich, *Politische,* 1967, pp. 47–49, makes the interesting point that the goal *neutrality* of Weber's definition of politics, by removing the goals from the sphere of the *a priori* given, invites conscious reflection on the nature of political goals, and so becomes an important precondition of goal *responsibility.*
6. GPS, p. 535.
7. P. 251.
8. GPS, p. 533.
9. GPS, p. 534.

Politik treibt, erstrebt Macht:—Macht entweder als Mittel im Dienst anderer Ziele ... oder Macht "um ihrer selbst willen": um das Prestigegefühl, das sie gibt, zu genießen" [10]; but he also condemns such a hypostatization of political means to political ends, and describes it as contrary to the ethic of the political sphere: "[es] gibt keine verderblichere Verzerrung der politischen Kraft, als das parvenümäßige Bramarbasieren mit Macht und die eitle Selbstbespiegelung in dem Gefühl der Macht, überhaupt jede Anbetung der Macht rein als solcher" [11].

2.2. Just as Weber is *able to* describe the tendency in question in a value-free way, he applies the same conscious neutrality to his description of the type of person who concentrates on the means of power and lacks all "goal responsibility". Already in *Parl. Reg.,* he mentions the American political "boss" as a paradigm of this type [12], and examines the "boss" system more closely in *Pol. Beruf* [13]. He emphasizes that the "boss" is wholly guided by considerations of power: "Der Boss hat keine festen politischen "Prinzipien", er ist vollkommen gesinnungslos ..." [14]. It seems clear—although the neutral character of the account prevents it from being expressed openly—that Weber regards this lack of political principles as disqualifying the "boss" from the title of politician by "vocation"; but it is interesting that Weber still draws attention to the *usefulness* of "bosses" as supporters of real political leaders: a system in which the "bosses" accept their limitations as politicians and do not to any significant degree pursue their own ambitions of holding public office, may be more propitious to politicians in the proper sense of the word, who have a strong sense of "goal responsibility", than for instance the classical system of "dignitaries". The complete indifference of the "boss" to political goals makes him an extraordinarily useful *instrument* of political innovation [15].

2.3. The example which is constantly in Weber's mind when he attacks and rejects the "power political" attitude, is doubtlessly that of Wilhelm II. The Kaiser's deficient sense of realities is in Weber's view accompanied by a fundamental dislike of committing himself to any long-term line of policy, and by a corresponding "Anpassung in der Auswahl aus den überhaupt möglichen letzten Stellungnahmen ... an die jeweiligen wirklichen oder scheinbaren Augenblickschancen einer von ihnen ..." [16]. Weber's dissatisfaction with Wilhelm II. was as long-lived as it was deep-rooted: a bitter remark concern-

10. GPS, p. 495.
11. GPS, p. 535.
12. GPS, p. 390.
13. GPS, pp. 527–28.
14. GPS, p. 528.
15. GPS, p. 528.
16. GAW, p. 515. The passage is a direct reference to German foreign policy since 1890.

275

ing the Kaiser in a letter from 1908 [17] is found in almost the same form, but more generally worded, in *Pol. Beruf* (1919) [18].

This identification of a concrete counterpart to the theoretical tension between political means and political ends is however only a special case. Far more general, but in principle expressing the same tension, is Weber's discussion of the relationship between bureaucracy and political leadership.

5.5.2.2. The danger of bureaucracy

1. For the individual politician, the problem remains that of striking a balance between "goal responsibility" and "power responsibility", between the loyalty towards the end and the knowledge of the means necessary to reach the desired result. Viewed quite generally, this problem may be seen as reflecting the elementary tension between the undemonstrable and the demonstrable, faith and knowledge, irrationality and rationality. In Weber's work, this antagonism is incorporated in huge contrasts. In his typology of sociological concepts, the two poles in their most extreme form are expressed as *charismatic* and *legal* authority ("Herrschaft") respectively [1]. On the level of concrete politics, we may accordingly distinguish between, on the one hand, the politician who sets his goals freely and, on the other, rational bureaucracy: the former acquires his political importance and power through his—more or less—charismatic qualities, his ability to communicate his *belief* in undemonstrable ideals to a band of supporters [2]; the political power of the latter, as Weber sees it, depends on its fund of objective *knowledge* [3].

2.1. In Weber's *systematic-historical* studies, the contrast between politicians and the bureaucracy often appears as an important phenomenon, usually as a sub-category of the conflict between the political *leader* and his staff [4].

In this connection, Weber uses the conflict between the politician and the party bureaucracy as an example [5].

17. "... der deutsche Kaiser hat Eitelkeit und begnügt sich mit dem *Schein* der Macht ..." (GPS [1], p. 456).
18. GPS, p. 535.
1. For the charismatic type, see for instance GAW, pp. 481–88; WG, pp. 179–88, 832–40. For the legal type, see for instance GAW, pp. 475–78; WG, pp. 160–64.
2. See for instance GPS, p. 496, where the "vocational" politician is assigned to the category of charismatic legitimacy.
3. "Der reinste Typus der legalen Herrschaft ist diejenige mittelst *bureaukratischen Verwaltungsstabs*" (WG, p. 162). *Cf.* WG, p. 164, where the specific advantages of bureaucracy are put down to its store of "Fachwissen"; and WG, pp. 165–66 and GPS, pp. 340–41, where Weber shows that the *political* power of bureaucracy rests on its possession of "Fachwissen" and "Dienstwissen", and particularly on the transformation of the latter into "Geheimwissen".
4. For instance WG, p. 196.
5. WG, p. 849.

2.1.1. The contrast in question is however not represented by Weber as a *stable* antagonism; on the contrary, it is a characteristic trait of these works that Weber often emphasizes the *inferiority* of the charismatic-political element when confronted with tendencies towards "Veralltäglichung", routine, bureaucratic regulations and regularity. Thus, the main section of Weber's treatment of "Herrschaftssoziologie" in WG closes with the words: "So geht mit der Rationalisierung der politischen und ökonomischen Bedarfsdeckung das Umsichgreifen der Disziplinierung als eine universelle Erscheinung unaufhaltsam vor sich und schränkt die Bedeutung des Charisma und des individuell differenzierten Handelns zunehmend ein" [6].

2.1.2. This development towards a bureaucratization of all fields of existence is apparently in Weber's eyes the inescapable condition, the *destiny* of modern civilization.

It is a fair supposition that the crystallization of this element of Weber's thought is connected with his inquiry into problems in the sociology of religion, starting with "Die protestantische Ethik und der "Geist" des Kapitalismus" which was published in 1904. In the *Vorbemerkung,* he describes the specifically *rational* traits of Western civilization; and in the course of his demonstration of the importance to modern capitalism of behaviour *motivated* by puritan religious thought, he already points to the necessity of modern economic rationality: "Der Puritaner *wollte* Berufsmensch sein,—wir *müssen* es sein [...] Nur wie "ein dünner Mantel, den man jederzeit abwerfen könnte" sollte ... die Sorge um die äußeren Güter um die Schultern ... [der] Heiligen liegen. Aber aus dem Mantel ließ das Verhängnis ein stahlhartes Gehäuse werden" [7]. This pessimistic view remained with Weber, and grew to embrace not only the field of economics but the whole spectrum of modern civilization. A few years later, at the 1909 congress of the *Verein,* Weber starts off his speech with the generally worded sentence: "... ich [bin] überzeugt von der Unaufhaltsamkeit des Fortschritts der bureaukratischen Mechanisierung" [8].

Weber does not intend this conviction to serve as a philosophy of history, but simply regards it as expressing *an apparently inescapable trend of development.* If rationalization and bureaucratization are said by him to be the "destiny" of the modern world, then only in the sense of their *empirical* predominance. But Weber's discussion of the phenomenon in WG—which is still marked by a deliberate attempt to remain on the ground of value freedom —reflects his belief that this predominance is indubitable and growing ever more certain. Here, he describes bureaucratization as a *late* phenomenon of

6. WG, p. 873. See also for instance GARS, p. 270 and WG, p. 851, where the fight between politician and party apparatus is clearly conceived as uneven.
7. PE I, p. 188.
8. GASS, p. 413.

civilization, which in its rise had important links with modern *mass* democracy [9], but which, once established, is almost impossible to destroy or to remove: "Eine einmal voll durchgeführte Bürokratie gehört zu den am schwersten zu zertrümmernden sozialen Gebilden" [10].

2.2. In Weber's *political* writings, we find similar passages, but here charged with an intense personal commitment. In *Parl. u. Reg.*, bureaucracy is again described as inescapable, an iron machine to which man is forced to *subject* himself [11]. Weber's vision of the bureaucratic system carried to its last conclusion is that of a thoroughly bureaucratized state like the Egyptian Middle Kingdom [12].

2.2.1. Weber sees any attempt to try to *stop* the development towards bureaucratization as the expression of a fatal lack of sense of realities; this development is "unaufhaltsam" and "unentrinnbar". But on the other hand, not even the recognition of this vast trend of development tempts him into proclaiming submission to it as a political duty or necessity: "... die zentrale Frage ist also nicht, wie wir das [bureaucracy] noch weiter fördern und beschleunigen, sondern was wir dieser Maschinerie *entgegenzusetzen* haben, um einen Rest des Menschentums freizuhalten von dieser ... Alleinherrschaft bureaukratischer Lebensideale" [13].

2.2.2. If the results of scholarship nourished Weber's pessimism, they also on the other hand show him the breach in the bureaucratic "Alleinherrschaft". In WG, he points out that although bureaucracy is the inevitable and highly developed, specifically modern *instrument* of politics, this does not entail that the bureaucrats must also possess and *exercise* the political power [14]. The problem which Weber in his role as politically committed individual sets himself, is consequently how to thwart the tendency of bureaucracy, of the *instrument* of political power, to usurp the political leadership. In this problem reappears the fundamental question: how can we ensure that the politician's occupation with the means of politics does not deaden his commitment to political ends?

3.1. The basic tenor of Weber's approach in his political writings to the problem of the power and the role of bureaucracy in the modern state is given concisely in a letter (of April, 1917) to Professor Ehrenberg: "Die Beamten ... sind *Techniker*. Und ihre Macht bleibt im rein parlamentarischen Staat genau so groß wie sonst, aber da, wo sie *hingehört*" [15]. Weber

---

9. WG, pp. 723, 738.
10. WG, p. 726.
11. GPS, pp. 318–20.
12. GPS, p. 320; *cf.* GASS, pp. 413–14.
13. GASS, p. 414; *cf.* GPS, p. 321.
14. WG, pp. 729–30.
15. GPS [1], p. 470.

repeatedly emphasizes in *Parl. u. Reg.* and in *Pol. Beruf* that the bureaucratic system, in spite of its indispensability in modern society, lacks the elementary political qualifications: a government official possesses a particular, and particularly useful, form of *knowledge,* and the specific dignity of his station rests on his ability and willingness to put this knowledge at the disposal of changing depositaries of political power, without distinction. But his activity does not and cannot demand of him that he should also *set* the goals which his knowledge serves to implement [16]; and consequently, he does not, in his role as member of the state bureaucracy, carry any kind of *responsibility* [17]. The "Ehre" of the bureaucratic order, its dignity, resides precisely in its *lack* of independent political commitment and independent opinions, and in the consequent lack of responsibility for such opinions: "Beharrt die vorgesetzte Stelle bei ihrer Anweisung, so ist es nicht nur seine [the bureaucrat's] Pflicht, sondern seine *Ehre,* sie so auszuführen, als ob sie seiner eigensten Überzeugung entspräche . . ." [18]

Accordingly, Weber sharply criticizes any tendency towards letting the administration work without control: the *"unkontrollierte* Beamtenherrschaft" must be avoided at any price [19]. But he adds to this criticism a positive discussion of the persons or organs which might effect the desired control.

Theoretically, Weber believes that the bureaucratic administration will accept orders from and submit to the control of any superior, whether this superior be eelected or appointed, a single person or a collective body [20]. However, he does not doubt that *"Politiker* . . . der Beamtenherrschaft das Gegengewicht geben [müssen]" [21]. "Politicians" in this context thus turn out to be those persons who agree to set political goals and to take personal responsibility, not only for the side effects resulting from the implementation of the goal but also for the choice of the goal as such.

3.2. Weber's political proposals on this point are derived wholly from the premises set out above: "Die Staatsform ist mir völlig Wurst, *wenn* nur Politiker . . . regieren", as he says in the letter quoted above [22]. In practice though, only two possibilities seem to present themselves as effective counterweights to bureaucracy: a head of state (monarch or president), or a parliament [23] (or possibly some combination of the two).

3.2.1. The traditional *monarch or empire* as a bulwark of political power in the state is viewed by Weber with profound distrust, partly because the

16. GPS, p. 342.
17. GPS, pp. 365, 512–13.
18. GPS, p. 323; *cf.* GPS, pp. 339–40, 365.
19. GPS, p. 342; *cf.* GPS,p . 430.
20. GPS, p. 323.
21. GPS, p. 340.
22. GPS [1], pp. 469–70.
23. GPS, p. 324.

monarchs in such a system are in a weak position and unfamiliar with the field of political conflict, partly because they are *irresponsible* in law [24]. His distrust is amply justified by his experience of "dilettierende Fatzkes wie Wilhelm II. und seinesgleichen" [25].

Because of this, the most reasonable solution seems to be to invest an elected *parliament* with the political power; and accordingly, this is the view propagated by Weber, in spite of certain misgivings, in his political essays and pamphlets from the years 1917–18. Emphatically, he states in *Parl. u. Reg.*: "Wer überhaupt die Zukunftsfrage der deutschen Staatsordnung anders stellt als dahin: *wie macht man das Parlament fähig zur Macht?*, der stellt sie von vornherein falsch. Denn alles andere ist Nebenwerk" [26]. In *Wahlr. u. Dem.*, we find similar passages [27].

3.2.2. Later events, however, seem to have disappointed Weber in his faith in parliament as a politically conscious, goal-setting state organ and, as such, as a counterweight to the bureaucratic administration. He had hoped that what he terms the "caesarist" element of the process of political selection, the *choice* of a leader on account of his charismatic (demagogic, etc.) qualities, would continue to be present within each of the political parties. Instead, he finds that the parties exhibit a steady tendency towards stifling any such charismatic element, and that the party organization tends to be introduced as an *intermediate link* between the electorate and the politicians: in short, the party machine does not serve as an instrument which allows the charismatic politician to subject the government bureaucracy to political control, but instead becomes an instrument of the bureaucratic or traditionalist control of the charismatic politician. Instead of "Führerdemokratie mit "Maschine" ", we have "führerlose Demokratie" [28].

3.2.3. In a later phase, therefore, Weber concentrates on getting the charismatic-caesaristic element incorporated in some other part of the government structure; and he accordingly advocates, during the elaboration of the Weimar constitution, giving more political importance to the office of the Reichspräsident, and particularly tries to ensure that it is filled by *popular election*. In the Constitutional Committee (headed by Hugo Preuß) which calls him in as an expert, he uses all his influence to this end [29], and repeats his demand for popular election of the Reichspräsident in a newspaper article,

---

24. See Weber's letter to his brother Alfred, of May 22nd, 1907 (DZA II, Rep. 92, No. 4), where this point is clearly stated.
25. GPS [1], p. 470.
26. GPS, p. 351; similarly, GPS, p. 342.
27. GPS, pp. 277, 279.
28. GPS p. 532.
29. On this point, *cf.* Mommsen, *Weber,* 1959, pp. 360–69.

after the first president, Ebert, has been chosen by the National Assembly [30]. His arguments in this article show that his main goal is still the same abstract one: to give *political leadership* better chances of development. Whether the medium permitting the realization of these chances is a parliament or the post of a caesaristic Reichspräsident, is a question of means and, as such, a subordinate one [31].

3.3. The account of Weber's concrete political proposals of course acquires its importance in the present context through the circumstance that they seem to be closely related to his abstract reflections on the essence of politics, especially on the necessity of protecting the freely goal-setting, and *insofar* responsible, element of the political process. The *commentaries* to these proposals will consequently only concern this methodological aspect, and disregard the numerous discussions of Weber's point of view from *political* premises.

3.3.1. In the first place, it seems natural to regard Weber's thoughts on bureaucracy and charisma, and on their concrete political incarnations, in the light of the discussion above [32] of the ideal type as a highly "charged" model. While it is hardly justified to accuse Weber of idealizing (in a normative sense) the two types, it is possible to hold the view that his analysis of the political facts, and the proposals based on this analysis, are too dependent on the *un*real, pure types of legitimacy [33]. The latent danger of neglecting the fundamentally partial character of the ideal type is made manifest by the fact that Weber strongly emphasizes and to a great extent lets his concrete proposals be guided by the antagonisms which are in his view inherent in constitutional problems defined in terms of ideal types.

3.3.2. In the light of this criticism, it is tempting to regard Weber's proposals as containing a deliberate *specialization* and *institutionalization* of the political functions: on the one side, the political leader, legitimated by his charisma, assuming the "goal responsibility"; on the other, the bureaucratic administration, the willing tool, assuming the "power responsibility"; and beneath them, the individual, under political tutelage, whose political function only amounts to the election of the leader. According to this interpretation, commitment and a sense of realities no longer form a personal, but only a national union, each incorporated in a *different* organ of government. Weber's expression "Führer mit "Maschine" " is taken quite literally.

3.3.2.1. This conclusion does not, however, seem warranted. As for the institutionalization, it is true that Weber's political writings usually stay on

---

30. "Der Reichspräsident", GPS, pp. 486–89.
31. GPS, pp. 487–88.
32. Pp. 234–36.
33. This criticism is made, for instance, by Bendix (*Portrait,* 1962, pp. 459, 485–86), Mommsen (*Weber,* 1959, p. 183) and Schulz (*Politisches Denken,* 1964, p. 344).

the macroanalytical level; but his attention must still be supposed to be
directed primarily at the *individual.* As a general indication of this, one
may point to his rejection of any collectivist reification of concepts like
"Staat", "Gesellschaft", etc. [34]; but moreover, he deliberately [35] *links up*
the macroanalysis of society with the level of the individual, the micro-
analytical level: "Ausnahmslos jede, wie immer geartete Ordnung der ge-
sellschaftlichen Beziehungen ist, wenn man sie *bewerten* will, letztlich auch
daraufhin zu prüfen, *welchem menschlichen Typus* sie ... die optimalen
Chancen gibt, zum herrschenden zu werden", Weber writes in *Wertfreiheit* [36]; and the same view is formulated concretely in a number of the discussions of the tension between bureaucracy and political leadership [37]. In
one place, Weber even directly claims that the political maturity of a nation
is a function of the chances offered to the *individual* citizen to participate
in the direction of the affairs of state [38]; and if his proposals remain on the
macroanalytical level, this should probably rather be explained by his recognition of the fact that one might in 1918 perhaps change this or that
institution, but not the mentality of a whole nation: "Es ist natürlich gar
nicht daran zu denken, daß irgendein ... Paragraph [in this case, concerning the powers of parliament] ... plötzlich "Führer" aus der Erde stampfen
würde ... Wohl aber lassen sich die unerläßlichen *Vorbedingungen* dafür
organisatorisch schaffen, und davon, daß dies geschieht, hängt in der Tat
alles ab" [39].

3.3.2.2. If we accept the view that Weber saw a close connection between
social institutions and the qualities of the individual, we are also able to
see the strong emphasis in his political writings on the *charismatic* element
in a broader context.

Already at the 1909 congress of the *Verein,* Weber connects the advance of
bureaucracy as an *institution* with the parallel growth of the orderly, bureaucratic *mentality;* and he similarly links up the question of the *institutional*
counterweight to bureaucracy with the problem of how to save the *individual*
from mental over-tidiness and narrowness: the main danger is "[die] Parzel-
lierung der Seele" [40]. Against this background, one may regard Weber's
political writings in the following years as attempts to create, by means of
institutional demands, the precondition of a *balance* not only of *organs* but
of *attitudes,* between "bureaukratische Lebensideale" and "aktive politische

34. *Cf. supra,* pp. 38–39.
35. P. 187.
36. GAW, p. 517.
37. For instance GPS, pp. 342, 386, 389, 430, 487.
38. GPS, p. 429. As early as the *Antrittsrede,* Weber discusses the enormous "*politische* Erziehungsarbeit" which is needed in Germany (GPS, p. 24).
39. GPS, p. 430.
40. GASS, p. 414.

Gestaltung", concentration on means and concentration on ends, "power responsibility" and "goal responsibility" [41]. According to this interpretation, Weber's discussion of political problems, whether they occur in his practical or in his theoretical writings, may always be seen as tentative answers to the fundamental question: "... wie heiße Leidenschaft und kühles Augenmaß miteinander in derselben Seele zusammengezwungen werden können?" [42].

5.5.3. The responsible ethic of conviction

1. Until now, the discussion of the responsibility of the politician, as defined by some sort of balance between commitment and a sense of realities, has only moved within a teleological system: although the "goal responsibility" is the responsibility for the maintenance and implementation of the goal, it is discharged by the attainment of a certain factual, "external" situation which represents the implementation of this goal.

There are good grounds for this delimitation. The immanent ethic of the political sphere should, as mentioned above [1], be seen as the reflection of the broad characterization of politics performed in the first section of this chapter. This characterization included the attainment of goals in a supra-individual context. The *goal* element does not in itself imply any variation from an ordinary "technical" calculation of ends and means; what constitutes the essential difference from such a "technical" calculation which only involves the value system of one individual or, alternatively, one conventionally fixed scale and ranking of values, is the *supra-individual* component: through it, an element of conflict is introduced into the discussion.

This element of conflict is neutralized, however, in the course of the argument. Weber does acknowledge its existence in the sense that he defines the specific instrument of politics, power, as the ability to implement a goal even against the wish of other persons, i. e., in a situation of conflict between individuals. But in so doing, he transposes all axiological conflicts to the teleological plane. An axiological conflict between the values of the politician and those of other persons is only important to the former to the extent that

41. Since the "decisionist" component in Weber's writings is mainly found in his *political* essays, while his strong emphasis on the sense of realities, the responsibility for the consequences, is found in the *methodological* and *ethical Pol. Beruf,* we find Mommsen, for instance (*Weber,* 1959, p. 50), on the basis of his sources, leaning towards an *irrationalist* interpretation of Weber's political ethic, whereas Aron (*Introduction,* 1963, p. 24), working from another angle, sees Weber as coming down strongly on the side of the ethic of responsibility defined in teleological terms.
42. GPS, p. 534.
1. Pp. 269-70.

it implies an empirical risk that he may have to resort to force to attain the goals he has set himself.

This again means that the politician, as characterized by Weber, cannot orient himself according to the ethic of conviction: the dilemma between the ethic of responsibility and the ethic of conviction only appears when the possibility of an axiological conflict is introduced; and by transforming this conflict into the definition of a specific *instrument,* Weber has already resolved the dilemma, since the essence of the ethic of conviction is precisely that it *refuses* to regard actions as means to external ends, and only judges them according to their intrinsic value. This transformation does not remove the tension between the political sphere and the value spheres constituting the normal value basis of the ethic of conviction, i. e., (mainly) the spheres of ethics and religion; but this tension *between* spheres cannot influence the definition of an ethic valid *inside* one such sphere (in this instance, the sphere of politics).

2.   This chain of arguments seems to be derived from Weber's own view of the essence of politics. Against this background, it appears downright confusing that Weber, towards the end of *Pol. Beruf,* categorically states that: "Ob man aber als Gesinnungsethiker oder als Verantwortungsethiker handeln *soll,* und wann das eine und das andere, darüber kann man niemandem Vorschriften machen" [2]. How are we to interpret this reappearance of a neutralized alternative, without jeopardizing the conclusions arrived at above?

2.1.   In order to find an answer to this question, it is necessary to examine Weber's subsequent discussion a little more closely. Here, we find him narrowing down the behaviour alternative which he had just set out, by distinguishing *two* ethics of conviction. Adherents of the first type are distinguished by their *complete* refusal to accept responsibility for the consequences of their actions; insofar, their attitude corresponds to the ethic of conviction

---

2. GPS, p. 546. Weber's statement does not explicitly apply only to the sphere of politics; and it would of course be far easier to understand if we were allowed to suppose that it simply concerned the behaviour possibilities of individuals in general. However, this solution seems excluded by the context (see for instance Weber's use of the term "Gesinnungs*politiker*" (my italics), which is not accompanied by any indication that Weber regards this attitude as illegitimate). A letter of March 22nd, 1916 from Weber to his wife Marianne points in the same direction (copy in DZA II, Rep. 92, No. 30, Vol. 2): here Weber explains the difference between the ethic of responsibility and the ethic of conviction, and illustrates his point by the following example: "Nun kann Jemand sagen: Deutschland soll, einerlei ob es siegt, den Amerikanern die Zähne zeigen, auch auf die Gefahr ruiniert zu werden. *Das ist dann nicht widerlegbar"* (my italics). In other words, the acceptance of the ethic of conviction as the political ethic cannot be proved wrong by scientific means.

defined above which rejects the teleological system as being fundamentally uninteresting. Weber dismisses this attitude with the words: "Das interessiert mich menschlich nicht sehr und erschüttert mich ganz und gar nicht" [3]; a rejection on apparently subjective ethical grounds. The description of the second type is so interesting that it is worthwhile quoting it in full:

"Während es unermeßlich erschütternd ist, wenn ein *reifer* Mensch–einerlei ob alt oder jung an Jahren—, der diese Verantwortung für die Folgen real und mit voller Seele empfindet und verantwortungsethisch handelt, an irgendeinem Punkte sagt: "Ich kann nicht anders, hier stehe ich". Das ist etwas, was menschlich echt ist und ergreift. Denn diese Lage muß freilich für *jeden* von uns, der nicht innerlich tot ist, irgendwann eintreten *können*. Insofern sind Gesinnungsethik und Verantwortungsethik nicht absolute Gegensätze, sondern Ergänzungen, die zusammen erst den echten Menschen ausmachen, den, der den "Beruf zur Politik" haben *kann*". [4]

What is remarkable in this passage is first of all the fact that Weber now provides his personal and subjective estimate with a theoretical framework. The second type described is apparently, unlike the first one, viewed by Weber as a reflection of qualities which he regards as necessary, *over and above* the traditional combination of commitment and a sense of realities in the ethic of responsibility, for political behaviour to be a true expression of the ethic of politics. If we compare this latter type of the ethic of conviction —which we can call the *responsible ethic of conviction*—with the traditional ethic of responsibility, we arrive at the following conclusions:

2.2. The responsible ethic of conviction is *like* the ethic of responsibility (and insofar *unlike* the types of the ethic of conviction discussed above) in that a person committed to it accepts his responsibility for the external consequences of his actions. On the other hand, it *differs* from the ethic of responsibility in that it does not invariably imply that the *actions* of the person in question are in accordance with this responsibility, since his behaviour is sometimes guided by axiological considerations. In fact, the attitude is a combination of the type referred to above [5] as the *passive ethic of responsibility* with an *active ethic of conviction*.

2.3. Since the latter component must be the complementary element which is in Weber's view necessary to the true politician, we can conclude that the precondition which Weber establishes for action in conformity with the ethic of politics is the *fundamental willingness to let oneself be guided in certain cases by the value axioms of other spheres* than the political one. Only those can have the "Beruf zur Politik" who do not only have this "Beruf", who in particular situations are able and willing to submit to *other* value systems.

This precondition again implies that the political ethic as defined by Weber does not only demand knowledge of the laws and regularities of the political

3. GPS, p. 547.
4. GPS, p. 547.
5. P. 261.

sphere; in other words, the "true" politician must not only be aware of the teleological system surrounding his political goal, but also of the *axiological* one. But this awareness again destroys the possibility referred to above of a relative harmony inside the political sphere. The possibilities of axiological conflict which were in the first instance absorbed by the definition of power as an instrument of politics, are resuscitated by Weber's demand that the politician should be aware of the relationship between the *political* calculation of ends and means and those of the *non-political* value spheres. Axiological value analysis becomes necessary to the politician. On the other hand, Weber's description of the responsible ethic of conviction means a rejection of the *pure* ethic of conviction, where the axiological analysis is the *only* relevant one: the acceptance of the responsibility for the consequences of one's actions demanded by the responsible ethic of conviction implies a knowledge of the consequences for which the responsibility is taken, i. e., a need for a *teleological* value analysis. A person committed to the responsible ethic of conviction, whether his actions be guided by the axioms of the political or of other value spheres, i. e., whether they be guided by teleological or by purely axiological considerations, should know the "cost" of these actions (in the form of tensions arising in relation to other value spheres). He has to make it clear to himself what ethical (religious, aesthetic, etc.) norms he is violating by, for instance, declaring war in the name of (political) national interest; and conversely, he must know what political demands he neglects by refusing on (for instance) ethical grounds to declare war or to use force at all in the situation. Since he is a politician, it is natural to assume that his starting point is political, i. e., that he is striving to attain a supra-individual goal. But even inside this chain of ends and means, he must constantly try to supplement the teleological value analysis by an axiological one. He must be aware of the means, of their side effects and of the further consequences of the goal; he must add to this an acknowledgement of the value irrationality of these teleological relations, i. e., that he is not justified in assimilating the axiological system to the teleological one; this acknowledgement will force him to examine the intrinsic axiological value of the means, the side effects and the goal according to the value system or systems to which he also remains committed outside the political sphere; and finally, he must recognize that his knowledge cannot reach beyond a certain point: that the paradox of consequences attaches to both end and means. Only after having elucidated all these points may he decide whether he can still accept working within the political sphere and submitting to its demands; only then can he take the responsibility for his decision and claim to have fulfilled the demands of the responsible ethic of conviction.

3.1. Thus, the political ethic as defined by Weber turns out to be, in the last resort, neither "Leidenschaft", political commitment, nor "Augenmaß", the ability to estimate correctly the means necessary to reach the goal set by the commitment; nor even the combination of these two qualities; but, in addition to these, "Klarheit", *awareness* of the "costs" of a concrete political commitment and of its realistic implementation, not only in relation to other political goals, but also in relation to other value spheres altogether. Political responsibility, under this construction, covers not only the political rationality of the actions, but also the decision to remain within the framework of political rationality at all. The politician who makes this decision *once and for all,* excludes himself from a deeper dimension of awareness; he transforms himself into a political "technician" [6].

3.2. Weber's definition of the responsible ethic of conviction as the ethic of politics acquires a particular significance because it endows the category of *knowledge,* and consequently science or at least the part of each individual devoted to the value of scientific inquiry, with a double aspect, a fundamental ambivalence in relation to the political sphere. A maximum of relevant knowledge is *necessary* to the politician's attainment of his goal; but at the same time, it is *dangerous* to him in his political role because it also represents the full recognition of the tension between the political and other value spheres, of the "axiological costs" which his political actions carry with them, and therefore—if he is committed to the responsible ethic of conviction —brings him nearer to the break with the political sphere which he theoretically acknowledges the possibility of. And it may not be unjustified to hear an echo of this at the same time defiant and pessimistic conclusion in Weber's own answer [7] to the question of what was his deepest motive for engaging in scholarship: "Ich will sehen, wieviel ich aushalten kann".

---

6. The passage from *Pol. Beruf* concerning the impingement of the ethic of conviction on responsible political action has been discussed by many scholars, but has usually been interpreted simply as emphasizing the importance of "goal responsibility". The interpretation advanced in the present work has not, as far as I know, been formulated explicitly by earlier commentators; but there are hints of it in Schelting's discussion (*Wissenschaftslehre,* 1934, p. 53); and Aron comes quite close to it: he distinguishes *two* antagonisms, which, in his view, are confused by Weber: on the one hand, the contrast between politics and pacifism; on the other one, that between deliberate action, based on a weighing of pros and cons, and immediate action, based on a definitive and unconditional behaviour premise. Aron's point is that the a-political side of the first antagonism (exemplified by pacifism) is not always identical with the "immediate" type of action, but may be found in conjunction with reflection and responsibility. The category implicitly defined in this way seems to be that which was referred to above as the responsible ethic of conviction.

7. Marianne Weber, *Lebensbild,* 1950, p. 731.

Appendix A. The relation of the concepts of power and "Herrschaft". The concept of "Herrschaft" (which will be translated here as "authority"[1]) is defined in WG as "die Chance, für einen Befehl bestimmten Inhalts bei angebbaren Personen Gehorsam zu finden"[2]. In many ways, Weber's work shows the concept of authority as competing with that of power as the specific characteristic of politics. This is undoubtedly, as pointed out by M. Hättich[3], due to the fact that Weber defines the explicit concept of "politics" narrowly and in close connection with the concept of state. Since the modern state is to a large extent characterized by submission, motivated by notions of legitimacy, to authority, the element of violence in practice subsides and is replaced by adaptation to de facto structures, and the concept of authority becomes similarly prominent: in Weber's work, authority is characteristic of politics in the narrow sense more or less in the same way that power is characteristic of politics in the broad sense.

This has led Hättich, for instance, to criticize the element of power in Weber's political sociology generally, and to propose a reformulation according to which the specific characteristic of politics is not power but *authority*[4]. This reformulation would, according to Hättich, not go beyond Weber's own lines of thought.

Hättich's point of view, which is on the face of it a very attractive one, still seems to me to possess certain fundamental weaknesses. In Weber's view, authority is clearly a *sub-category* of power[5]. In comparison with the general category, it appears to be limited in two respects: first, it involves the notion of an *command* which is *obeyed;* and secondly, it tends to include an element of *internalization*.

The narrowing down of the concept to include only relations of command and submission excludes a number of other ways of striving to achieve supra-individual goals, for instance some of the non-violent exercises of power mentioned above; furthermore, foreign policy, which, unlike domestic policy, is not characterized by formal commands (laws, regulations, etc.) demanding to be obeyed, is thereby excluded from the characterization of politics by means of its specific instrument or element.

While the first of the two limiting conditions set out above is quite obvious from the definition, the second one is more implicit. One may, however, point to a passage like the following: "Ein bestimmtes Minimum an Gehorchen*wollen,* also: *Interesse* (äußerem oder innerem) am Gehorchen, gehört zu jedem echten Herrschaftsverhältnis"[6]. In fact, the concept of authority contains the suggestion that *legitimacy* is the only certain basis of authority[7].

Even though one must exclude the possibility that submission to authority may be completely voluntary in all cases (if so, authority could no longer be regarded as a sub-category of power, since the latter concept implies that the purposes are carried out *even against resistance*), the "internalizing" component of the concept of legitimacy leads us into twilight zones between (subjectively) free will and necessity. This may be justified in an empirical sociology of politics, particularly

1. The German term is difficult to translate; the important point seems to be the stress laid on the *mutual* character of the relationship: the will to govern is matched by a wish to comply.
2. WG, p. 38; *cf.* WG, pp. 157, 695.
3. Hättich, *Politische,* 1967, pp. 43–44.
4. *Ibid.,* pp. 45–46.
5. WG, pp. 38, 691.
6. WG, p. 157.
7. WG, p. 157.

if it concentrates on domestic politics; but by weakening the import of the theoretical acceptance of the need for violent action in this way, Hättich's reformulation of the definition cuts the logical connection with the wider, fundamental concept of politics, and consequently with the "politico-ethical" conclusions which may be drawn from the latter. As I see it, Hättich makes an important contribution to the re-organization of a number of Weber's sub-categories; but his attempt at a reformulation ignores the deeper connection in Weber's work between politics as a narrow concept of political sociology, and the category of politics in the broad sense, i. e., as an elementary dimension of human behaviour and the conditions of this dimension of behaviour in certain situations. Hättich, in advocating a reformulation which is in itself a fruitful one, unwittingly departs from Weber's basic line of thought.

General conclusions

In the introduction, an attempt was made to show how the general plan of the present work could be seen as reflecting the various possible relations beteeen scientific inquiry and values. As will have become evident, this general plan is matched by an inner coherence, although of a different kind, in the work of Max Weber.

In Weber's eyes, the demand for the value freedom of scientific inquiry presupposes the existence both of undemonstrable values and of objective knowledge. The attainment of the latter is in its turn dependent on the adoption of valuational aspects in a theoretical value relation; and the scientific treatment of values, the value analysis, is at the same time a result of and a condition for the fruitfulness of this value relation. In the concepts formed as ideal types, value relation and value analysis are joined together with the aim of furthering research into problems of society. And social science, defined and equipped in this fashion, forms the necessary basis of meaningful political practice.

On the face of it, it is the respect for and interest in *values,* the subjective element, which creates the inner unity of all these relations. In each of the fields, this is the element which is the object of Weber's special attention. The principle of the value freedom of scientific inquiry turns out to be, to a large extent, a demand for the "science freedom" of the value sphere; the objectivity of the results of scientific inquiry is almost exclusively defined by means of an intense discussion of the theoretical value relation; to the value analysis, subjective value orientation is the only object; in the ideal type it is also a constitutive conceptual element; and the specific problem of politics is the attainment of freely chosen goals in spite of the inertia of the status quo.

However, it would be unjustified to regard Weber's methodology as being only guided by a concern for subjective elements. In the discussion, the objective element, *knowledge,* constantly stands as an independent factor, equal in rank, alongside the subjective one: The acknowledgement of the independence of the value sphere leads to the affirmation of objective science, and to the recognition of the necessity of value relation to safeguarding it. The analysis of and by means of values is both based on and results in a rational clarification of their structure and consequences. The political goals are implemented not only against, but also inside an existing situation and is dependent on a clear recognition of actual possibilities.

Rather than the dominance of the subjective or the objective element, Weber's methodology expresses his fundamental view of the two elements as at the same time diametrical contrasts and complementary aspects. It is precisely the endeavour of the scholar to eradicate practical valuations from his level of study which shows him the limits of science concerning values and its dependence on them; and the constant struggle of the politician to implement his goals in the last resort points to theoretical clarity as the essential political ethic. To Max Weber, values and science are two closed spheres containing the key to each other.

Bibliography

This bibliography lays no claim to completeness. Far more has been written on Weber, even on his methodology, even in recent years. Below, I have simply listed all the material quoted in the foregoing (with one or two, I hope pardonable, exceptions), as well as a number of other books and articles which I have felt to be of value to me in the course of my studies.

Shortened titles have been added, in brackets, if they are actually used in the text.

1. Weber's own writings.

1.1. Published writings, including published letters.

Gesammelte Aufsätze zur Religionssoziologie, I–III, Tübingen 1920–21 (photographic reprint, 1963 (Vol. I) and 1966 (Vols. II–III) respectively). (GARS I–III).

Gesammelte Aufsätze zur Sozial- und Wirtschaftsgeschichte (ed. Marianne Weber), Tübingen 1924.

Gesammelte Aufsätze zur Soziologie und Sozialpolitik (ed. Marianne Weber), Tübingen 1924. (GASS).

Gesammelte Aufsätze zur Wissenschaftslehre (2. ed.) (ed. Johannes Winckelmann), Tübingen 1951.
This edition has a number of editorial notes and a very full index.

Gesammelte Aufsätze zur Wissenschaftslehre (3. ed.) (ed. Johannes Winckelmann), Tübingen 1968. (GAW).

Die protestantische Ethik (2. ed.) (ed. Johannes Winckelmann), Munich/Hamburg 1969. (PE I).

Äußerungen zur Werturteilsdiskussion im Ausschuß des Vereins für Sozialpolitik, (printed for private circulation), pp. 83–120. (*Gutachten*).

Jugendbriefe (ed. Marianne Weber), Tübingen 1936.

Methodologische Schriften (ed., intr. Johannes Winckelmann), Frankfurt a/Main 1968. (*Meth. Schr.*).

Gesammelte Politische Schriften, Munich 1921. (GPS[1]).
This edition, on pp. 451–88, contains a number of Weber's letters on political questions, which are not reprinted in later editions.

Gesammelte Politische Schriften (2. ed.) (ed. Johannes Winckelmann, intr. Theodor Heuß), Tübingen 1958. (GPS).

Gesammelte Politische Schriften (3. ed.) (ed. Johannes Winckelmann, intr. Theodor Heuß), Tübingen 1971.

Staatssoziologie (ed. Johannes Winckelmann), Berlin 1956.
This edition, of certain of Weber's writings which are also found elsewhere, contains a useful introduction and some very full editorial footnotes.

Wirtschaft und Gesellschaft. Grundriß der verstehenden Soziologie, I–II (Studienausgabe) (ed. Johannes Winckelmann), Cologne/Berlin 1964. (WG).

Baumgarten, Eduard, *Max Weber. Werk und Person,* Tübingen 1964. (Baumgarten, *Weber,* 1964).
Pp. 88–139, 224–33, 321–24, 433–41 contain reprints of some of Weber's writings which are difficult to get hold of otherwise. Pp. 398–401, 429, 448–49, 490–97, 500–06, 531–32, 532–33, 633–35, 644–48 contain hitherto unpublished letters and fragments of writings by Weber.

Weber, Max, Letter to Carl Petersen of April 14th, 1920, reprinted in Frye, Bruce B., "A Letter From Max Weber", *Journal of Modern History,* Vol. 39 (1967), pp. 119–25.

1.2. Completely or partly unpublished letters, manuscripts, etc.

Collection of letters, manuscripts, etc. in the archives of the Max Weber Institute, Munich.

Collection of letters, notes, etc., in the Repository no. 92, German Central Archives, Historical Section II (Rep. 92, Deutsches Zentralarchiv, Historische Abteilung II), Merseburg, GDR.
This is the most important collection of Weber's letters, original or in Marianne Weber's copies.

1.3. Translations.

Economy and Society (ed. Günther Roth, Claus Wittich, intr. Günther Roth), New York 1968.

Essais sur la théorie de la science (transl., ed., intr. Julien Freund), Paris 1965.

Makt og byåkrati (transl. Dag Østerberg, intr. Egil Fivelsdal), Oslo 1971.

The Methodology of the Social Sciences (ed., transl. Edward A. Shils & Henry A. Finch, intr. Edward A. Shils), Glencoe, Ill. 1949. (Weber (Shils, Finch), *Methodology,* 1949).

Le savant et le politique (transl. Julien Freund, intr. Raymond Aron), Paris 1963.

From Max Weber (transl., ed., intr. H.H.Gerth & C. Wright Mills), London 1948.

2. Secondary literature.

Abramowski, Günter, *Das Geschichtsbild Max Webers* (Kieler Historische Studien, Vol. I), Stuttgart 1966. (Abramowski, *Geschichtsbild,* 1966).

Äußerungen zur Werturteilsdiskussion im Ausschuß des Vereins für Sozialpolitik, 1913 (printed for private circulation). (*Äußerungen,* 1913).

Albert, Hans, "Theorie und Praxis. Max Weber und das Problem der Wertfreiheit und der Rationalität", Oldemeyer, Ernst (ed.), *Die Philosophie und die Wissenschaften (Simon Moser zum 65. Geburtstag),* Meisenheim a/Glan 1967, pp. 246–72. (Albert, *Th. und Prax.,* 1967).

Albert, Hans, *Traktat über kritische Vernunft,* Tübingen 1968. (Albert, *Traktat,* 1968).

Albert, Hans, "Das Werturteilsproblem im Lichte der logischen Analyse", *Zeitschrift für die gesamte Staatswissenschaft,* Vol. 112 (1956), pp. 410–39, reprinted in and quoted from Gäfgen, Gérard (ed.), *Grundlagen der Wirtschaftspolitik,* Cologne/Berlin 1966, pp. 25–52.

Albert, Hans, "Wissenschaft und Politik. Zum Problem der Anwendbarkeit einer wertfreien Sozialwissenschaft", Topitsch, Ernst (ed), *Probleme der Wissenschaftstheorie (Festschrift für Victor Kraft),* Vienna 1960, pp. 201–32.

Aron, Raymond, "Introduction", Weber, Max, *Le savant et le politique* (transl. Julien Freund), Paris 1963, pp. 7–52. (Aron, *Introduction,* 1963).

293

Aron, Raymond, "Max Weber und die Machtpolitik", Stammer, Otto (ed.), *Max Weber und die Soziologie heute* (Verhandlungen des 15. deutschen Soziologentages), Tübingen 1965, pp. 103–20. (Aron, *Machtpolitik,* 1965).

Baumgarten, Eduard, *Max Weber. Werk und Person,* Tübingen 1964. (Baumgarten, *Weber,* 1964).

Becker, Howard, *Through Values to Social Interpretation. Essays on Social Contexts, Actions, Types and Prospects,* Durham (N. Car.) 1950.

Bendix, Reinhard, "The Age of Ideology: Persistent and changing", Apter, David F. (ed.), *Ideology and Discontent* (International Yearbook of Political Behaviour Research, Vol. V), 1964, pp. 294–327.

Bendix, Reinhard, *Max Weber. An Intellectual Portrait,* New York (Anchor Books, Doubleday) 1962. (Bendix, *Portrait,* 1962).

Bendix, Reinhard, "Max Weber's Sociology today", *international social science journal,* Vol. XVII (1965), pp. 9–22.

Bergstraesser, Arnold, "Max Weber, der Nationalstaat und die Politik", *Politik in Wissenschaft und Bildung* (Freiburger Studien zu Politik und Soziologie), Freiburg i. B. 1961, pp. 63–75.

Boese, Franz, *Geschichte des Vereins für Sozialpolitik 1872–1932,* Berlin 1939. (Boese, *Geschichte des VfS,* 1939).

Brecht, Arnold, *Political Theory. The Foundations of Twentieth-Century Political Thought,* Princeton (N. J.) 1959. (Brecht, *Theory,* 1959).

Brentano, Lujo, "Die Meinungsverschiedenheiten unter den Volkswirtschaftslehrern", *Cosmopolis,* Vol. II (April-June 1896), pp. 241–60, reprinted with an introduction as "Ueber Werturteile in der Volkswirtschaftslehre", *Archiv für Sozialwissenschaft und Sozialpolitik,* Vol. XXXIII (1911), pp. 695–714.

Cohn, Jonas, "Die Erkenntnis der Werte und das Vorrecht der Bejahung. Betrachtungen, angeknüpft an Max Webers Lehre von der Wertfreiheit der Wissenschaft", *Logos,* Vol. X (1921–22), pp. 195–226.

Dahrendorf, Ralf, "Sozialwissenschaft und Werturteil", *Pfade aus Utopia,* Munich 1967, pp. 74–88. (Dahrendorf, *Werturteil,* 1967).

Easton, David, *The Political System. An Inquiry into the State of Political Science,* New York 1953.

Franz Eulenburg, "Gesellschaft und Natur", *Archiv für Sozialwissenschaft und Sozialpolitik,* Vol. XXI (1905), pp. 519–55.

Ferber, Christian v., *Die Gewalt in der Politik,* Stuttgart 1970. (Ferber, *Gewalt,* 1970).

Ferber, Christian v., "Der Werturteilsstreit 1909/1959. Versuch einer wissenschaftsgeschichtlichen Interpretation", *Kölner Zeitschrift für Soziologie und Sozialpsychologie,* Vol. 11 (1959), pp. 21–37, reprinted in and quoted from Topitsch, Ernst (ed.), *Logik der Sozialwissenschaften,* Cologne/Berlin 1965, pp. 165–80.

Fleischmann, Eugène, "De Weber à Nietzsche", *Archives Européennes de Sociologie,* Vol. V (1964), pp. 190–238.

Francis, Emerich, "Kultur und Gesellschaft in der Soziologie Max Webers", Karl Engisch, Bernhard Pfister, Johannes Winckelmann (eds.), *Max Weber. Gedächtnisschrift der Ludwig-Maximilians-Universität München zur 100. Wiederkehr seines Geburtstages 1964,* Berlin 1966, pp. 89–114. (Francis, *Kultur,* 1966).

Freund, Julien, *Sociologie de Max Weber,* Paris 1966.

Friedrich, Carl J., *Man and his Government. An Empirical Theory of Politics,* New York 1963.

Gide, Charles & Rist, Charles, *Histoire des doctrines économiques depuis les physiocrates jusqu'à nos jours* (6. ed.), Paris 1944.

Gouldner, Alvin W., "Anti-Minotaur: The Myth of a Value-Free Sociology", *Social Problems* 9 (1962), reprinted in and quoted from Horowitz, Irving L. (ed.), *The New Sociology,* New York 1964, pp. 196–217.

Habermas, Jürgen, *Zur Logik der Sozialwissenschaften* (Philosophische Rundschau, Sonderheft (Beiheft 5)), Tübingen 1967.

Hättich, Manfred, "Der Begriff des Politischen bei Max Weber", *Politische Viertel-jahresschrift*, Vol. 8 (1967), pp. 40–50. (Hättich, *Politische*, 1967).

Henrich, Dieter, *Die Einheit der Wissenschaftslehre Max Webers*, Tübingen 1952. (Henrich, *Einheit*, 1952).

Heuß, Alfred, "Max Weber und das Problem der Universalgeschichte", *Zur Theorie der Weltgeschichte*, Berlin 1968, pp. 49–83.

Honigsheim, Paul, "Die Gründung der deutschen Gesellschaft für Soziologie in ihren geistesgeschichtlichen Zusammenhängen", *Kölner Zeitschrift für Soziologie und Sozialpsychologie*, Vol. 11 (1959), pp. 3–10.

Honigsheim, Paul, "Max Weber als Soziologe", *Kölner Vierteljahreshefte für Sozial-wissenschaften* (Reihe A: Soziologische Hefte), Vol. 1 (1921), pp. 32–41.

Hughes, H. Stuart, *Consciousness and Society*, New York 1958 (Hughes, *Consciousness*, 1958).

Janoska-Bendl, Judith, *Methodologische Aspekte des Idealtypus*, Berlin 1965. (Janoska-Bendl, *Idealtypus*, 1965).

Jaspers, Karl, "Bemerkungen zu Max Webers politischem Denken", *Antidoron. Edgar Salin zum 70. Geburtstag*, Tübingen 1962, pp. 200–214.

Jaspers, Karl, *Max Weber. Politiker. Forscher. Philosoph*, Munich 1958.

Jellinek, Georg, *Das Recht des modernen Staates. I: Allgemeine Staatslehre*, Berlin 1900.

Jonas, Friedrich, *Geschichte der Soziologie IV*, Reinbek bei Hamburg 1968. (Jonas, *Geschichte*, 1968).

König, René, "Einige Überlegungen zur Frage der "Werturteilsfreiheit" bei Max Weber", *Kölner Zeitschrift für Soziologie und Sozialpsychologie*, Vol. 16 (1964), pp. 1–29.

König, René & Johannes Winckelmann (eds.), *Max Weber zum Gedächtnis. Materialien zur Bewertung von Werk und Persönlichkeit*, Cologne/Opladen 1963.

Kraft, Jürgen. *Das Verhältnis von Nationalökonomie und Soziologie bei Franz Oppen-heimer, Werner Sombart, Max Weber und in der sozialwissenschaftlichen System-bildung des 19. Jahrhunderts*, Diss. Göttingen 1961.

Loewenstein, Karl, *Max Webers staatspolitische Auffassungen in der Sicht unserer Zeit*, Frankfurt a/Main/Bonn 1965.

Löwith, Karl, "Max Weber und Karl Marx", *Archiv für Sozialwissenschaft und Sozial-politik*, Vol. 67 (1932), pp. 53–99, 175–214, reprinted (with alterations) in and quoted from Löwith, Karl, *Gesammelte Abhandlungen. Zur Kritik der geschicht-lichen Existenz*, Stuttgart 1960, pp. 1–67. (Löwith, *Weber u. Marx*, 1960).

Loos, Fritz, *Zur Wert- und Rechtslehre Max Webers*, Tübingen 1970. (Loos, *Wertlehre*, 1970).

Lübbe, Hermann, "Die Freiheit der Theorie. Max Weber über Wissenschaft als Beruf", *Archiv für Rechts- und Sozialphilosophie*, Vol. 48 (1962), pp. 343–65.

Mayer, J. P., *Max Weber and German Politics. A study in political sociology* (2. ed.), London 1956.

Menger, Carl, *Untersuchungen über die Methode der Socialwissenschaften und der politischen Oekonomie insbesondere*, Leipzig 1883. (Menger, *Untersuchungen*, 1883).

Menger, Carl, *Die Irrthümer des Historismus in der deutschen Nationaloekonomie*, Vienna 1884. (Menger, *Irrthümer*, 1884).

Mommsen, Wolfgang J., "Universalgeschichtliches und politisches Denken bei Max Weber", *Historische Zeitschrift*, Vol. 201 (1965), pp. 557–612. (Mommsen, *Pol. Denken*, 1965).

Mommsen, Wolfgang J., *Max Weber und die deutsche Politik 1890–1920*, Tübingen 1959. (Mommsen, *Weber*, 1959).

Myrdal, Gunnar, *The Political Element in the Development of Economic Theory*, London 1953. (Myrdal, *Pol. Element*, 1953).

Myrdal, Gunnar, *Das politische Element in der nationalökonomischen Doktrinbildung* (2. ed), Hannover 1963.

Oppenheimer, Hans, *Die Logik der soziologischen Begriffsbildung mit besonderer Berücksichtigung von Max Weber* (Heidelberger Abhandlungen zur Philosophie und ihrer Geschichte, 5), Tübingen 1925.

Parsons, Talcott, *The Structure of Social Action, II*, New York 1937.

Parsons, Talcott, "Wertgebundenheit und Objektivität in den Sozialwissenschaften. Eine Interpretation der Beiträge Max Webers", Stammer, Otto (ed.), *Max Weber und die Soziologie heute* (Verhandlungen des 15. deutschen Soziologentages), Tübingen 1965, pp. 39–64.

Pfister, Bernhard, *Die Entwicklung zum Idealtypus. Eine methodologische Untersuchung über das Verhältnis von Theorie und Geschichte bei Menger, Schmoller und Max Weber*, Tübingen 1928. (Pfister, *Idealtypus*, 1928).

Radbruch, Gustav, *Grundzüge der Rechtsphilosophie*, Leipzig 1914.

Rasmussen, Erik, *Komparativ Politik I–II*, Copenhagen 1968–69.

Rickert, Heinrich, *Der Gegenstand der Erkenntnis*, Freiburg i. B. 1892.

Rickert, Heinrich, *Die Grenzen der naturwissenschaftlichen Begriffsbildung*, Tübingen 1902. (Rickert, *Grenzen*, 1902). 2. ed., Tübingen 1913 (Rickert, *Grenzen²*, 1913). 5. ed., Tübingen 1929 (Rickert, *Grenzen⁵*, 1929).

Rickert, Heinrich, *Kulturwissenschaft und Naturwissenschaft*, Freiburg i. B. 1899.

Rickert, Heinrich, *Zur Lehre von der Definition*, Freiburg i. B. 1888.

Rickert, Heinrich, "Max Weber und seine Stellung zur Wissenschaft", *Logos*, Vol. XV (1926), pp. 222–37.

Runciman, W. G., *Social Science and Political Theory*, Cambridge 1963.

Salin, Edgar, *Politische Ökonomie*, Tübingen/Zürich 1967.

Schelting, Alexander v., "Die logische Theorie der historischen Kulturwissenschaft von Max Weber und im besonderen sein Begriff des Idealtypus", *Archiv für Sozialwissenschaft und Sozialpolitik*, Vol. 49 (1922), pp. 623–752.

Schelting, Alexander v., *Max Webers Wissenschaftslehre*, Tübingen 1934. (Schelting, *Wissenschaftslehre*, 1934).

Schieder, Theodor, *Gesellschaft und Staat im Wandel unserer Zeit*, Munich 1958.

Schmoller, Gustav v., "Zur Methodologie der Staats- und Sozialwissenschaften", *Schmollers Jahrbuch für Gesetzgebung, Verwaltung und Volkswirtschaft*, Leipzig 1883, pp. 239–58. (Schmoller, *Methodologie*, 1883).

Schmoller, Gustav v., *Die Volkswirtschaft, die Volkswirtschaftslehre und ihre Methode* (ed., intr. Aug. Skalweit), Frankfurt a/Main 1949. (Schmoller, *Volkswirtschaftslehre*, 1949).

Schulz, Gerhard, "Geschichtliche Theorie und politisches Denken bei Max Weber", *Vierteljahreshefte für Zeitgeschichte*, Vol. 12 (1964), pp. 325–50. (Schulz, *Politisches Denken*, 1964).

Simey, T. S., *Social Science and Social Purpose*, London 1968. (Simey, *Social Science*, 1968).

Simmel, Georg, *Einleitung in die Moralwissenschaft, I–II*, Berlin 1892–93. (Simmel, *Moralwissenschaft*, 1892–93).

Simmel, Georg, *Die Probleme der Geschichtsphilosophie*, Leipzig 1892.

Stammer, Otto (ed.), *Max Weber und die Soziologie heute* (Verhandlungen des 15. deutschen Soziologentages), Tübingen 1965.(Stammer (ed.), *Weber*, 1965).

Strauss, Leo, "What is Political Philosophy?", *Journal of Politics*, Vol. 19 (1957), pp. 343–68. (Strauss, *Pol. Phil.*, 1957).

Strauss, Leo, *Natural Right and History*, Chicago 1953. (Strauss, *Nat. Right*, 1953).

Strzelewicz, Willy, *Die Grenzen der Wissenschaft bei Max Weber*, Diss. phil. Frankfurt 1933.

Tenbruck, Friedrich H., "Die Genesis der Methodologie Max Webers", *Kölner Zeitschrift für Soziologie und Sozialpsychologie*, Vol. 11 (1959), pp. 573–630.

Troeltsch, Ernst, *Der Historismus und seine Probleme*, Tübingen 1922 (photographic reprint 1961). (Troeltsch, *Historismus*, 1922).

Verhandlungen des Ersten Deutschen Soziologentages vom 19.–22. Oktober 1910 in Frankfurt a.M. (Schriften der Deutschen Gesellschaft für Soziologie, I. Serie, Vol. I), Tübingen 1911.

Verhandlungen des Vereins für Socialpolitik in Wien 1909 (Schriften des Vereins für Socialpolitik, Vol. 132), Leipzig 1910.

Verhandlungen des Vereins für Sozialpolitik in Nürnberg 1911 (Schriften des Vereins für Sozialpolitik, Vol. 138), Leipzig 1912.

Voegelin, Eric, *The New Science of Politics. An Introduction,* Chicago 1952. (Voegelin, *Politics,* 1952).

Walther, Andreas, "Max Weber als Soziologe", *Jahrbuch für Soziologie* (ed. G. Salomon), Vol. 2, Karlsruhe 1926, pp. 1–65.

Weber, Marianne, *Max Weber. Ein Lebensbild,* (2. ed.), Heidelberg 1950. (Marianne Weber, *Lebensbild,* 1950).

Wegener, Walther, *Die Quellen der Wissenschaftsauffassung Max Webers und die Problematik der Werturteilsfreiheit der Nationalökonomie,* Berlin 1962. (Wegener, *Wissenschaftsauffassung,* 1962).

Weippert, Georg, "Die idealtypische Sinn- und Wesenserfassung und die Denkgebilde der formalen Theorie. Zur Logik des "Idealtypus" und der "rationalen Schemata" ", *Zeitschrift für die gesamte Staatswissenschaft,* Vol. 100 (1940), pp. 257–308.

Wiese, Leopold v., "Die deutsche Gesellschaft für Soziologie. Persönliche Eindrücke in den ersten fünfzig Jahren", *Kölner Zeitschrift für Soziologie und Sozialpsychologie,* Vol. 11 (1959), pp. 11–20.

Winckelmann, Johannes, *Legitimität und Legalität in Max Webers Herrschaftssoziologie,* Tübingen 1952. (Winckelmann, *Legitimität,* 1952).

Winckelmann, Johannes, "Max Webers Verständnis von Mensch und Gesellschaft", Karl Engisch, Bernhard Pfister, Johannes Winckelmann, *Max Weber. Gedächtnisschrift . . .,* Berlin 1966.

Windelband, Wilhelm, "Geschichte und Naturwissenschaft" (1894), *Präludien. Aufsätze und Reden zur Philosophie und ihrer Geschichte II* (5. ed.), Tübingen 1914 (photographic reprint 1924), pp. 136–60.

Windelband, Wilhelm, "Normen und Naturgesetze" (1882), *Präludien. Aufsätze und Reden zur Einleitung in die Philosophie,* Freiburg i. B./Tübingen 1884, pp. 211–46. (Windelband, *Normen,* 1884).

Windelband, Wilhelm, *Ueber Willensfreiheit,* Tübingen 1904.

3. Bibliographies.

Weber, Max, *Schriften zur theoretischen Soziologie, zur Soziologie der Politik und Verfassung* (ed., intr. Max Graf zu Solms) (Civitas Gentium. Quellenschriften zur Soziologie und Kulturphilosophie (ed. Max Graf zu Solms), Vol. I), Frankfurt a/Main 1947, pp. 274–88.

Weber, Max, *Aus den Schriften zur Religionssoziologie* (ed., intr. M. Ernst Graf zu Solms) (Civitas Gentium. Quellenschriften zur Soziologie und Kulturphilosophie (ed. Max Graf zu Solms), Vol. II), Frankfurt a/Main 1948, pp. 325–28.

Gerth, H. H. & Hedwig Ide, "Bibliography on Max Weber", *Social Research,* Vol. 16 (1949), pp. 70–89.

Weber, Max, *Soziologie. Weltgeschichtliche Analysen. Politik* (4. ed.) (ed. Johannes Winckelmann, intr. Eduard Baumgarten), Stuttgart 1968, pp. 490–510.

Weinreich, Marcel, *Max Weber, l'homme et le savant. Études sur ses idées directrices,* Paris 1938, pp. 189–205.

Comparative table of pages

S,F   Max Weber (transl. Edward A. Shils, Henry A. Finch), *The Methodology of the Social Sciences,* New York (The Free Press) 1949.

GAW	S,F	GAW	S,F	GAW	S,F
146	49–50	195	94–95	243	140–41
147	50–51	196	95	244	141–42
148	51–52	197	95–96	245	142–43
149	52–53	198	96–97	246	143–44
150	53–54	199	97–98	247	144–45
151	54–55	200	98–99	248	145–46
152	55–56	201	99–100	249	146–47
153	56–57	202	100–01	250	147–48
154	57–58	203	101–02	251	149–50
155	58–59	204	102–03	252	150
156	59	205	103–04	253	150–51
157	59–60	206	104–05	254	152
158	60–61	207	105–06	255	152–53
159	61–62	208	106	256	153–54
160	62–63	209	106–07	257	154–55
161	63–64	210	107–08	258	155–56
162	64–65	211	108–09	259	156–57
163	65–66	212	109–10	260	157–58
164	66–67	213	110–11	261	158–59
165	67	214	111–12	262	159–60
166	67–68			263	160–61
167	68–69	215	113–14	264	161–62
168	69–70	216	114–15	265	162–63
169	70–71	217	115–16	266	164
170	71–72	218	116–17	267	164–65
171	72–73	219	117–18	268	165–66
172	73–74	220	118–19	269	166–68
173	74–75	221	119–20	270	168
174	75	222	120–21	271	168–69
175	75–76	223	121–22	272	169–70
176	76–77	224	122	273	170–71
177	77–78	225	122–24	274	171–72
178	78–79	226	124–25	275	172–73
179	79–80	227	125–26	276	173–74
180	80–81	228	126–27	277	174–75
181	81–82	229	127–28	278	175–76
182	82–83	230	128–29	279	176–77
183	83–84	231	129–30	280	177–79
184	84–85	232	130	281	179
185	85	233	130–31	282	179–80
186	85–86	234	131–32	283	180–81
187	86–87	235	132–33	284	181–82
188	87–88	236	133–34	285	182–84
189	88–89	237	134–35	286	184
190	89–90	238	135–36	287	184–86
191	90–91	239	136–37	288	186–87
192	91–92	240	137–38	289	187–88
193	92–93	241	138–39	290	188
194	93–94	242	139–40		

Comparative table of pages

Weber   *From Max Weber: Essays in Sociology* (transl. H. H. Gerth, C. Wright Mills), London (Routledge & Kegan Paul) 1948.

ES   Max Weber, *Economy and Society* (various transl.), New York (Bedminster Press) 1968.

GAW	Weber	GPS	Weber	GPS	Weber	WG	ES
582	129	493	77	521	103–04	3	3–4
583	129–30	494	77–78	522	104–05	4	4–6
584	130–31	495	78–79	523	105–06	5	6–7
585	131–32	496	79–80	524	106–07	6	7–8
586	132–33	497	80–81	525	107–08	7	8–10
587	133–34	498	81–82	526	108–09	8	10–11
588	134–35	499	82–83	527	109	9	11–13
589	135	500	83–84	528	109–10	10	13–14
590	135–36	501	84–85	529	110–11	11	14–16
591	136–37	502	85–86	530	111–12	12	16–17
592	137–38	503	86–87	531	112–13	13	17–19
593	138–39	504	87–88	532	113–14	14	19–20
594	139–40	505	88–89	533	114–15	15	20–22
595	140–41	506	89–90	534	115–16		
596	141–42	507	90	535	116–17	160	216–17
597	142	508	90–91	536	117–18	161	217–19
598	142–43	509	91–92	537	118–19	162	219–20
599	143–44	510	92–93	538	119	163	220–22
600	144–45	511	93–94	539	119–20	164	222–23
601	145–46	512	94–95	540	120–21	165	223–25
602	146–47	513	95–96	541	121–22	166	225–26
603	147–48	514	96–97	542	122–23		
604	148	515	97–98	543	123–24	657	901–02
605	148–49	516	98–99	544	124–25	658	902–03
606	149–50	517	99–100	545	125–26	659	903–04
607	150–51	518	100–01	546	126–27	660	904–05
608	151–52	519	101–02	547	127–28	661	905–07
609	152–53	520	102–03	548	128	662	907–08
610	153–54					663	908–09
611	154–55					664	909–10
612	155						
613	155–56					674	921–22
						675	922–23
						676	923–24
						677	924–25
						678	925–26
						688	937–38
						689	938–39
						691	941–42
						692	942–43
						693	943–44
						694	944–45
						695	945–47
						696	947–48

Index of names

300

Sombart, W. 168n

Tobler, M. 180n
Toennies, F. 44n, 180n

Voßler, K. 17n, 34n, 38n
Weber, A. 55n, 135n, 279n
Weber, Marianne 18n, 70n, 95n, 164n, 283n
Wilbrandt, R. 194n

Index of other persons referred to in the text

Aristotle 42n

Babeuf, G. 182n
Bashkirtseff, M. 111
Bush, Wilh. 136

Caesar 115, 116
Croce, B. 39n

Darwin, Ch. 82n
Dilthey, W. 39n, 83–84
Duverger, M. 102n

Easton, D. 243
Ebert, Fr. 280
Eisner, K. 271
Eulenburg, F. 9

Fichte, J. G. 9
Foerster, F. W. 258, 259
Fr. Wilhelm IV 226
Fuchs, C. J. 18n

Gide, A. 128n
Gierke, O. v. 38
Goethe, J. W. v. 106, 138
Goldscheid, R. 18–19
Gottl-Ottlilienfeld, Fr. v. 99n

Hegel, Fr. 39
Hildebrand, B. 79
Hume, D. 17
Husserl, G. 11n

Jaffé, E. 9, 22
Jellinek, G. 17, 209, 210n

Kant, I. 17, 48
Knapp, G. F. 18n
Knies, K. 39n, 80, 95

Lamprecht, K. 38
Lask, E. 11n
Liefmann, R. 41, 53
Locke, John 75

Marx, Karl 39n, 110, 111, 132
Meinecke, Fr. 84n
Menger, C. 81–83, 101, 209
Meyer, Ed. 107n, 123, 135
Mill, J. S. 186n
Mommsen, Th. 77, 159
More, Th. 143
Münsterberg, H. 102, 119

Newton, I. 82n

Ostwald, W. 18

Philippovich, E. v. 18n
Plato 42n
Preuß, H. 279

Richelieu, A. J. du P. de 252
Rickert, H. 9, 11, 12, 13, 17, 32n, 38, 45, 48, 49n, 50, 68, 83n, 84–101, 103–04, 106, 107n, 109, 114n, 116–21, 124–34, 136–39, 142–44, 152, 162n, 164, 204, 206–09, 211–15, 218n, 225
Robinson Crusoe 217
Roscher, W. 38, 42n, 45, 79, 95, 102
Rousseau, J. J. 149

Salisbury, Lord 264–65
Schmoller, G. v. 18, 19n, 20, 51–52, 80–83, 181, 187, 205–06, 209, 225, 248n
Schopenhauer, A. 172
Schultze-Gävernitz, A. v. 34n
Simmel, G. 16, 32n, 40, 49–50, 84n, 86n, 87n, 95, 109
Solvay, E. 39n
Sombart, W. 9, 18, 20, 22, 66n
Stammler, R. 18, 39n, 53, 126
St. Thomas Aquinas 42n

Tolstoy, L. 44
Treitschke, H. v. 77, 159
Trotski, L. 252

Wilhelm II 263n, 269n, 271, 274–75, 279
Wilson, W. 206n
Windelband, W. 11, 48, 50, 69n, 84, 87, 95
Wundt, W. 11n, 18, 39, 42n, 107–08

Young, M. 182n